POE DAMERON

STAR WARS

LEGEND LOST

POE DAMERON
STAR WARS

LEGEND LOST

Writer	**CHARLES SOULE**
Artist	**ANGEL UNZUETA**
Color Artists	**FRANK D'ARMATA** (#7) &
	ARIF PRIANTO (#14-19)
Letterer	**VC's JOE CARAMAGNA**
Cover Art	**PHIL NOTO**

Assistant Editor	**HEATHER ANTOS**
Editor	**JORDAN D. WHITE**
Executive Editor	**C.B. CEBULSKI**

Editor in Chief	**AXEL ALONSO**
Chief Creative Officer	**JOE QUESADA**
President	**DAN BUCKLEY**

For Lucasfilm:

Senior Editor	**FRANK PARISI**
Creative Director	**MICHAEL SIGLAIN**
Lucasfilm Story Group	**JAMES WAUGH, LELAND CHEE,**
	MATT MARTIN

Collection Editor	**JENNIFER GRÜNWALD**
Assistant Editor	**CAITLIN O'CONNELL**
Associate Managing Editor	**KATERI WOODY**
Editor, Special Projects	**MARK D. BEAZLEY**
VP Production & Special Projects	**JEFF YOUNGQUIST**
SVP Print, Sales & Marketing	**DAVID GABRIEL**
Book Designer	**ADAM DEL RE**

STAR WARS: POE DAMERON VOL. 3 — LEGEND LOST. Contains material originally published in magazine form as STAR WARS: POE DAMERON #7 and #14-19. First printing 2017. ISBN# 978-1-302-90742-6. Published by MARVEL WORLDWIDE, INC.; a subsidiary of MARVEL ENTERTAINMENT, LLC. OFFICE OF PUBLICATION: 135 West 50th Street, New York, NY 10020. STAR WARS and related text and illustrations are trademarks and/or copyrights, in the United States and other countries, of Lucasfilm Ltd. and/or its affiliates: © & TM Lucasfilm Ltd. No similarity between any of the names, characters, persons, and/or institutions in this magazine with those of any living or dead person or institution is intended, and any such similarity which may exist is purely coincidental. Marvel and its logos are TM Marvel Characters, Inc. Printed in the U.S.A. DAN BUCKLEY, President, Marvel Entertainment; JOE QUESADA, Chief Creative Officer; TOM BREVOORT, SVP of Publishing; DAVID BOGART, SVP of Business Affairs & Operations, Publishing & Partnership; C.B. CEBULSKI, VP of Brand Management & Development, Asia; DAVID GABRIEL, SVP of Sales & Marketing, Publishing; JEFF YOUNGQUIST, VP of Production & Special Projects; DAN CARR, Executive Director of Publishing Technology; ALEX MORALES, Director of Publishing Operations; SUSAN CRESPI, Production Manager; STAN LEE, Chairman Emeritus. For information regarding advertising in Marvel Comics or on Marvel.com, please contact Vit DeBellis, Integrated Sales Manager, at vdebellis@marvel.com. For Marvel subscription inquiries, please call 888-511-5480. Manufactured between 9/8/2017 and 10/9/2017 by QUAD/GRAPHICS WASECA, WASECA, MN, USA.

10 9 8 7 6 5 4 3 2 1

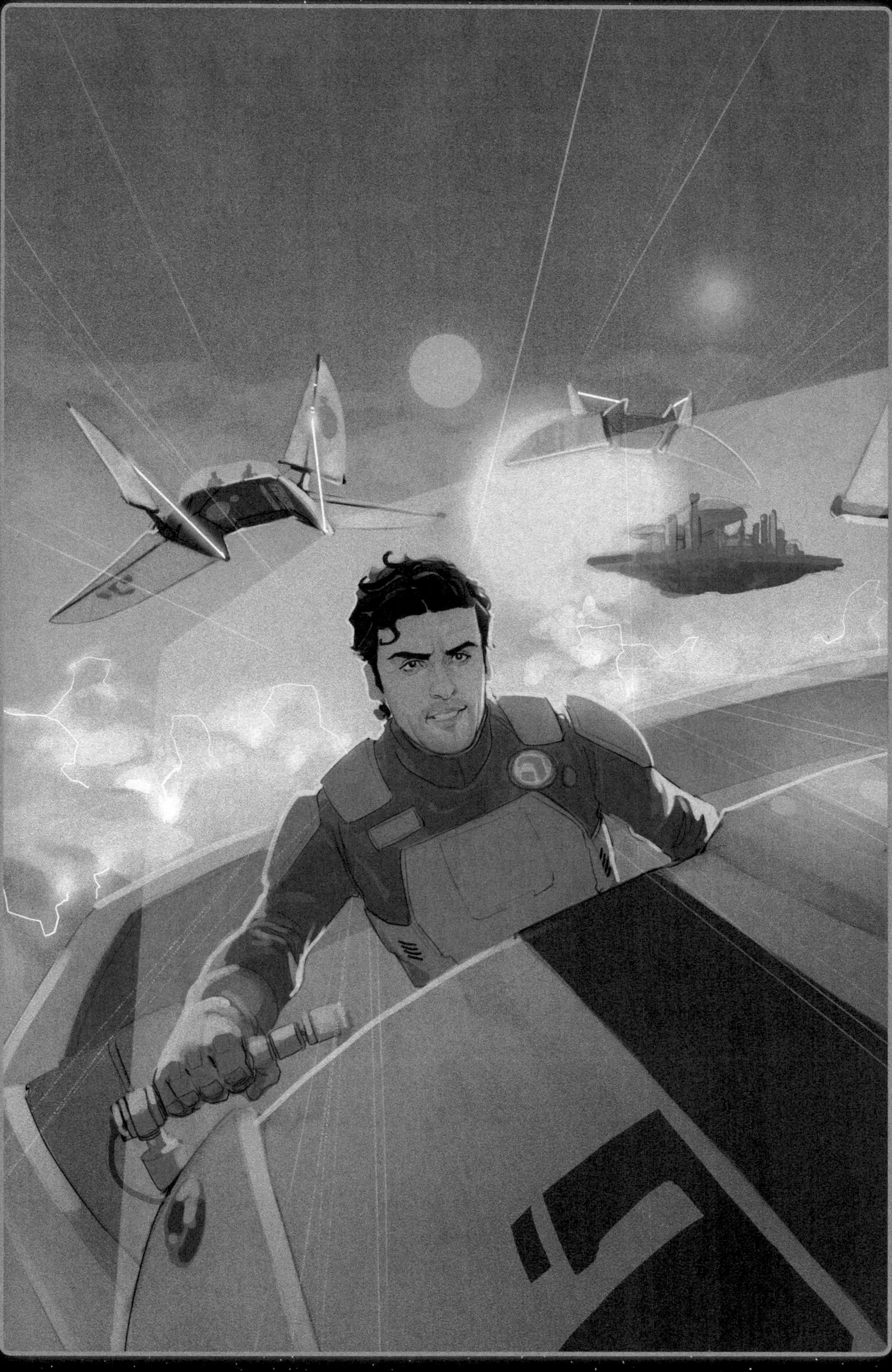

7

THE GATHERING STORM

It is a time of uncertainty in the galaxy. Standing against the oppression of the First Order is the Resistance, including Poe Dameron and his team of ace pilots — Black Squadron.

General Leia Organa is the leader of the Resistance, working out of a secret base on the planet D'Qar. The Resistance fighters, including Poe and the pilots of the Black Squadron, hail from across the galaxy and are dedicated to fighting the First Order and tyranny in all its forms.

Poe has been occupied with information-gathering and rescue missions on behalf of the Resistance. He has been thrown into the most dangerous prison in the galaxy, come face-to-face with evil agents, and survived piloting in incredibly treacherous conditions. Now, he receives a message from his past....

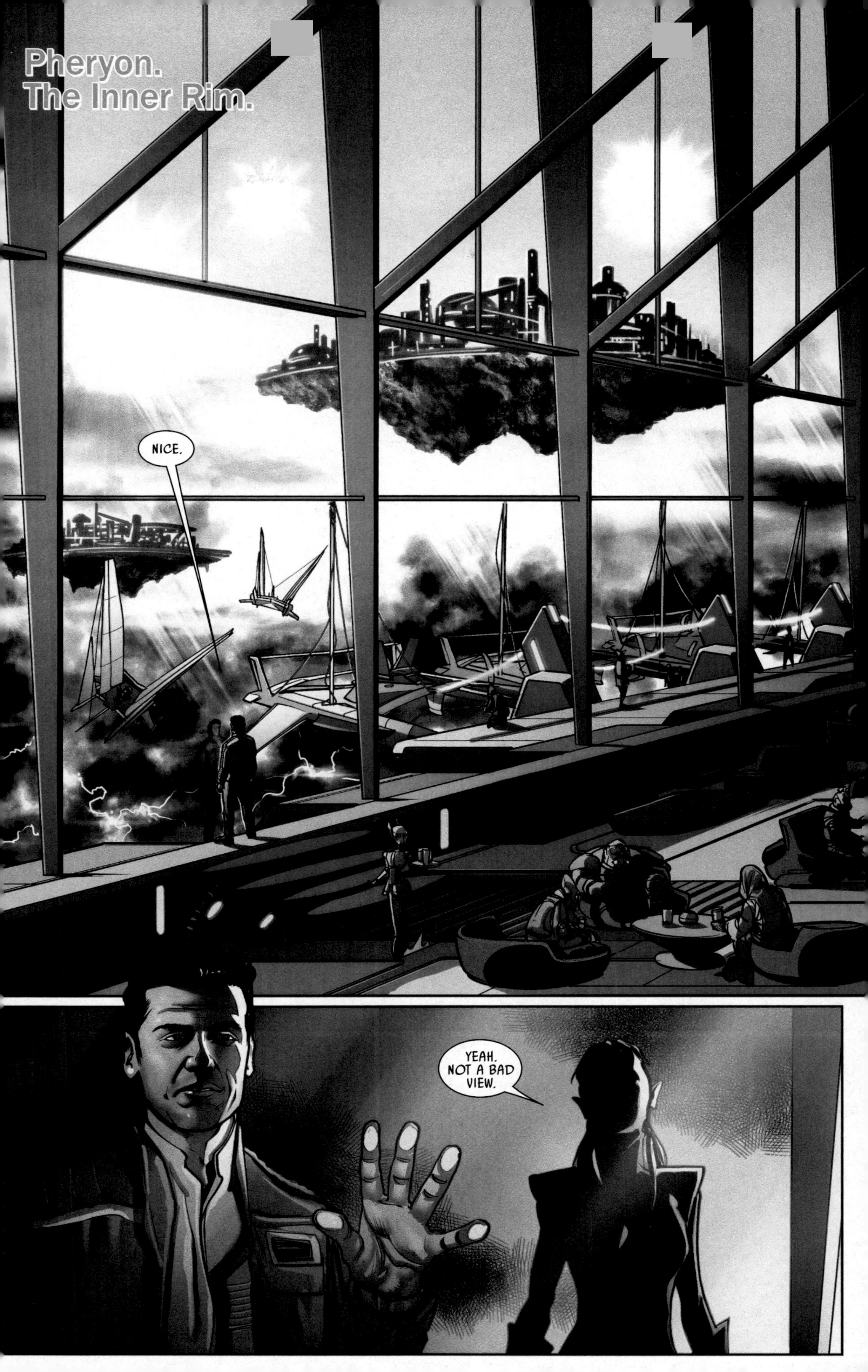
Pheryon.
The Inner Rim.
NICE.
YEAH. NOT A BAD VIEW.

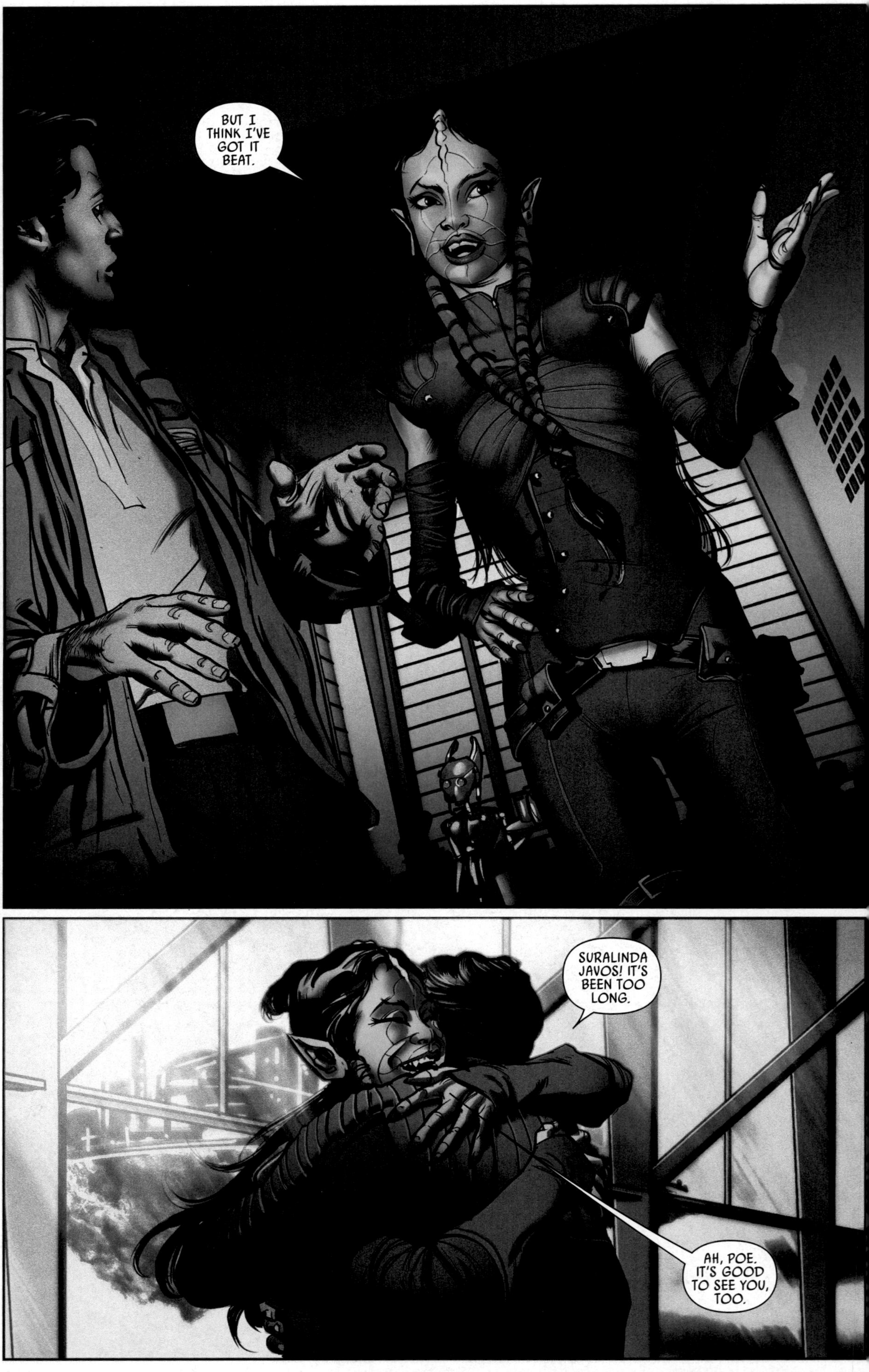
BUT I THINK I'VE GOT IT BEAT.
SURALINDA JAVOS! IT'S BEEN TOO LONG.
AH, POE. IT'S GOOD TO SEE YOU, TOO.

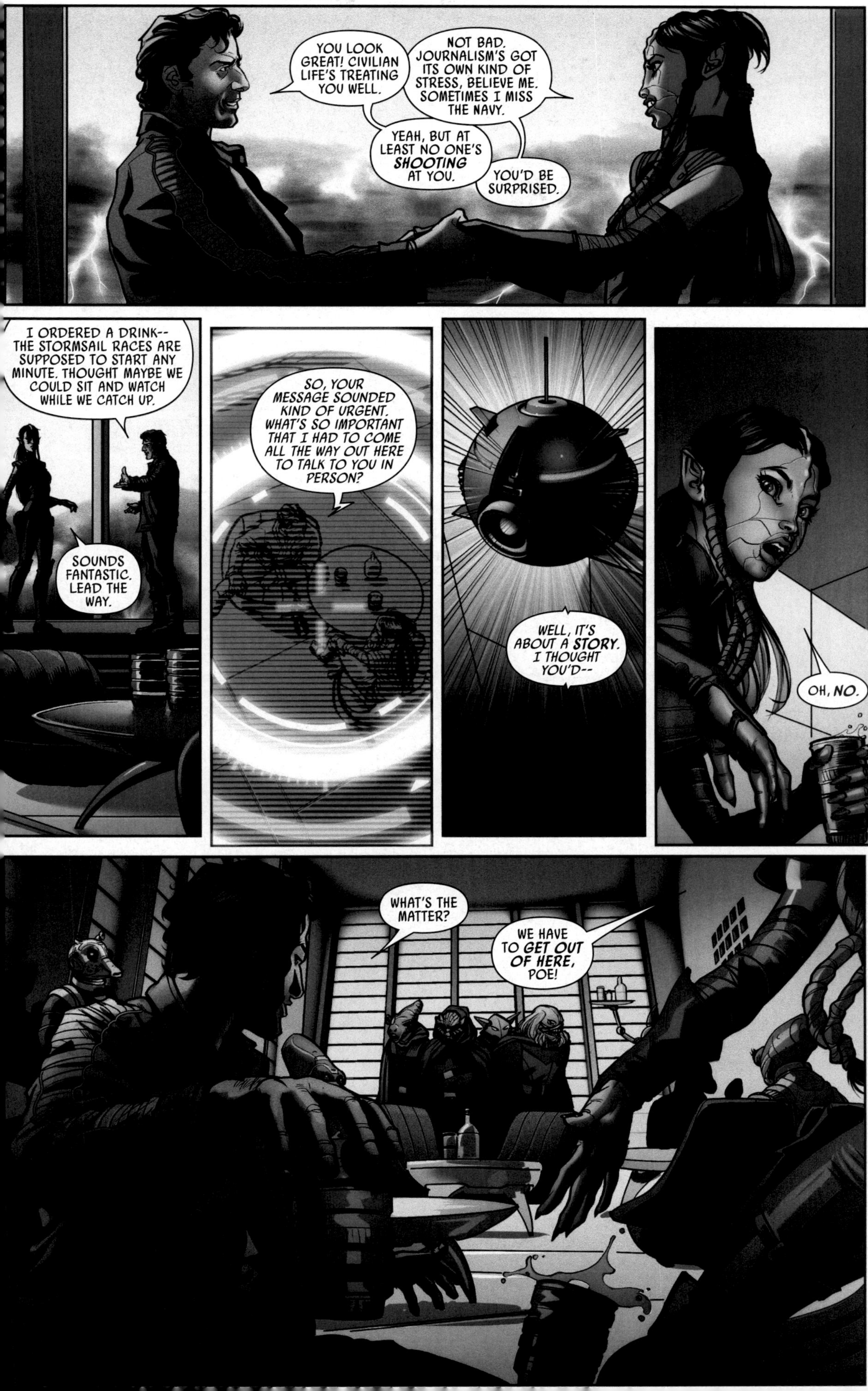
YOU LOOK GREAT! CIVILIAN LIFE'S TREATING YOU WELL.
NOT BAD. JOURNALISM'S GOT ITS OWN KIND OF STRESS, BELIEVE ME. SOMETIMES I MISS THE NAVY.
YEAH, BUT AT LEAST NO ONE'S SHOOTING AT YOU.
YOU'D BE SURPRISED.
I ORDERED A DRINK-- THE STORMSAIL RACES ARE SUPPOSED TO START ANY MINUTE. THOUGHT MAYBE WE COULD SIT AND WATCH WHILE WE CATCH UP.
SOUNDS FANTASTIC. LEAD THE WAY.
SO, YOUR MESSAGE SOUNDED KIND OF URGENT. WHAT'S SO IMPORTANT THAT I HAD TO COME ALL THE WAY OUT HERE TO TALK TO YOU IN PERSON?
WELL, IT'S ABOUT A STORY. I THOUGHT YOU'D--
OH, NO.
WHAT'S THE MATTER?
WE HAVE TO GET OUT OF HERE, POE!

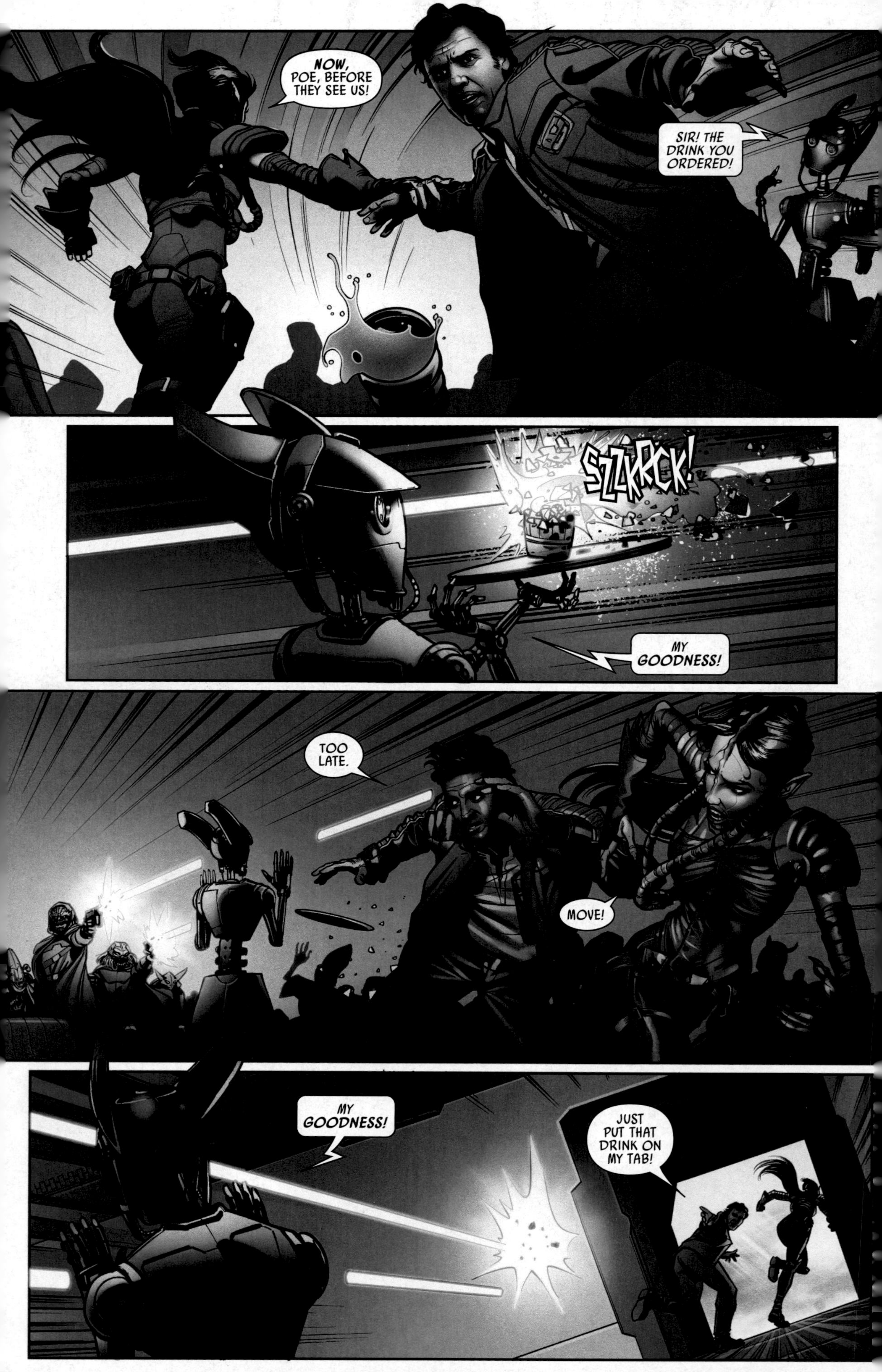
NOW, POE, BEFORE THEY SEE US!
SIR! THE DRINK YOU ORDERED!
SZZKRRCK!
MY GOODNESS!
TOO LATE.
MOVE!
MY GOODNESS!
JUST PUT THAT DRINK ON MY TAB!

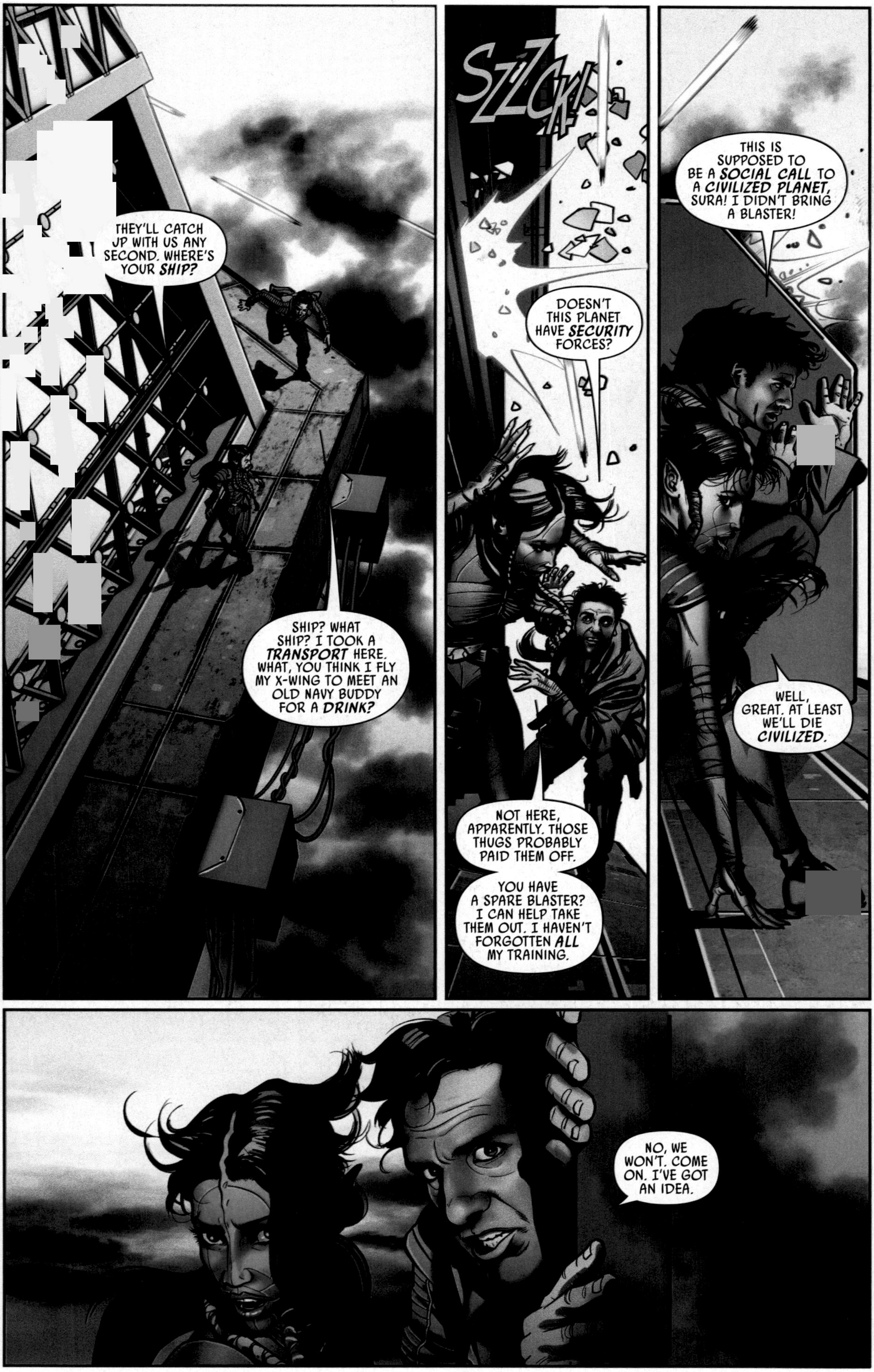
THEY'LL CATCH UP WITH US ANY SECOND. WHERE'S YOUR SHIP?
SHIP? WHAT SHIP? I TOOK A TRANSPORT HERE. WHAT, YOU THINK I FLY MY X-WING TO MEET AN OLD NAVY BUDDY FOR A DRINK?
SZZCK!
DOESN'T THIS PLANET HAVE SECURITY FORCES?
NOT HERE, APPARENTLY. THOSE THUGS PROBABLY PAID THEM OFF.
YOU HAVE A SPARE BLASTER? I CAN HELP TAKE THEM OUT. I HAVEN'T FORGOTTEN ALL MY TRAINING.
THIS IS SUPPOSED TO BE A SOCIAL CALL TO A CIVILIZED PLANET, SURA! I DIDN'T BRING A BLASTER!
WELL, GREAT. AT LEAST WE'LL DIE CIVILIZED.
NO, WE WON'T. COME ON. I'VE GOT AN IDEA.

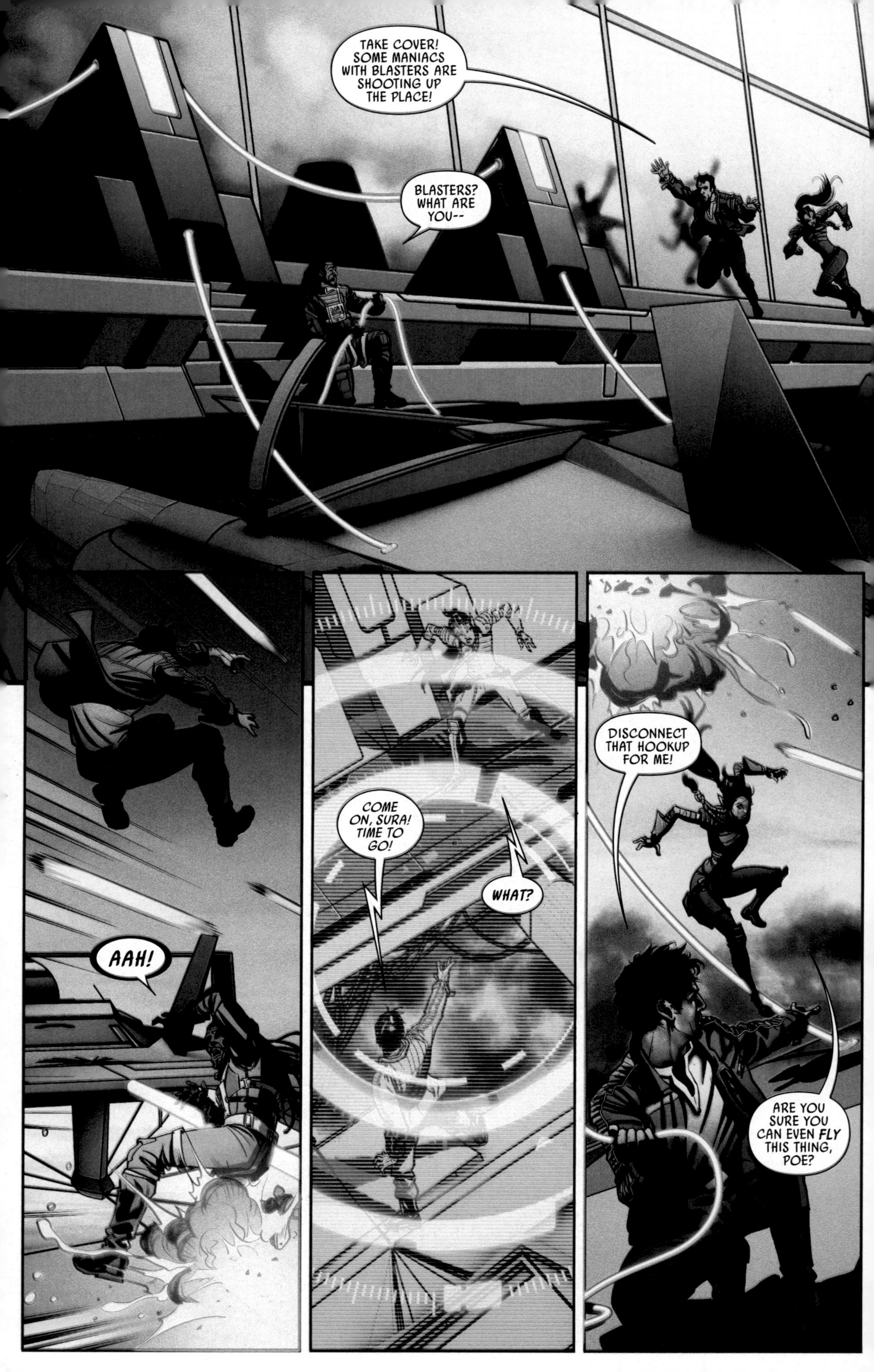
TAKE COVER! SOME MANIACS WITH BLASTERS ARE SHOOTING UP THE PLACE!
BLASTERS? WHAT ARE YOU--
AAH!
COME ON, SURA! TIME TO GO!
WHAT?
DISCONNECT THAT HOOKUP FOR ME!
ARE YOU SURE YOU CAN EVEN FLY THIS THING, POE?

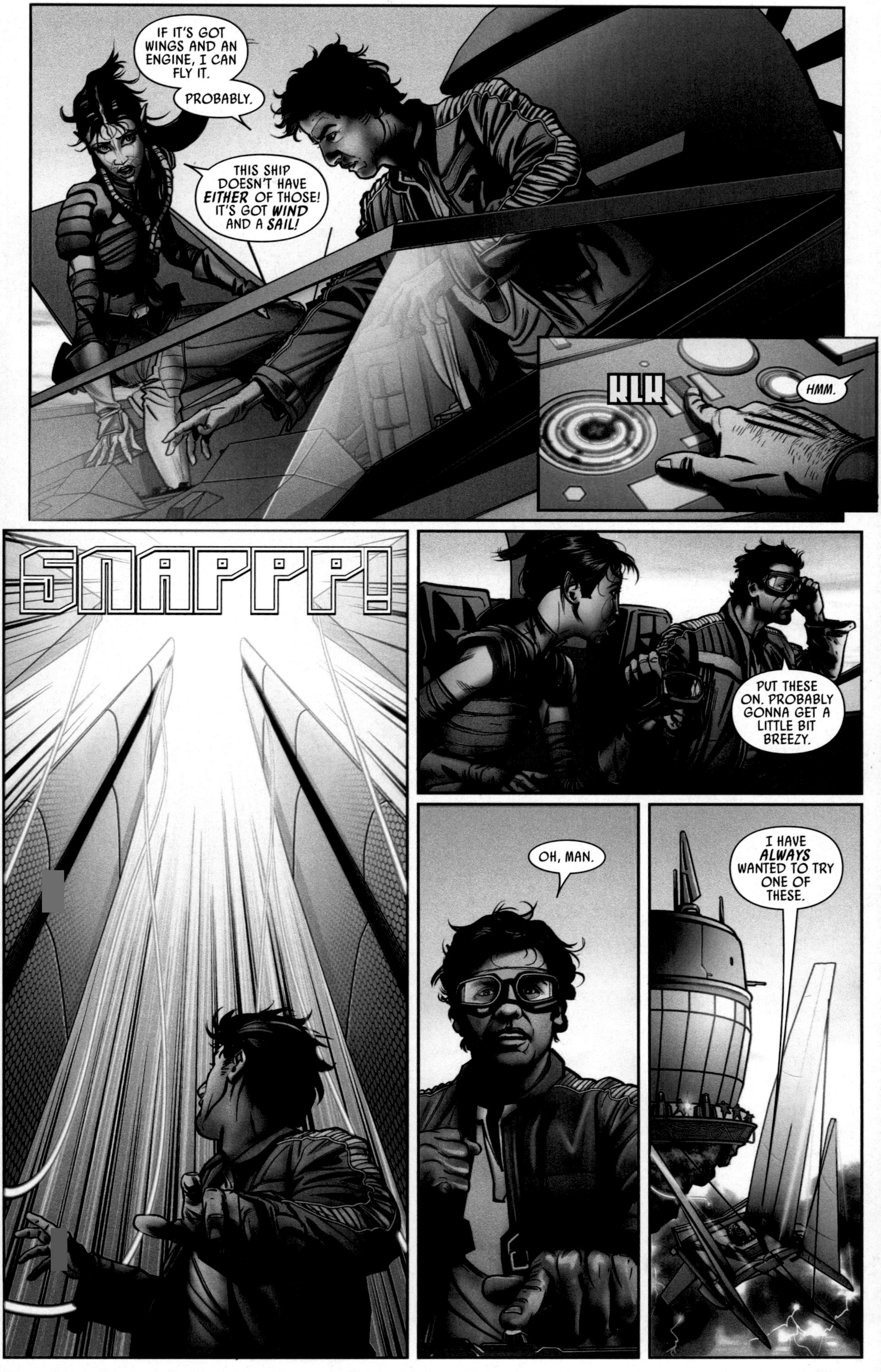
IF IT'S GOT WINGS AND AN ENGINE, I CAN FLY IT.
PROBABLY.
THIS SHIP DOESN'T HAVE *EITHER* OF THOSE! IT'S GOT *WIND* AND A *SAIL!*
KLK
HMM.
SNAPPP!
PUT THESE ON. PROBABLY GONNA GET A LITTLE BIT BREEZY.
OH, MAN.
I HAVE *ALWAYS* WANTED TO TRY ONE OF THESE.

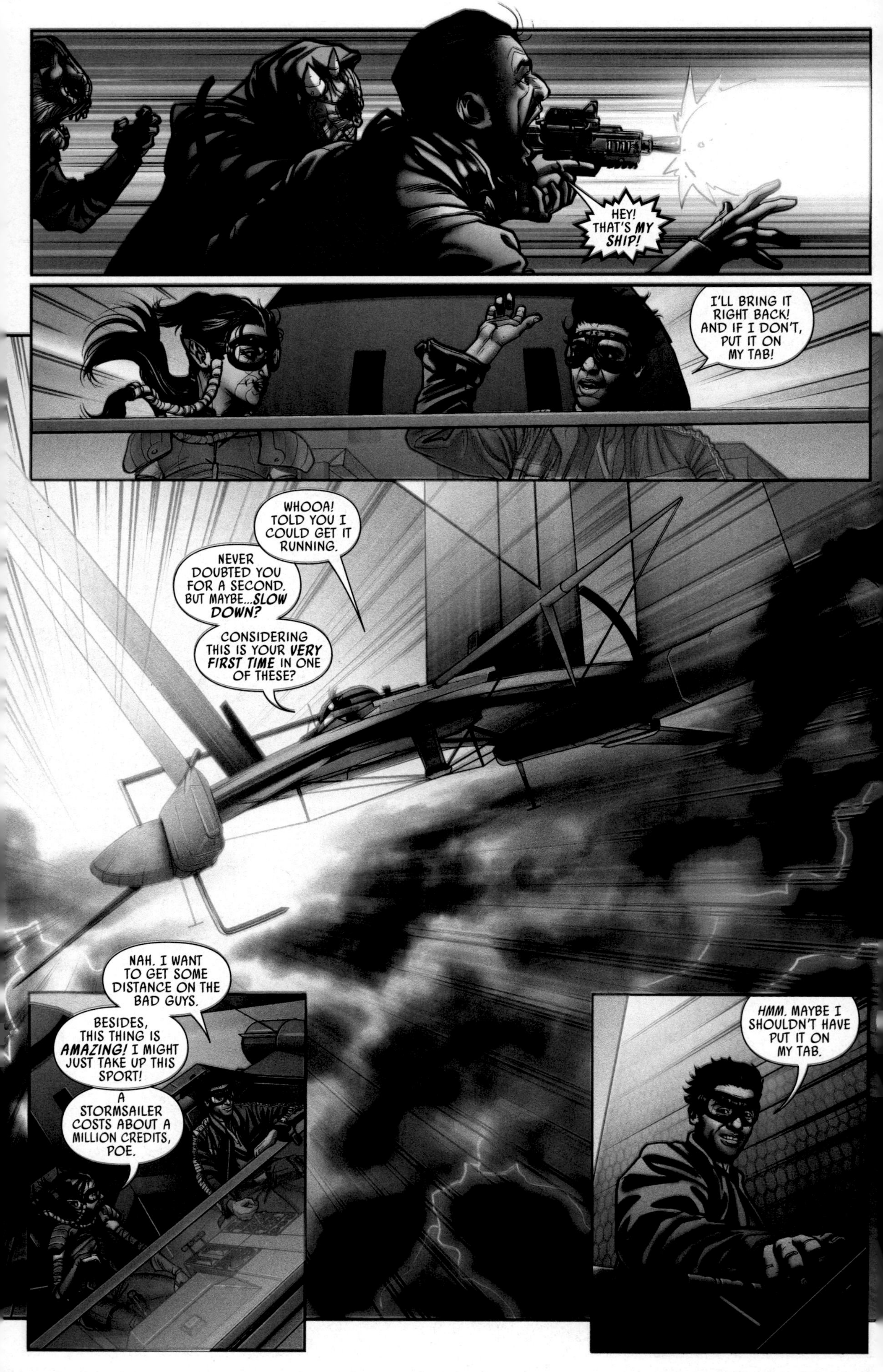
HEY! THAT'S MY SHIP!
I'LL BRING IT RIGHT BACK! AND IF I DON'T, PUT IT ON MY TAB!
WHOOA! TOLD YOU I COULD GET IT RUNNING.
NEVER DOUBTED YOU FOR A SECOND. BUT MAYBE...SLOW DOWN?
CONSIDERING THIS IS YOUR VERY FIRST TIME IN ONE OF THESE?
NAH. I WANT TO GET SOME DISTANCE ON THE BAD GUYS.
BESIDES, THIS THING IS AMAZING! I MIGHT JUST TAKE UP THIS SPORT!
A STORMSAILER COSTS ABOUT A MILLION CREDITS, POE.
HMM. MAYBE I SHOULDN'T HAVE PUT IT ON MY TAB.

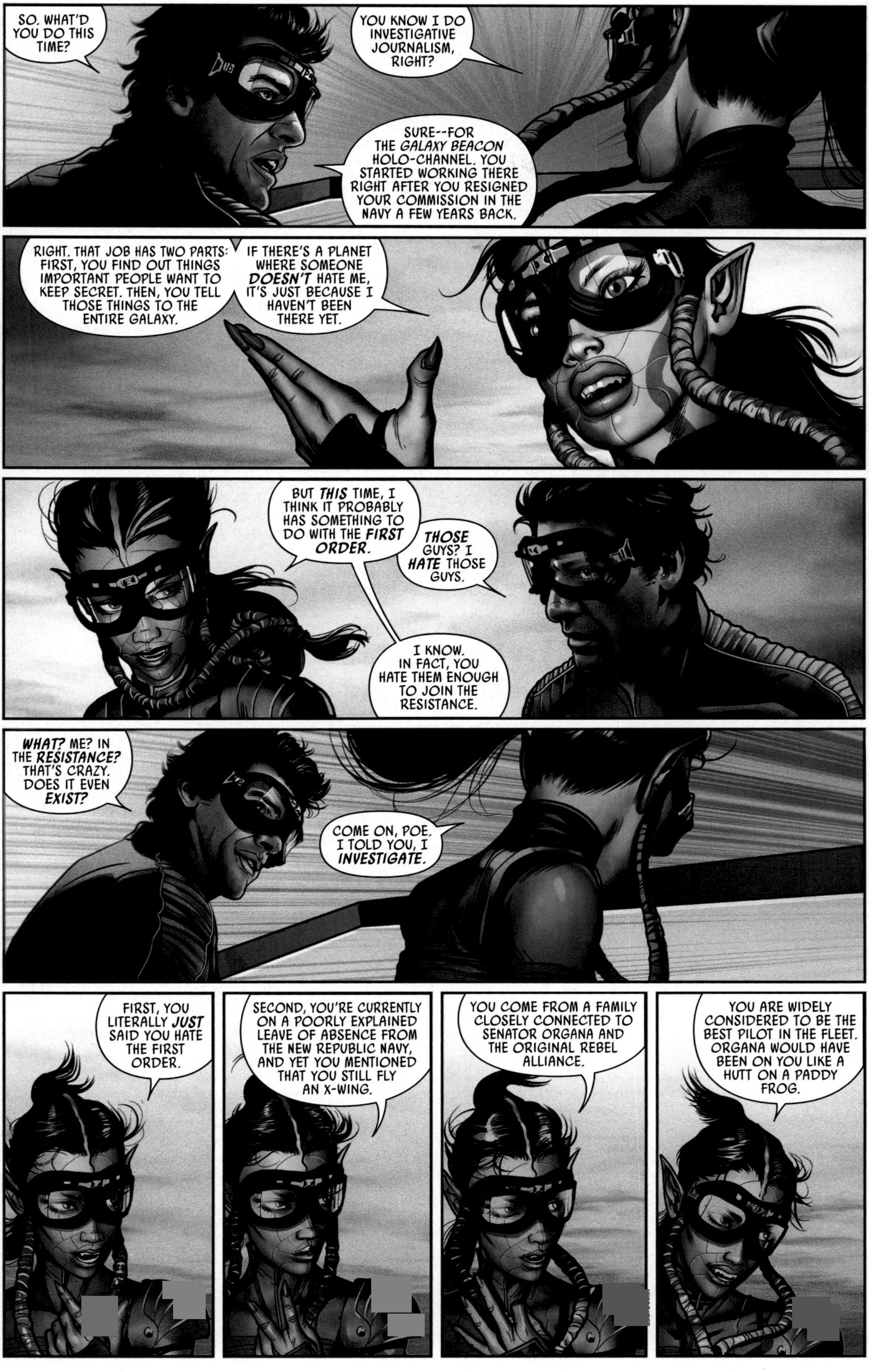
SO, WHAT'D YOU DO THIS TIME?
YOU KNOW I DO INVESTIGATIVE JOURNALISM, RIGHT?
SURE--FOR THE GALAXY BEACON HOLO-CHANNEL. YOU STARTED WORKING THERE RIGHT AFTER YOU RESIGNED YOUR COMMISSION IN THE NAVY A FEW YEARS BACK.
RIGHT. THAT JOB HAS TWO PARTS: FIRST, YOU FIND OUT THINGS IMPORTANT PEOPLE WANT TO KEEP SECRET. THEN, YOU TELL THOSE THINGS TO THE ENTIRE GALAXY.
IF THERE'S A PLANET WHERE SOMEONE DOESN'T HATE ME, IT'S JUST BECAUSE I HAVEN'T BEEN THERE YET.
BUT THIS TIME, I THINK IT PROBABLY HAS SOMETHING TO DO WITH THE FIRST ORDER.
THOSE GUYS? I HATE THOSE GUYS.
I KNOW. IN FACT, YOU HATE THEM ENOUGH TO JOIN THE RESISTANCE.
WHAT? ME? IN THE RESISTANCE? THAT'S CRAZY. DOES IT EVEN EXIST?
COME ON, POE. I TOLD YOU, I INVESTIGATE.
FIRST, YOU LITERALLY JUST SAID YOU HATE THE FIRST ORDER.
SECOND, YOU'RE CURRENTLY ON A POORLY EXPLAINED LEAVE OF ABSENCE FROM THE NEW REPUBLIC NAVY, AND YET YOU MENTIONED THAT YOU STILL FLY AN X-WING.
YOU COME FROM A FAMILY CLOSELY CONNECTED TO SENATOR ORGANA AND THE ORIGINAL REBEL ALLIANCE.
YOU ARE WIDELY CONSIDERED TO BE THE BEST PILOT IN THE FLEET. ORGANA WOULD HAVE BEEN ON YOU LIKE A HUTT ON A PADDY FROG.

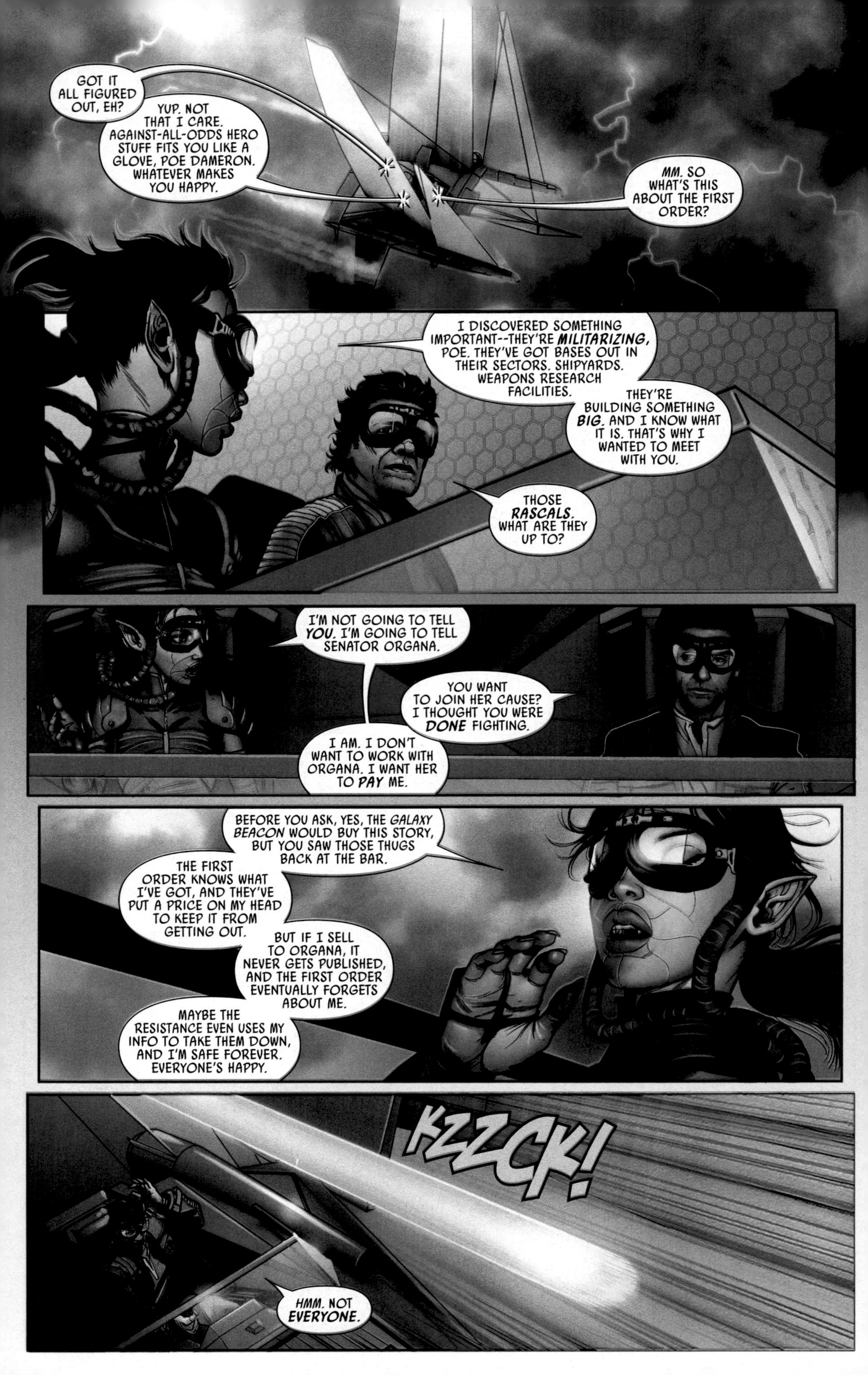
GOT IT ALL FIGURED OUT, EH?
YUP. NOT THAT I CARE. AGAINST-ALL-ODDS HERO STUFF FITS YOU LIKE A GLOVE, POE DAMERON. WHATEVER MAKES YOU HAPPY.
MM. SO WHAT'S THIS ABOUT THE FIRST ORDER?
I DISCOVERED SOMETHING IMPORTANT--THEY'RE *MILITARIZING*, POE. THEY'VE GOT BASES OUT IN THEIR SECTORS. SHIPYARDS. WEAPONS RESEARCH FACILITIES.
THEY'RE BUILDING SOMETHING *BIG*. AND I KNOW WHAT IT IS. THAT'S WHY I WANTED TO MEET WITH YOU.
THOSE *RASCALS*. WHAT ARE THEY UP TO?
I'M NOT GOING TO TELL *YOU*. I'M GOING TO TELL SENATOR ORGANA.
YOU WANT TO JOIN HER CAUSE? I THOUGHT YOU WERE *DONE* FIGHTING.
I AM. I DON'T WANT TO WORK WITH ORGANA. I WANT HER TO *PAY* ME.
BEFORE YOU ASK, YES, THE *GALAXY BEACON* WOULD BUY THIS STORY, BUT YOU SAW THOSE THUGS BACK AT THE BAR.
THE FIRST ORDER KNOWS WHAT I'VE GOT, AND THEY'VE PUT A PRICE ON MY HEAD TO KEEP IT FROM GETTING OUT.
BUT IF I SELL TO ORGANA, IT NEVER GETS PUBLISHED, AND THE FIRST ORDER EVENTUALLY FORGETS ABOUT ME.
MAYBE THE RESISTANCE EVEN USES MY INFO TO TAKE THEM DOWN, AND I'M SAFE FOREVER. EVERYONE'S HAPPY.
KZZCK!
HMM. NOT *EVERYONE*.

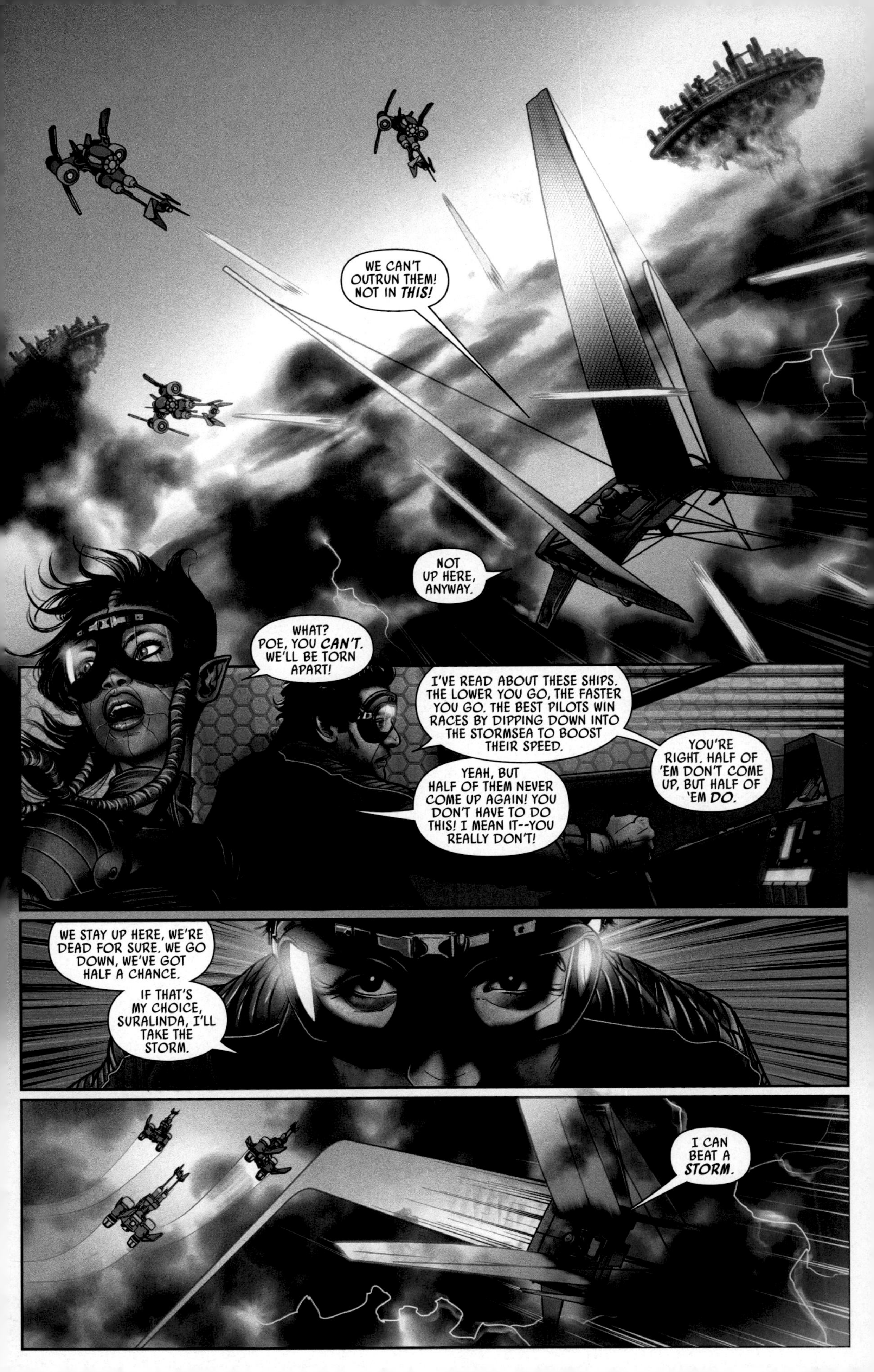
WE CAN'T OUTRUN THEM! NOT IN THIS!
NOT UP HERE, ANYWAY.
WHAT? POE, YOU CAN'T. WE'LL BE TORN APART!
I'VE READ ABOUT THESE SHIPS. THE LOWER YOU GO, THE FASTER YOU GO. THE BEST PILOTS WIN RACES BY DIPPING DOWN INTO THE STORMSEA TO BOOST THEIR SPEED.
YEAH, BUT HALF OF THEM NEVER COME UP AGAIN! YOU DON'T HAVE TO DO THIS! I MEAN IT--YOU REALLY DON'T!
YOU'RE RIGHT. HALF OF 'EM DON'T COME UP, BUT HALF OF 'EM DO.
WE STAY UP HERE, WE'RE DEAD FOR SURE. WE GO DOWN, WE'VE GOT HALF A CHANCE.
IF THAT'S MY CHOICE, SURALINDA, I'LL TAKE THE STORM.
I CAN BEAT A STORM.

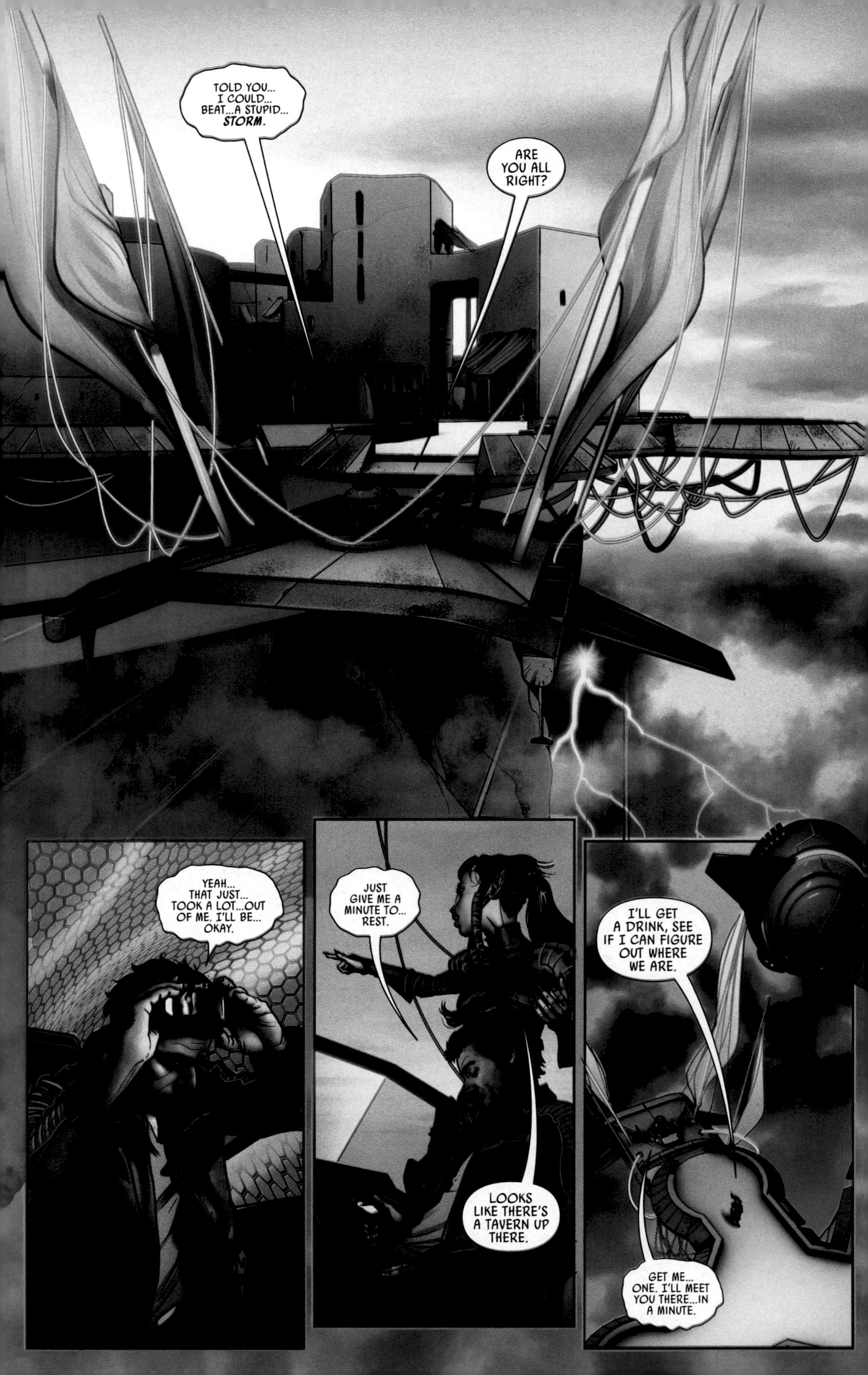
TOLD YOU... I COULD... BEAT...A STUPID... STORM.
ARE YOU ALL RIGHT?
YEAH... THAT JUST... TOOK A LOT...OUT OF ME. I'LL BE... OKAY.
JUST GIVE ME A MINUTE TO... REST.
LOOKS LIKE THERE'S A TAVERN UP THERE.
I'LL GET A DRINK, SEE IF I CAN FIGURE OUT WHERE WE ARE.
GET ME... ONE. I'LL MEET YOU THERE...IN A MINUTE.

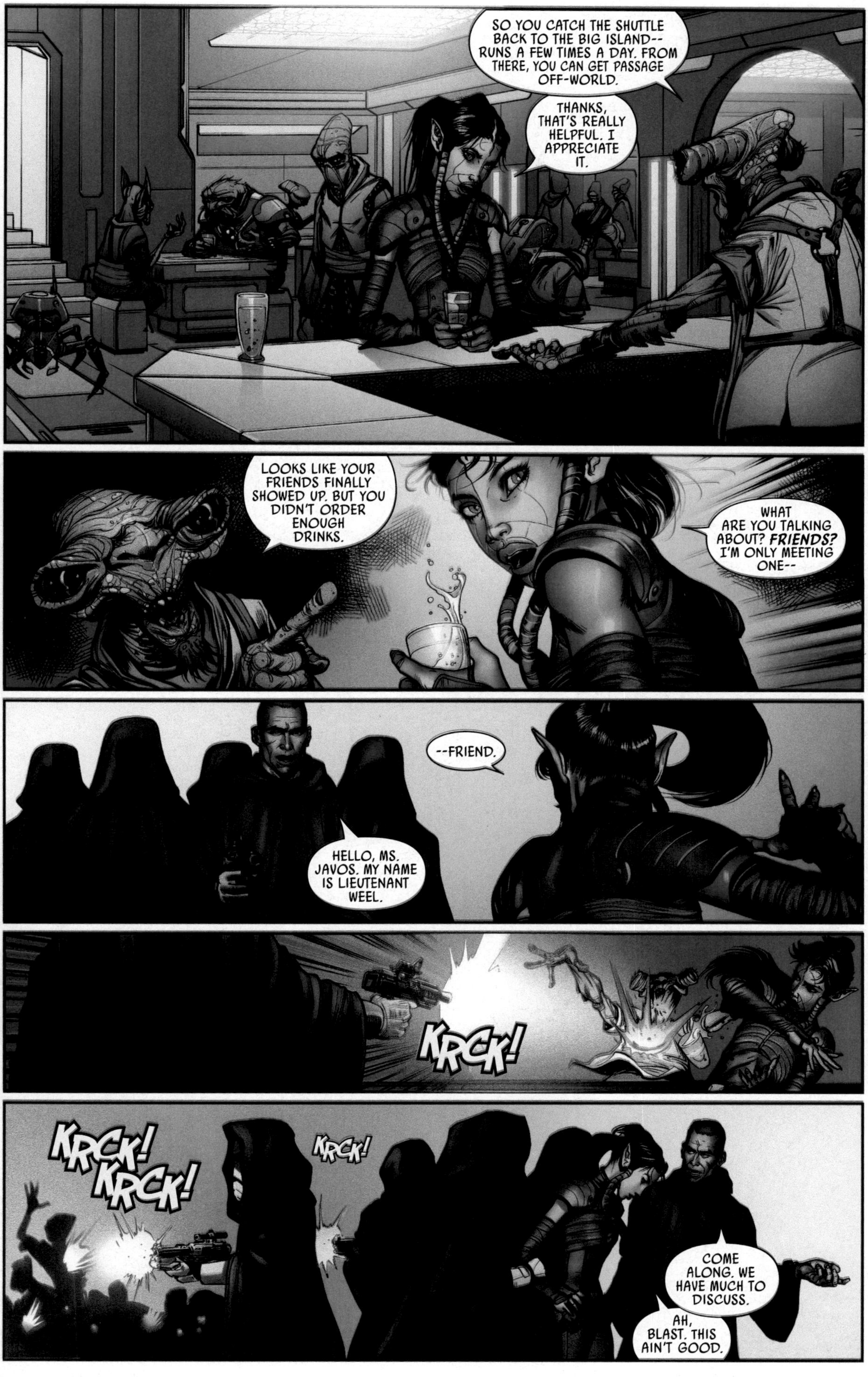
SO YOU CATCH THE SHUTTLE BACK TO THE BIG ISLAND-- RUNS A FEW TIMES A DAY. FROM THERE, YOU CAN GET PASSAGE OFF-WORLD.
THANKS, THAT'S REALLY HELPFUL. I APPRECIATE IT.
LOOKS LIKE YOUR FRIENDS FINALLY SHOWED UP. BUT YOU DIDN'T ORDER ENOUGH DRINKS.
WHAT ARE YOU TALKING ABOUT? ***FRIENDS?*** I'M ONLY MEETING ONE--
--FRIEND.
HELLO, MS. JAVOS. MY NAME IS LIEUTENANT WEEL.
KRCK!
KRCK! KRCK!
KRCK!
COME ALONG. WE HAVE MUCH TO DISCUSS.
AH, BLAST. THIS AIN'T GOOD.

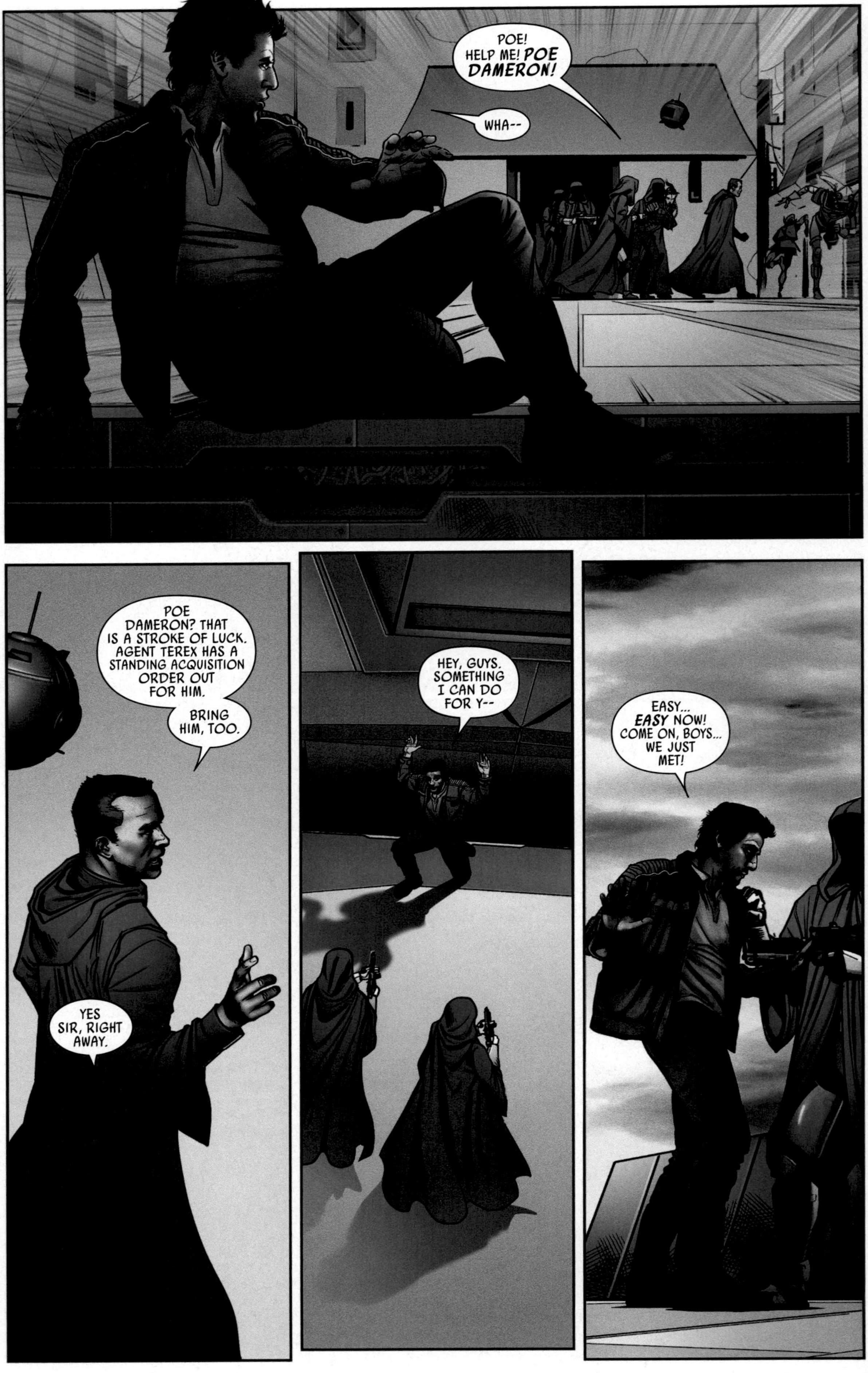

POE! HELP ME! POE DAMERON!
WHA--
POE DAMERON? THAT IS A STROKE OF LUCK. AGENT TEREX HAS A STANDING ACQUISITION ORDER OUT FOR HIM.
BRING HIM, TOO.
YES SIR, RIGHT AWAY.
HEY, GUYS. SOMETHING I CAN DO FOR Y--
EASY... EASY NOW! COME ON, BOYS... WE JUST MET!

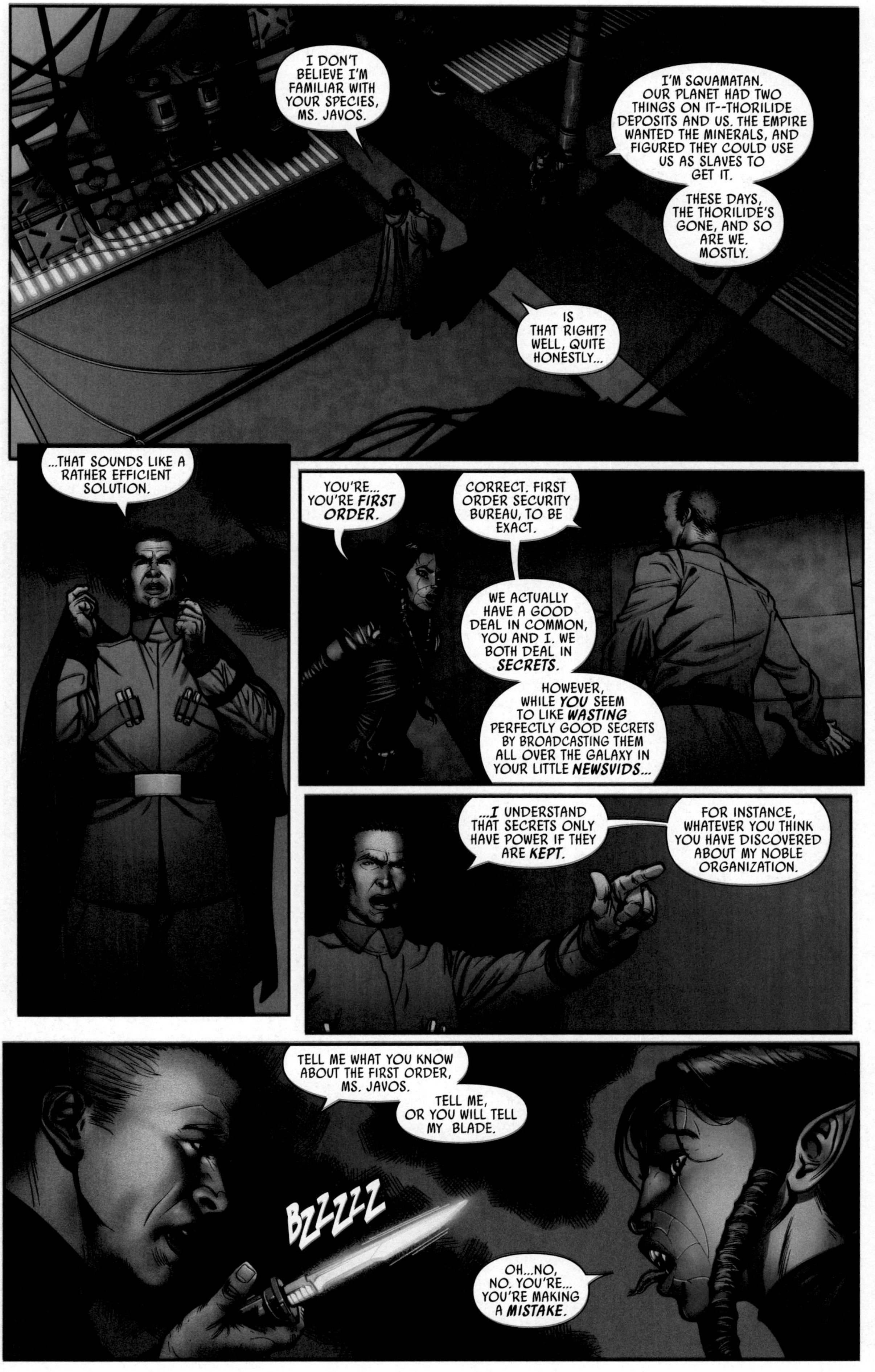
I DON'T BELIEVE I'M FAMILIAR WITH YOUR SPECIES, MS. JAVOS.
I'M SQUAMATAN. OUR PLANET HAD TWO THINGS ON IT--THORILIDE DEPOSITS AND US. THE EMPIRE WANTED THE MINERALS, AND FIGURED THEY COULD USE US AS SLAVES TO GET IT.
THESE DAYS, THE THORILIDE'S GONE, AND SO ARE WE. MOSTLY.
IS THAT RIGHT? WELL, QUITE HONESTLY...
...THAT SOUNDS LIKE A RATHER EFFICIENT SOLUTION.
YOU'RE... YOU'RE FIRST ORDER.
CORRECT. FIRST ORDER SECURITY BUREAU, TO BE EXACT.
WE ACTUALLY HAVE A GOOD DEAL IN COMMON, YOU AND I. WE BOTH DEAL IN SECRETS.
HOWEVER, WHILE YOU SEEM TO LIKE WASTING PERFECTLY GOOD SECRETS BY BROADCASTING THEM ALL OVER THE GALAXY IN YOUR LITTLE NEWSVIDS...
...I UNDERSTAND THAT SECRETS ONLY HAVE POWER IF THEY ARE KEPT.
FOR INSTANCE, WHATEVER YOU THINK YOU HAVE DISCOVERED ABOUT MY NOBLE ORGANIZATION.
TELL ME WHAT YOU KNOW ABOUT THE FIRST ORDER, MS. JAVOS.
TELL ME, OR YOU WILL TELL MY BLADE.
BZZZZZ
OH...NO, NO. YOU'RE... YOU'RE MAKING A MISTAKE.

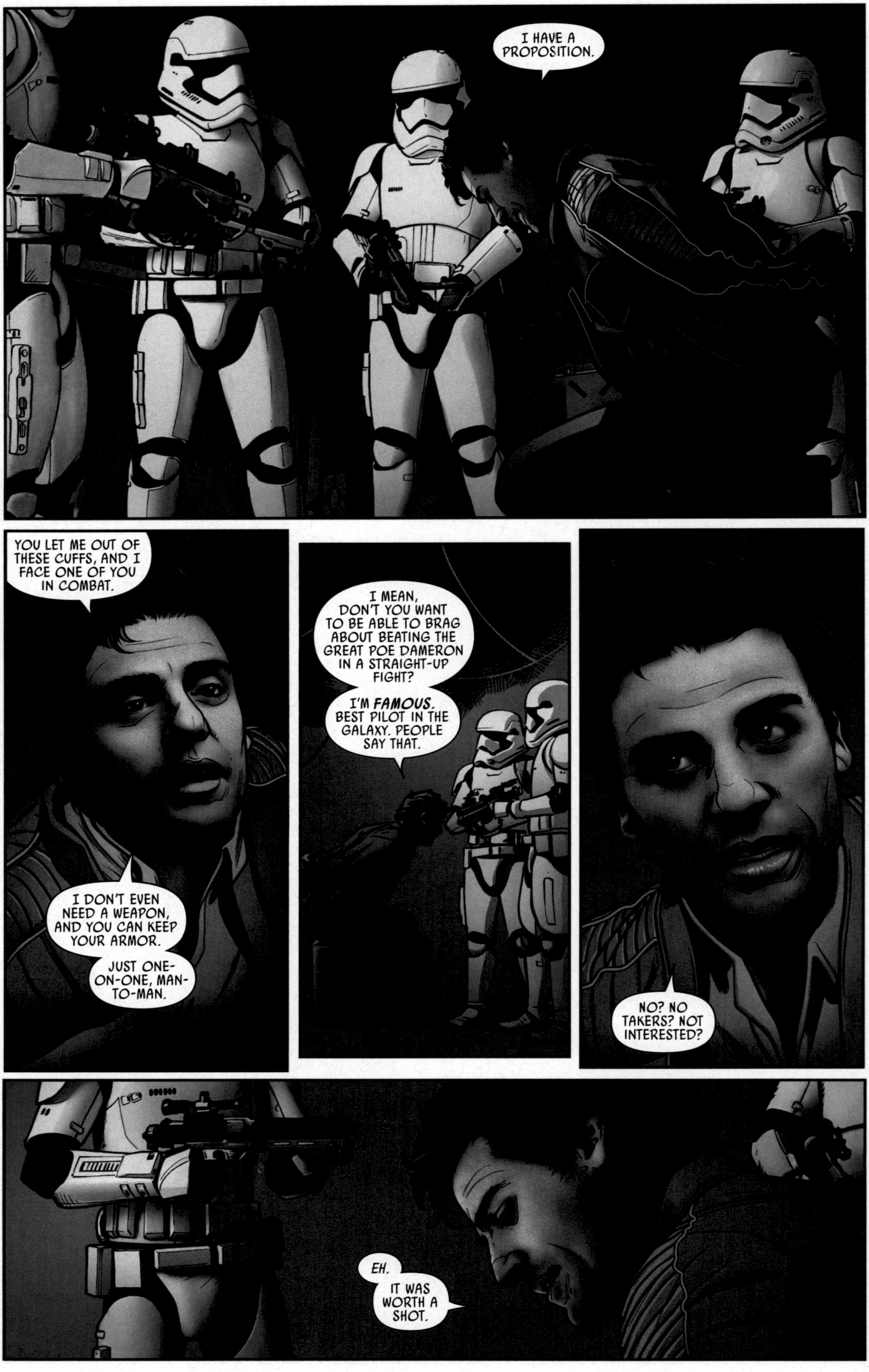
I HAVE A PROPOSITION.
YOU LET ME OUT OF THESE CUFFS, AND I FACE ONE OF YOU IN COMBAT.
I DON'T EVEN NEED A WEAPON, AND YOU CAN KEEP YOUR ARMOR.
JUST ONE-ON-ONE, MAN-TO-MAN.
I MEAN, DON'T YOU WANT TO BE ABLE TO BRAG ABOUT BEATING THE GREAT POE DAMERON IN A STRAIGHT-UP FIGHT?
I'M *FAMOUS.* BEST PILOT IN THE GALAXY. PEOPLE SAY THAT.
NO? NO TAKERS? NOT INTERESTED?
EH.
IT WAS WORTH A SHOT.

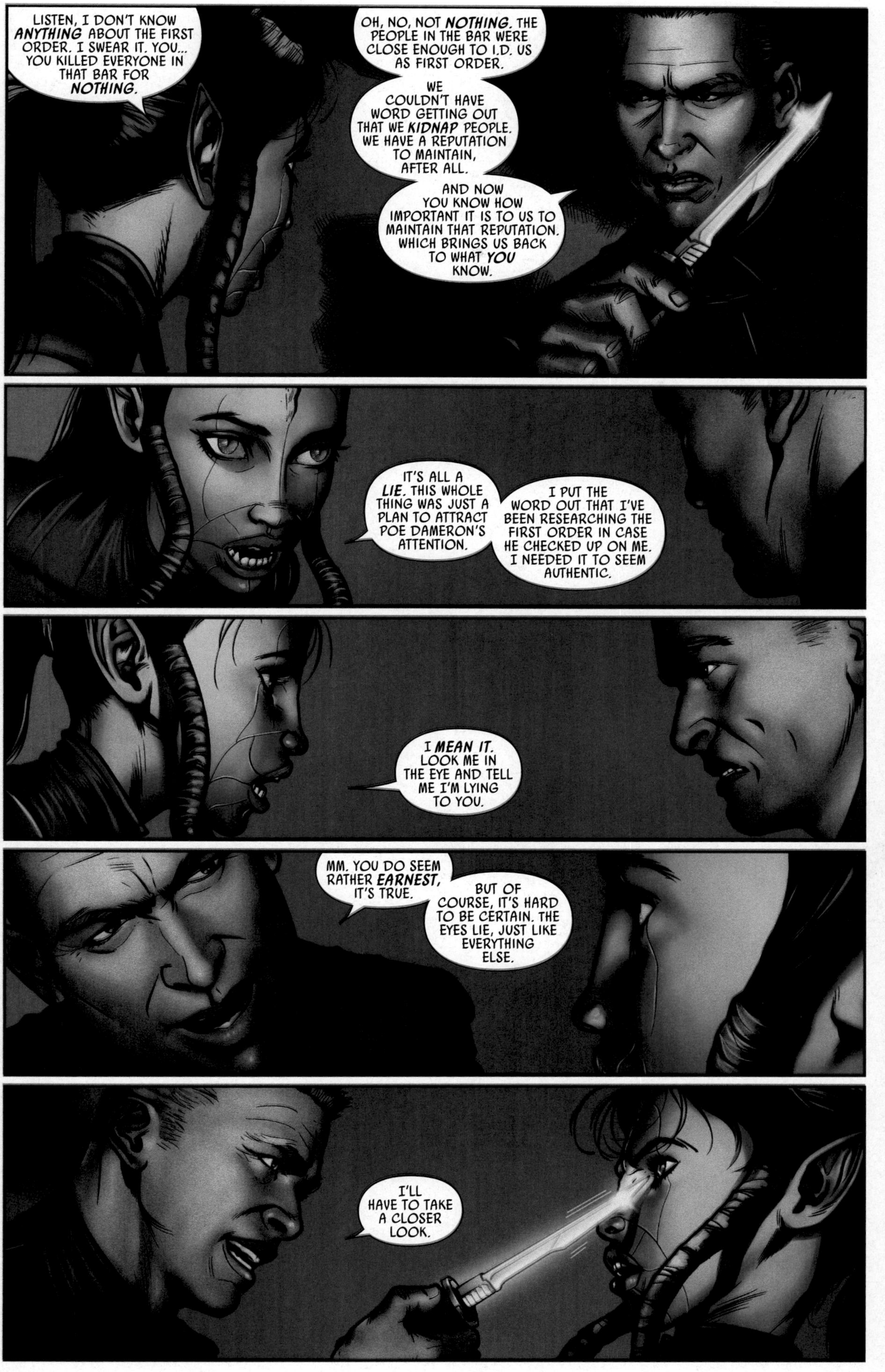
LISTEN, I DON'T KNOW ANYTHING ABOUT THE FIRST ORDER. I SWEAR IT. YOU... YOU KILLED EVERYONE IN THAT BAR FOR NOTHING.
OH, NO, NOT NOTHING. THE PEOPLE IN THE BAR WERE CLOSE ENOUGH TO I.D. US AS FIRST ORDER.
WE COULDN'T HAVE WORD GETTING OUT THAT WE KIDNAP PEOPLE. WE HAVE A REPUTATION TO MAINTAIN, AFTER ALL.
AND NOW YOU KNOW HOW IMPORTANT IT IS TO US TO MAINTAIN THAT REPUTATION. WHICH BRINGS US BACK TO WHAT YOU KNOW.
IT'S ALL A LIE. THIS WHOLE THING WAS JUST A PLAN TO ATTRACT POE DAMERON'S ATTENTION.
I PUT THE WORD OUT THAT I'VE BEEN RESEARCHING THE FIRST ORDER IN CASE HE CHECKED UP ON ME. I NEEDED IT TO SEEM AUTHENTIC.
I MEAN IT. LOOK ME IN THE EYE AND TELL ME I'M LYING TO YOU.
MM. YOU DO SEEM RATHER EARNEST, IT'S TRUE.
BUT OF COURSE, IT'S HARD TO BE CERTAIN. THE EYES LIE, JUST LIKE EVERYTHING ELSE.
I'LL HAVE TO TAKE A CLOSER LOOK.

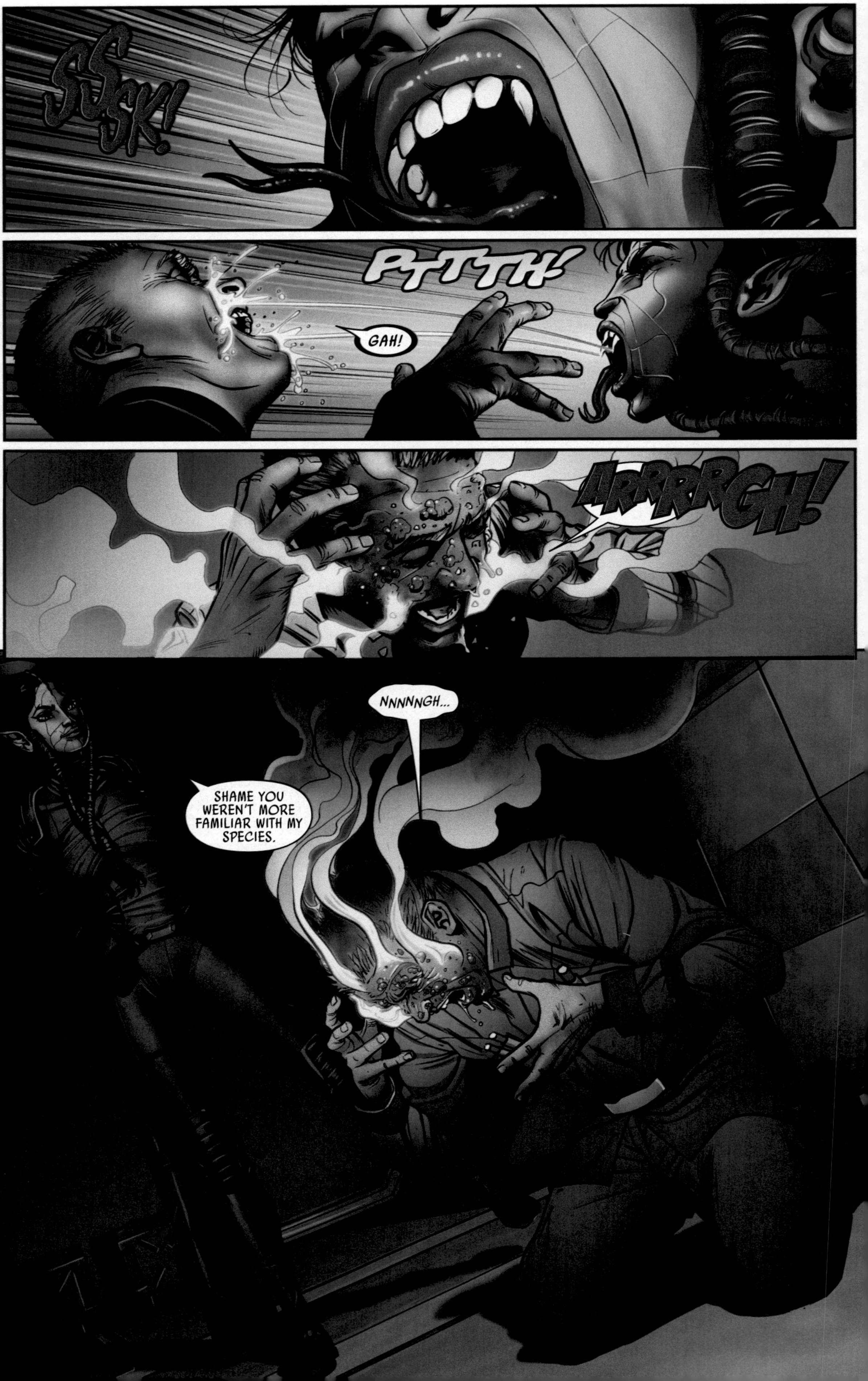
SSSK!
PTTTH!
GAH!
ARRRRGH!
NNNNNGH...
SHAME YOU WEREN'T MORE FAMILIAR WITH MY SPECIES.

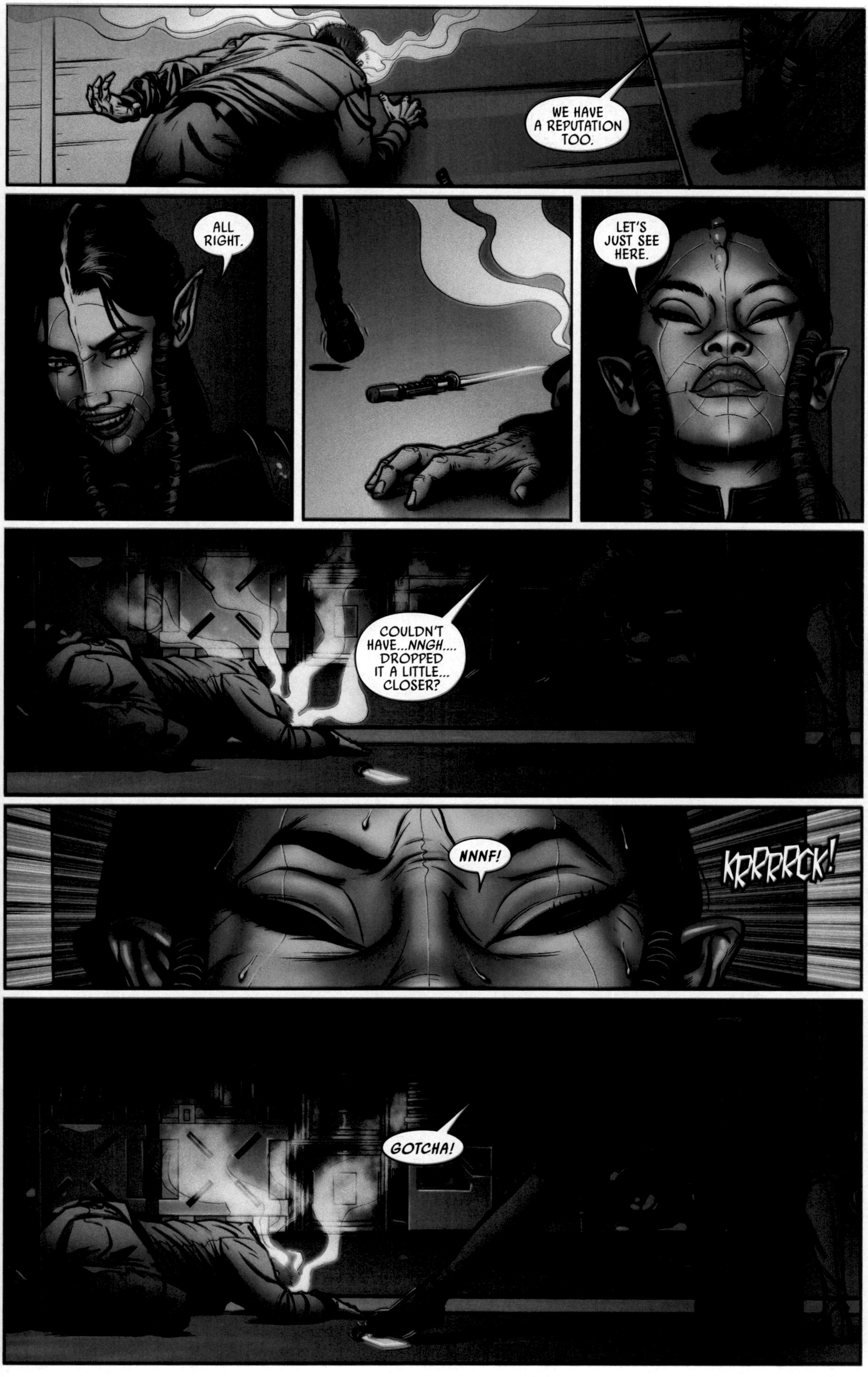
WE HAVE A REPUTATION TOO.
ALL RIGHT.
LET'S JUST SEE HERE.
COULDN'T HAVE...NNGH.... DROPPED IT A LITTLE... CLOSER?
NNNF!
KRRRRCK!
GOTCHA!

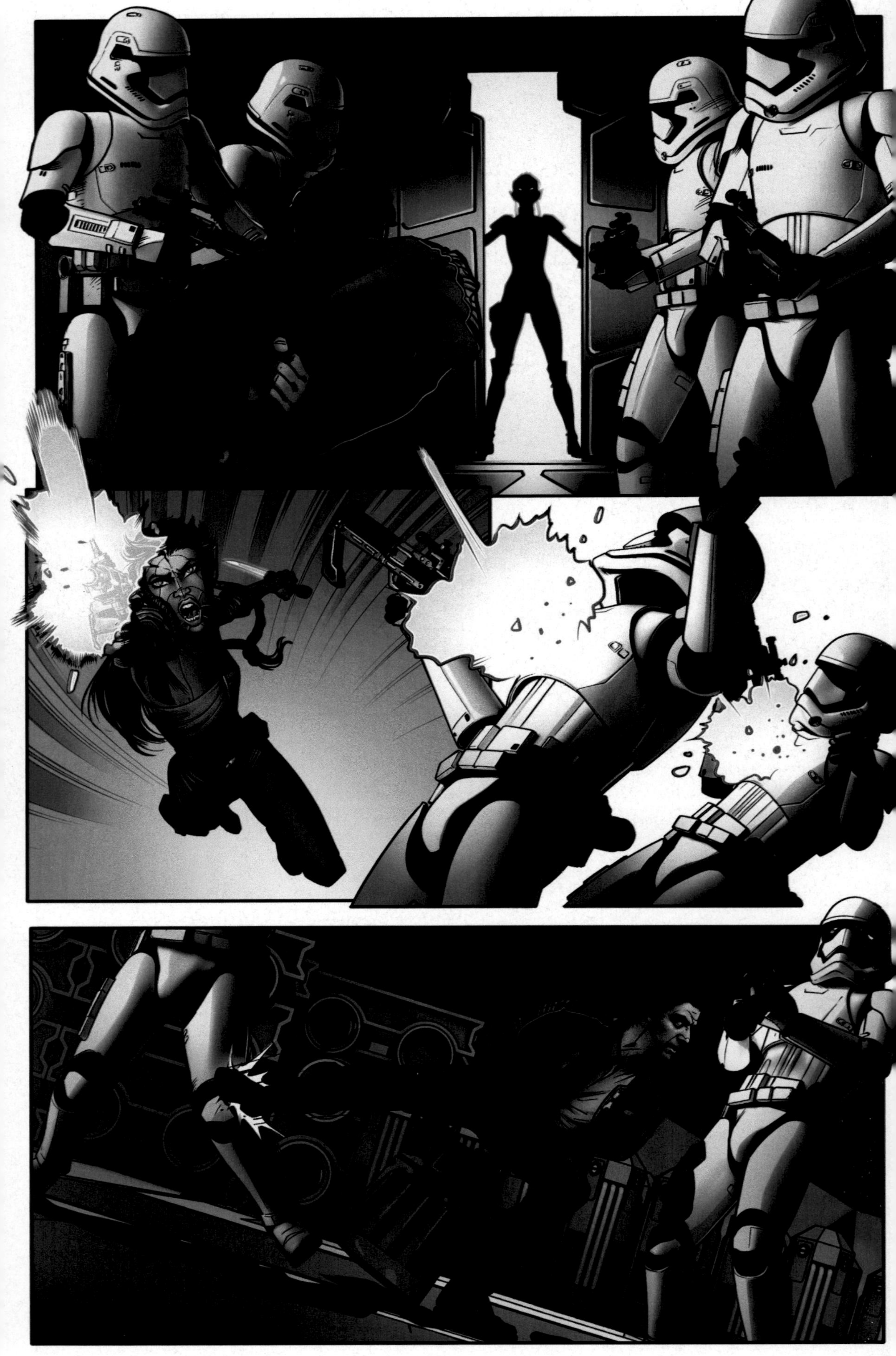

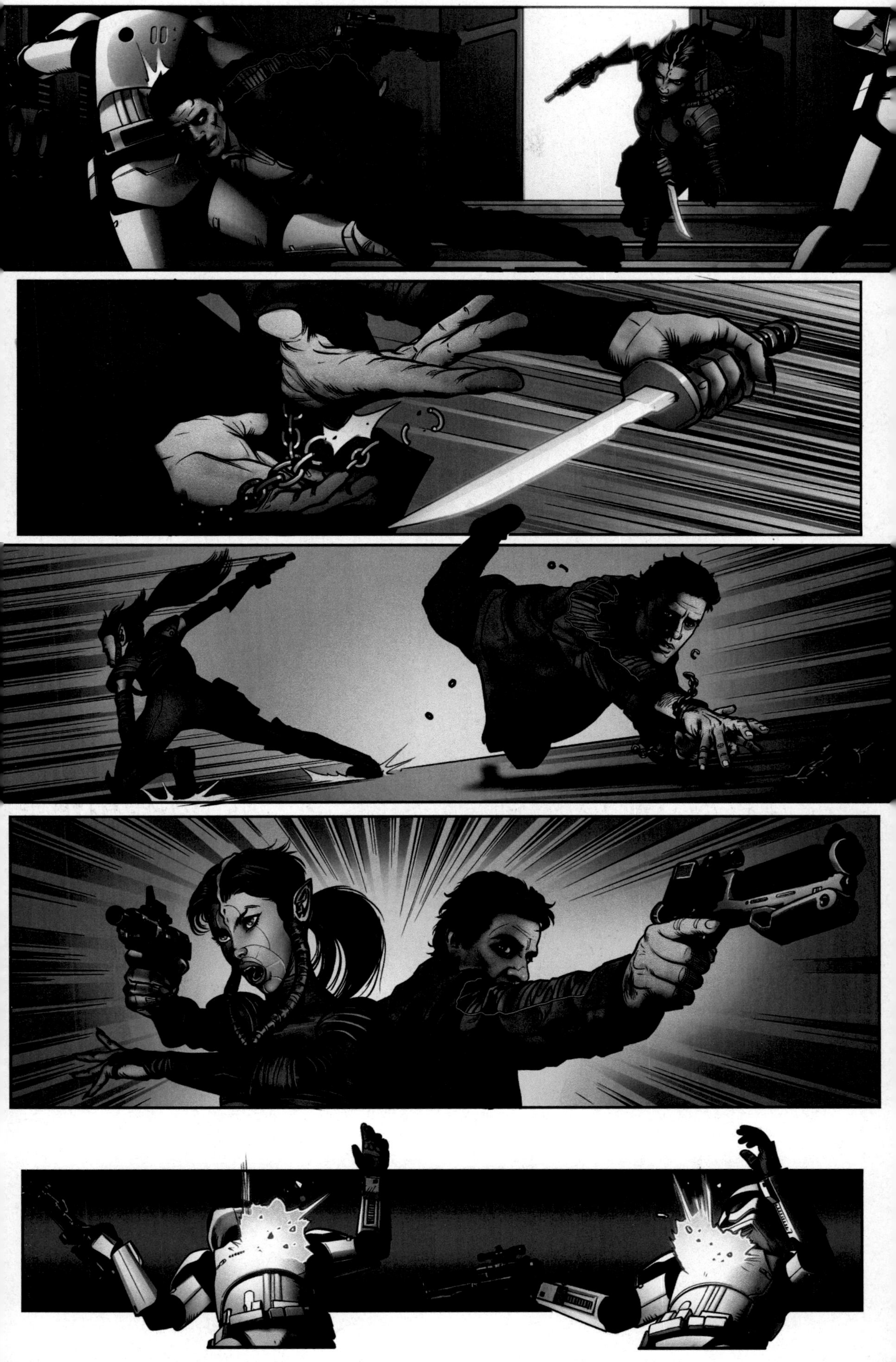

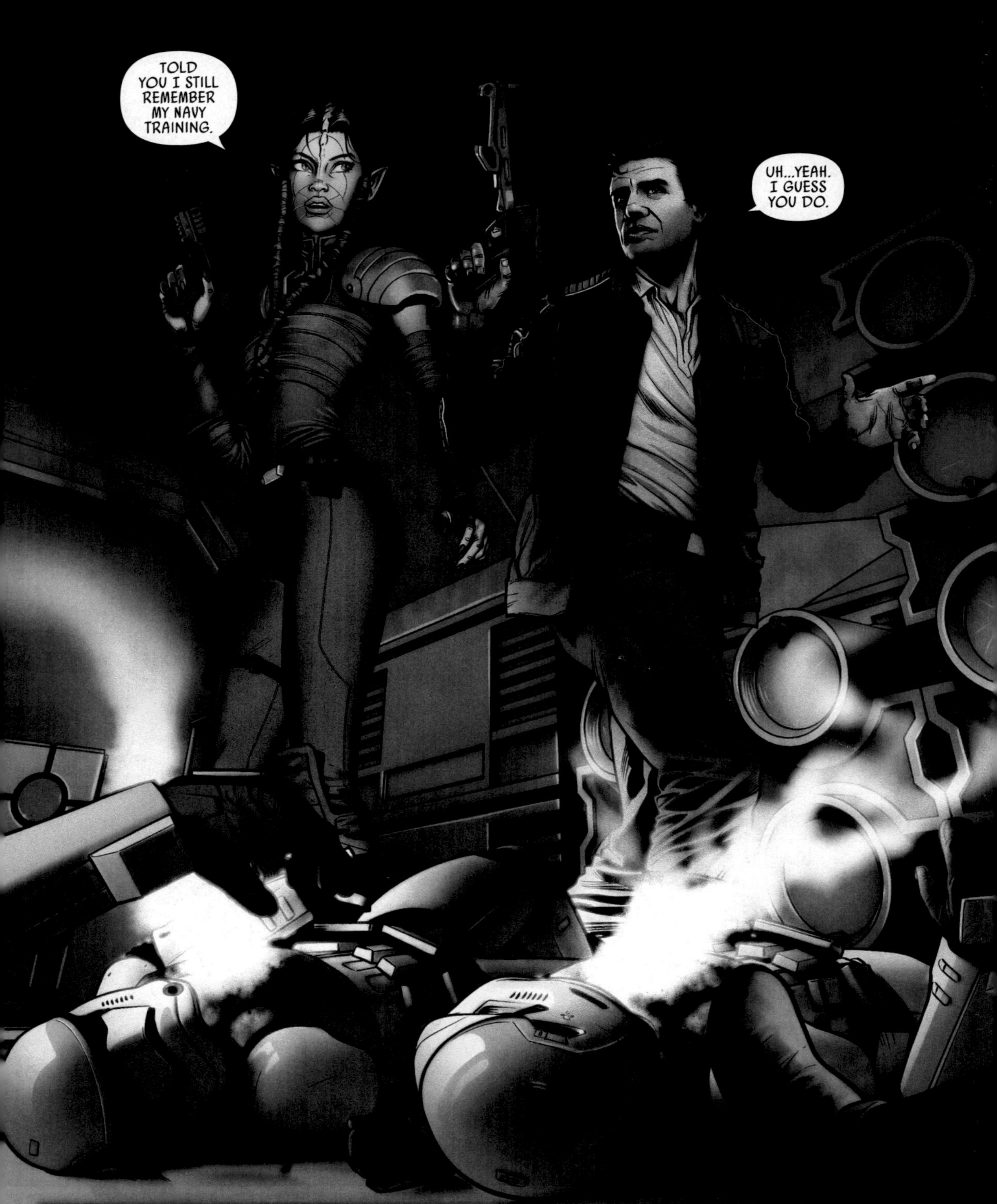
TOLD YOU I STILL REMEMBER MY NAVY TRAINING.
UH...YEAH. I GUESS YOU DO.

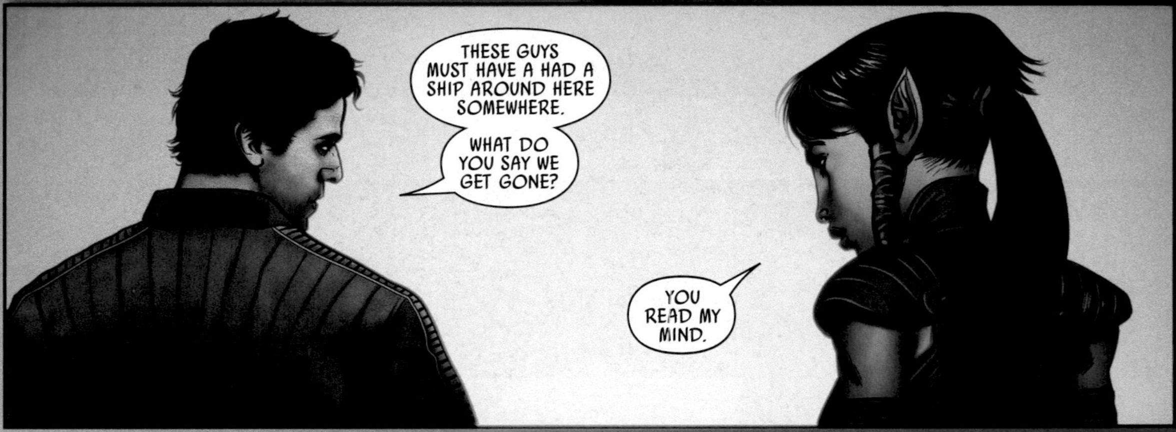
THESE GUYS MUST HAVE A HAD A SHIP AROUND HERE SOMEWHERE.
WHAT DO YOU SAY WE GET GONE?
YOU READ MY MIND.

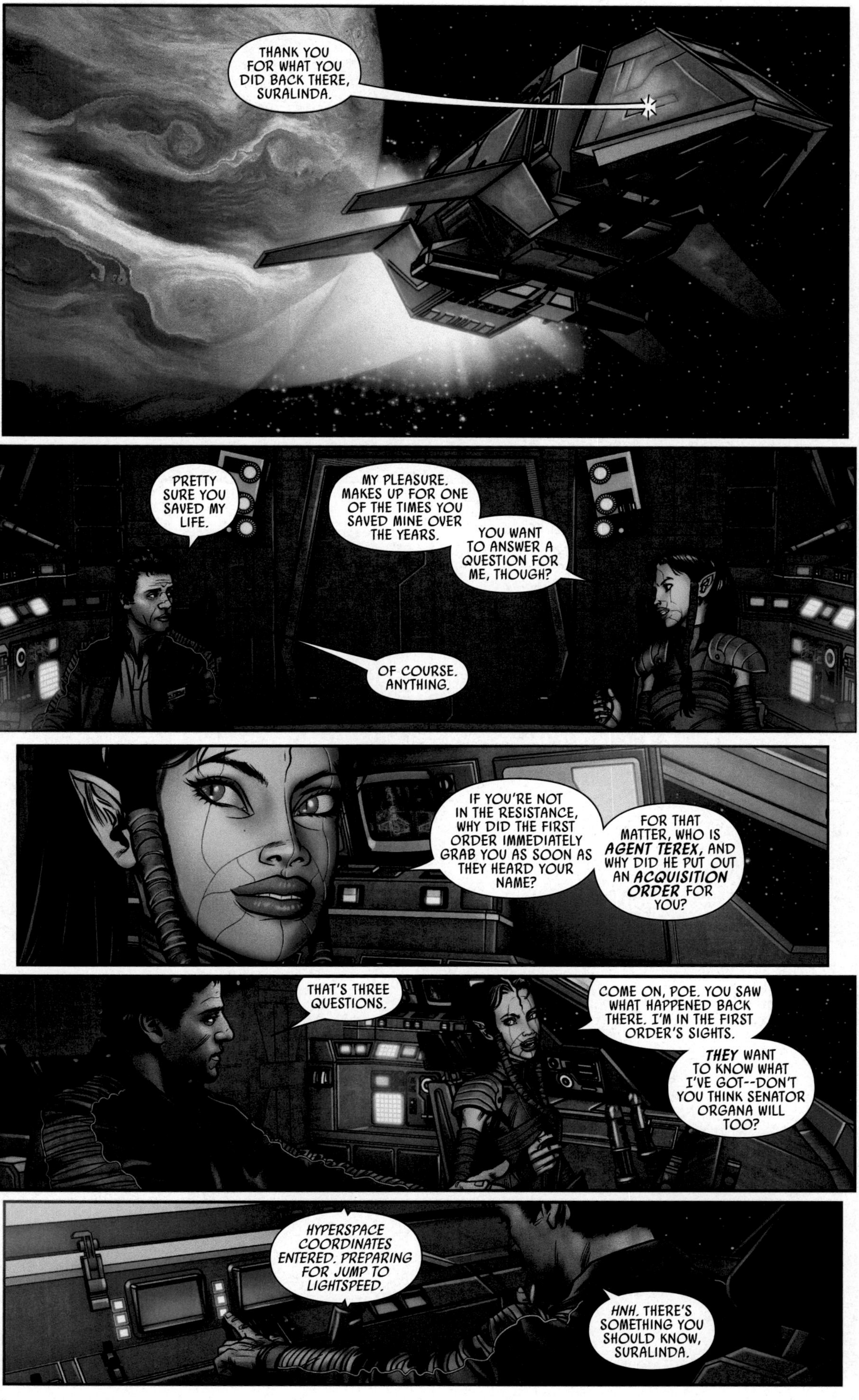
THANK YOU FOR WHAT YOU DID BACK THERE, SURALINDA.
PRETTY SURE YOU SAVED MY LIFE.
MY PLEASURE. MAKES UP FOR ONE OF THE TIMES YOU SAVED MINE OVER THE YEARS.
YOU WANT TO ANSWER A QUESTION FOR ME, THOUGH?
OF COURSE. ANYTHING.
IF YOU'RE NOT IN THE RESISTANCE, WHY DID THE FIRST ORDER IMMEDIATELY GRAB YOU AS SOON AS THEY HEARD YOUR NAME?
FOR THAT MATTER, WHO IS ***AGENT TEREX,*** AND WHY DID HE PUT OUT AN ***ACQUISITION ORDER*** FOR YOU?
THAT'S THREE QUESTIONS.
COME ON, POE. YOU SAW WHAT HAPPENED BACK THERE. I'M IN THE FIRST ORDER'S SIGHTS.
THEY WANT TO KNOW WHAT I'VE GOT--DON'T YOU THINK SENATOR ORGANA WILL TOO?
HYPERSPACE COORDINATES ENTERED. PREPARING FOR JUMP TO LIGHTSPEED.
HNH. THERE'S SOMETHING YOU SHOULD KNOW, SURALINDA.

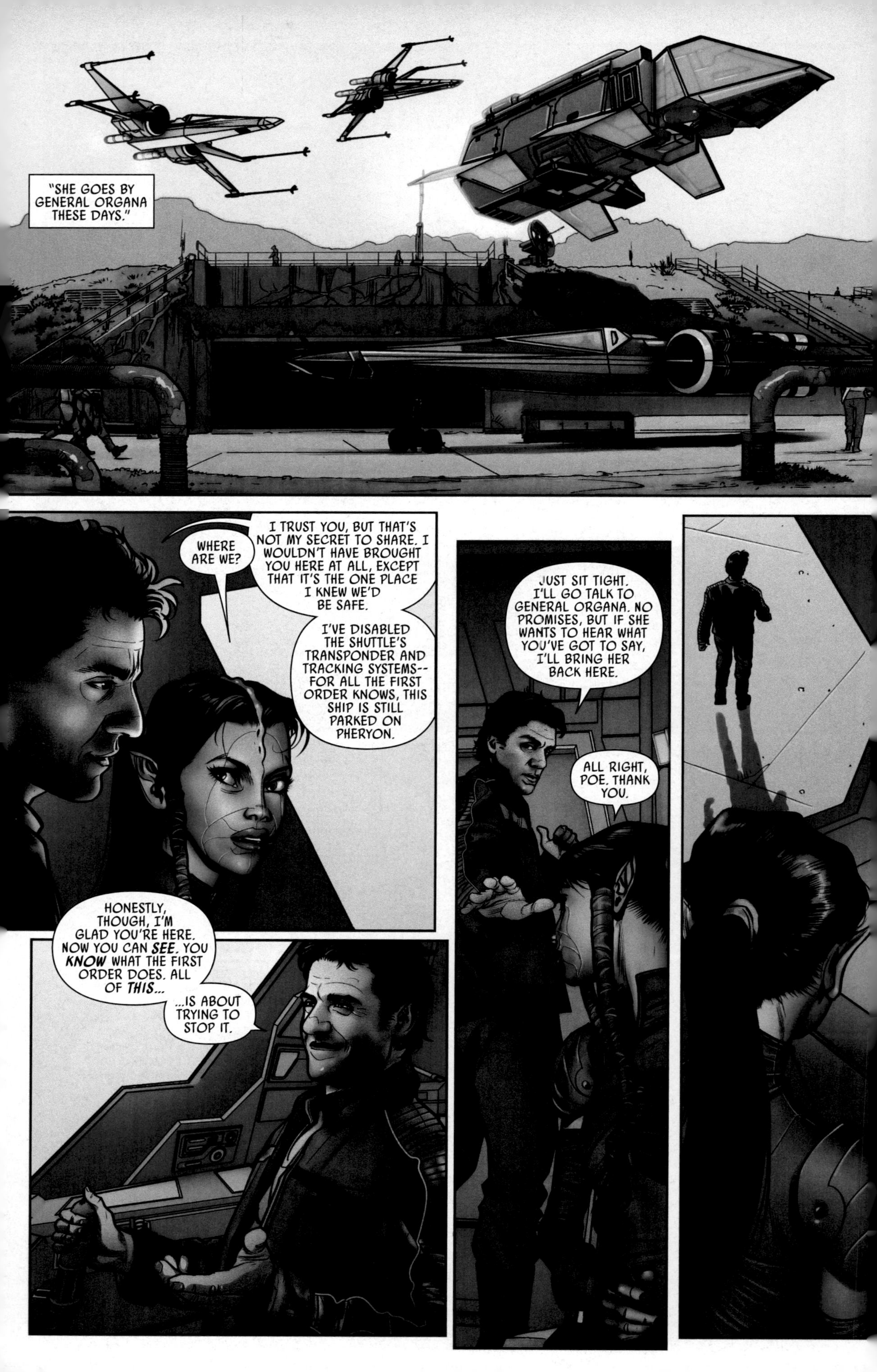
"SHE GOES BY GENERAL ORGANA THESE DAYS."
WHERE ARE WE?
I TRUST YOU, BUT THAT'S NOT MY SECRET TO SHARE. I WOULDN'T HAVE BROUGHT YOU HERE AT ALL, EXCEPT THAT IT'S THE ONE PLACE I KNEW WE'D BE SAFE.
I'VE DISABLED THE SHUTTLE'S TRANSPONDER AND TRACKING SYSTEMS-- FOR ALL THE FIRST ORDER KNOWS, THIS SHIP IS STILL PARKED ON PHERYON.
HONESTLY, THOUGH, I'M GLAD YOU'RE HERE. NOW YOU CAN SEE. YOU KNOW WHAT THE FIRST ORDER DOES. ALL OF THIS...
...IS ABOUT TRYING TO STOP IT.
JUST SIT TIGHT. I'LL GO TALK TO GENERAL ORGANA. NO PROMISES, BUT IF SHE WANTS TO HEAR WHAT YOU'VE GOT TO SAY, I'LL BRING HER BACK HERE.
ALL RIGHT, POE. THANK YOU.

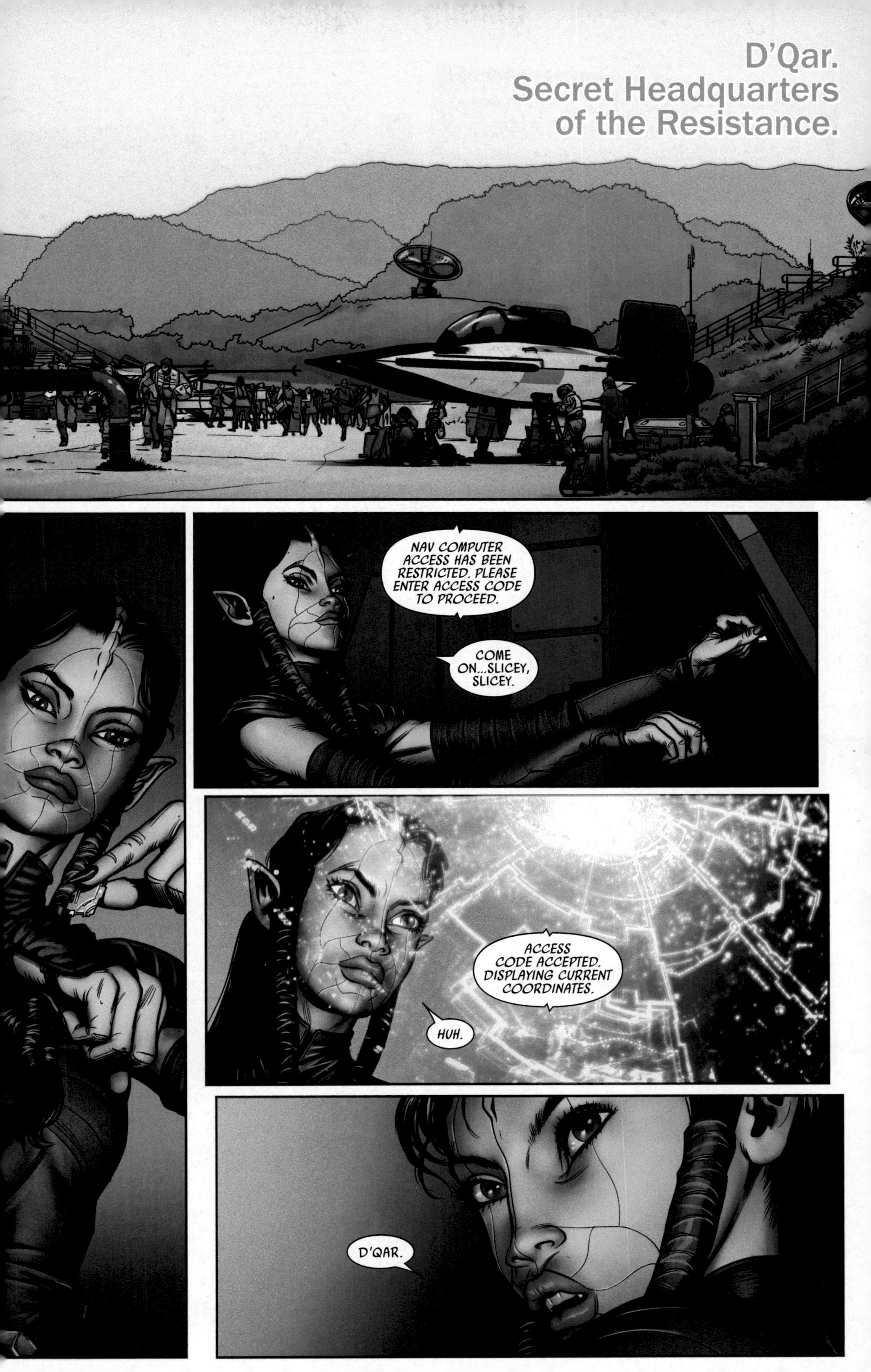
D'Qar.
Secret Headquarters of the Resistance.
NAV COMPUTER ACCESS HAS BEEN RESTRICTED. PLEASE ENTER ACCESS CODE TO PROCEED.
COME ON...SLICEY, SLICEY.
ACCESS CODE ACCEPTED. DISPLAYING CURRENT COORDINATES.
HUH.
D'QAR.

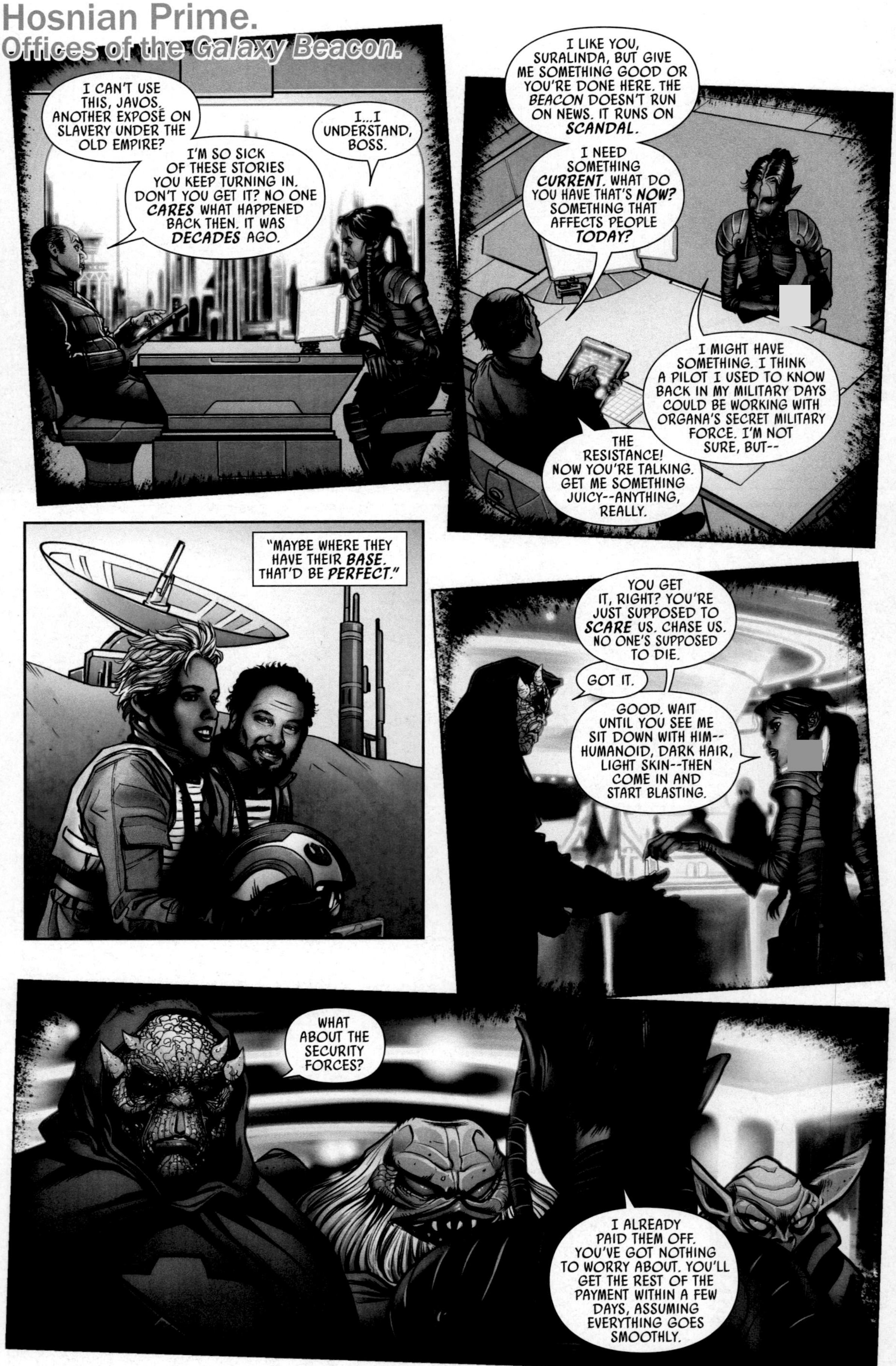
Hosnian Prime.
Offices of the Galaxy Beacon.
I CAN'T USE THIS, JAVOS. ANOTHER EXPOSÉ ON SLAVERY UNDER THE OLD EMPIRE?
I'M SO SICK OF THESE STORIES YOU KEEP TURNING IN. DON'T YOU GET IT? NO ONE CARES WHAT HAPPENED BACK THEN. IT WAS DECADES AGO.
I...I UNDERSTAND, BOSS.
I LIKE YOU, SURALINDA, BUT GIVE ME SOMETHING GOOD OR YOU'RE DONE HERE. THE BEACON DOESN'T RUN ON NEWS. IT RUNS ON SCANDAL.
I NEED SOMETHING CURRENT. WHAT DO YOU HAVE THAT'S NOW? SOMETHING THAT AFFECTS PEOPLE TODAY?
I MIGHT HAVE SOMETHING. I THINK A PILOT I USED TO KNOW BACK IN MY MILITARY DAYS COULD BE WORKING WITH ORGANA'S SECRET MILITARY FORCE. I'M NOT SURE, BUT--
THE RESISTANCE! NOW YOU'RE TALKING. GET ME SOMETHING JUICY--ANYTHING, REALLY.
"MAYBE WHERE THEY HAVE THEIR BASE. THAT'D BE PERFECT."
YOU GET IT, RIGHT? YOU'RE JUST SUPPOSED TO SCARE US. CHASE US. NO ONE'S SUPPOSED TO DIE.
GOT IT.
GOOD. WAIT UNTIL YOU SEE ME SIT DOWN WITH HIM--HUMANOID, DARK HAIR, LIGHT SKIN--THEN COME IN AND START BLASTING.
WHAT ABOUT THE SECURITY FORCES?
I ALREADY PAID THEM OFF. YOU'VE GOT NOTHING TO WORRY ABOUT. YOU'LL GET THE REST OF THE PAYMENT WITHIN A FEW DAYS, ASSUMING EVERYTHING GOES SMOOTHLY.

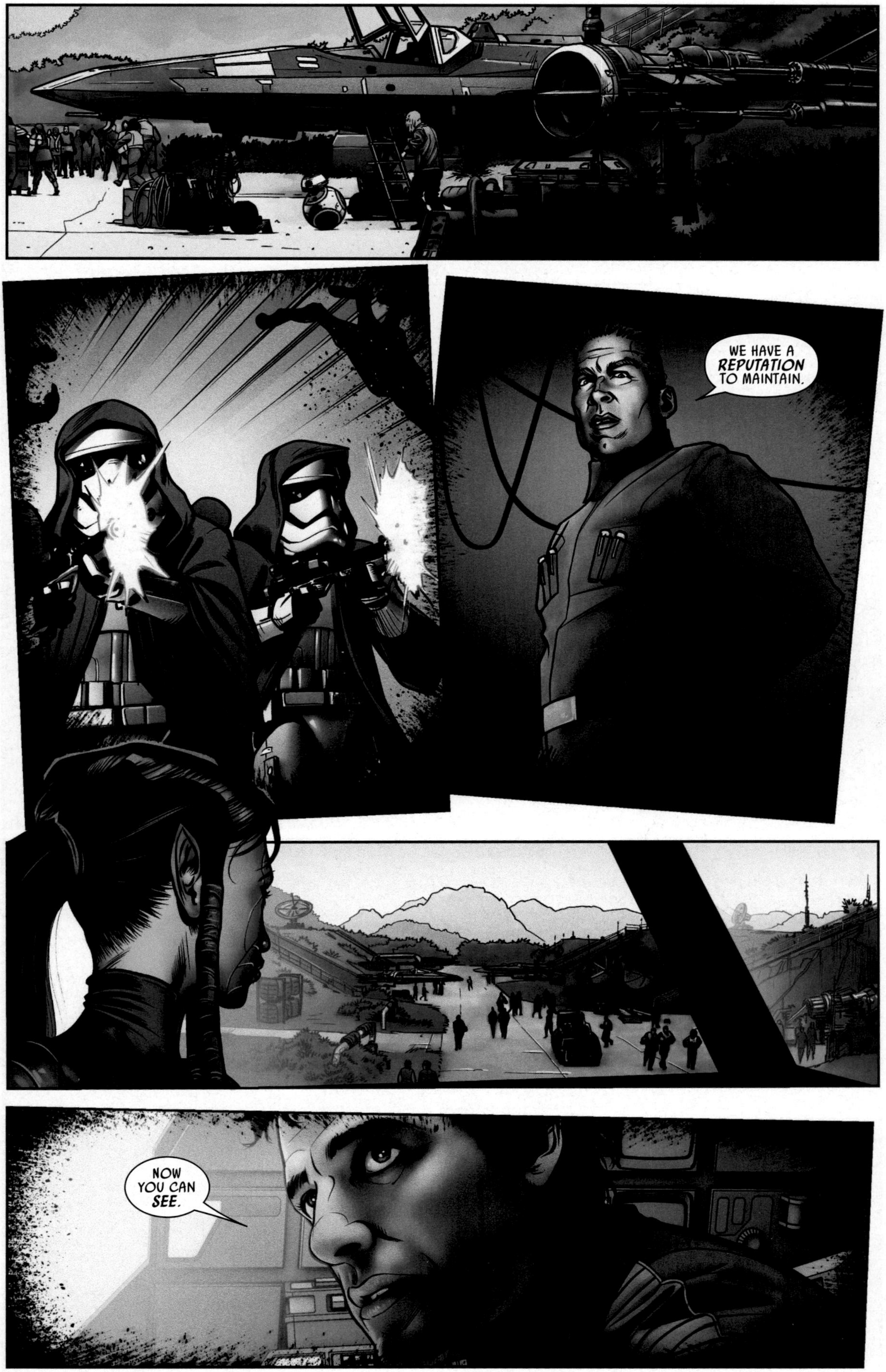
WE HAVE A REPUTATION TO MAINTAIN.
NOW YOU CAN SEE.

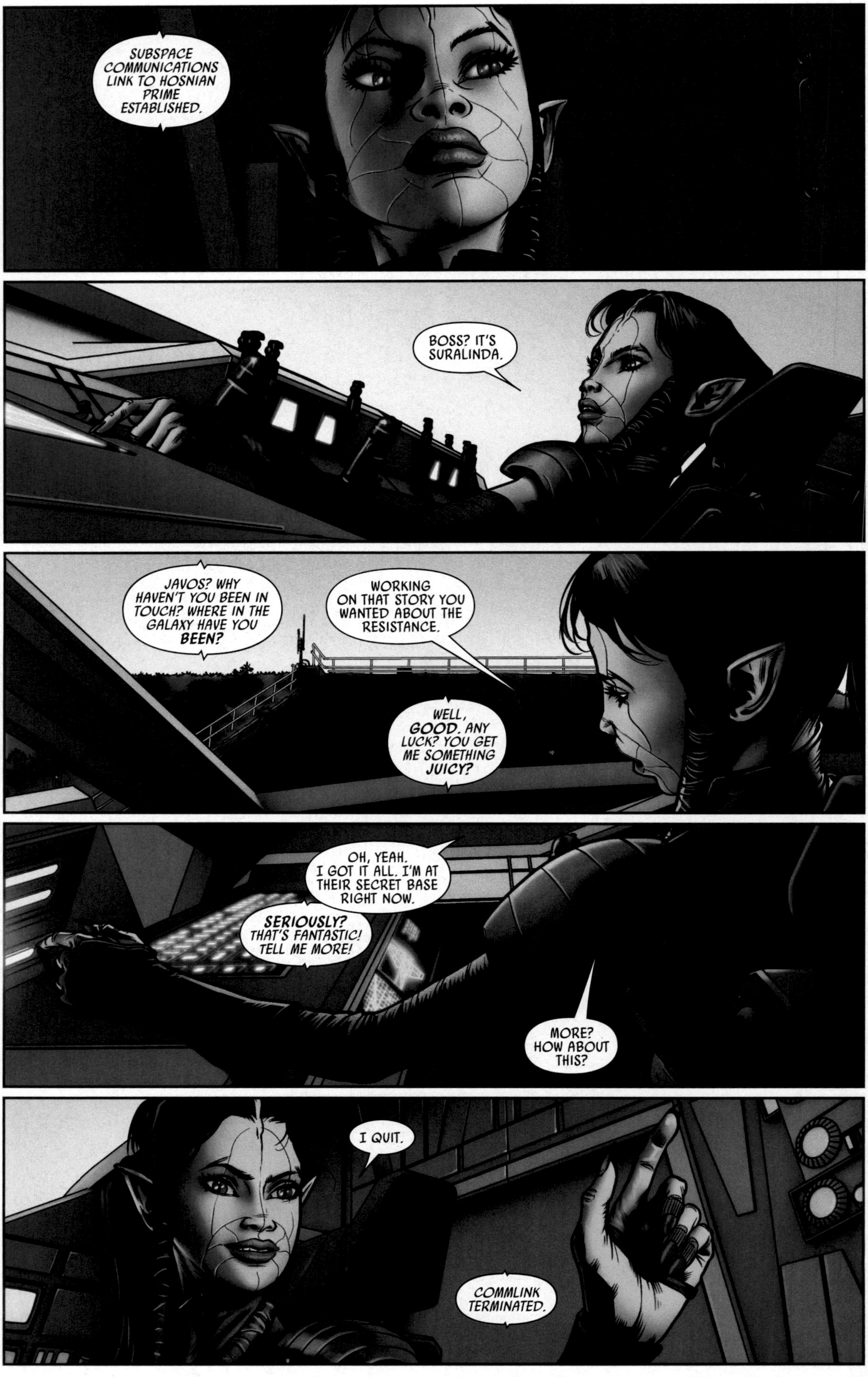
SUBSPACE COMMUNICATIONS LINK TO HOSNIAN PRIME ESTABLISHED.
BOSS? IT'S SURALINDA.
JAVOS? WHY HAVEN'T YOU BEEN IN TOUCH? WHERE IN THE GALAXY HAVE YOU **BEEN?**
WORKING ON THAT STORY YOU WANTED ABOUT THE RESISTANCE.
WELL, **GOOD.** ANY LUCK? YOU GET ME SOMETHING **JUICY?**
OH, YEAH. I GOT IT ALL. I'M AT THEIR SECRET BASE RIGHT NOW.
SERIOUSLY? THAT'S FANTASTIC! TELL ME MORE!
MORE? HOW ABOUT THIS?
I QUIT.
COMMLINK TERMINATED.

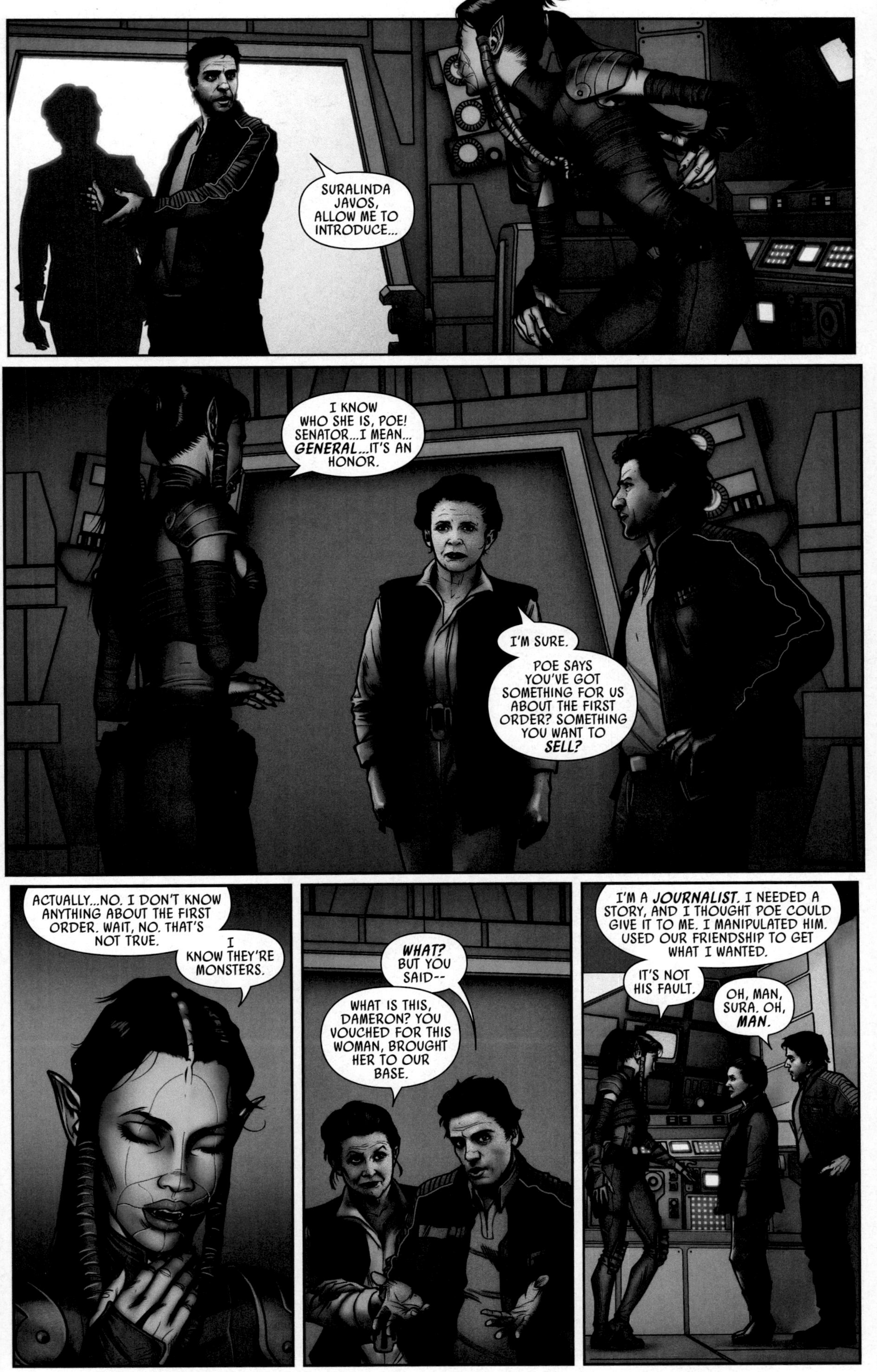
SURALINDA JAVOS, ALLOW ME TO INTRODUCE...
I KNOW WHO SHE IS, POE! SENATOR...I MEAN... GENERAL...IT'S AN HONOR.
I'M SURE.
POE SAYS YOU'VE GOT SOMETHING FOR US ABOUT THE FIRST ORDER? SOMETHING YOU WANT TO SELL?
ACTUALLY...NO. I DON'T KNOW ANYTHING ABOUT THE FIRST ORDER. WAIT, NO. THAT'S NOT TRUE.
I KNOW THEY'RE MONSTERS.
WHAT? BUT YOU SAID--
WHAT IS THIS, DAMERON? YOU VOUCHED FOR THIS WOMAN, BROUGHT HER TO OUR BASE.
I'M A JOURNALIST. I NEEDED A STORY, AND I THOUGHT POE COULD GIVE IT TO ME. I MANIPULATED HIM. USED OUR FRIENDSHIP TO GET WHAT I WANTED.
IT'S NOT HIS FAULT.
OH, MAN, SURA. OH, MAN.

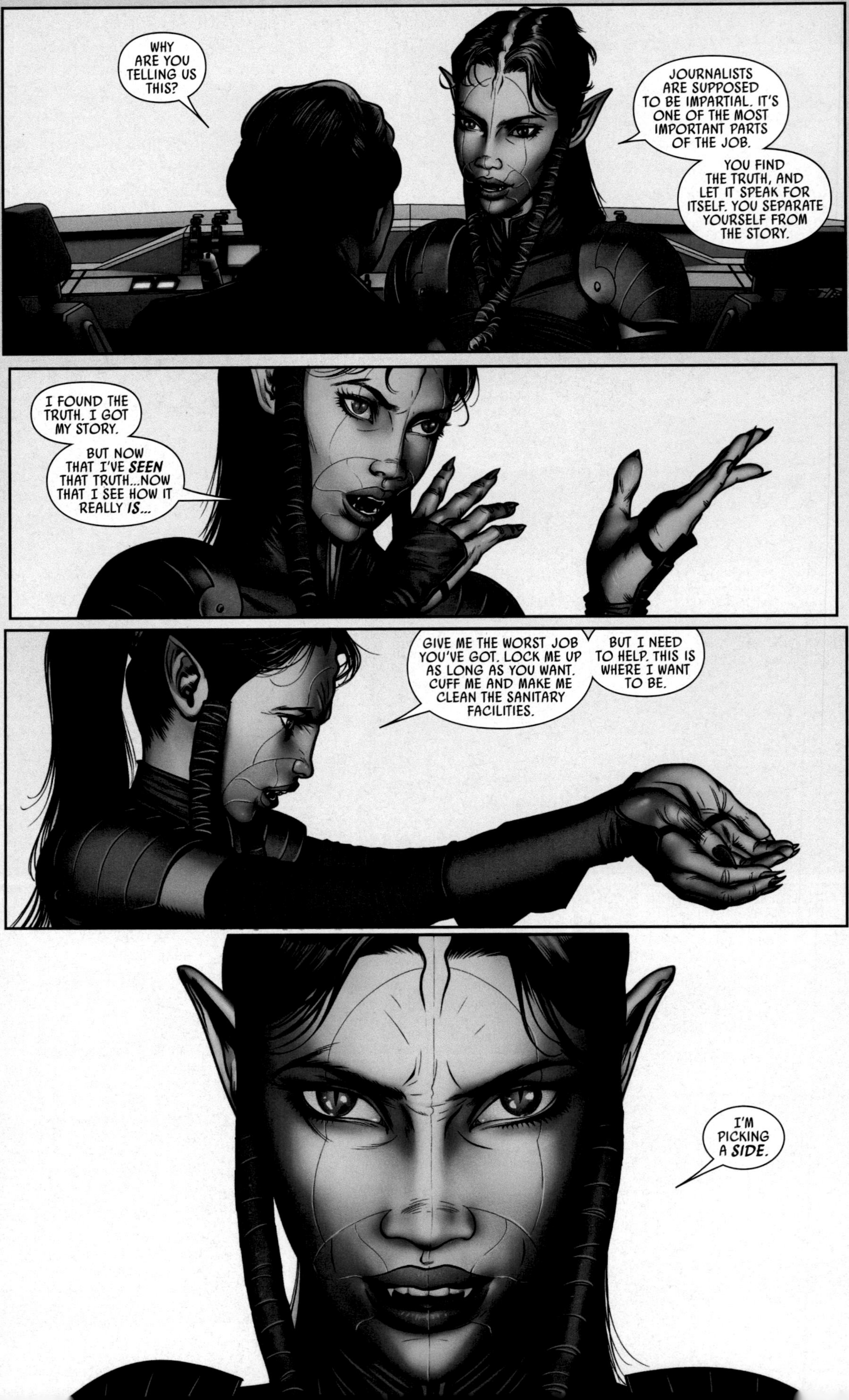
WHY ARE YOU TELLING US THIS?
JOURNALISTS ARE SUPPOSED TO BE IMPARTIAL. IT'S ONE OF THE MOST IMPORTANT PARTS OF THE JOB.
YOU FIND THE TRUTH, AND LET IT SPEAK FOR ITSELF. YOU SEPARATE YOURSELF FROM THE STORY.
I FOUND THE TRUTH. I GOT MY STORY.
BUT NOW THAT I'VE ***SEEN*** THAT TRUTH...NOW THAT I SEE HOW IT REALLY ***IS...***
GIVE ME THE WORST JOB YOU'VE GOT. LOCK ME UP AS LONG AS YOU WANT. CUFF ME AND MAKE ME CLEAN THE SANITARY FACILITIES.
BUT I NEED TO HELP. THIS IS WHERE I WANT TO BE.
I'M PICKING A ***SIDE.***

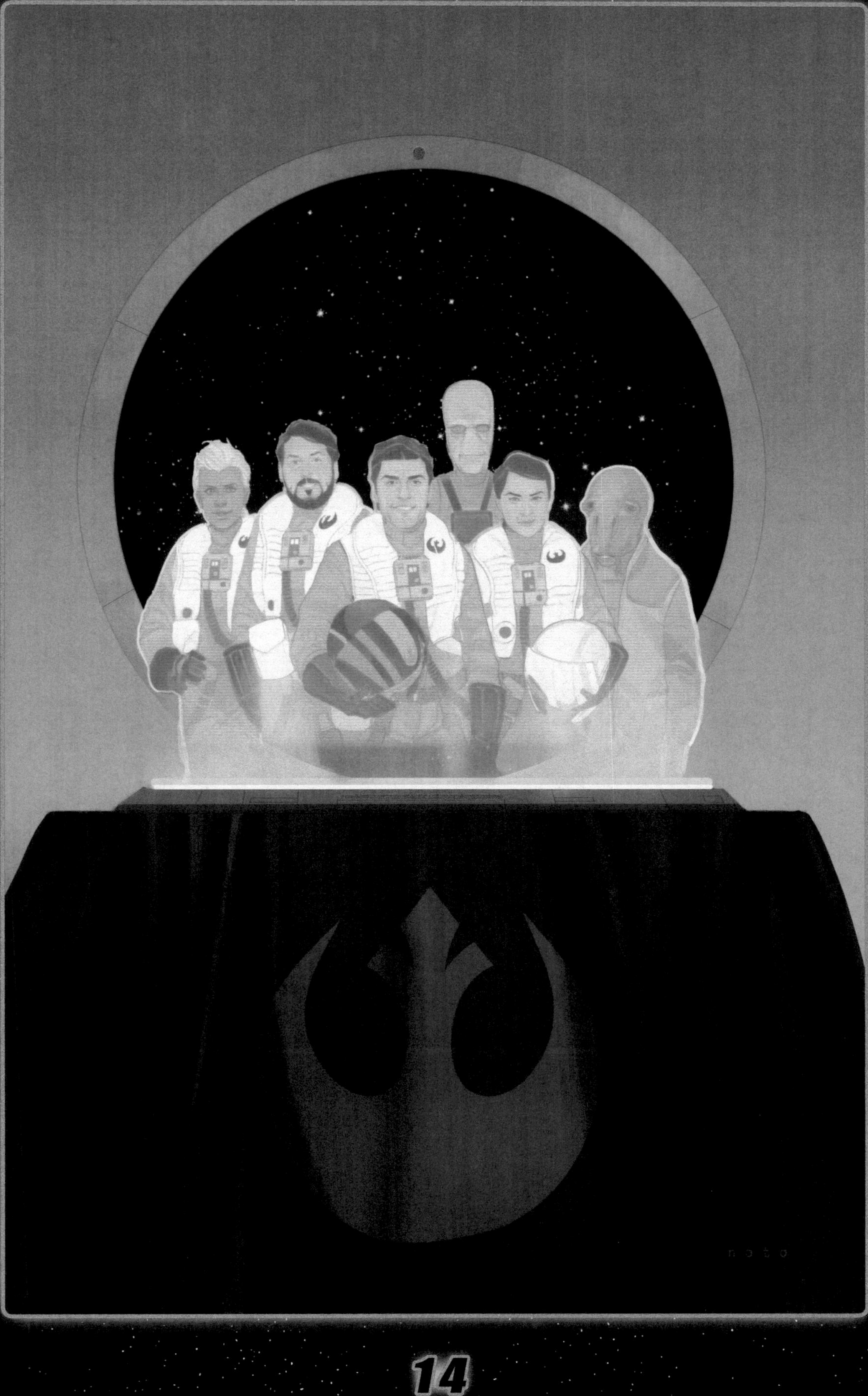
noto
14

Book III
LEGEND LOST

It is a time of uncertainty in the galaxy. Standing against the oppression of the First Order is General Organa's Resistance, including Poe Dameron and his team of pilots — Black Squadron.

Poe Dameron and his team have recently emerged from a bittersweet victory. Through a combination of luck and skill, they defeated the ruthless crime lord Terex, although in the process they lost one of their own, grizzled veteran pilot L'ulo. Terex was taken prisoner by his former employers, the evil First Order, who intend to punish him for defying their commands.

Now, back at the hidden Resistance base, Black Squadron and their comrades have come together to mourn their loss, while in a First Order prison cell Terex awaits his fate....

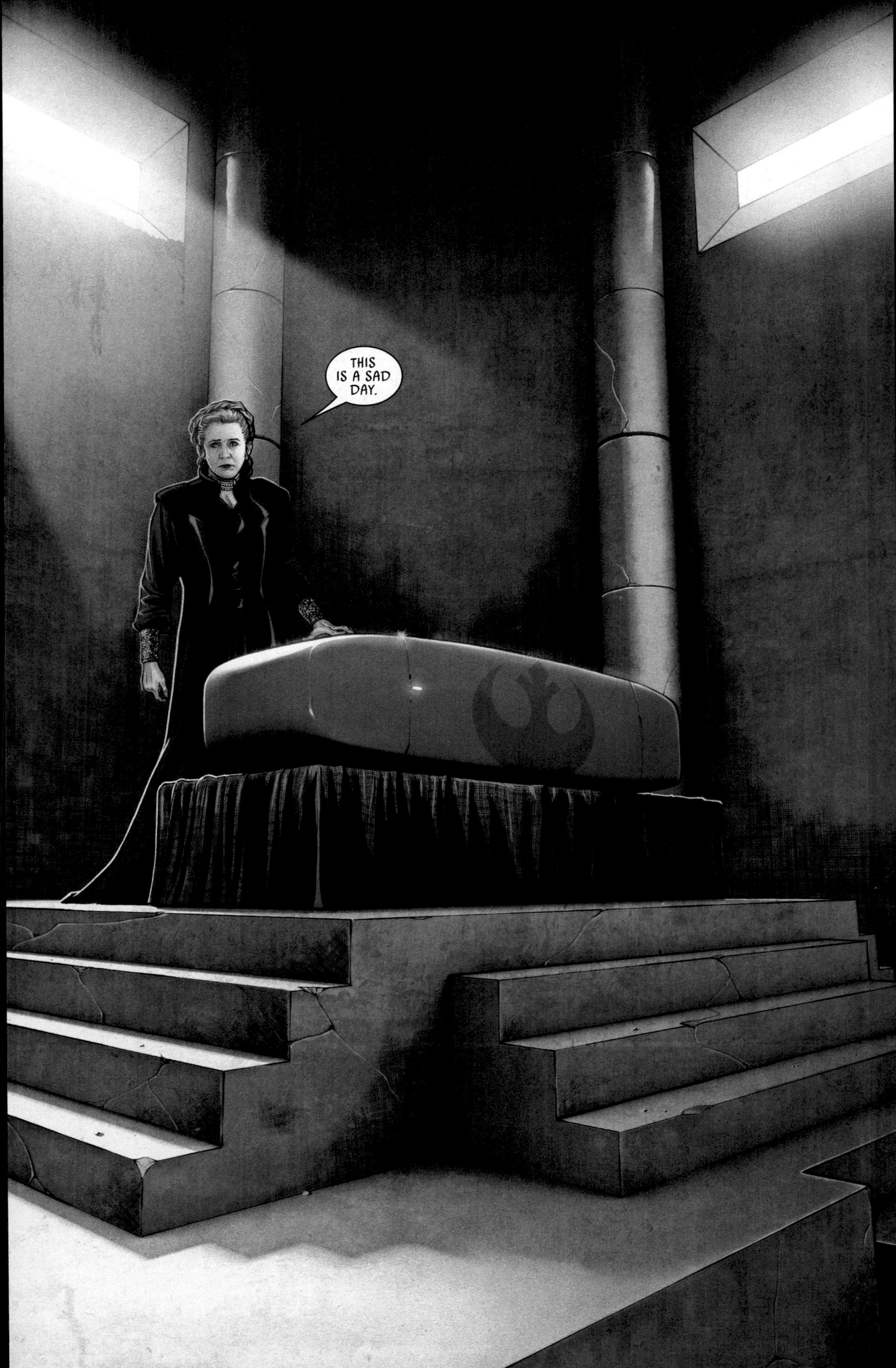
THIS IS A SAD DAY.

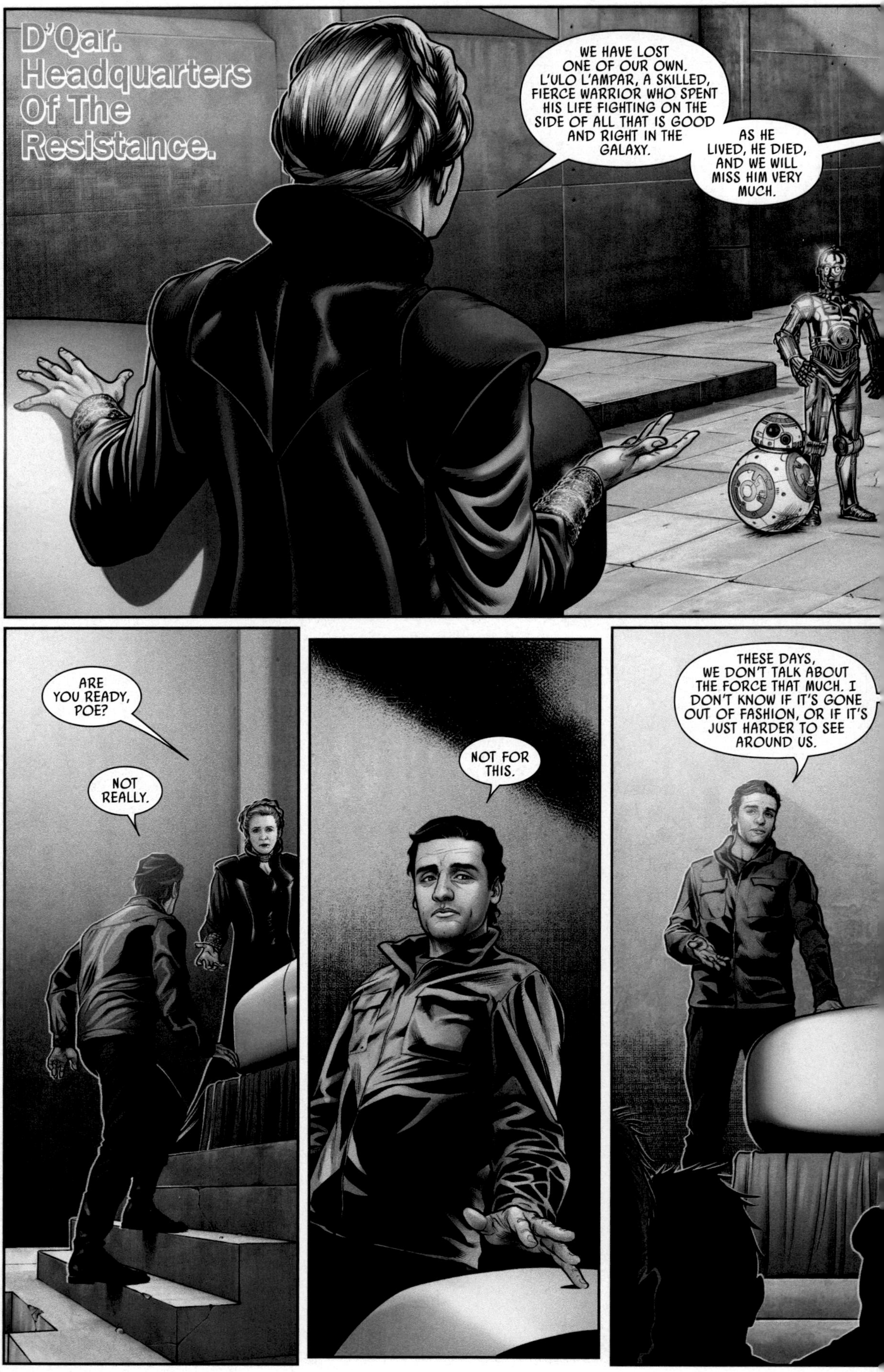
D'Qar. Headquarters Of The Resistance.
WE HAVE LOST ONE OF OUR OWN. L'ULO L'AMPAR, A SKILLED, FIERCE WARRIOR WHO SPENT HIS LIFE FIGHTING ON THE SIDE OF ALL THAT IS GOOD AND RIGHT IN THE GALAXY.
AS HE LIVED, HE DIED, AND WE WILL MISS HIM VERY MUCH.
ARE YOU READY, POE?
NOT REALLY.
NOT FOR THIS.
THESE DAYS, WE DON'T TALK ABOUT THE FORCE THAT MUCH. I DON'T KNOW IF IT'S GONE OUT OF FASHION, OR IF IT'S JUST HARDER TO SEE AROUND US.

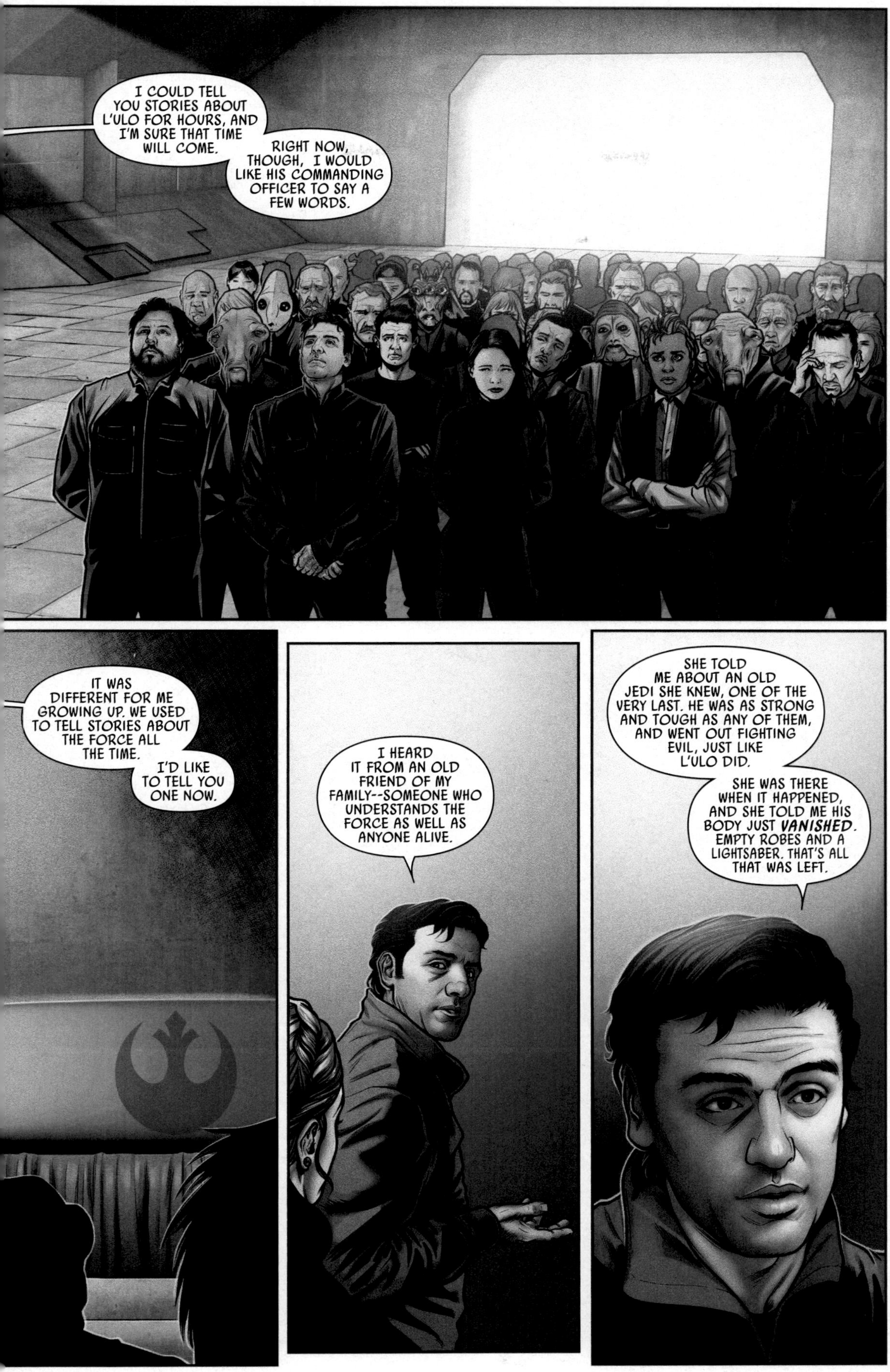
I COULD TELL YOU STORIES ABOUT L'ULO FOR HOURS, AND I'M SURE THAT TIME WILL COME.
RIGHT NOW, THOUGH, I WOULD LIKE HIS COMMANDING OFFICER TO SAY A FEW WORDS.
IT WAS DIFFERENT FOR ME GROWING UP. WE USED TO TELL STORIES ABOUT THE FORCE ALL THE TIME.
I'D LIKE TO TELL YOU ONE NOW.
I HEARD IT FROM AN OLD FRIEND OF MY FAMILY--SOMEONE WHO UNDERSTANDS THE FORCE AS WELL AS ANYONE ALIVE.
SHE TOLD ME ABOUT AN OLD JEDI SHE KNEW, ONE OF THE VERY LAST. HE WAS AS STRONG AND TOUGH AS ANY OF THEM, AND WENT OUT FIGHTING EVIL, JUST LIKE L'ULO DID.
SHE WAS THERE WHEN IT HAPPENED, AND SHE TOLD ME HIS BODY JUST *VANISHED*. EMPTY ROBES AND A LIGHTSABER. THAT'S ALL THAT WAS LEFT.

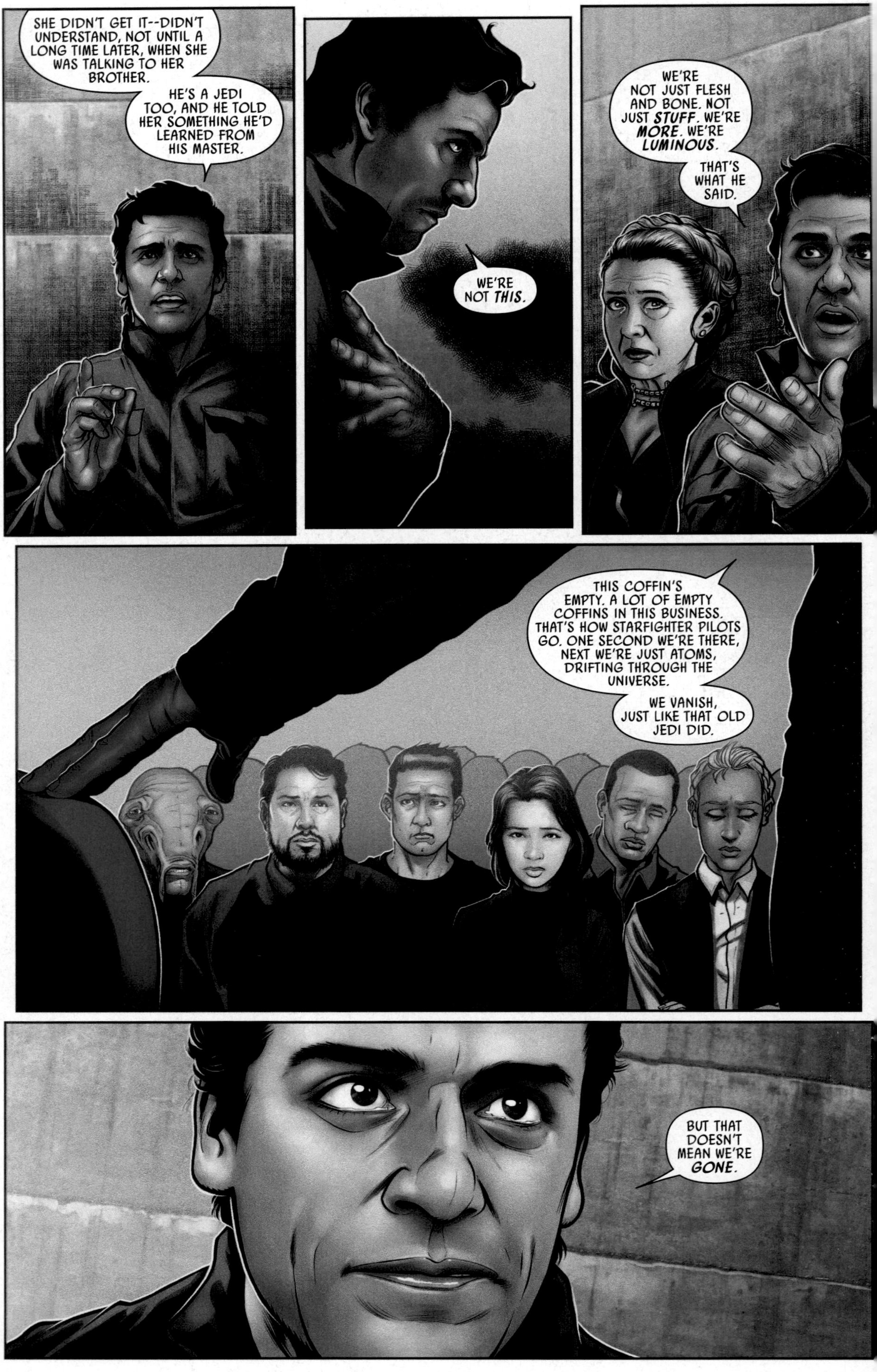
SHE DIDN'T GET IT--DIDN'T UNDERSTAND, NOT UNTIL A LONG TIME LATER, WHEN SHE WAS TALKING TO HER BROTHER.
HE'S A JEDI TOO, AND HE TOLD HER SOMETHING HE'D LEARNED FROM HIS MASTER.
WE'RE NOT *THIS*.
WE'RE NOT JUST FLESH AND BONE. NOT JUST *STUFF*. WE'RE *MORE*. WE'RE *LUMINOUS*.
THAT'S WHAT HE SAID.
THIS COFFIN'S EMPTY. A LOT OF EMPTY COFFINS IN THIS BUSINESS. THAT'S HOW STARFIGHTER PILOTS GO. ONE SECOND WE'RE THERE, NEXT WE'RE JUST ATOMS, DRIFTING THROUGH THE UNIVERSE.
WE VANISH, JUST LIKE THAT OLD JEDI DID.
BUT THAT DOESN'T MEAN WE'RE *GONE*.

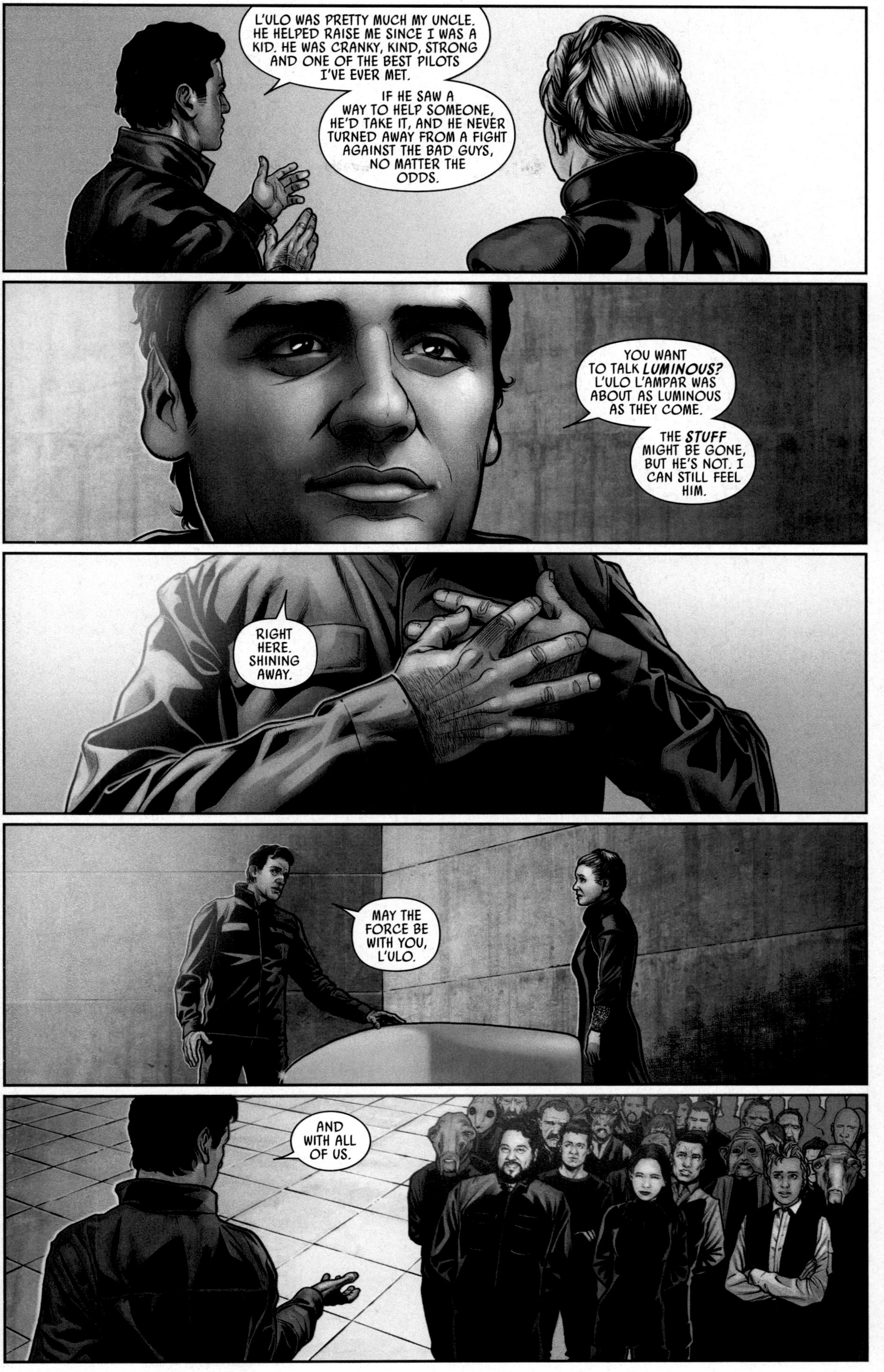
L'ULO WAS PRETTY MUCH MY UNCLE. HE HELPED RAISE ME SINCE I WAS A KID. HE WAS CRANKY, KIND, STRONG AND ONE OF THE BEST PILOTS I'VE EVER MET.
IF HE SAW A WAY TO HELP SOMEONE, HE'D TAKE IT, AND HE NEVER TURNED AWAY FROM A FIGHT AGAINST THE BAD GUYS, NO MATTER THE ODDS.
YOU WANT TO TALK LUMINOUS? L'ULO L'AMPAR WAS ABOUT AS LUMINOUS AS THEY COME.
THE STUFF MIGHT BE GONE, BUT HE'S NOT. I CAN STILL FEEL HIM.
RIGHT HERE. SHINING AWAY.
MAY THE FORCE BE WITH YOU, L'ULO.
AND WITH ALL OF US.

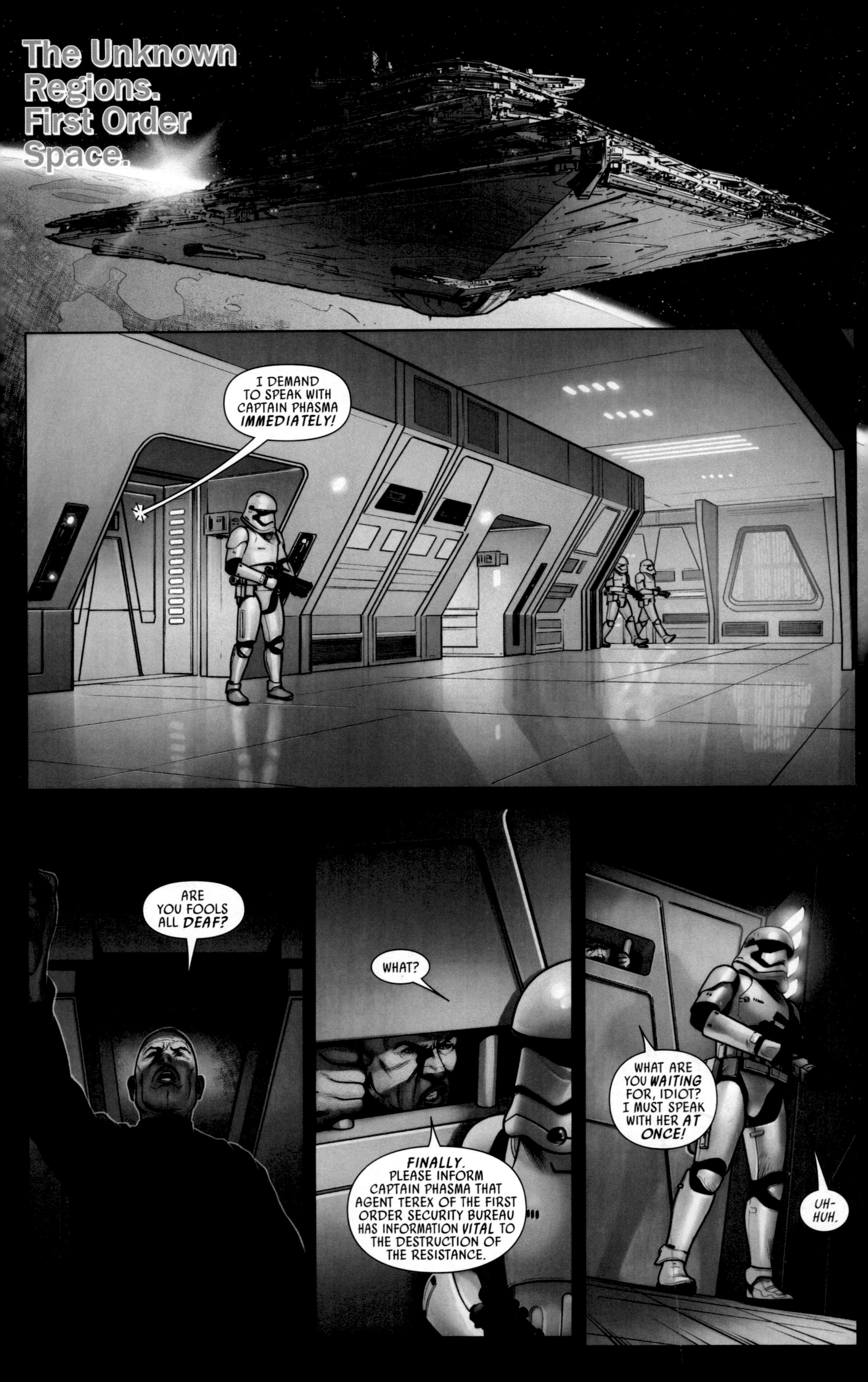
The Unknown Regions. First Order Space.
I DEMAND TO SPEAK WITH CAPTAIN PHASMA IMMEDIATELY!
ARE YOU FOOLS ALL DEAF?
WHAT?
FINALLY. PLEASE INFORM CAPTAIN PHASMA THAT AGENT TEREX OF THE FIRST ORDER SECURITY BUREAU HAS INFORMATION VITAL TO THE DESTRUCTION OF THE RESISTANCE.
WHAT ARE YOU WAITING FOR, IDIOT? I MUST SPEAK WITH HER AT ONCE!
UH-HUH.

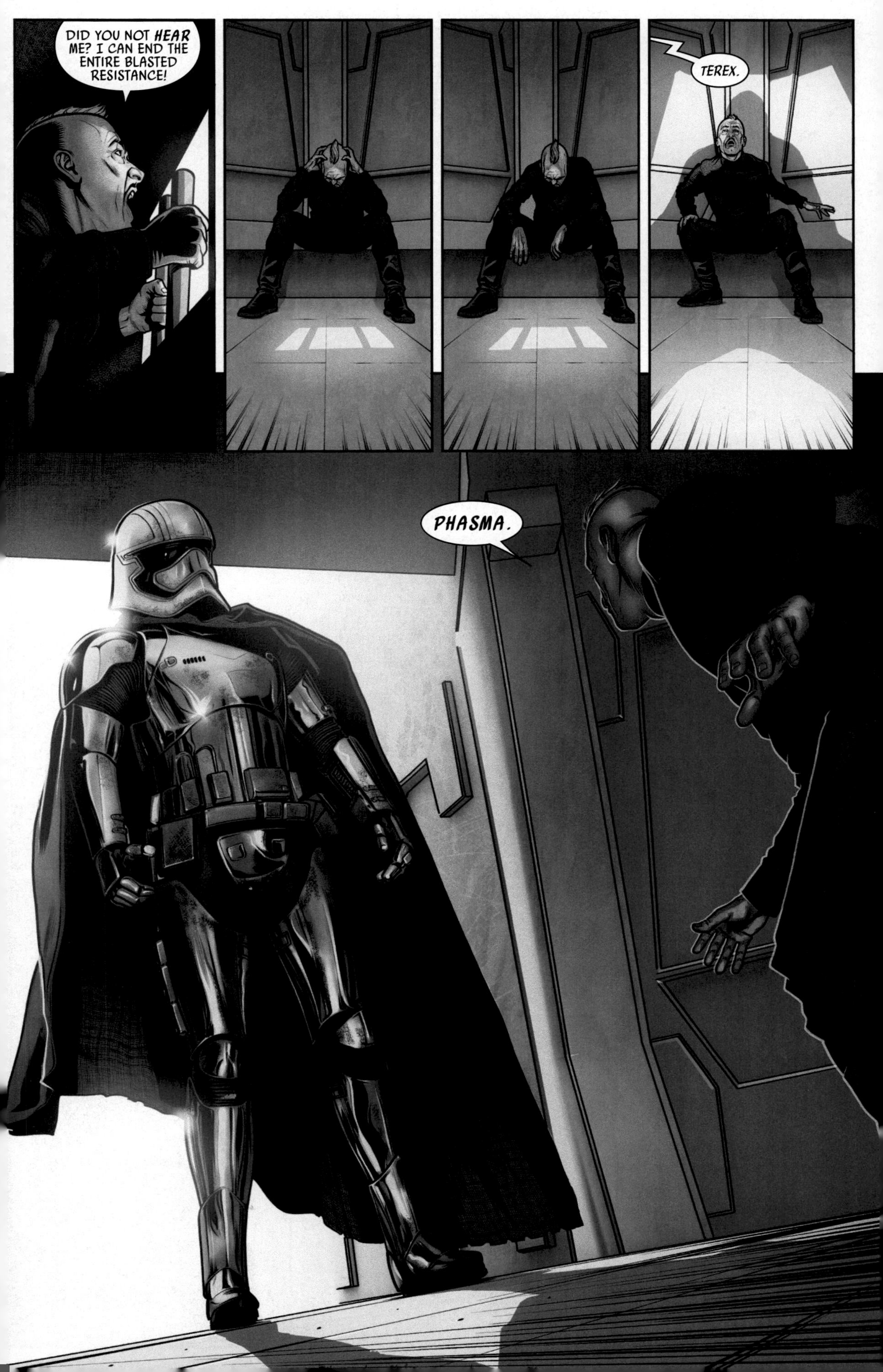
DID YOU NOT HEAR ME? I CAN END THE ENTIRE BLASTED RESISTANCE!
TEREX.
PHASMA.

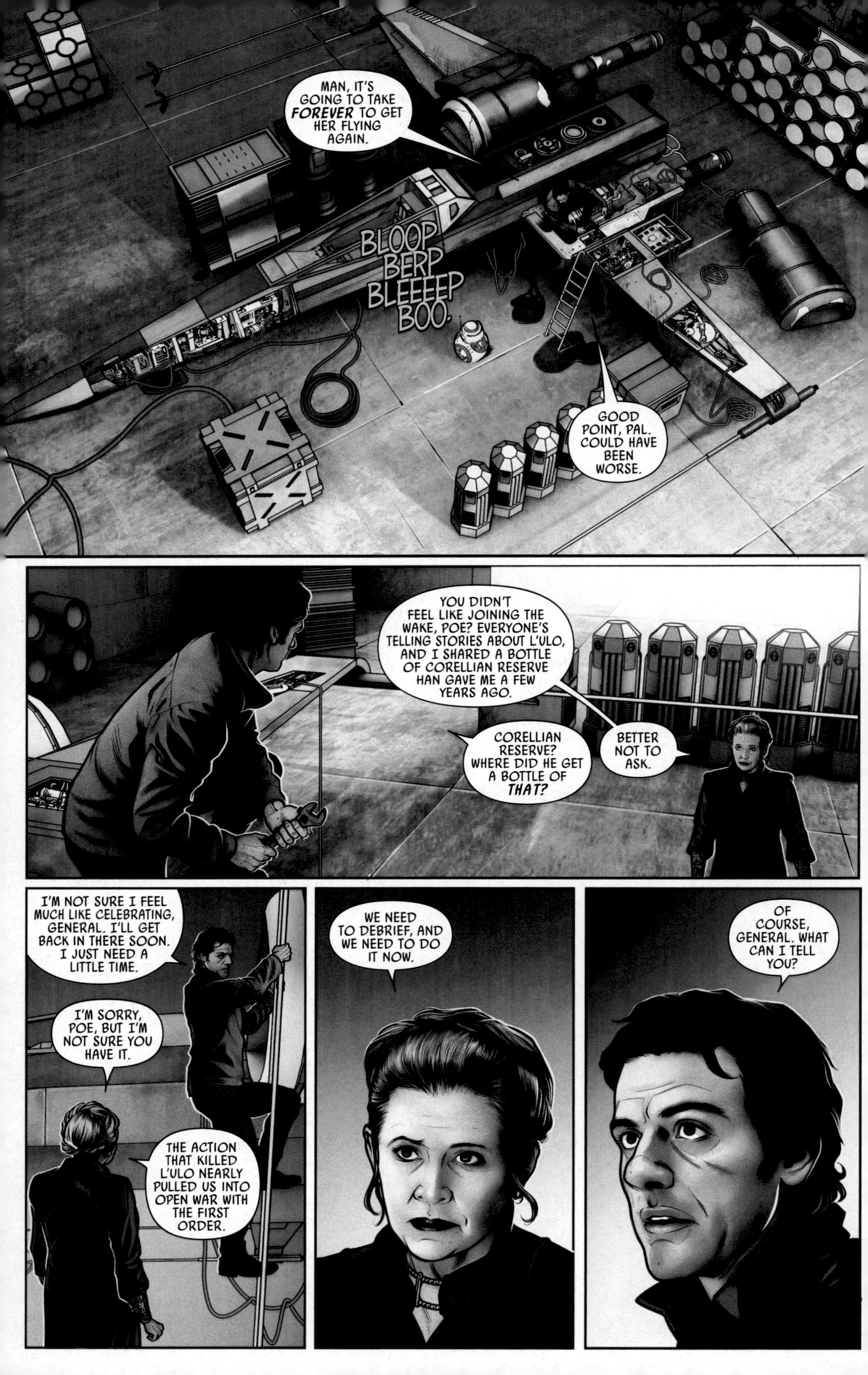
MAN, IT'S GOING TO TAKE *FOREVER* TO GET HER FLYING AGAIN.
BLOOP BERP BLEEEEP BOO.
GOOD POINT, PAL. COULD HAVE BEEN WORSE.
YOU DIDN'T FEEL LIKE JOINING THE WAKE, POE? EVERYONE'S TELLING STORIES ABOUT L'ULO, AND I SHARED A BOTTLE OF CORELLIAN RESERVE HAN GAVE ME A FEW YEARS AGO.
CORELLIAN RESERVE? WHERE DID HE GET A BOTTLE OF *THAT?*
BETTER NOT TO ASK.
I'M NOT SURE I FEEL MUCH LIKE CELEBRATING, GENERAL. I'LL GET BACK IN THERE SOON. I JUST NEED A LITTLE TIME.
I'M SORRY, POE, BUT I'M NOT SURE YOU HAVE IT.
THE ACTION THAT KILLED L'ULO NEARLY PULLED US INTO OPEN WAR WITH THE FIRST ORDER.
WE NEED TO DEBRIEF, AND WE NEED TO DO IT NOW.
OF COURSE, GENERAL. WHAT CAN I TELL YOU?

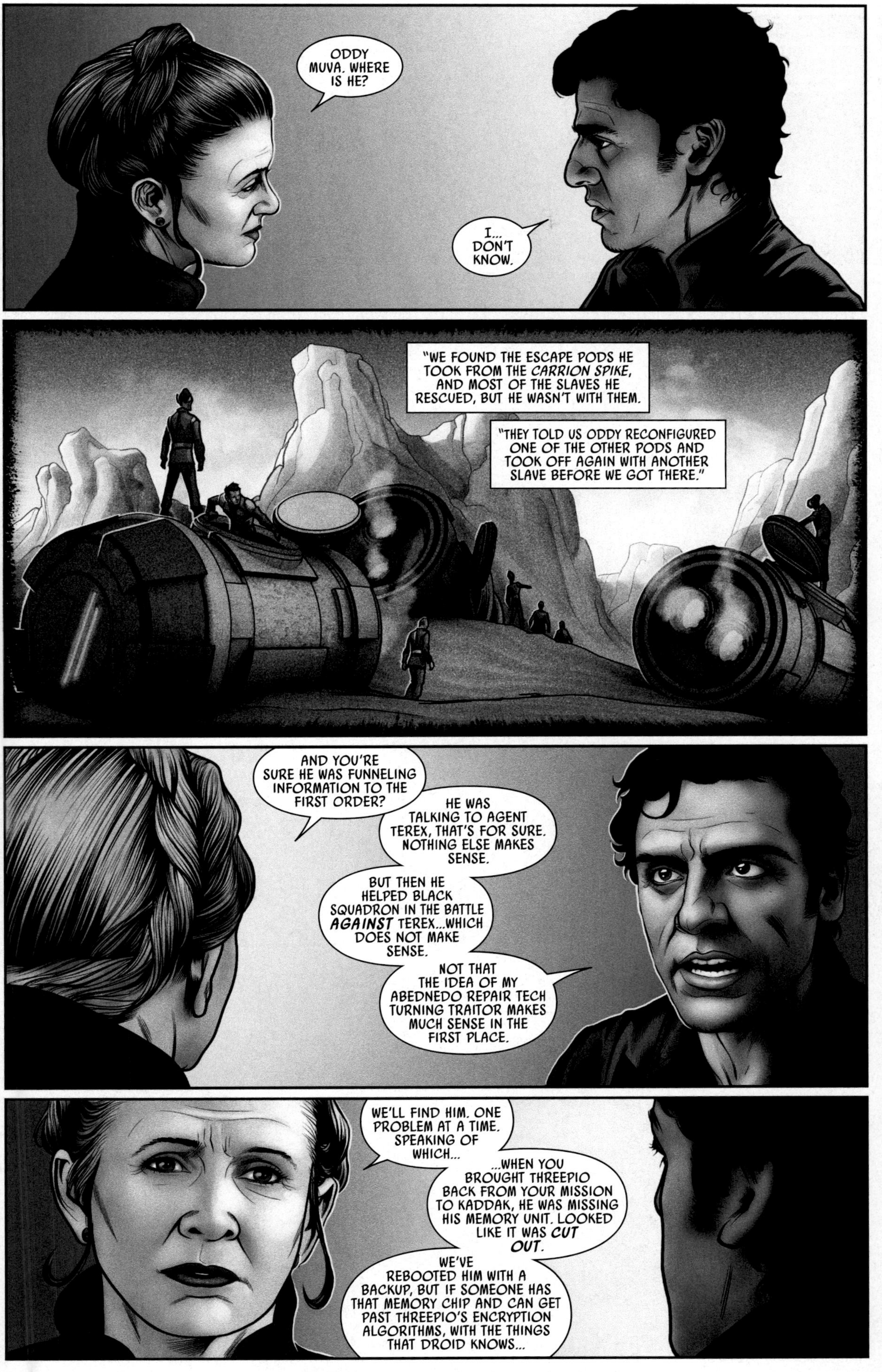
ODDY MUVA. WHERE IS HE?
I... DON'T KNOW.
"WE FOUND THE ESCAPE PODS HE TOOK FROM THE *CARRION SPIKE*, AND MOST OF THE SLAVES HE RESCUED, BUT HE WASN'T WITH THEM.
"THEY TOLD US ODDY RECONFIGURED ONE OF THE OTHER PODS AND TOOK OFF AGAIN WITH ANOTHER SLAVE BEFORE WE GOT THERE."
AND YOU'RE SURE HE WAS FUNNELING INFORMATION TO THE FIRST ORDER?
HE WAS TALKING TO AGENT TEREX, THAT'S FOR SURE. NOTHING ELSE MAKES SENSE.
BUT THEN HE HELPED BLACK SQUADRON IN THE BATTLE ***AGAINST*** TEREX...WHICH DOES NOT MAKE SENSE.
NOT THAT THE IDEA OF MY ABEDNEDO REPAIR TECH TURNING TRAITOR MAKES MUCH SENSE IN THE FIRST PLACE.
WE'LL FIND HIM. ONE PROBLEM AT A TIME. SPEAKING OF WHICH...
...WHEN YOU BROUGHT THREEPIO BACK FROM YOUR MISSION TO KADDAK, HE WAS MISSING HIS MEMORY UNIT. LOOKED LIKE IT WAS ***CUT OUT***.
WE'VE REBOOTED HIM WITH A BACKUP, BUT IF SOMEONE HAS THAT MEMORY CHIP AND CAN GET PAST THREEPIO'S ENCRYPTION ALGORITHMS, WITH THE THINGS THAT DROID KNOWS...

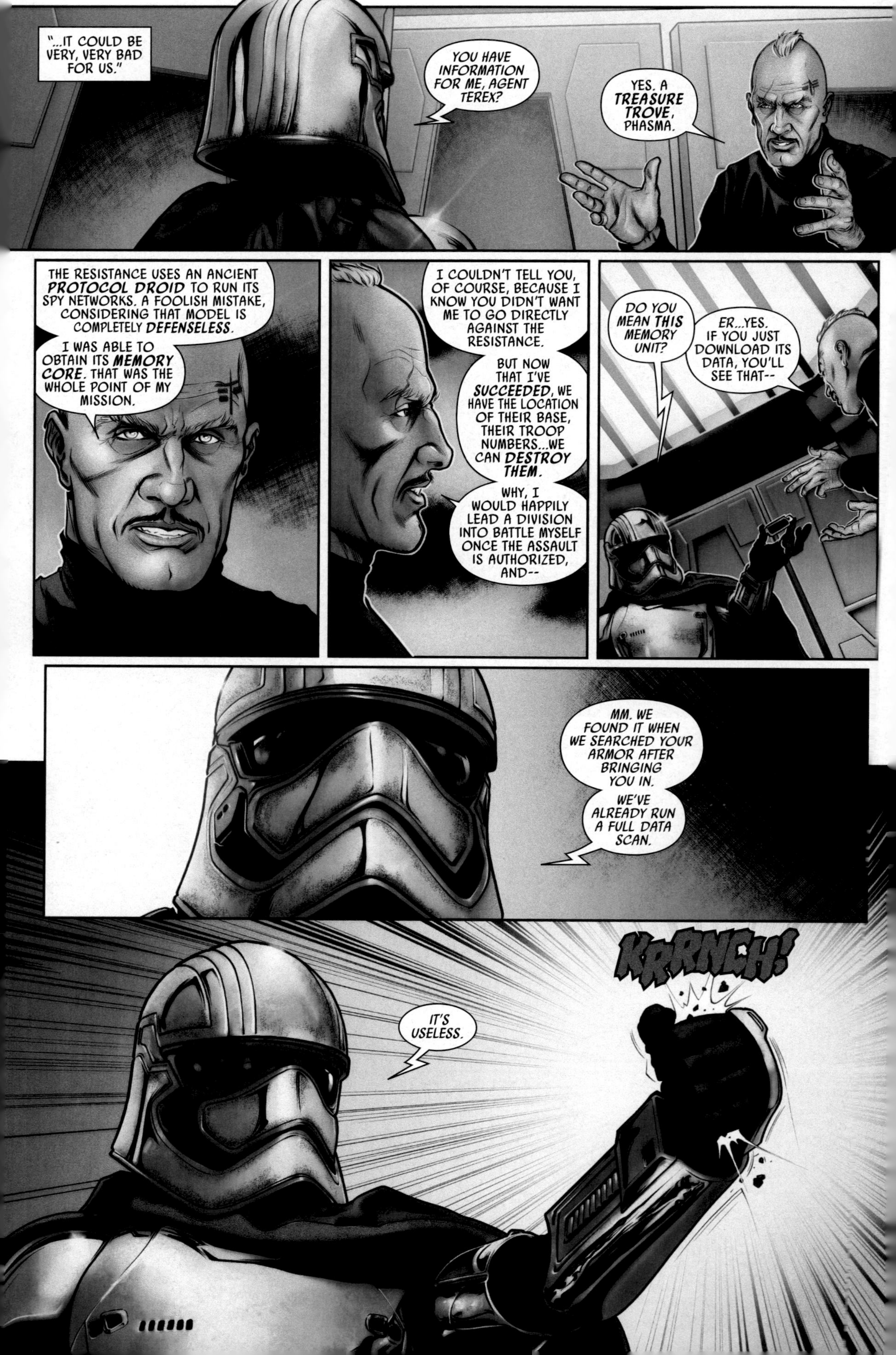
"...IT COULD BE VERY, VERY BAD FOR US."
YOU HAVE INFORMATION FOR ME, AGENT TEREX?
YES. A TREASURE TROVE, PHASMA.
THE RESISTANCE USES AN ANCIENT PROTOCOL DROID TO RUN ITS SPY NETWORKS. A FOOLISH MISTAKE, CONSIDERING THAT MODEL IS COMPLETELY DEFENSELESS.
I WAS ABLE TO OBTAIN ITS MEMORY CORE. THAT WAS THE WHOLE POINT OF MY MISSION.
I COULDN'T TELL YOU, OF COURSE, BECAUSE I KNOW YOU DIDN'T WANT ME TO GO DIRECTLY AGAINST THE RESISTANCE.
BUT NOW THAT I'VE SUCCEEDED, WE HAVE THE LOCATION OF THEIR BASE, THEIR TROOP NUMBERS...WE CAN DESTROY THEM.
WHY, I WOULD HAPPILY LEAD A DIVISION INTO BATTLE MYSELF ONCE THE ASSAULT IS AUTHORIZED, AND--
DO YOU MEAN THIS MEMORY UNIT?
ER...YES. IF YOU JUST DOWNLOAD ITS DATA, YOU'LL SEE THAT--
MM. WE FOUND IT WHEN WE SEARCHED YOUR ARMOR AFTER BRINGING YOU IN.
WE'VE ALREADY RUN A FULL DATA SCAN.
KRRNCH!
IT'S USELESS.

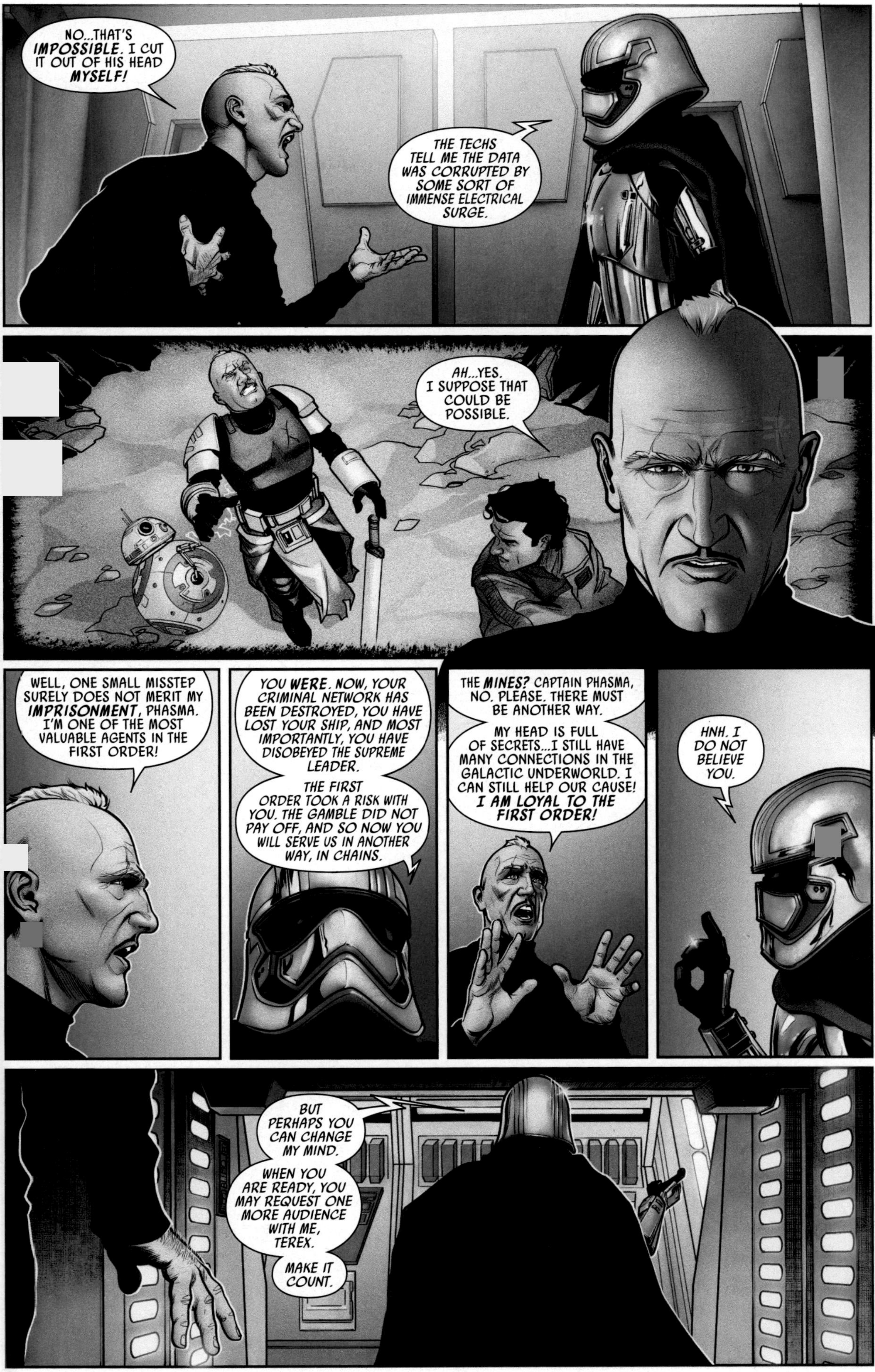
NO...THAT'S IMPOSSIBLE. I CUT IT OUT OF HIS HEAD MYSELF!
THE TECHS TELL ME THE DATA WAS CORRUPTED BY SOME SORT OF IMMENSE ELECTRICAL SURGE.
AH...YES. I SUPPOSE THAT COULD BE POSSIBLE.
WELL, ONE SMALL MISSTEP SURELY DOES NOT MERIT MY IMPRISONMENT, PHASMA. I'M ONE OF THE MOST VALUABLE AGENTS IN THE FIRST ORDER!
YOU WERE. NOW, YOUR CRIMINAL NETWORK HAS BEEN DESTROYED, YOU HAVE LOST YOUR SHIP, AND MOST IMPORTANTLY, YOU HAVE DISOBEYED THE SUPREME LEADER.
THE FIRST ORDER TOOK A RISK WITH YOU. THE GAMBLE DID NOT PAY OFF, AND SO NOW YOU WILL SERVE US IN ANOTHER WAY, IN CHAINS.
THE MINES? CAPTAIN PHASMA, NO. PLEASE. THERE MUST BE ANOTHER WAY.
MY HEAD IS FULL OF SECRETS...I STILL HAVE MANY CONNECTIONS IN THE GALACTIC UNDERWORLD. I CAN STILL HELP OUR CAUSE! I AM LOYAL TO THE FIRST ORDER!
HNH. I DO NOT BELIEVE YOU.
BUT PERHAPS YOU CAN CHANGE MY MIND.
WHEN YOU ARE READY, YOU MAY REQUEST ONE MORE AUDIENCE WITH ME, TEREX.
MAKE IT COUNT.

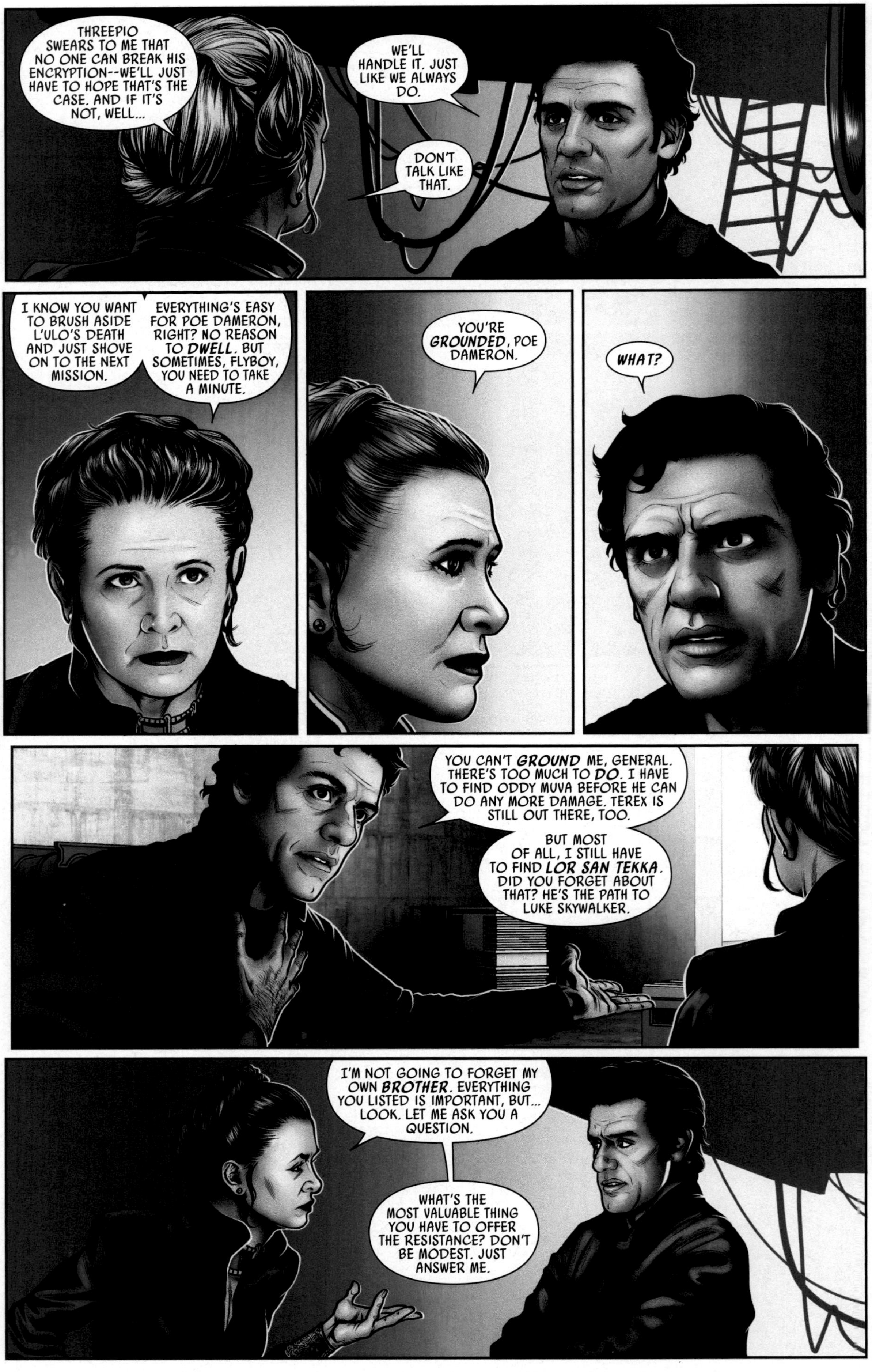
THREEPIO SWEARS TO ME THAT NO ONE CAN BREAK HIS ENCRYPTION--WE'LL JUST HAVE TO HOPE THAT'S THE CASE. AND IF IT'S NOT, WELL...
WE'LL HANDLE IT. JUST LIKE WE ALWAYS DO.
DON'T TALK LIKE THAT.
I KNOW YOU WANT TO BRUSH ASIDE L'ULO'S DEATH AND JUST SHOVE ON TO THE NEXT MISSION.
EVERYTHING'S EASY FOR POE DAMERON, RIGHT? NO REASON TO DWELL. BUT SOMETIMES, FLYBOY, YOU NEED TO TAKE A MINUTE.
YOU'RE GROUNDED, POE DAMERON.
WHAT?
YOU CAN'T GROUND ME, GENERAL. THERE'S TOO MUCH TO DO. I HAVE TO FIND ODDY MUVA BEFORE HE CAN DO ANY MORE DAMAGE. TEREX IS STILL OUT THERE, TOO.
BUT MOST OF ALL, I STILL HAVE TO FIND LOR SAN TEKKA. DID YOU FORGET ABOUT THAT? HE'S THE PATH TO LUKE SKYWALKER.
I'M NOT GOING TO FORGET MY OWN BROTHER. EVERYTHING YOU LISTED IS IMPORTANT, BUT... LOOK. LET ME ASK YOU A QUESTION.
WHAT'S THE MOST VALUABLE THING YOU HAVE TO OFFER THE RESISTANCE? DON'T BE MODEST. JUST ANSWER ME.

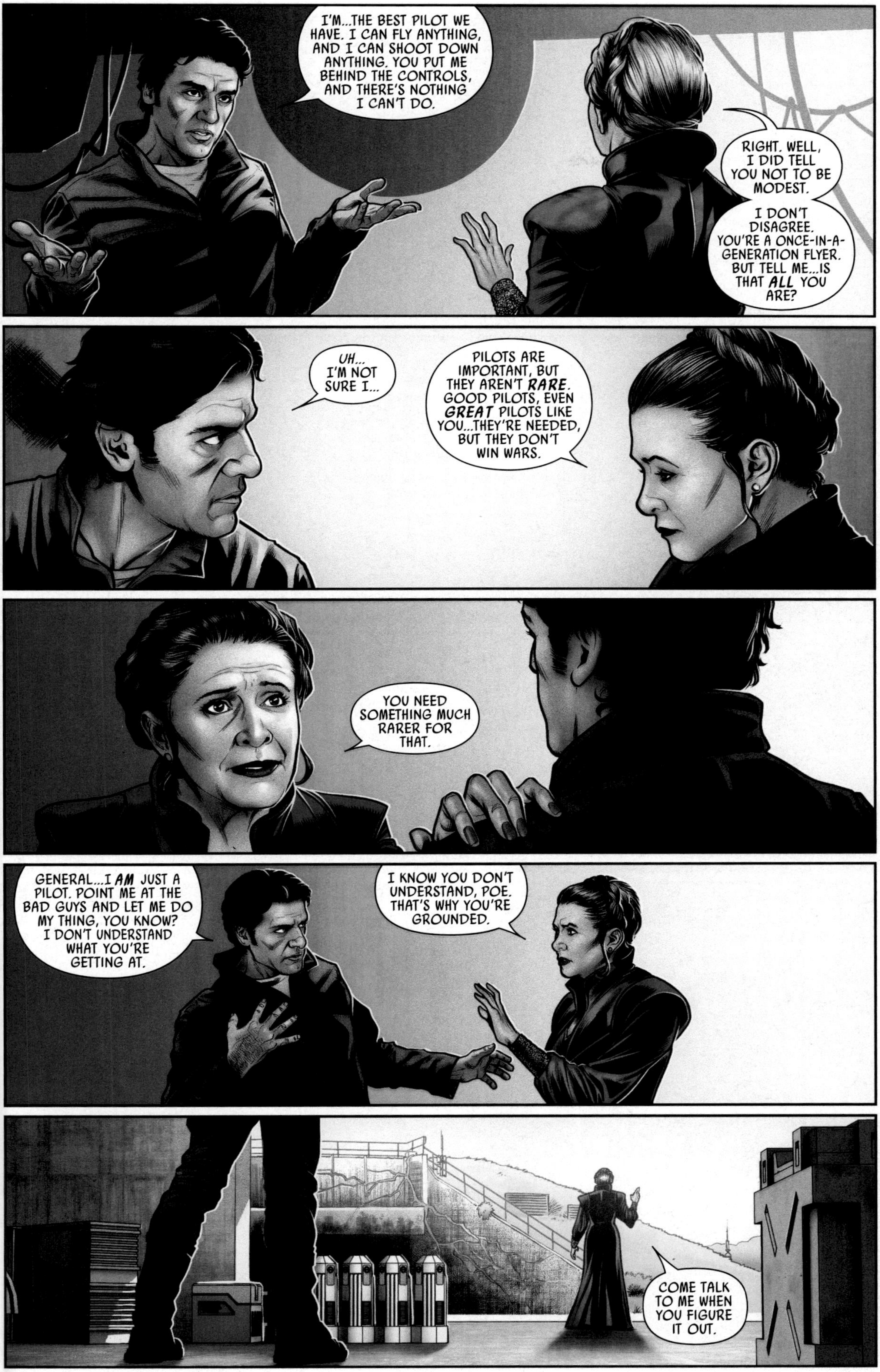
I'M...THE BEST PILOT WE HAVE. I CAN FLY ANYTHING, AND I CAN SHOOT DOWN ANYTHING. YOU PUT ME BEHIND THE CONTROLS, AND THERE'S NOTHING I CAN'T DO.
RIGHT. WELL, I DID TELL YOU NOT TO BE MODEST.
I DON'T DISAGREE. YOU'RE A ONCE-IN-A-GENERATION FLYER. BUT TELL ME...IS THAT ALL YOU ARE?
UH... I'M NOT SURE I...
PILOTS ARE IMPORTANT, BUT THEY AREN'T RARE. GOOD PILOTS, EVEN GREAT PILOTS LIKE YOU...THEY'RE NEEDED, BUT THEY DON'T WIN WARS.
YOU NEED SOMETHING MUCH RARER FOR THAT.
GENERAL...I AM JUST A PILOT. POINT ME AT THE BAD GUYS AND LET ME DO MY THING, YOU KNOW? I DON'T UNDERSTAND WHAT YOU'RE GETTING AT.
I KNOW YOU DON'T UNDERSTAND, POE. THAT'S WHY YOU'RE GROUNDED.
COME TALK TO ME WHEN YOU FIGURE IT OUT.

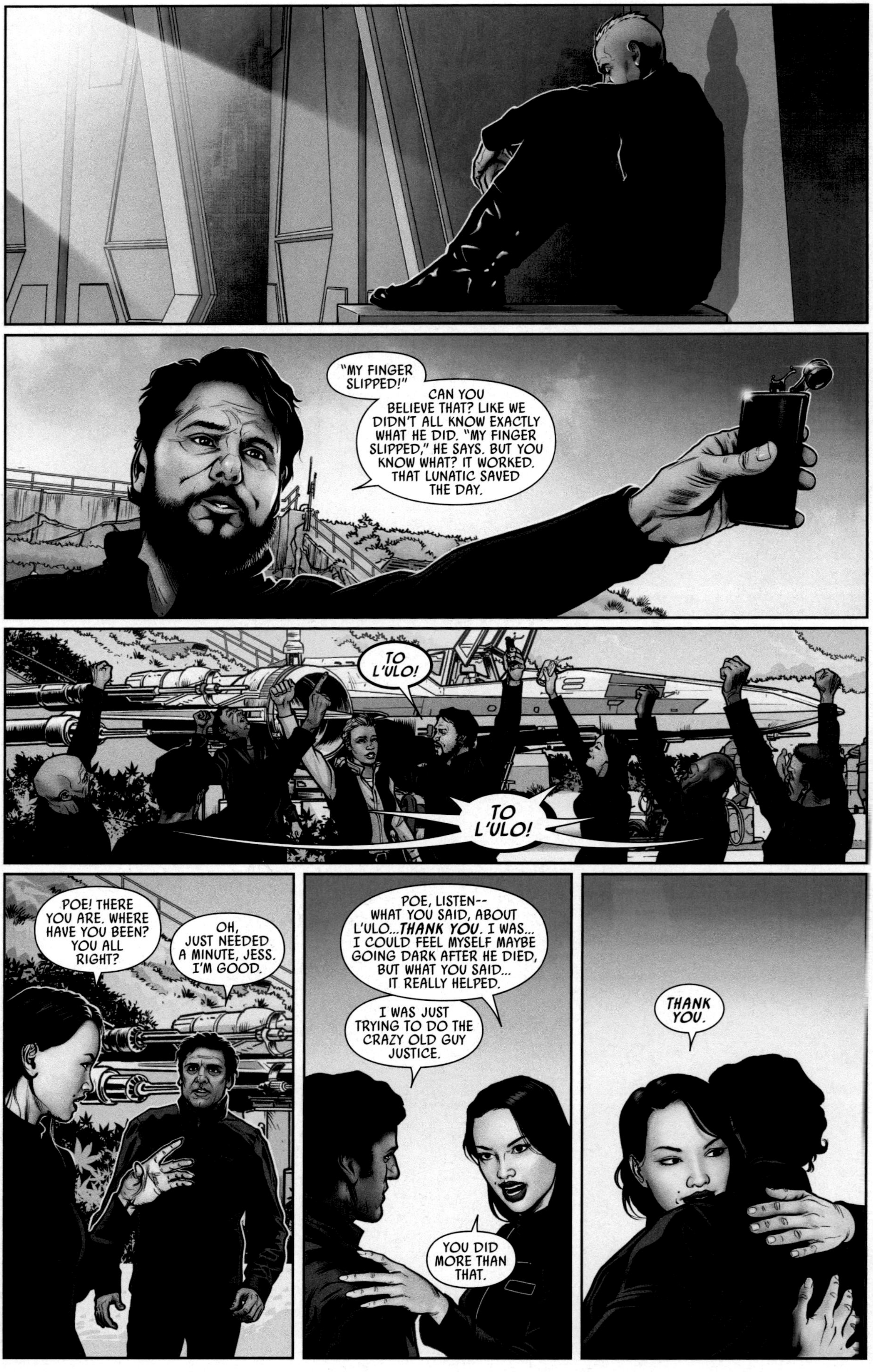
"MY FINGER SLIPPED!"
CAN YOU BELIEVE THAT? LIKE WE DIDN'T ALL KNOW EXACTLY WHAT HE DID. "MY FINGER SLIPPED," HE SAYS. BUT YOU KNOW WHAT? IT WORKED. THAT LUNATIC SAVED THE DAY.
TO L'ULO!
TO L'ULO!
POE! THERE YOU ARE. WHERE HAVE YOU BEEN? YOU ALL RIGHT?
OH, JUST NEEDED A MINUTE, JESS. I'M GOOD.
POE, LISTEN-- WHAT YOU SAID, ABOUT L'ULO... *THANK YOU*. I WAS... I COULD FEEL MYSELF MAYBE GOING DARK AFTER HE DIED, BUT WHAT YOU SAID... IT REALLY HELPED.
I WAS JUST TRYING TO DO THE CRAZY OLD GUY JUSTICE.
YOU DID MORE THAN THAT.
THANK YOU.

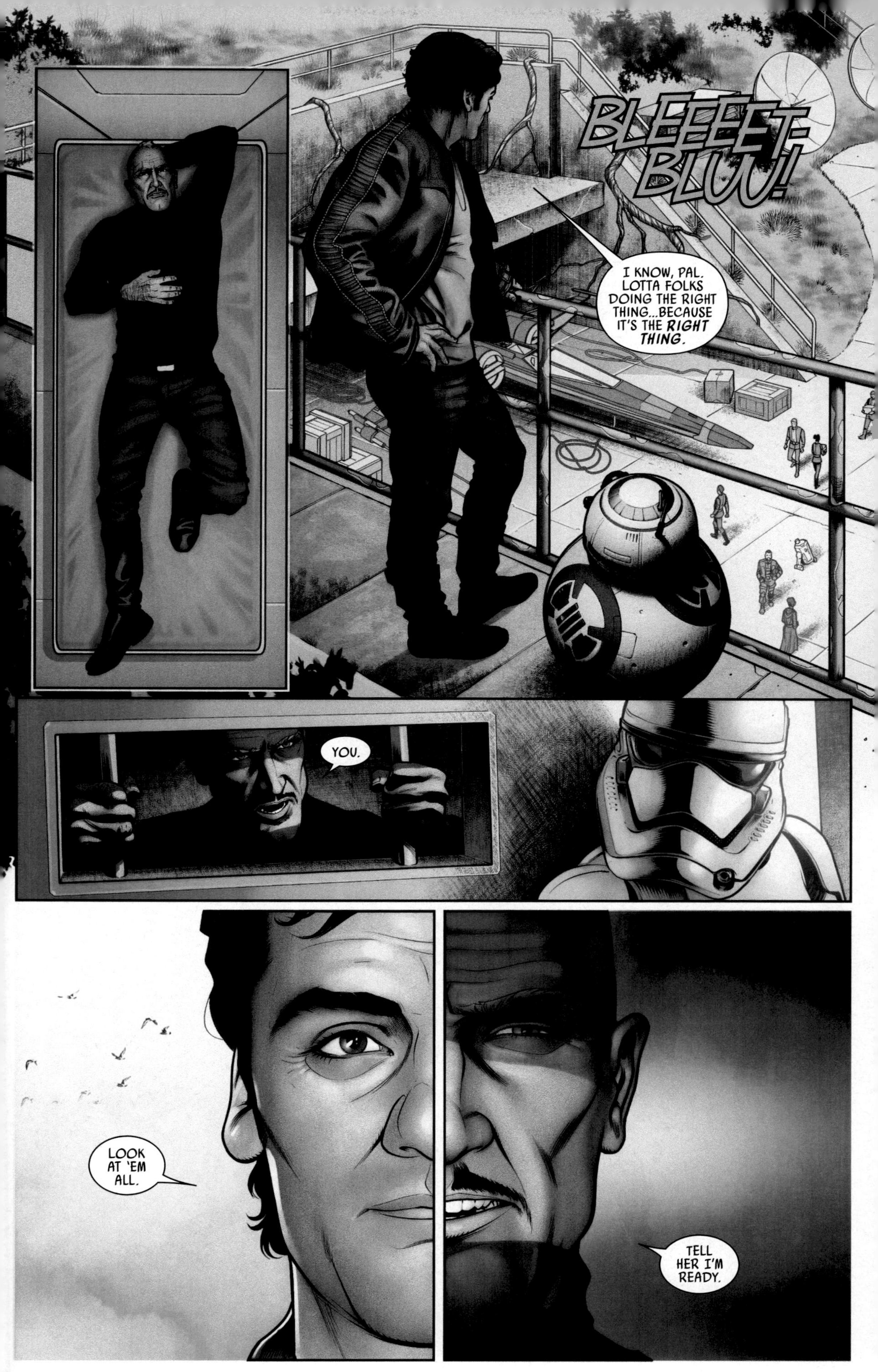
BLEEEEET-BLUU!
I KNOW, PAL. LOTTA FOLKS DOING THE RIGHT THING...BECAUSE IT'S THE RIGHT THING.
YOU.
LOOK AT 'EM ALL.
TELL HER I'M READY.

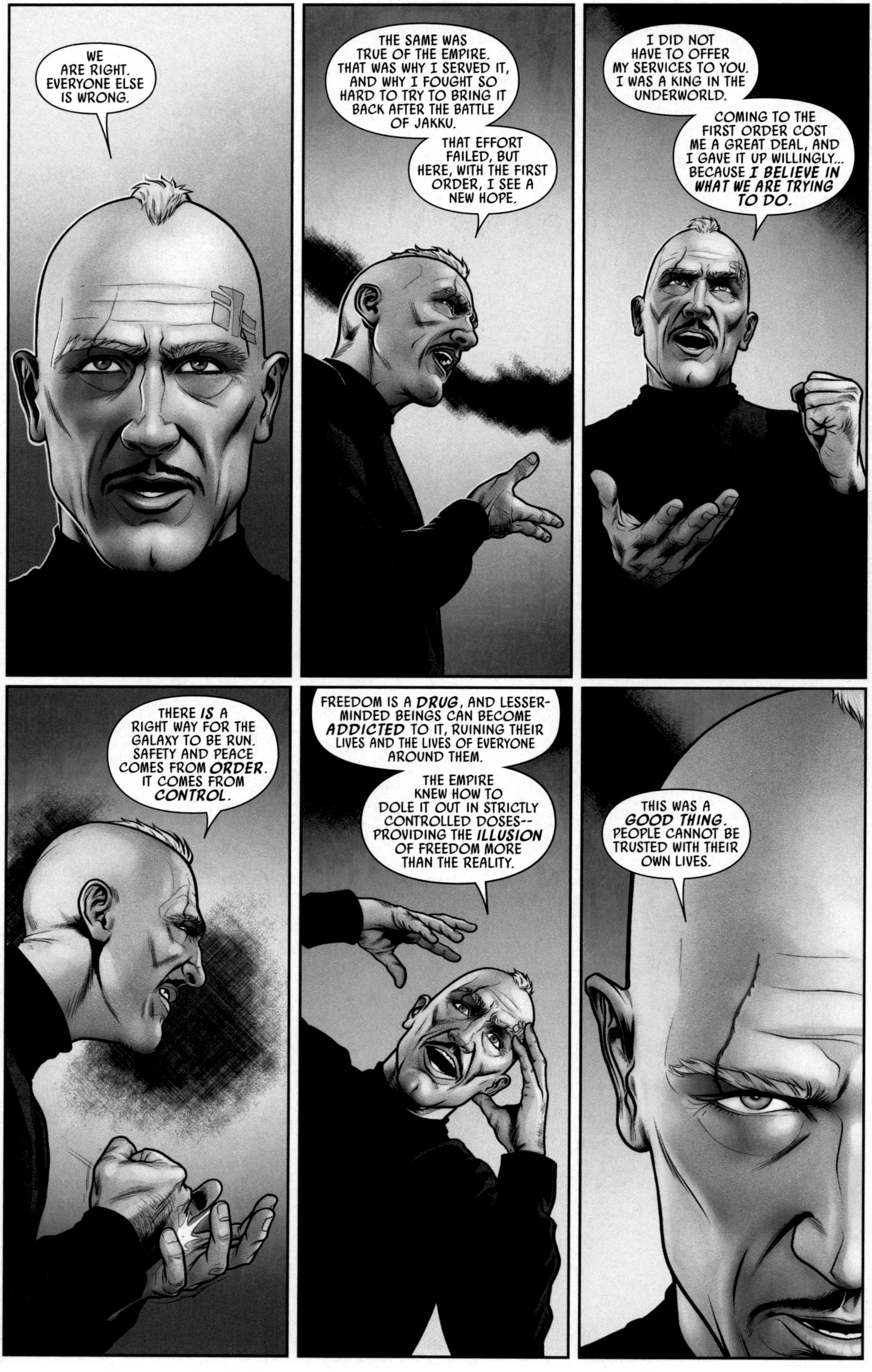
WE ARE RIGHT. EVERYONE ELSE IS WRONG.
THE SAME WAS TRUE OF THE EMPIRE. THAT WAS WHY I SERVED IT, AND WHY I FOUGHT SO HARD TO TRY TO BRING IT BACK AFTER THE BATTLE OF JAKKU.
THAT EFFORT FAILED, BUT HERE, WITH THE FIRST ORDER, I SEE A NEW HOPE.
I DID NOT HAVE TO OFFER MY SERVICES TO YOU. I WAS A KING IN THE UNDERWORLD.
COMING TO THE FIRST ORDER COST ME A GREAT DEAL, AND I GAVE IT UP WILLINGLY... BECAUSE I BELIEVE IN WHAT WE ARE TRYING TO DO.
THERE IS A RIGHT WAY FOR THE GALAXY TO BE RUN. SAFETY AND PEACE COMES FROM ORDER. IT COMES FROM CONTROL.
FREEDOM IS A DRUG, AND LESSER-MINDED BEINGS CAN BECOME ADDICTED TO IT, RUINING THEIR LIVES AND THE LIVES OF EVERYONE AROUND THEM.
THE EMPIRE KNEW HOW TO DOLE IT OUT IN STRICTLY CONTROLLED DOSES-- PROVIDING THE ILLUSION OF FREEDOM MORE THAN THE REALITY.
THIS WAS A GOOD THING. PEOPLE CANNOT BE TRUSTED WITH THEIR OWN LIVES.

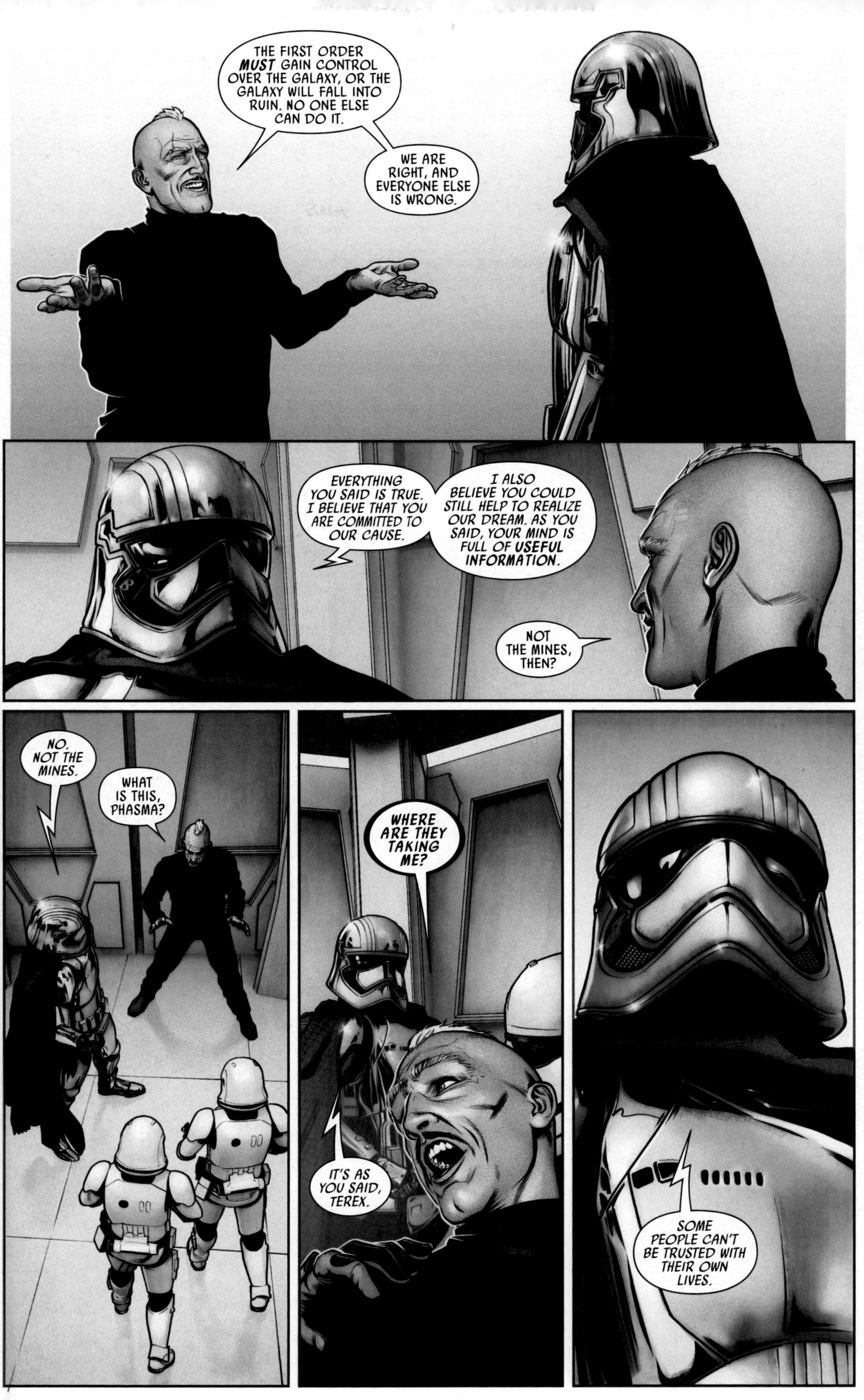
THE FIRST ORDER MUST GAIN CONTROL OVER THE GALAXY, OR THE GALAXY WILL FALL INTO RUIN. NO ONE ELSE CAN DO IT.
WE ARE RIGHT, AND EVERYONE ELSE IS WRONG.
EVERYTHING YOU SAID IS TRUE. I BELIEVE THAT YOU ARE COMMITTED TO OUR CAUSE.
I ALSO BELIEVE YOU COULD STILL HELP TO REALIZE OUR DREAM. AS YOU SAID, YOUR MIND IS FULL OF USEFUL INFORMATION.
NOT THE MINES, THEN?
NO. NOT THE MINES.
WHAT IS THIS, PHASMA?
WHERE ARE THEY TAKING ME?
IT'S AS YOU SAID, TEREX.
SOME PEOPLE CAN'T BE TRUSTED WITH THEIR OWN LIVES.

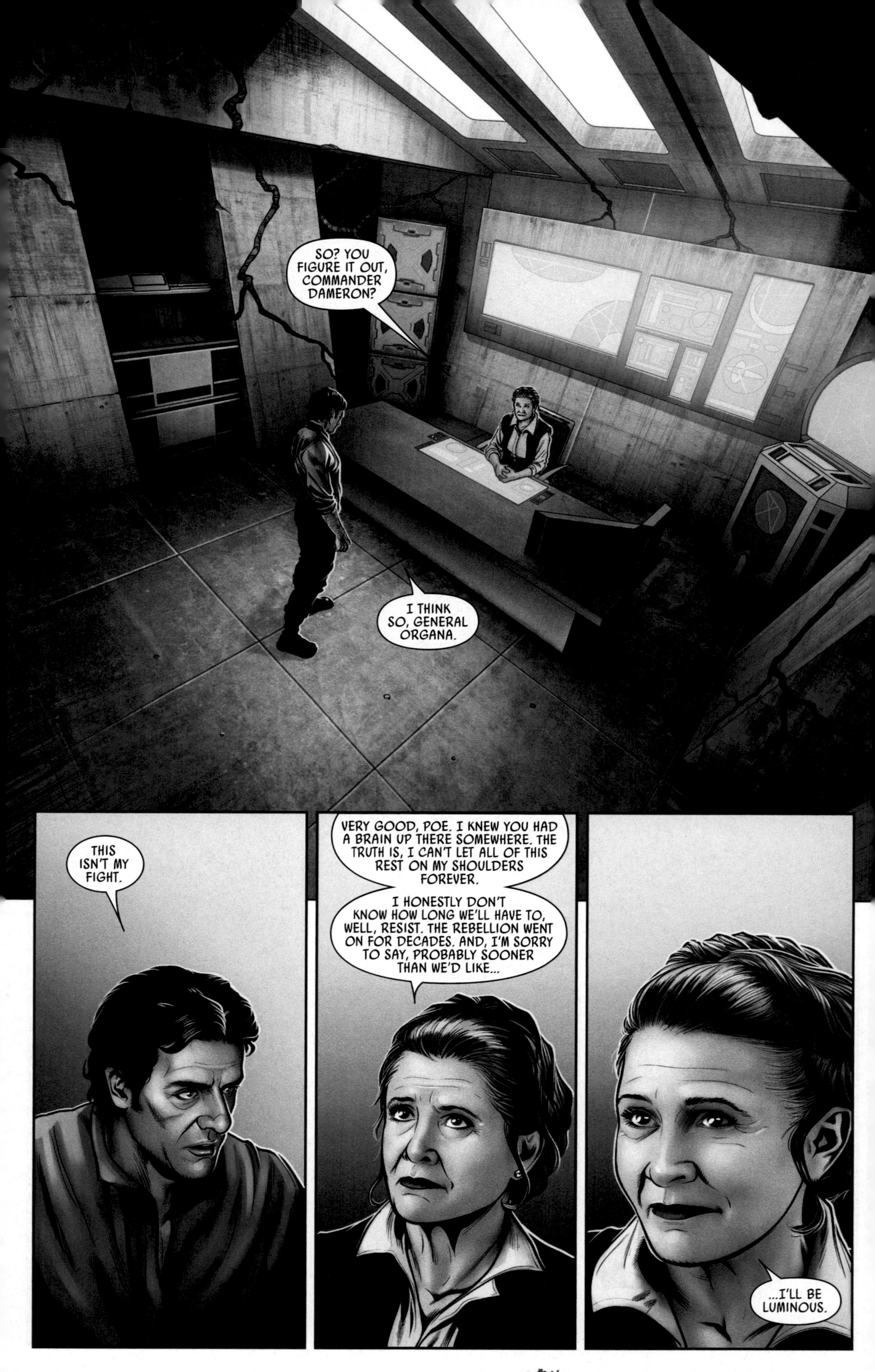
SO? YOU FIGURE IT OUT, COMMANDER DAMERON?
I THINK SO, GENERAL ORGANA.
THIS ISN'T MY FIGHT.
VERY GOOD, POE. I KNEW YOU HAD A BRAIN UP THERE SOMEWHERE. THE TRUTH IS, I CAN'T LET ALL OF THIS REST ON MY SHOULDERS FOREVER.
I HONESTLY DON'T KNOW HOW LONG WE'LL HAVE TO, WELL, RESIST. THE REBELLION WENT ON FOR DECADES. AND, I'M SORRY TO SAY, PROBABLY SOONER THAN WE'D LIKE...
...I'LL BE LUMINOUS.

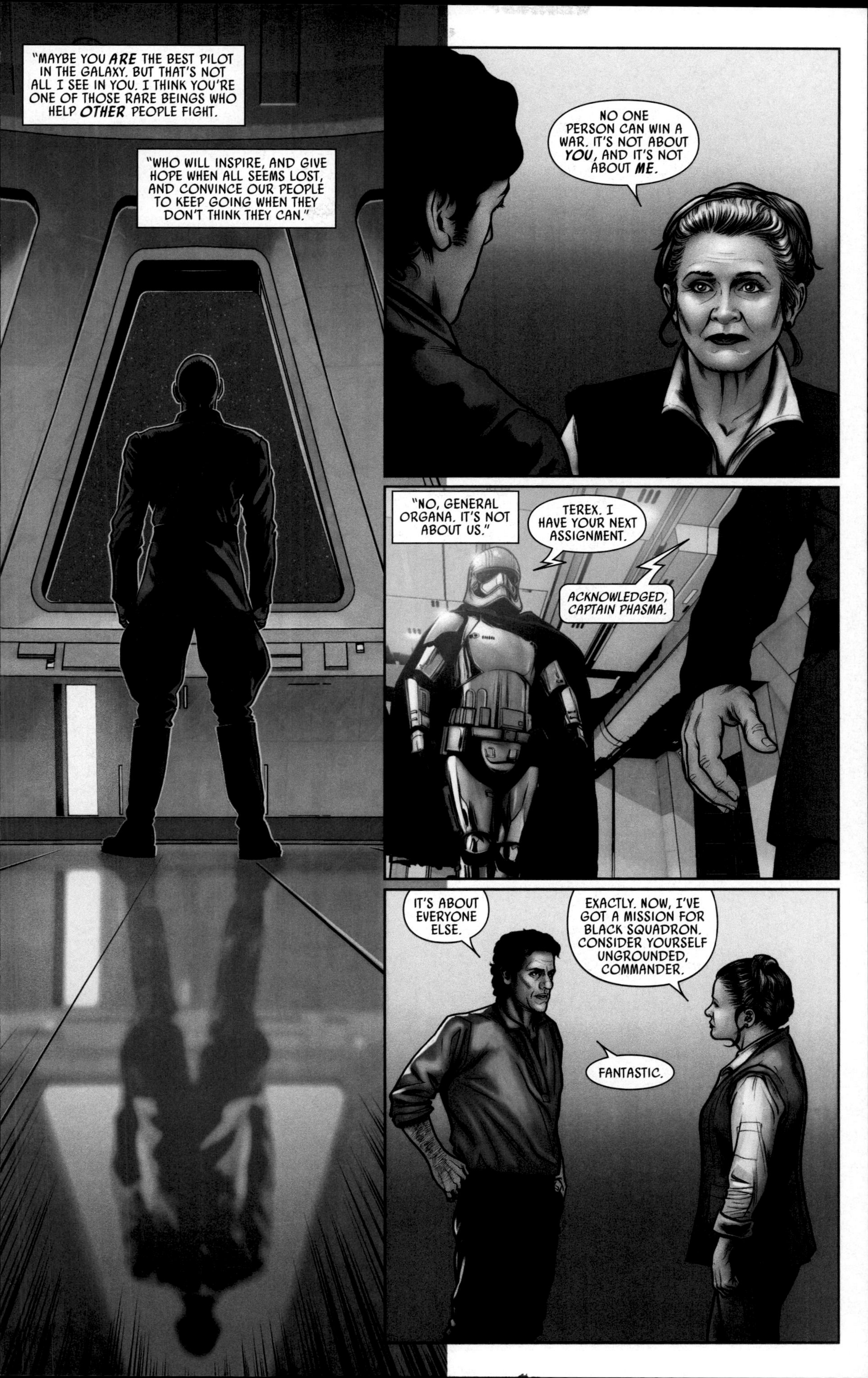
"MAYBE YOU ARE THE BEST PILOT IN THE GALAXY. BUT THAT'S NOT ALL I SEE IN YOU. I THINK YOU'RE ONE OF THOSE RARE BEINGS WHO HELP OTHER PEOPLE FIGHT.
"WHO WILL INSPIRE, AND GIVE HOPE WHEN ALL SEEMS LOST, AND CONVINCE OUR PEOPLE TO KEEP GOING WHEN THEY DON'T THINK THEY CAN."
NO ONE PERSON CAN WIN A WAR. IT'S NOT ABOUT YOU, AND IT'S NOT ABOUT ME.
"NO, GENERAL ORGANA. IT'S NOT ABOUT US."
TEREX. I HAVE YOUR NEXT ASSIGNMENT.
ACKNOWLEDGED, CAPTAIN PHASMA.
IT'S ABOUT EVERYONE ELSE.
EXACTLY. NOW, I'VE GOT A MISSION FOR BLACK SQUADRON. CONSIDER YOURSELF UNGROUNDED, COMMANDER.
FANTASTIC.

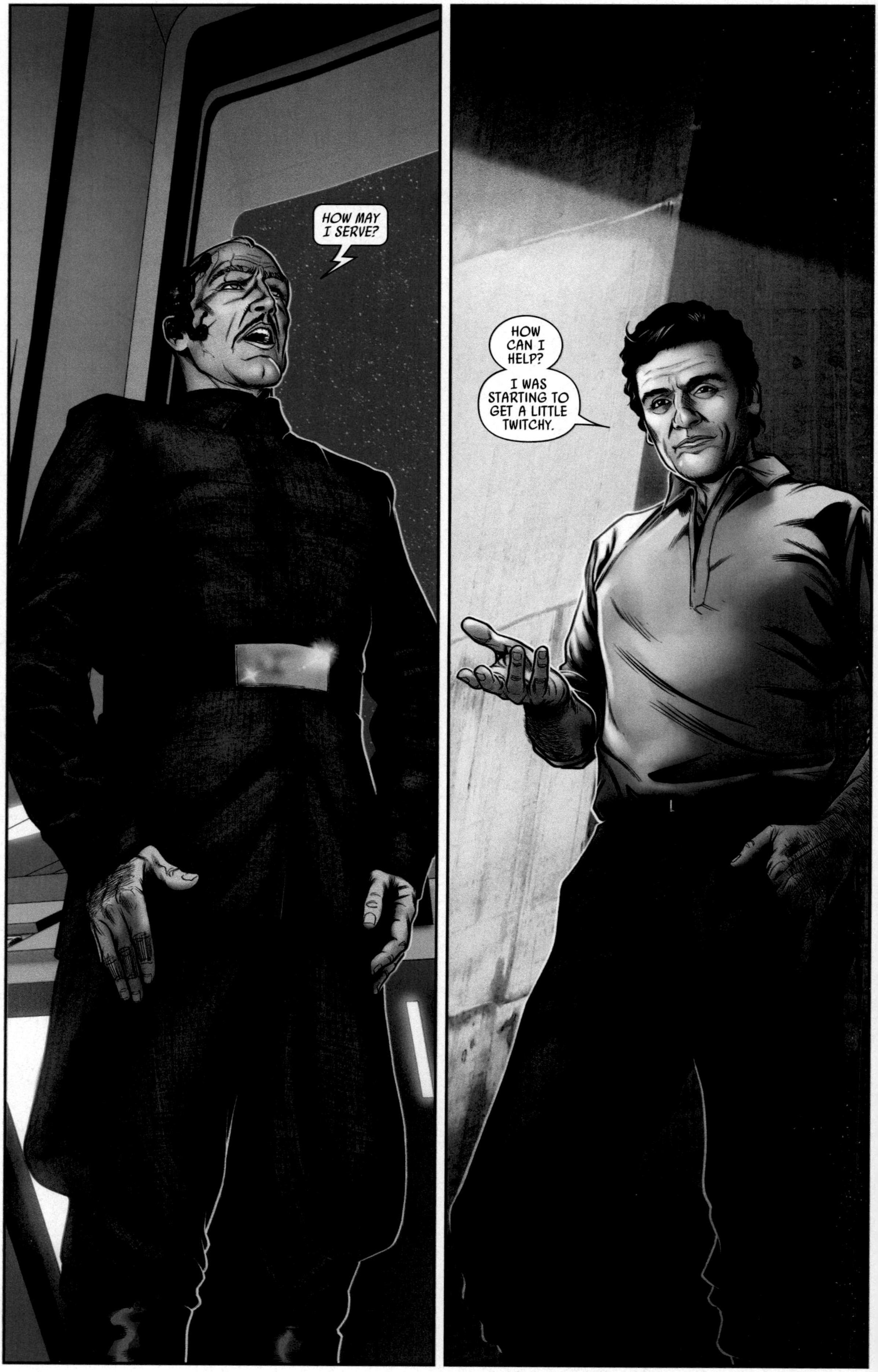
HOW MAY I SERVE?
HOW CAN I HELP?
I WAS STARTING TO GET A LITTLE TWITCHY.

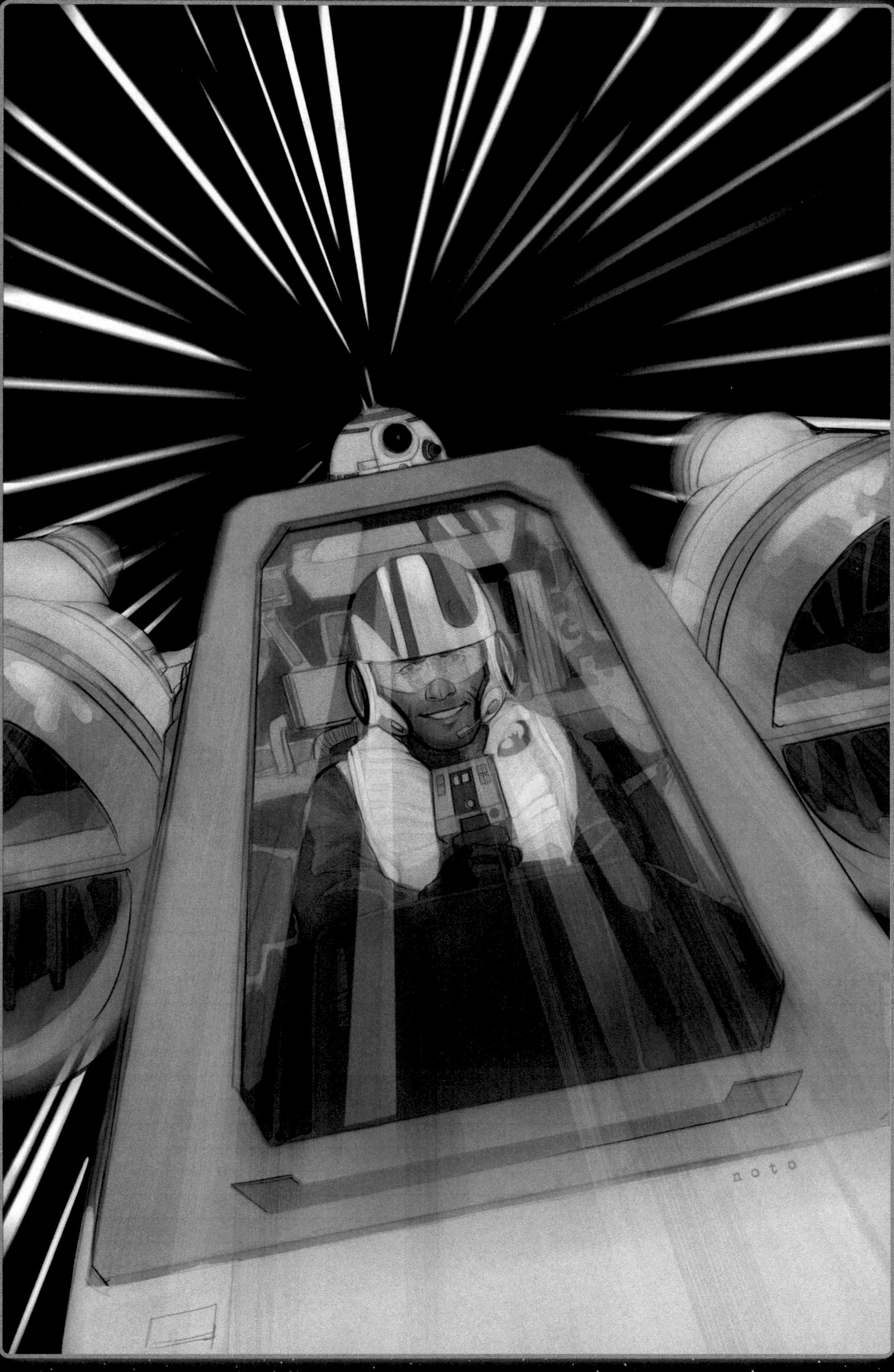
noto

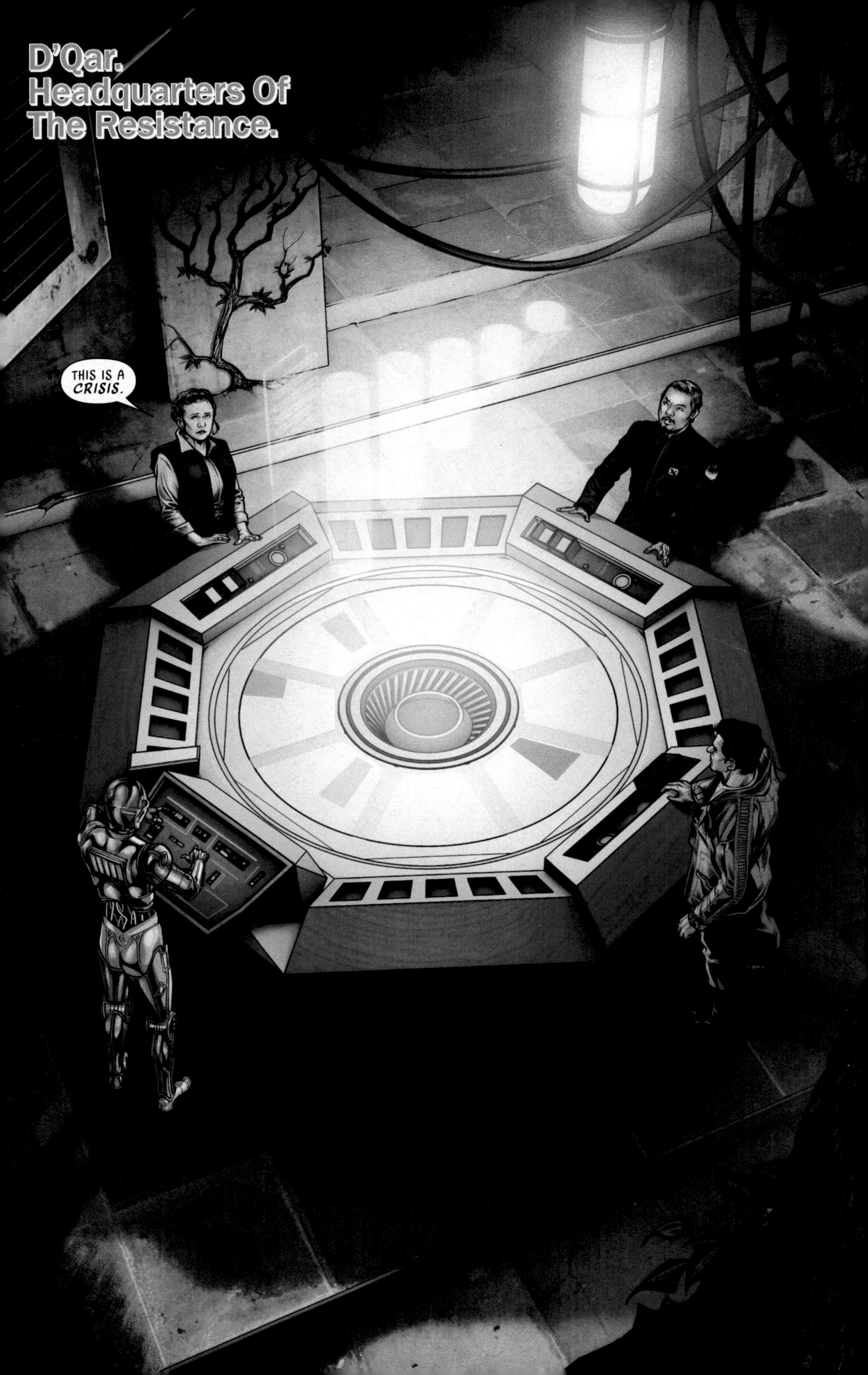
D'Qar. Headquarters Of The Resistance.
THIS IS A CRISIS.

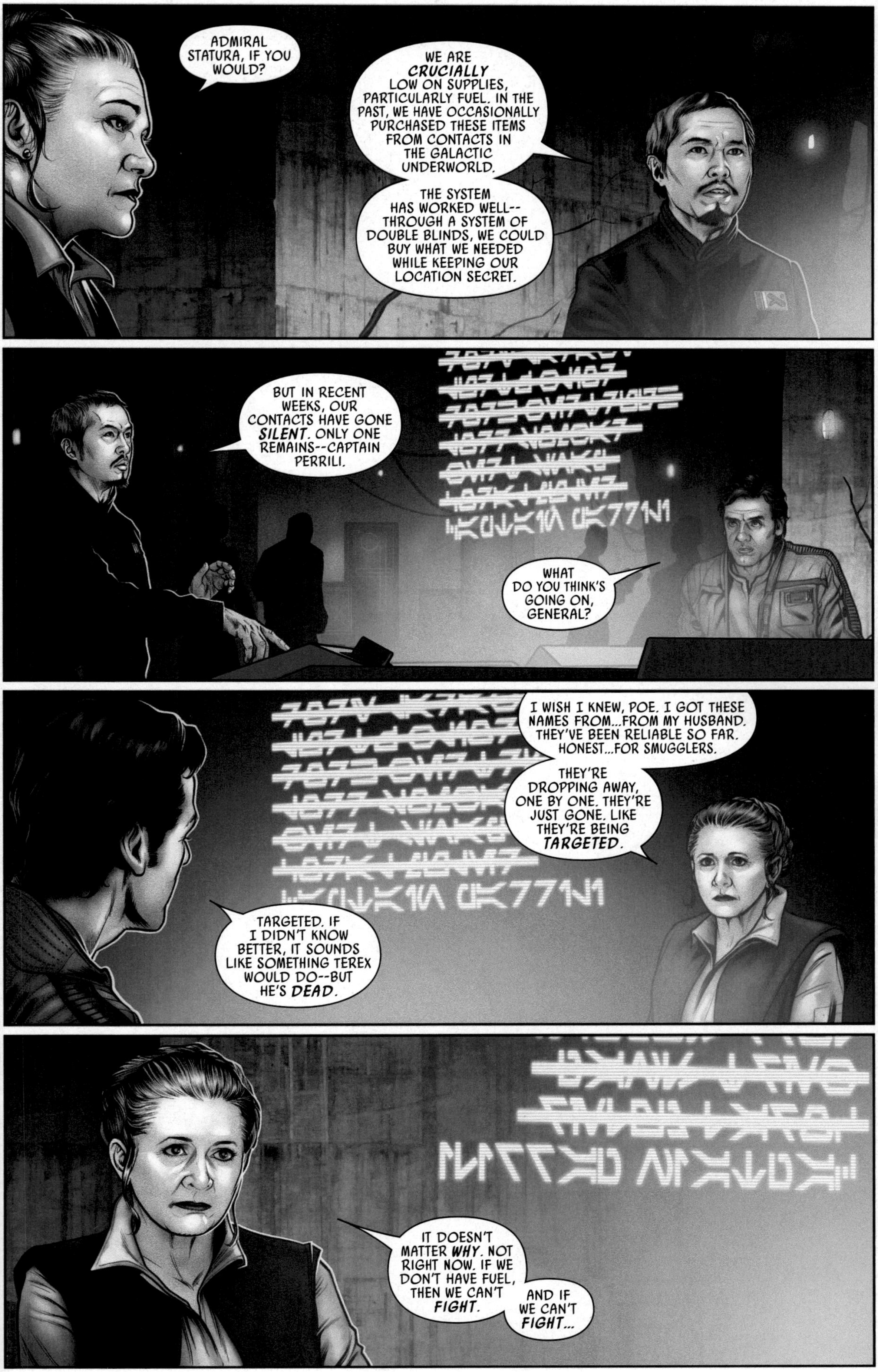
ADMIRAL STATURA, IF YOU WOULD?
WE ARE CRUCIALLY LOW ON SUPPLIES, PARTICULARLY FUEL. IN THE PAST, WE HAVE OCCASIONALLY PURCHASED THESE ITEMS FROM CONTACTS IN THE GALACTIC UNDERWORLD.
THE SYSTEM HAS WORKED WELL--THROUGH A SYSTEM OF DOUBLE BLINDS, WE COULD BUY WHAT WE NEEDED WHILE KEEPING OUR LOCATION SECRET.
BUT IN RECENT WEEKS, OUR CONTACTS HAVE GONE SILENT. ONLY ONE REMAINS--CAPTAIN PERRILI.
WHAT DO YOU THINK'S GOING ON, GENERAL?
I WISH I KNEW, POE. I GOT THESE NAMES FROM...FROM MY HUSBAND. THEY'VE BEEN RELIABLE SO FAR. HONEST...FOR SMUGGLERS.
THEY'RE DROPPING AWAY, ONE BY ONE. THEY'RE JUST GONE. LIKE THEY'RE BEING TARGETED.
TARGETED. IF I DIDN'T KNOW BETTER, IT SOUNDS LIKE SOMETHING TEREX WOULD DO--BUT HE'S DEAD.
IT DOESN'T MATTER WHY. NOT RIGHT NOW. IF WE DON'T HAVE FUEL, THEN WE CAN'T FIGHT.
AND IF WE CAN'T FIGHT...

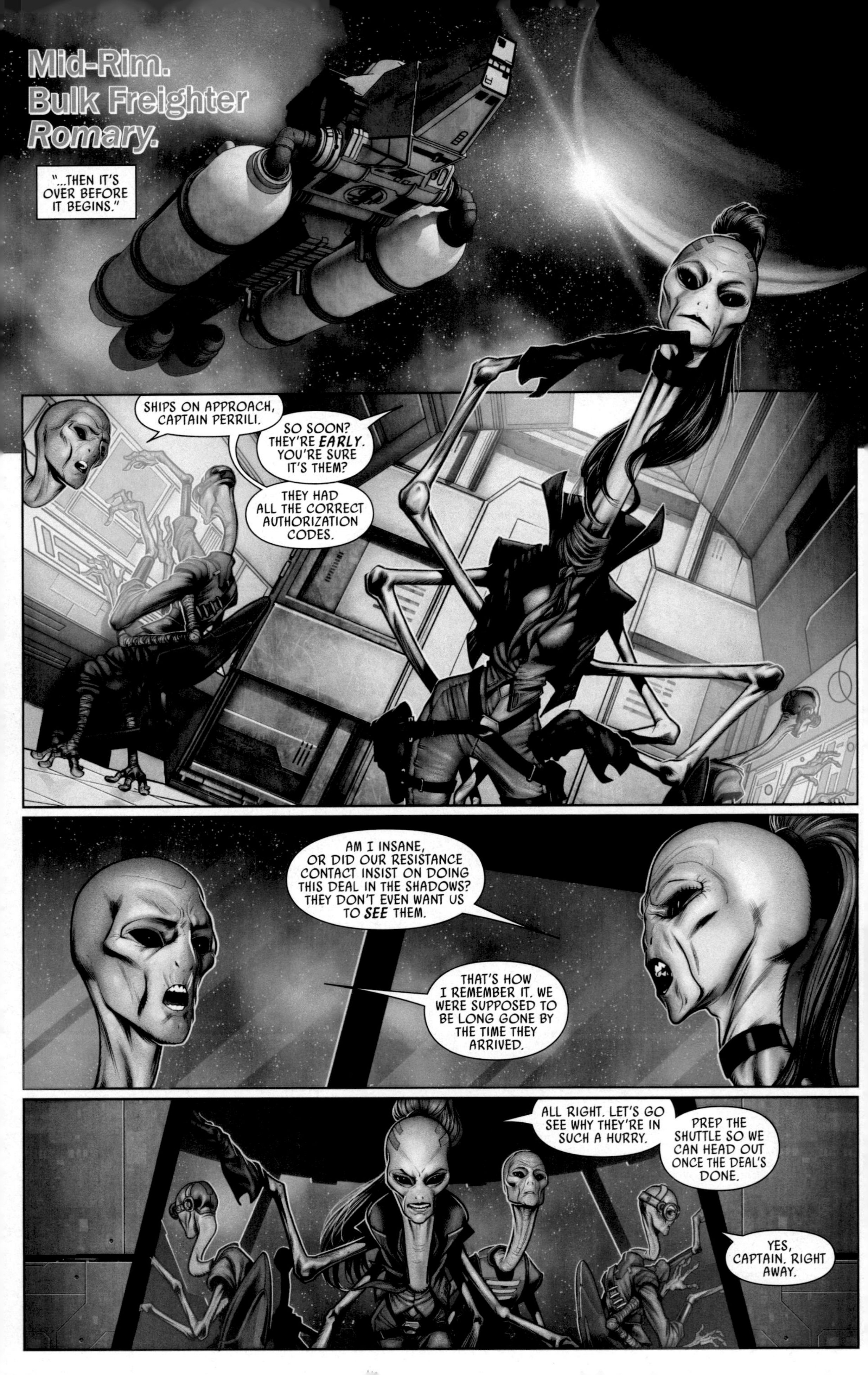
Mid-Rim.
Bulk Freighter
Romary.
"...THEN IT'S OVER BEFORE IT BEGINS."
SHIPS ON APPROACH, CAPTAIN PERRILI.
SO SOON? THEY'RE EARLY. YOU'RE SURE IT'S THEM?
THEY HAD ALL THE CORRECT AUTHORIZATION CODES.
AM I INSANE, OR DID OUR RESISTANCE CONTACT INSIST ON DOING THIS DEAL IN THE SHADOWS? THEY DON'T EVEN WANT US TO SEE THEM.
THAT'S HOW I REMEMBER IT. WE WERE SUPPOSED TO BE LONG GONE BY THE TIME THEY ARRIVED.
ALL RIGHT. LET'S GO SEE WHY THEY'RE IN SUCH A HURRY.
PREP THE SHUTTLE SO WE CAN HEAD OUT ONCE THE DEAL'S DONE.
YES, CAPTAIN. RIGHT AWAY.

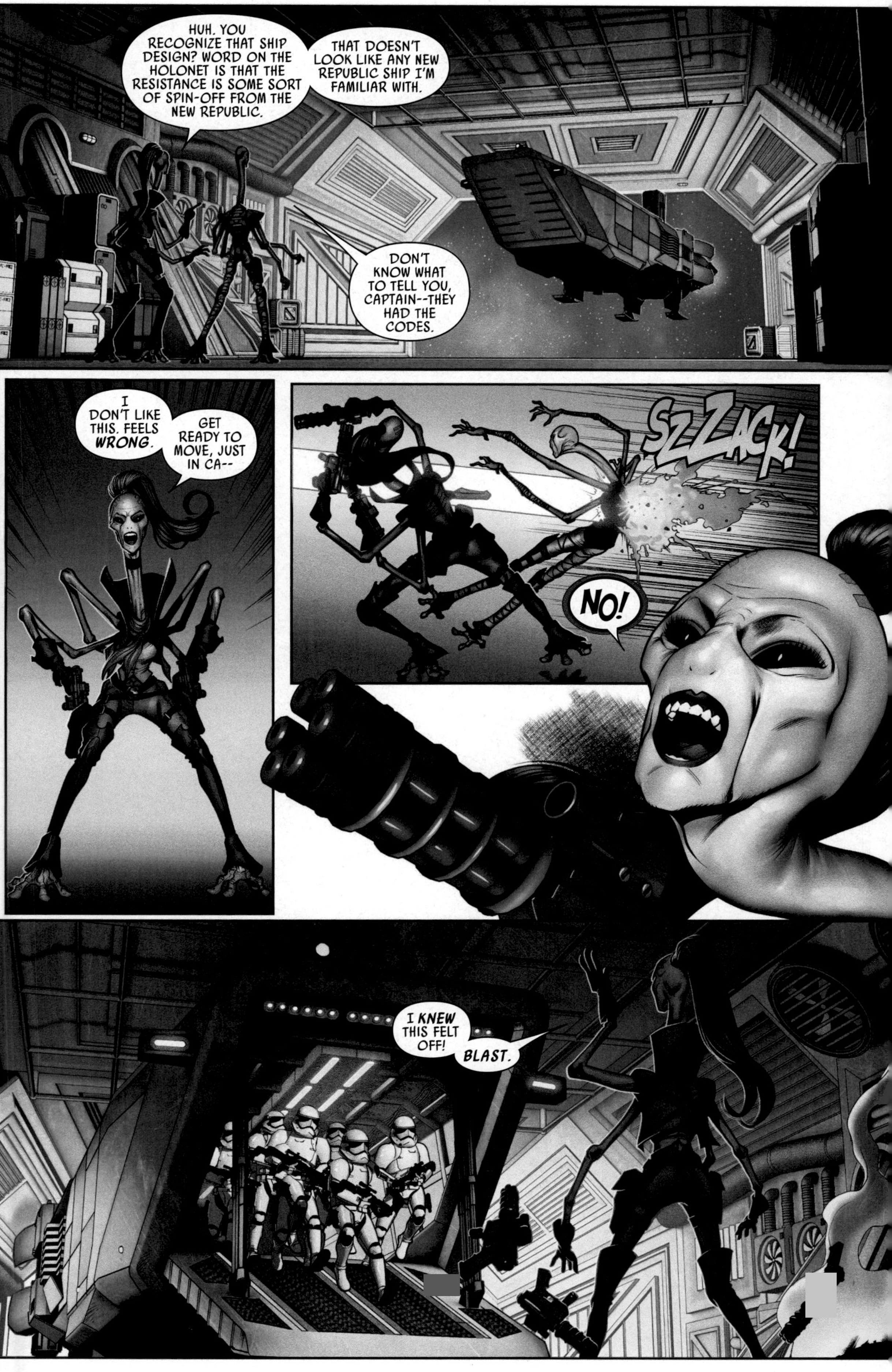
HUH. YOU RECOGNIZE THAT SHIP DESIGN? WORD ON THE HOLONET IS THAT THE RESISTANCE IS SOME SORT OF SPIN-OFF FROM THE NEW REPUBLIC.
THAT DOESN'T LOOK LIKE ANY NEW REPUBLIC SHIP I'M FAMILIAR WITH.
DON'T KNOW WHAT TO TELL YOU, CAPTAIN--THEY HAD THE CODES.
I DON'T LIKE THIS. FEELS *WRONG*.
GET READY TO MOVE, JUST IN CA--
SZZACK!
NO!
I *KNEW* THIS FELT OFF!
BLAST.

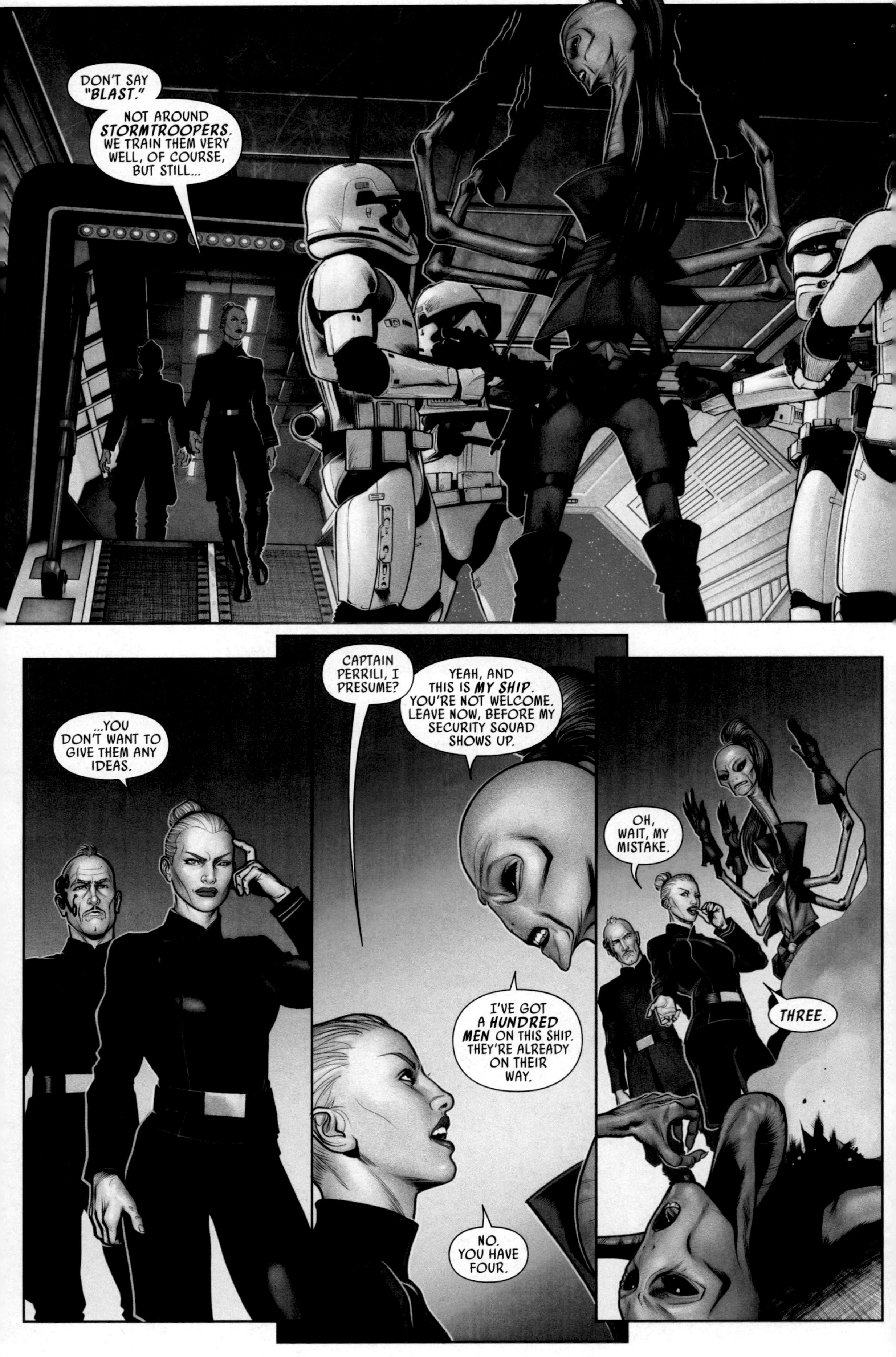
DON'T SAY "BLAST."
NOT AROUND STORMTROOPERS. WE TRAIN THEM VERY WELL, OF COURSE, BUT STILL...
...YOU DON'T WANT TO GIVE THEM ANY IDEAS.
CAPTAIN PERRILI, I PRESUME?
YEAH, AND THIS IS MY SHIP. YOU'RE NOT WELCOME. LEAVE NOW, BEFORE MY SECURITY SQUAD SHOWS UP.
I'VE GOT A HUNDRED MEN ON THIS SHIP. THEY'RE ALREADY ON THEIR WAY.
NO. YOU HAVE FOUR.
OH, WAIT, MY MISTAKE.
THREE.

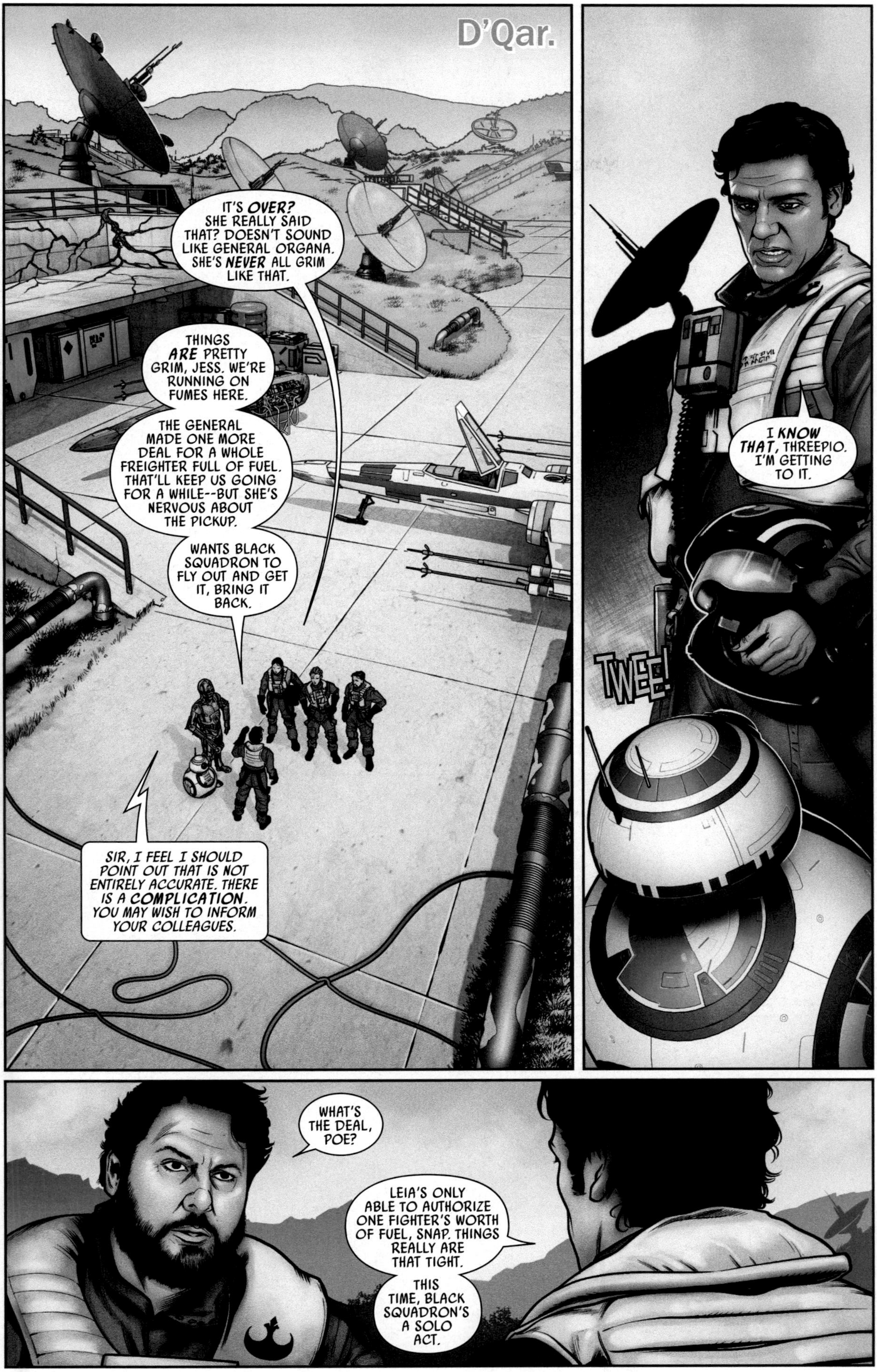
D'Qar.
IT'S OVER? SHE REALLY SAID THAT? DOESN'T SOUND LIKE GENERAL ORGANA. SHE'S NEVER ALL GRIM LIKE THAT.
THINGS ARE PRETTY GRIM, JESS. WE'RE RUNNING ON FUMES HERE.
THE GENERAL MADE ONE MORE DEAL FOR A WHOLE FREIGHTER FULL OF FUEL. THAT'LL KEEP US GOING FOR A WHILE--BUT SHE'S NERVOUS ABOUT THE PICKUP.
WANTS BLACK SQUADRON TO FLY OUT AND GET IT, BRING IT BACK.
SIR, I FEEL I SHOULD POINT OUT THAT IS NOT ENTIRELY ACCURATE. THERE IS A COMPLICATION. YOU MAY WISH TO INFORM YOUR COLLEAGUES.
I KNOW THAT, THREEPIO. I'M GETTING TO IT.
TWEE!
WHAT'S THE DEAL, POE?
LEIA'S ONLY ABLE TO AUTHORIZE ONE FIGHTER'S WORTH OF FUEL, SNAP. THINGS REALLY ARE THAT TIGHT.
THIS TIME, BLACK SQUADRON'S A SOLO ACT.

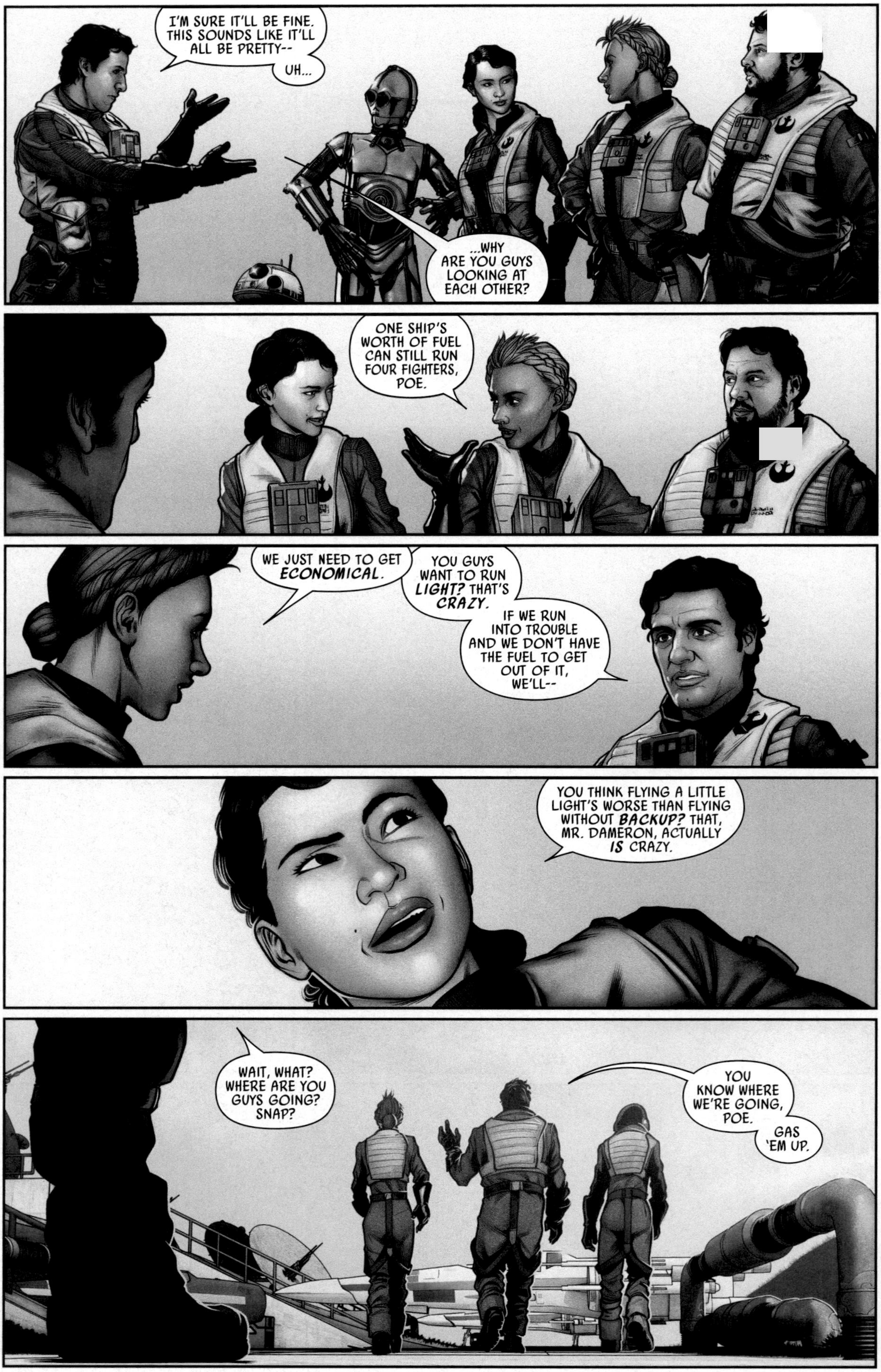

I'M SURE IT'LL BE FINE. THIS SOUNDS LIKE IT'LL ALL BE PRETTY--
UH...
...WHY ARE YOU GUYS LOOKING AT EACH OTHER?
ONE SHIP'S WORTH OF FUEL CAN STILL RUN FOUR FIGHTERS, POE.
WE JUST NEED TO GET ECONOMICAL.
YOU GUYS WANT TO RUN LIGHT? THAT'S CRAZY.
IF WE RUN INTO TROUBLE AND WE DON'T HAVE THE FUEL TO GET OUT OF IT, WE'LL--
YOU THINK FLYING A LITTLE LIGHT'S WORSE THAN FLYING WITHOUT BACKUP? THAT, MR. DAMERON, ACTUALLY IS CRAZY.
WAIT, WHAT? WHERE ARE YOU GUYS GOING? SNAP?
YOU KNOW WHERE WE'RE GOING, POE.
GAS 'EM UP.

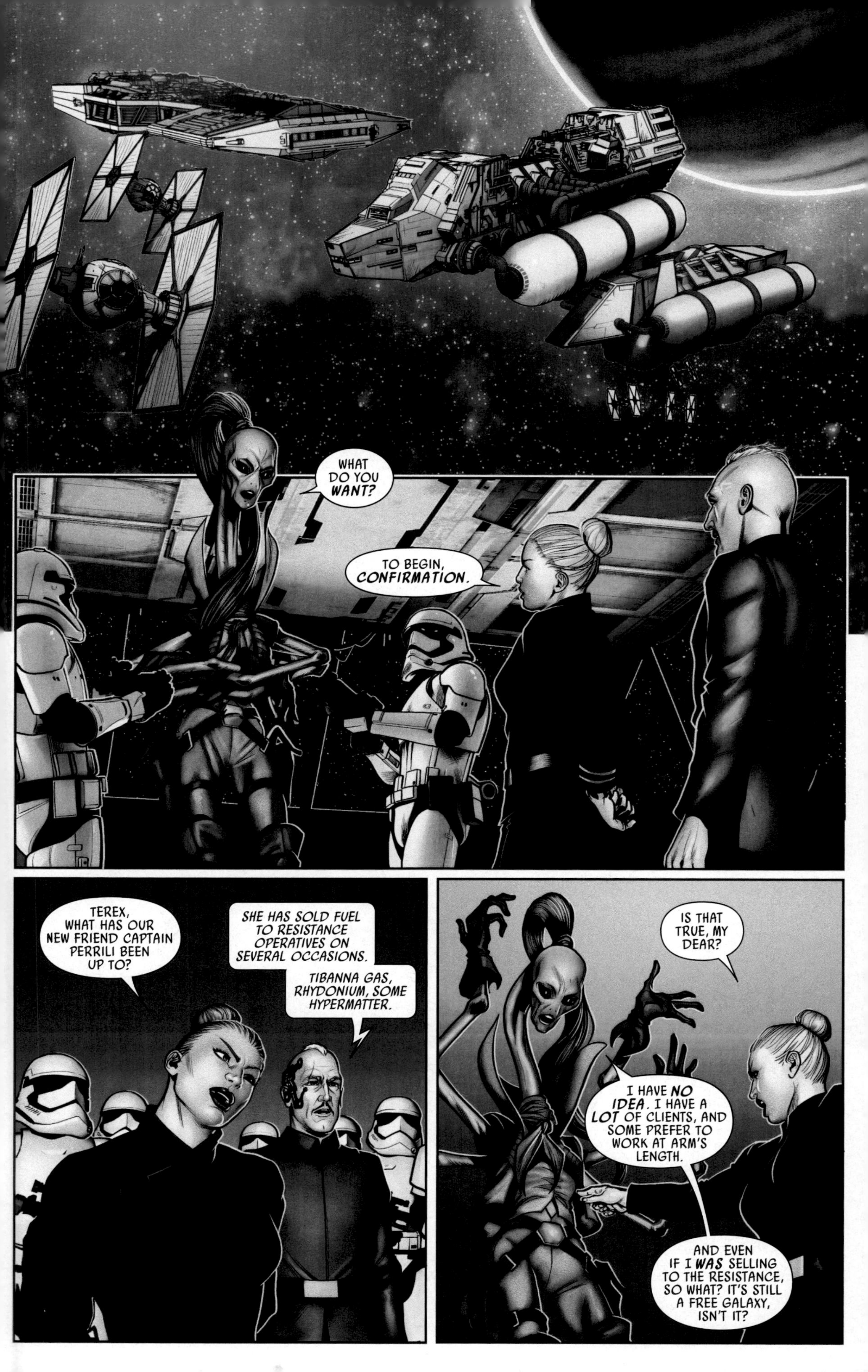
WHAT DO YOU WANT?
TO BEGIN, CONFIRMATION.
TEREX, WHAT HAS OUR NEW FRIEND CAPTAIN PERRILI BEEN UP TO?
SHE HAS SOLD FUEL TO RESISTANCE OPERATIVES ON SEVERAL OCCASIONS.
TIBANNA GAS, RHYDONIUM, SOME HYPERMATTER.
IS THAT TRUE, MY DEAR?
I HAVE NO IDEA. I HAVE A LOT OF CLIENTS, AND SOME PREFER TO WORK AT ARM'S LENGTH.
AND EVEN IF I WAS SELLING TO THE RESISTANCE, SO WHAT? IT'S STILL A FREE GALAXY, ISN'T IT?

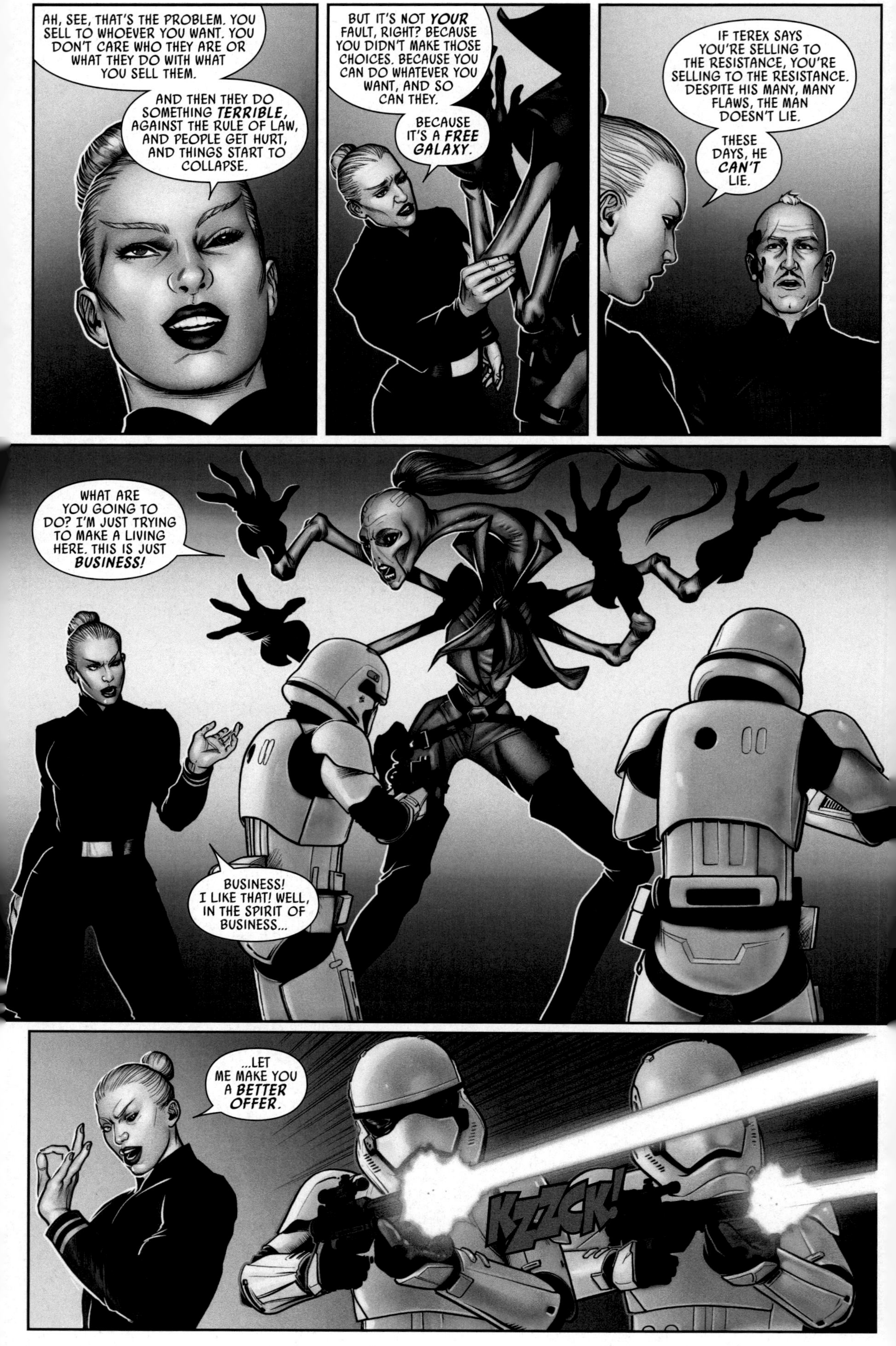
AH, SEE, THAT'S THE PROBLEM. YOU SELL TO WHOEVER YOU WANT. YOU DON'T CARE WHO THEY ARE OR WHAT THEY DO WITH WHAT YOU SELL THEM.
AND THEN THEY DO SOMETHING TERRIBLE, AGAINST THE RULE OF LAW, AND PEOPLE GET HURT, AND THINGS START TO COLLAPSE.
BUT IT'S NOT YOUR FAULT, RIGHT? BECAUSE YOU DIDN'T MAKE THOSE CHOICES. BECAUSE YOU CAN DO WHATEVER YOU WANT, AND SO CAN THEY.
BECAUSE IT'S A FREE GALAXY.
IF TEREX SAYS YOU'RE SELLING TO THE RESISTANCE, YOU'RE SELLING TO THE RESISTANCE. DESPITE HIS MANY, MANY FLAWS, THE MAN DOESN'T LIE.
THESE DAYS, HE CAN'T LIE.
WHAT ARE YOU GOING TO DO? I'M JUST TRYING TO MAKE A LIVING HERE. THIS IS JUST BUSINESS!
BUSINESS! I LIKE THAT! WELL, IN THE SPIRIT OF BUSINESS...
...LET ME MAKE YOU A BETTER OFFER.
KZZCK!

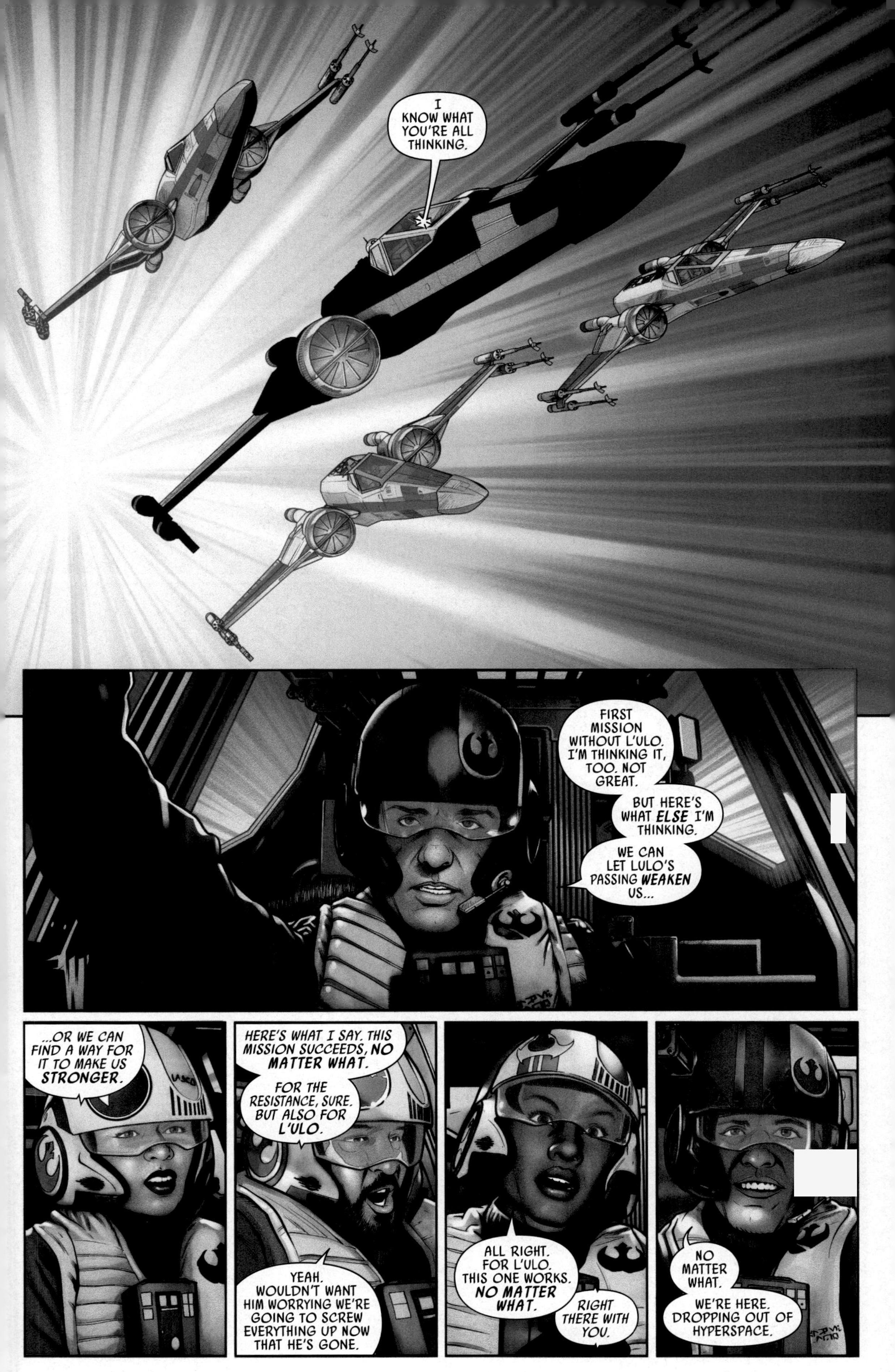
I KNOW WHAT YOU'RE ALL THINKING.
FIRST MISSION WITHOUT L'ULO. I'M THINKING IT, TOO. NOT GREAT.
BUT HERE'S WHAT ELSE I'M THINKING.
WE CAN LET LULO'S PASSING WEAKEN US...
...OR WE CAN FIND A WAY FOR IT TO MAKE US STRONGER.
HERE'S WHAT I SAY. THIS MISSION SUCCEEDS, NO MATTER WHAT.
FOR THE RESISTANCE, SURE. BUT ALSO FOR L'ULO.
YEAH. WOULDN'T WANT HIM WORRYING WE'RE GOING TO SCREW EVERYTHING UP NOW THAT HE'S GONE.
ALL RIGHT. FOR L'ULO. THIS ONE WORKS. NO MATTER WHAT.
RIGHT THERE WITH YOU.
NO MATTER WHAT.
WE'RE HERE. DROPPING OUT OF HYPERSPACE.

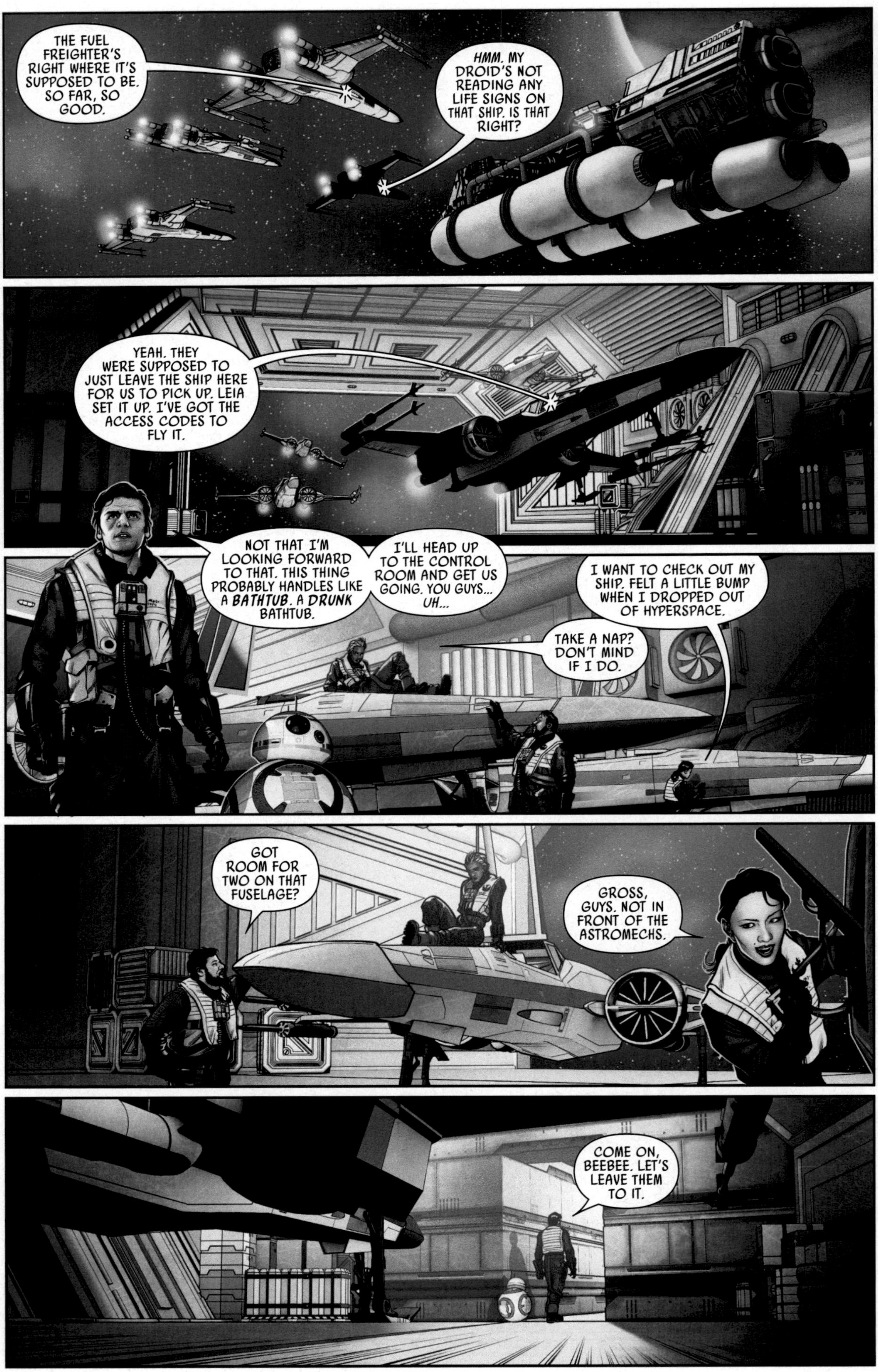
THE FUEL FREIGHTER'S RIGHT WHERE IT'S SUPPOSED TO BE. SO FAR, SO GOOD.
HMM. MY DROID'S NOT READING ANY LIFE SIGNS ON THAT SHIP. IS THAT RIGHT?
YEAH. THEY WERE SUPPOSED TO JUST LEAVE THE SHIP HERE FOR US TO PICK UP. LEIA SET IT UP. I'VE GOT THE ACCESS CODES TO FLY IT.
NOT THAT I'M LOOKING FORWARD TO THAT. THIS THING PROBABLY HANDLES LIKE A BATHTUB. A DRUNK BATHTUB.
I'LL HEAD UP TO THE CONTROL ROOM AND GET US GOING. YOU GUYS... UH...
I WANT TO CHECK OUT MY SHIP. FELT A LITTLE BUMP WHEN I DROPPED OUT OF HYPERSPACE.
TAKE A NAP? DON'T MIND IF I DO.
GOT ROOM FOR TWO ON THAT FUSELAGE?
GROSS, GUYS. NOT IN FRONT OF THE ASTROMECHS.
COME ON, BEEBEE. LET'S LEAVE THEM TO IT.

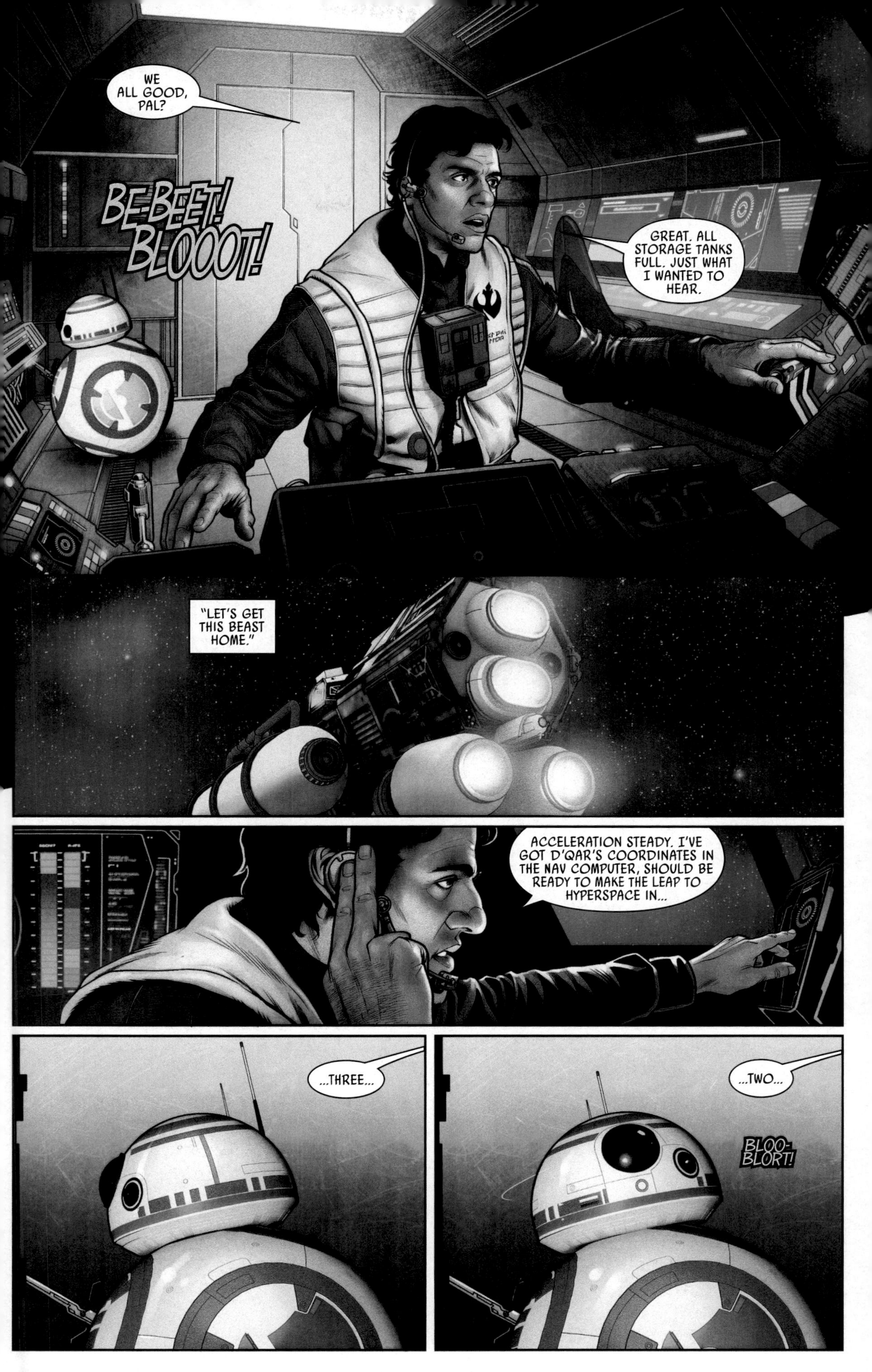
WE ALL GOOD, PAL?
BE-BEET! BLOOOT!
GREAT. ALL STORAGE TANKS FULL. JUST WHAT I WANTED TO HEAR.
"LET'S GET THIS BEAST HOME."
ACCELERATION STEADY. I'VE GOT D'QAR'S COORDINATES IN THE NAV COMPUTER, SHOULD BE READY TO MAKE THE LEAP TO HYPERSPACE IN...
...THREE...
...TWO...
BLOO-BLORT!

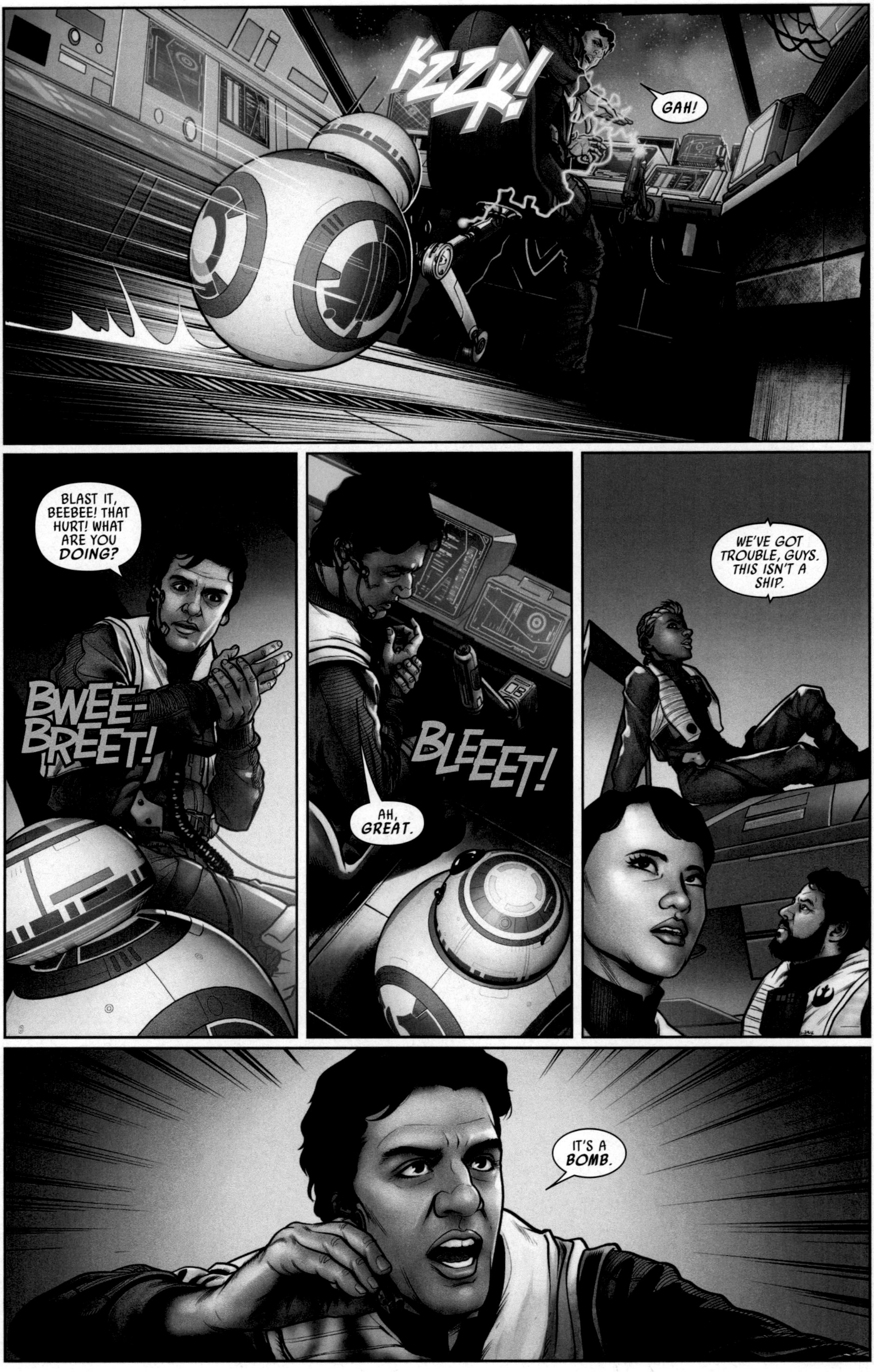
KZZK!
GAH!
BLAST IT, BEEBEE! THAT HURT! WHAT ARE YOU DOING?
BWEE-BREET!
BLEEET!
AH, GREAT.
WE'VE GOT TROUBLE, GUYS. THIS ISN'T A SHIP.
IT'S A BOMB.

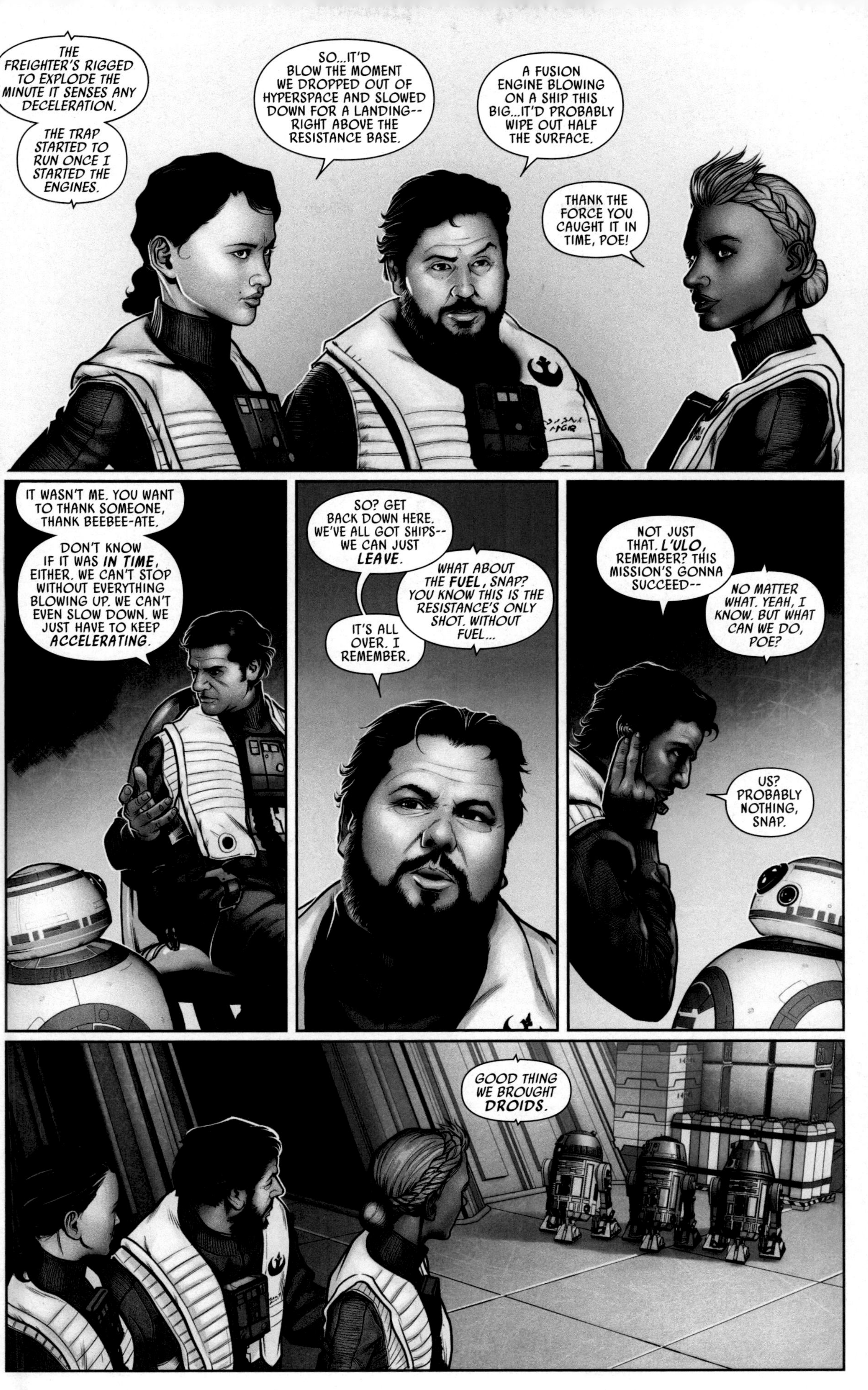
THE FREIGHTER'S RIGGED TO EXPLODE THE MINUTE IT SENSES ANY DECELERATION.
THE TRAP STARTED TO RUN ONCE I STARTED THE ENGINES.
SO...IT'D BLOW THE MOMENT WE DROPPED OUT OF HYPERSPACE AND SLOWED DOWN FOR A LANDING--RIGHT ABOVE THE RESISTANCE BASE.
A FUSION ENGINE BLOWING ON A SHIP THIS BIG...IT'D PROBABLY WIPE OUT HALF THE SURFACE.
THANK THE FORCE YOU CAUGHT IT IN TIME, POE!
IT WASN'T ME. YOU WANT TO THANK SOMEONE, THANK BEEBEE-ATE.
DON'T KNOW IF IT WAS *IN TIME*, EITHER. WE CAN'T STOP WITHOUT EVERYTHING BLOWING UP. WE CAN'T EVEN SLOW DOWN. WE JUST HAVE TO KEEP *ACCELERATING*.
SO? GET BACK DOWN HERE. WE'VE ALL GOT SHIPS--WE CAN JUST *LEAVE*.
WHAT ABOUT THE *FUEL*, SNAP? YOU KNOW THIS IS THE RESISTANCE'S ONLY SHOT. WITHOUT FUEL...
IT'S ALL OVER. I REMEMBER.
NOT JUST THAT. *L'ULO*, REMEMBER? THIS MISSION'S GONNA SUCCEED--
NO MATTER WHAT. YEAH, I KNOW. BUT WHAT CAN WE DO, POE?
US? PROBABLY NOTHING, SNAP.
GOOD THING WE BROUGHT *DROIDS*.

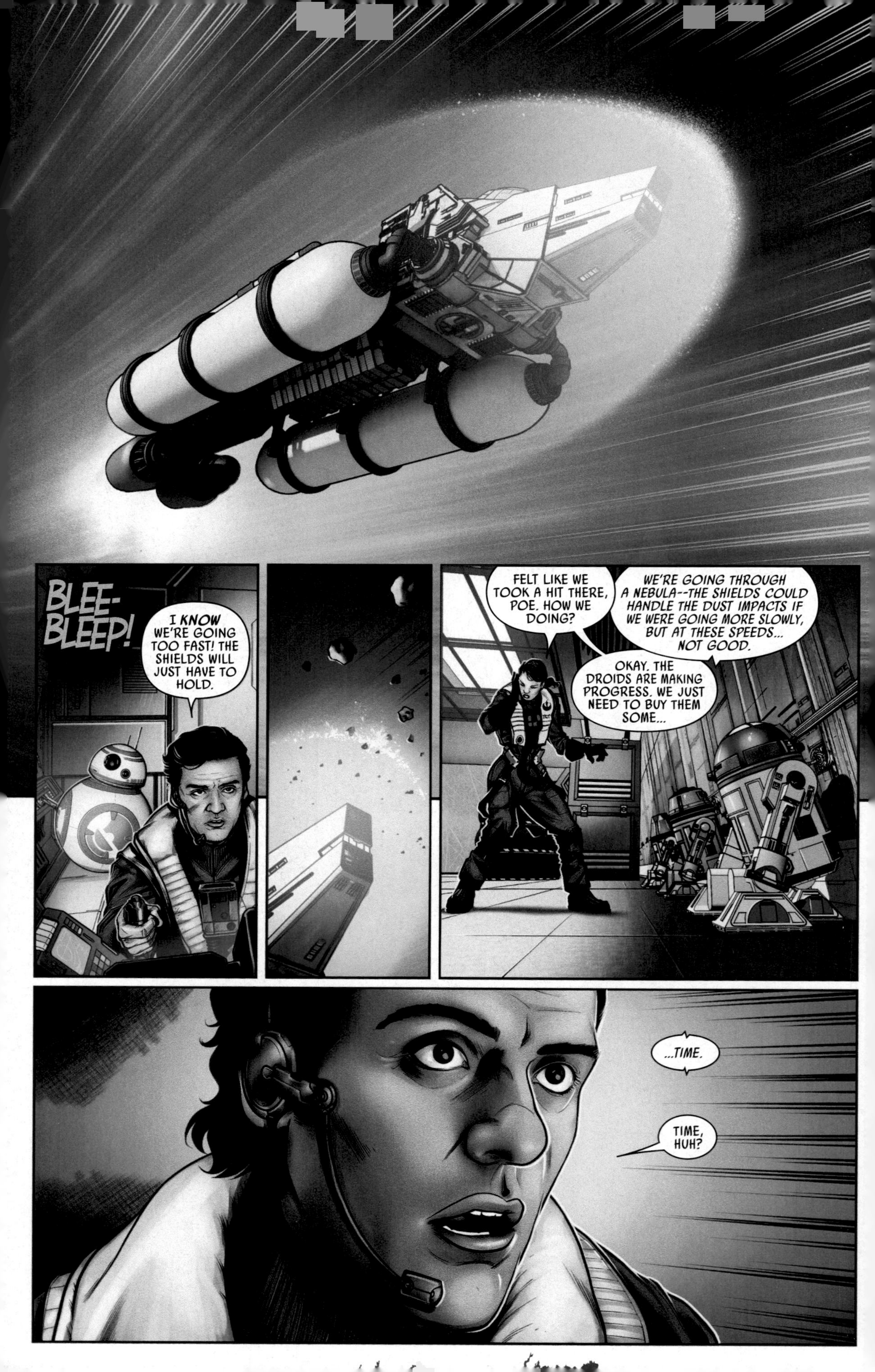
BLEE-BLEEP!
I KNOW WE'RE GOING TOO FAST! THE SHIELDS WILL JUST HAVE TO HOLD.
FELT LIKE WE TOOK A HIT THERE, POE. HOW WE DOING?
WE'RE GOING THROUGH A NEBULA--THE SHIELDS COULD HANDLE THE DUST IMPACTS IF WE WERE GOING MORE SLOWLY, BUT AT THESE SPEEDS... NOT GOOD.
OKAY. THE DROIDS ARE MAKING PROGRESS. WE JUST NEED TO BUY THEM SOME...
...TIME.
TIME, HUH?

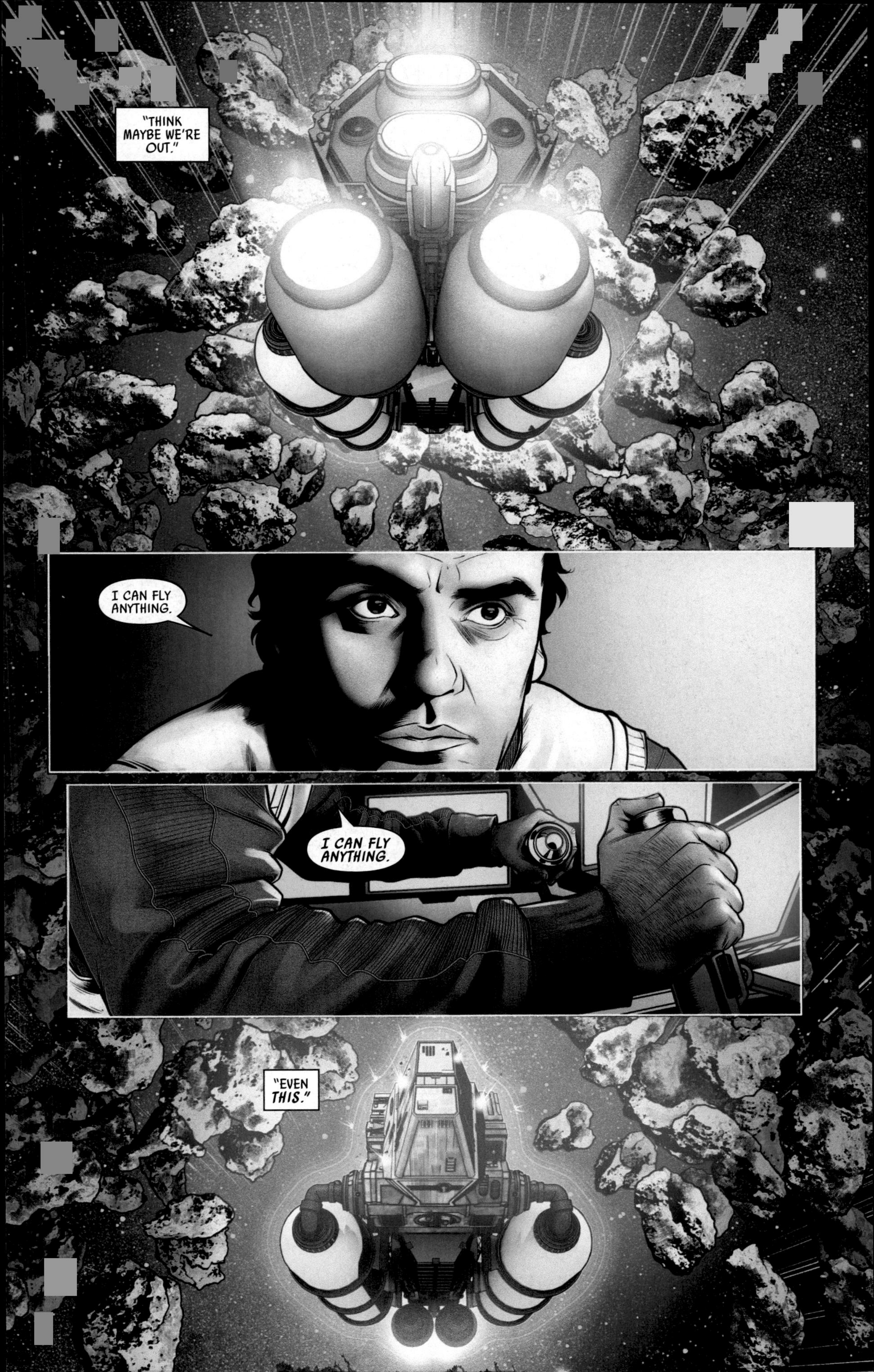
"THINK MAYBE WE'RE OUT."
I CAN FLY ANYTHING.
I CAN FLY ANYTHING.
"EVEN THIS."

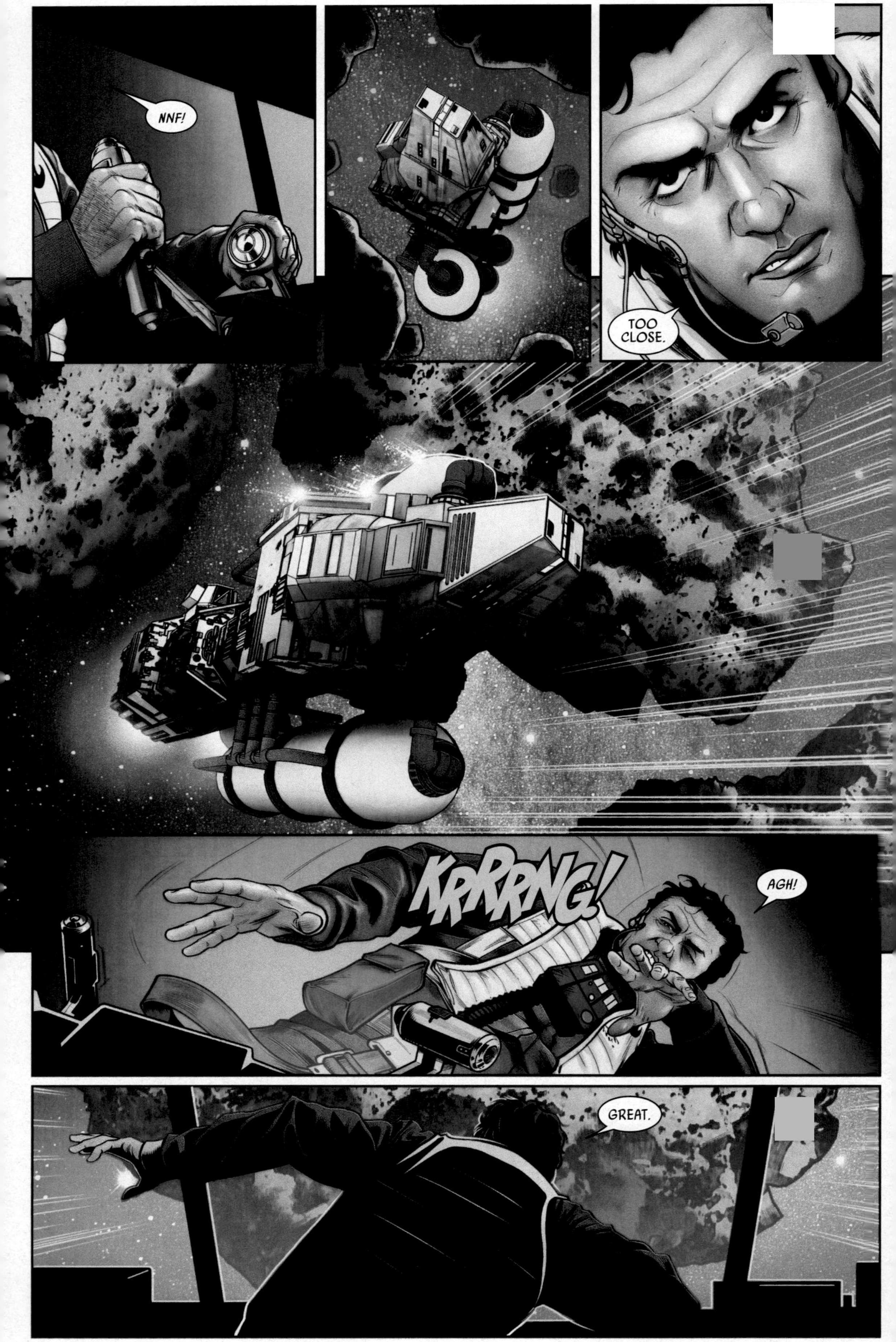
NNF!
TOO CLOSE.
KRRRNG!
AGH!
GREAT.

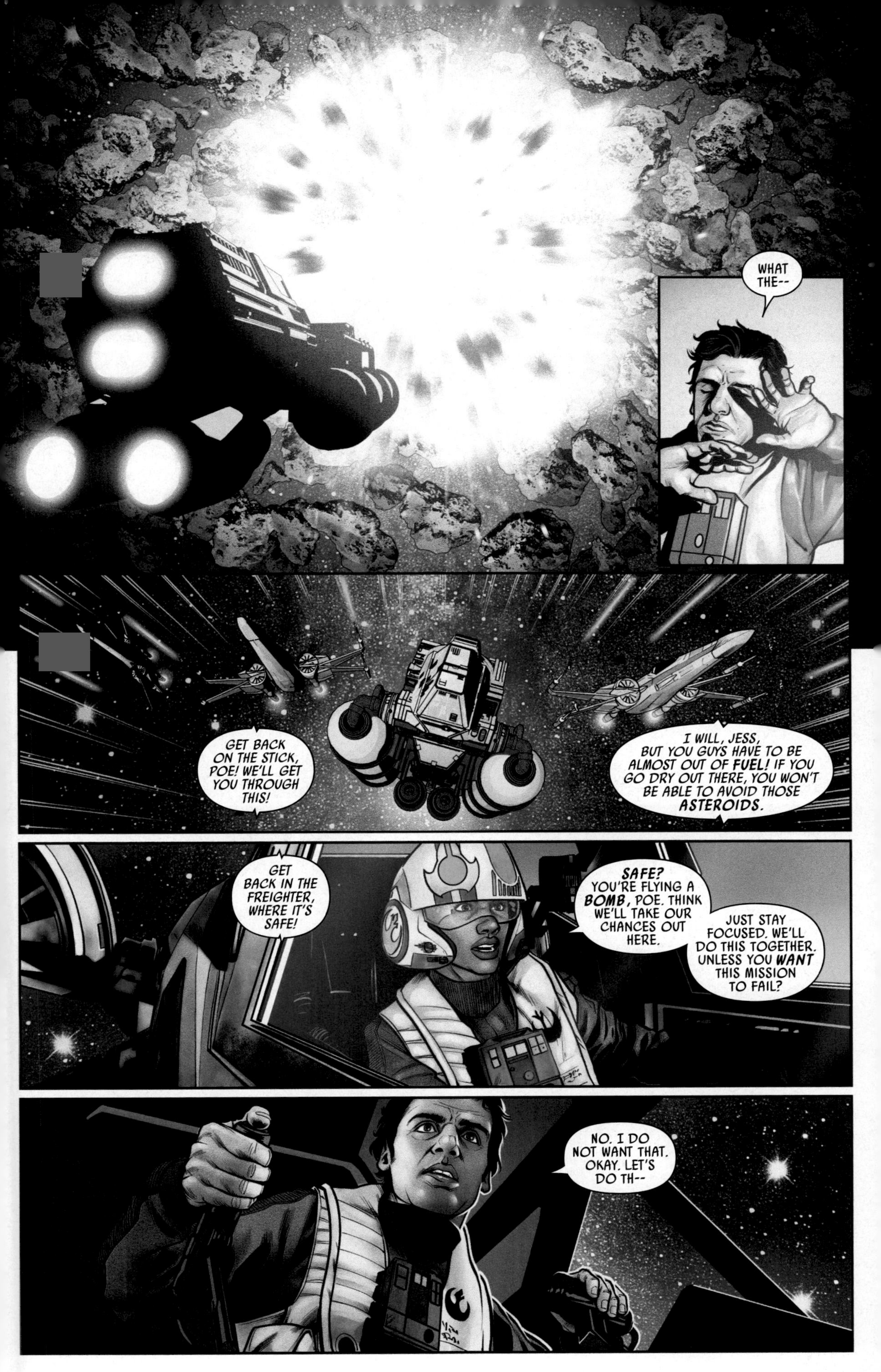
WHAT THE--
GET BACK ON THE STICK, POE! WE'LL GET YOU THROUGH THIS!
I WILL, JESS, BUT YOU GUYS HAVE TO BE ALMOST OUT OF FUEL! IF YOU GO DRY OUT THERE, YOU WON'T BE ABLE TO AVOID THOSE ASTEROIDS.
GET BACK IN THE FREIGHTER, WHERE IT'S SAFE!
SAFE? YOU'RE FLYING A BOMB, POE. THINK WE'LL TAKE OUR CHANCES OUT HERE.
JUST STAY FOCUSED. WE'LL DO THIS TOGETHER. UNLESS YOU WANT THIS MISSION TO FAIL?
NO. I DO NOT WANT THAT. OKAY. LET'S DO TH--

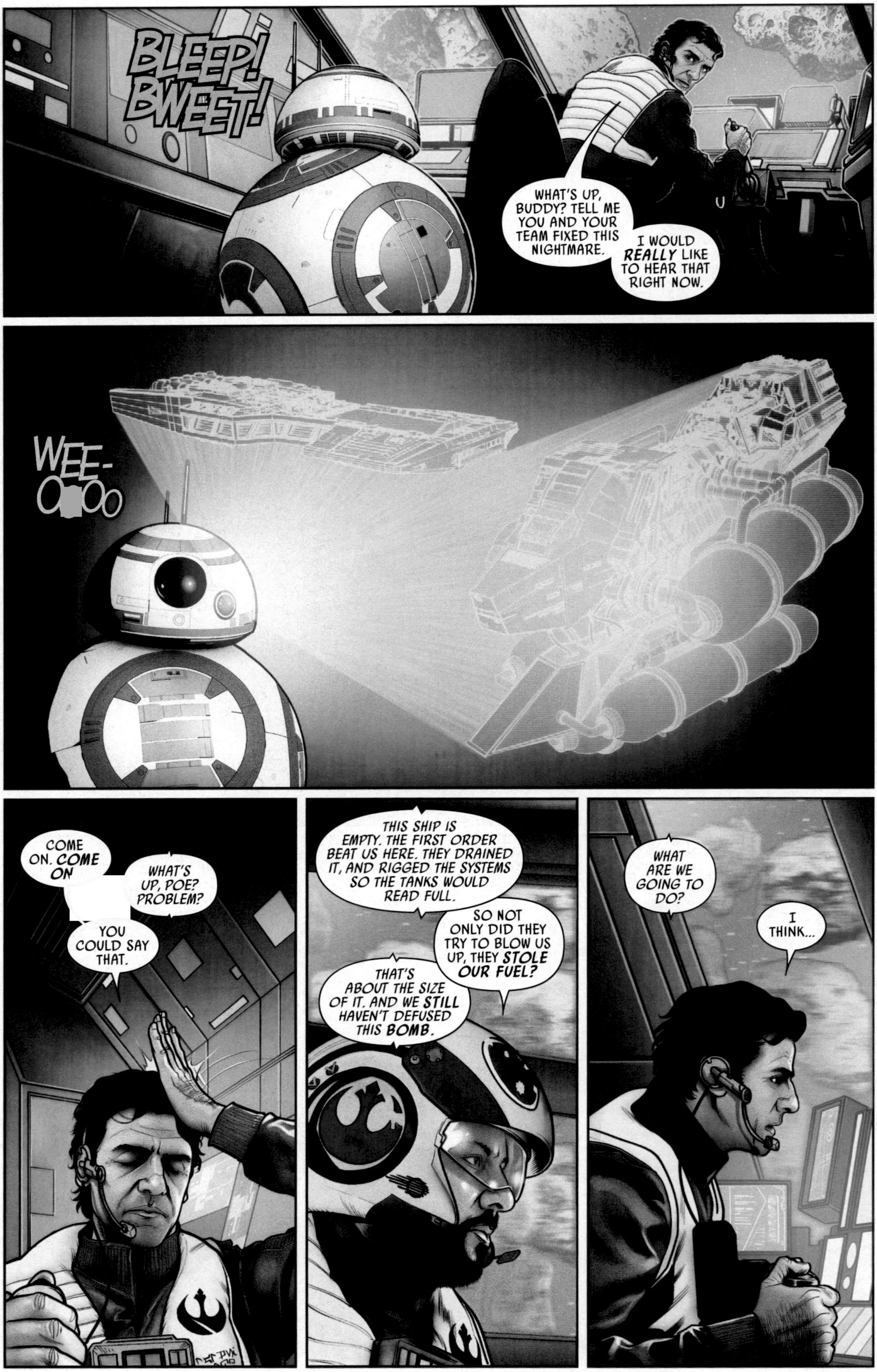
BLEEP! BWEET!
WHAT'S UP, BUDDY? TELL ME YOU AND YOUR TEAM FIXED THIS NIGHTMARE.
I WOULD REALLY LIKE TO HEAR THAT RIGHT NOW.
WEE-
O OO
COME ON. COME ON
WHAT'S UP, POE? PROBLEM?
YOU COULD SAY THAT.
THIS SHIP IS EMPTY. THE FIRST ORDER BEAT US HERE. THEY DRAINED IT, AND RIGGED THE SYSTEMS SO THE TANKS WOULD READ FULL.
SO NOT ONLY DID THEY TRY TO BLOW US UP, THEY STOLE OUR FUEL?
THAT'S ABOUT THE SIZE OF IT. AND WE STILL HAVEN'T DEFUSED THIS BOMB.
WHAT ARE WE GOING TO DO?
I THINK...

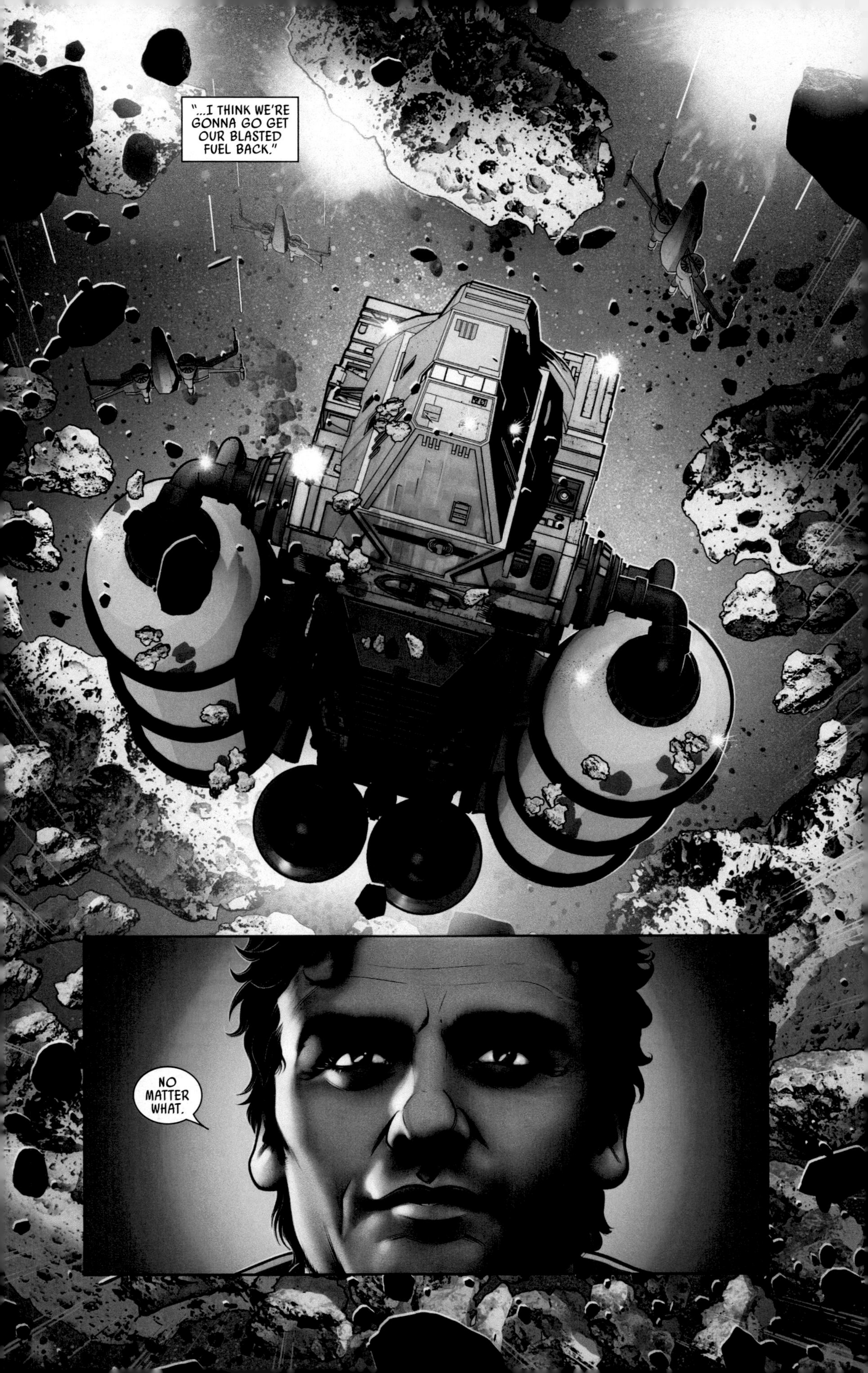
"...I THINK WE'RE GONNA GO GET OUR BLASTED FUEL BACK."
NO MATTER WHAT.

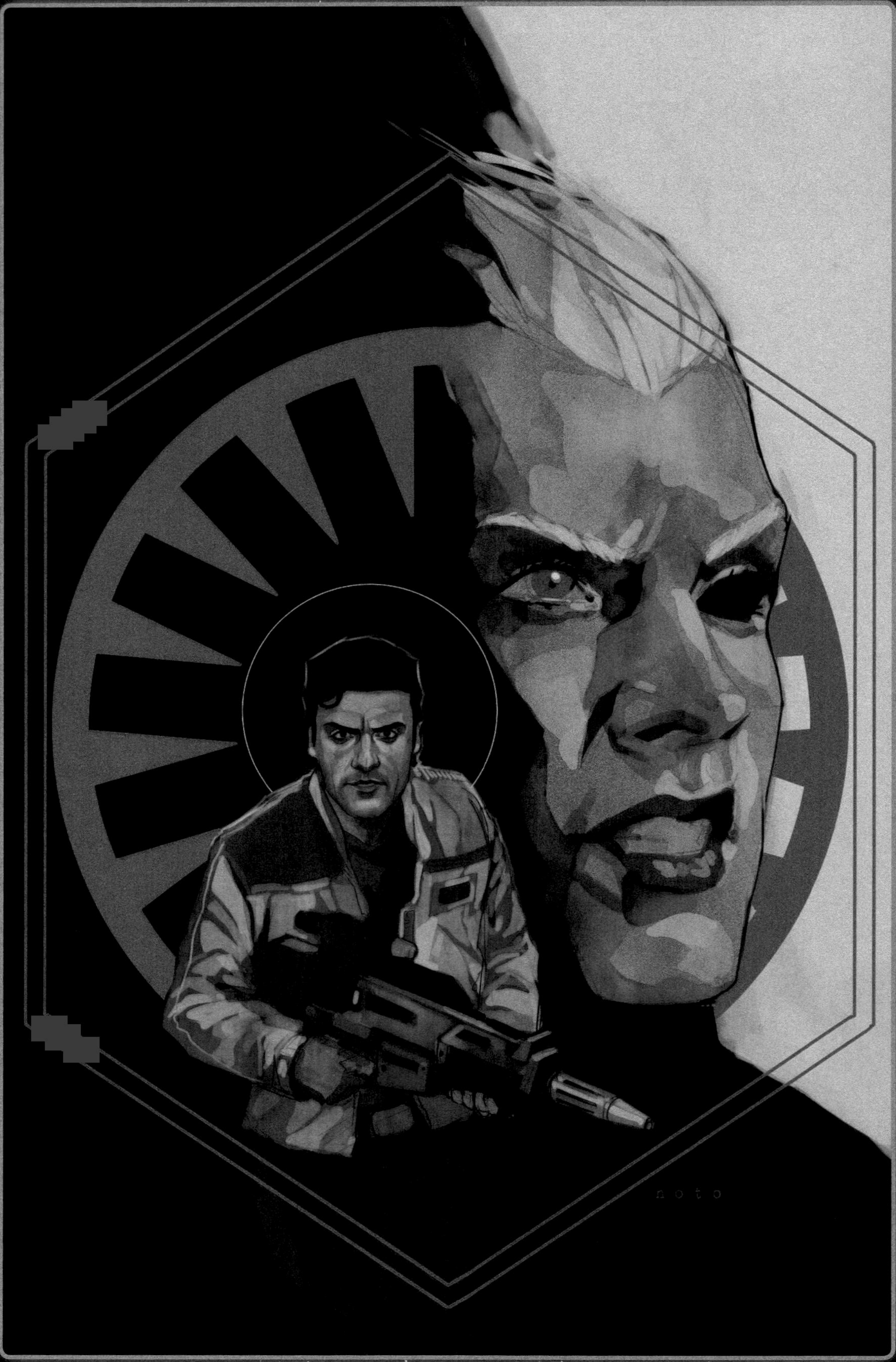
noto

16

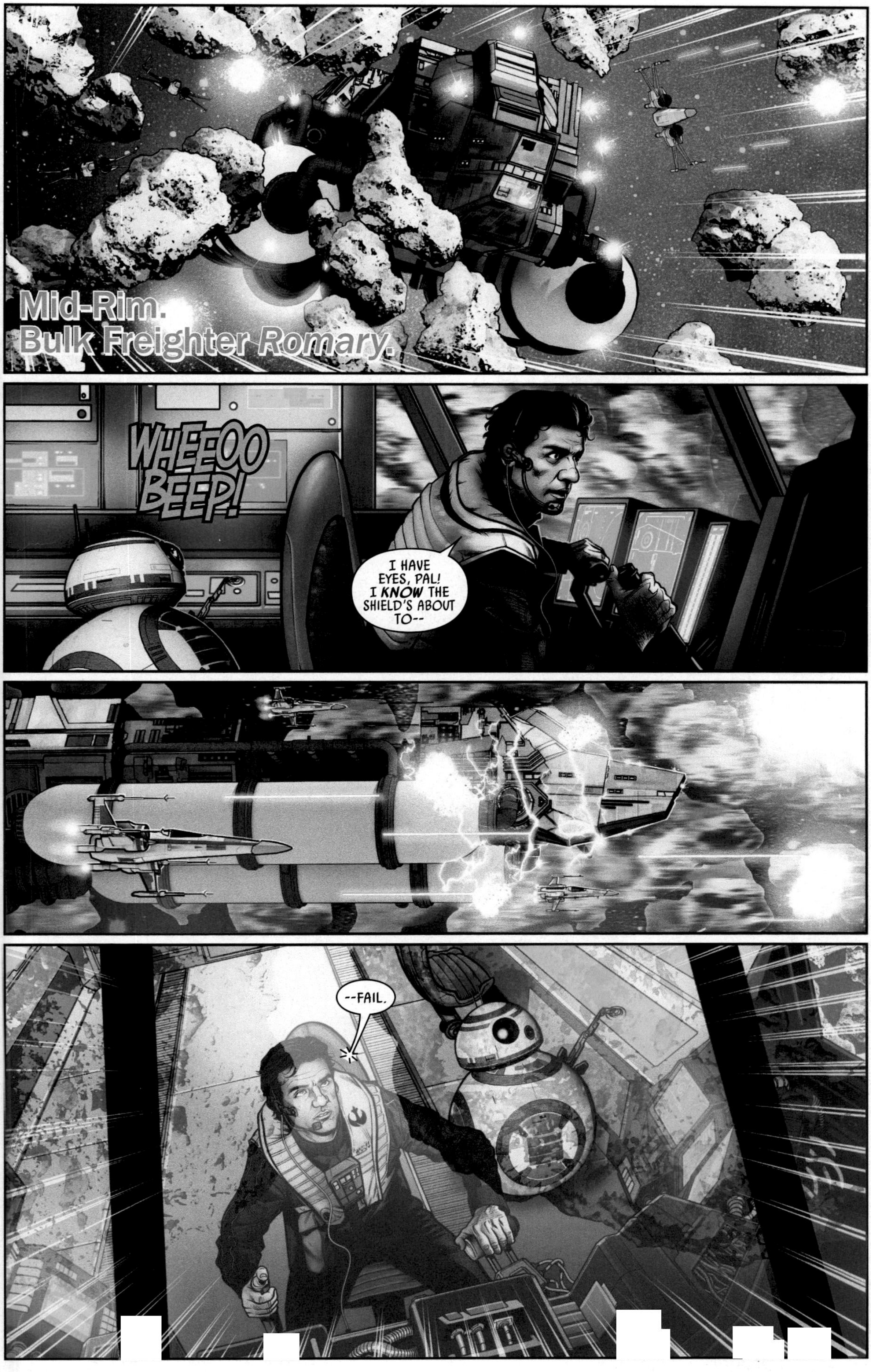
Mid-Rim.
Bulk Freighter Romary.
WHEEOO BEEP!
I HAVE EYES, PAL! I KNOW THE SHIELD'S ABOUT TO--
--FAIL.

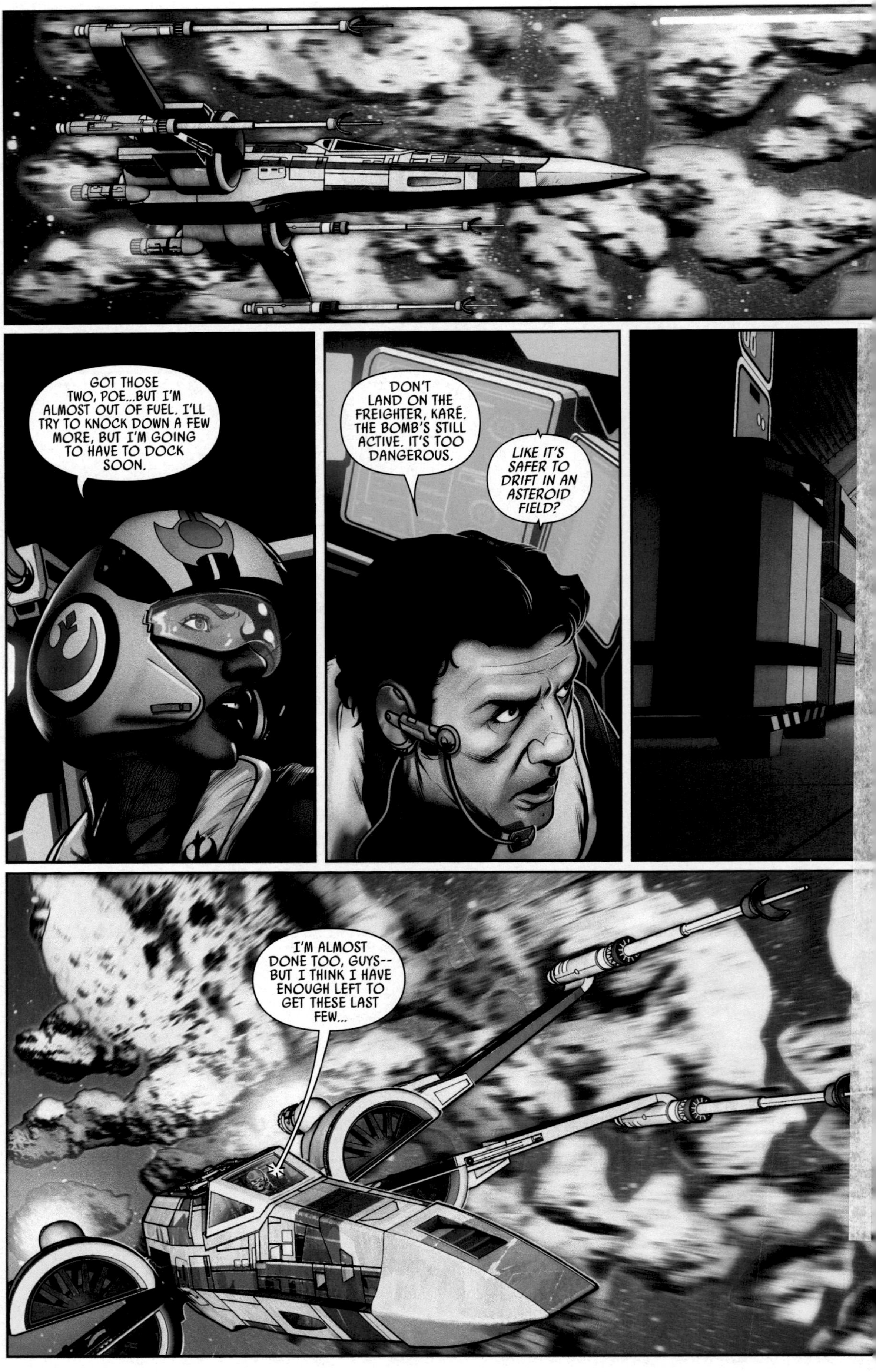
GOT THOSE TWO, POE...BUT I'M ALMOST OUT OF FUEL. I'LL TRY TO KNOCK DOWN A FEW MORE, BUT I'M GOING TO HAVE TO DOCK SOON.
DON'T LAND ON THE FREIGHTER, KARÉ. THE BOMB'S STILL ACTIVE. IT'S TOO DANGEROUS.
LIKE IT'S SAFER TO DRIFT IN AN ASTEROID FIELD?
I'M ALMOST DONE TOO, GUYS-- BUT I THINK I HAVE ENOUGH LEFT TO GET THESE LAST FEW...

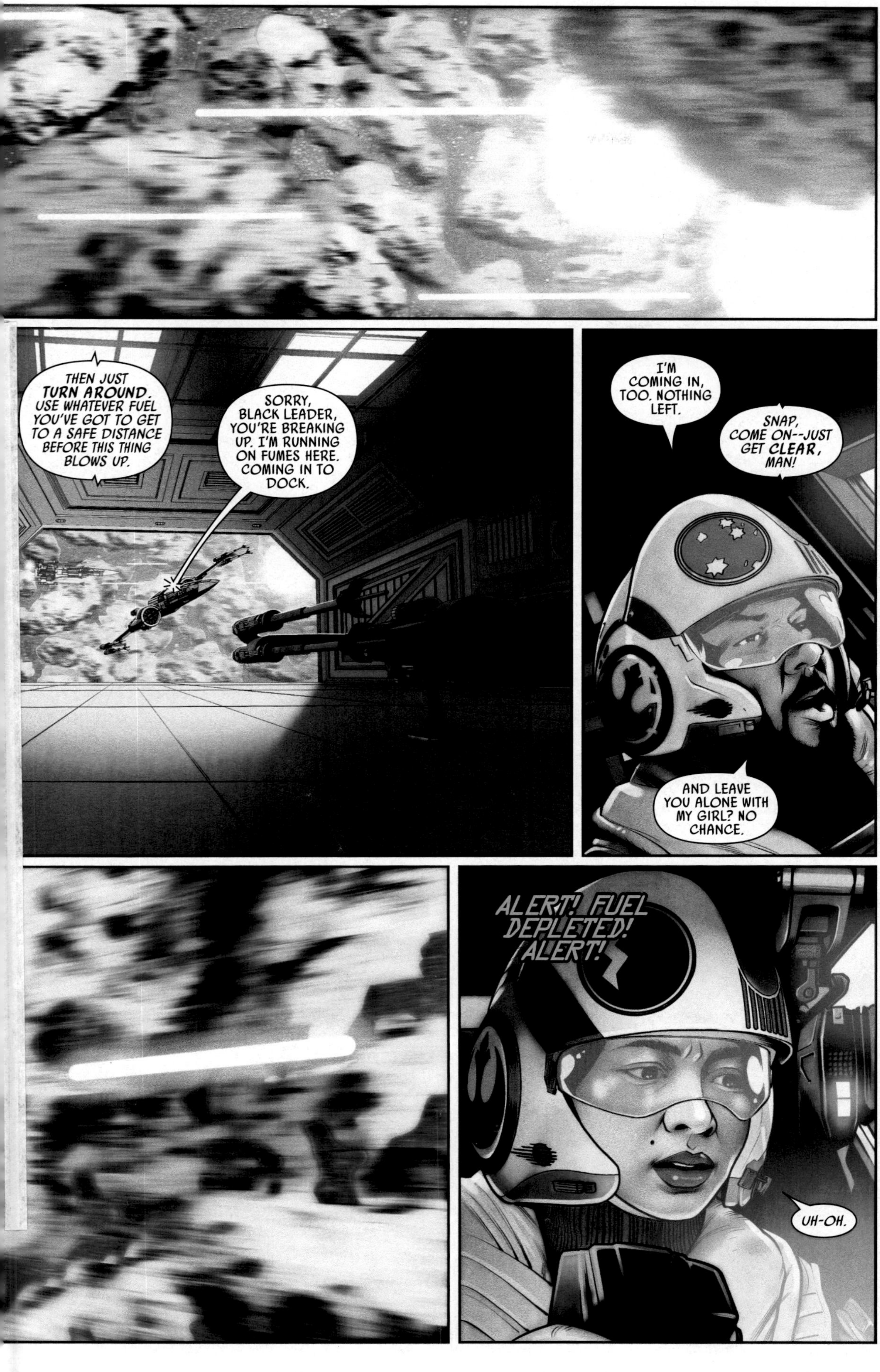

THEN JUST TURN AROUND. USE WHATEVER FUEL YOU'VE GOT TO GET TO A SAFE DISTANCE BEFORE THIS THING BLOWS UP.
SORRY, BLACK LEADER, YOU'RE BREAKING UP. I'M RUNNING ON FUMES HERE. COMING IN TO DOCK.
I'M COMING IN, TOO. NOTHING LEFT.
SNAP, COME ON--JUST GET CLEAR, MAN!
AND LEAVE YOU ALONE WITH MY GIRL? NO CHANCE.
ALERT! FUEL DEPLETED! ALERT!
UH-OH.

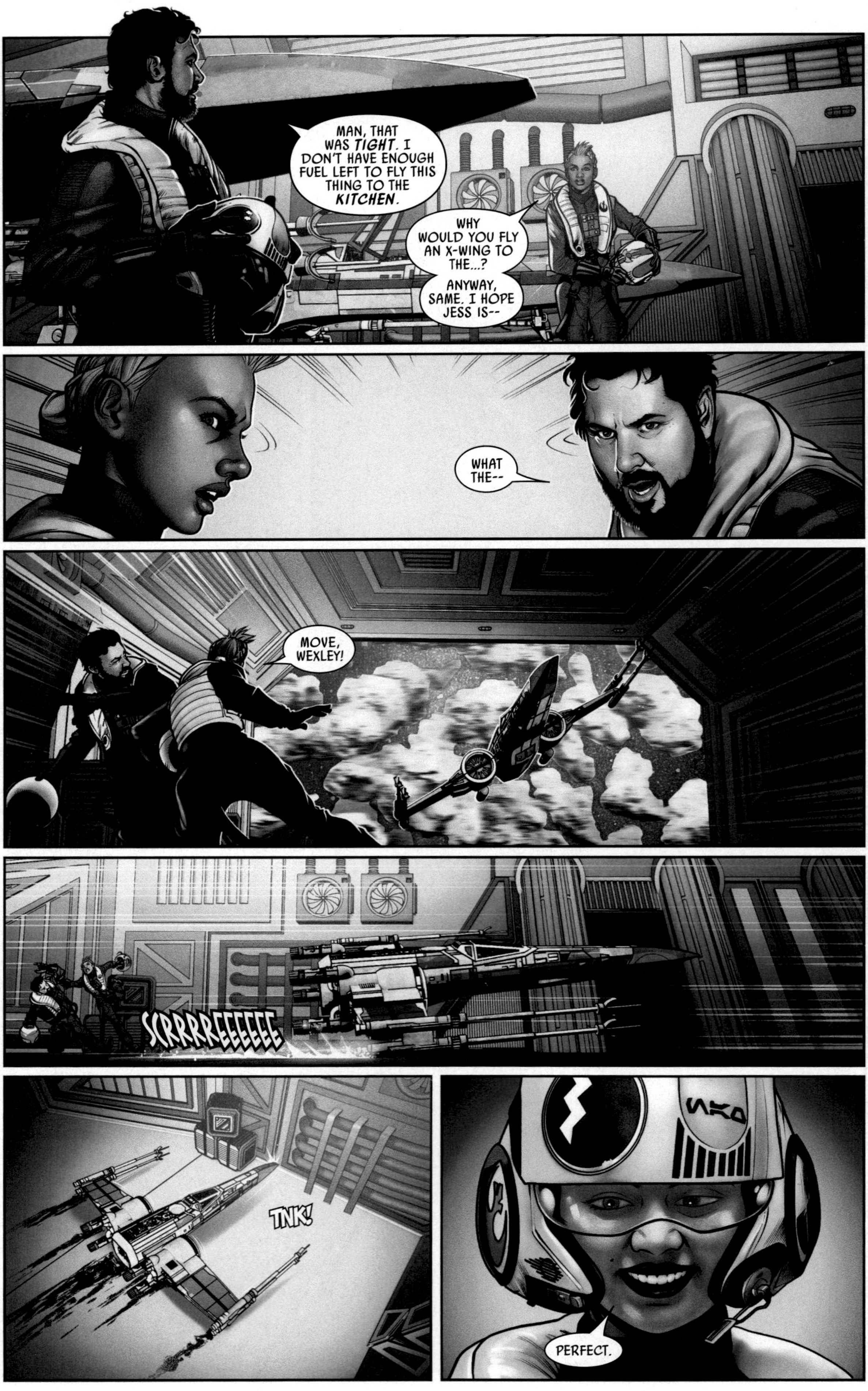

MAN, THAT WAS TIGHT. I DON'T HAVE ENOUGH FUEL LEFT TO FLY THIS THING TO THE KITCHEN.
WHY WOULD YOU FLY AN X-WING TO THE...?
ANYWAY, SAME. I HOPE JESS IS--
WHAT THE--
MOVE, WEXLEY!
SCRRRREEEEEEE
TNK!
PERFECT.

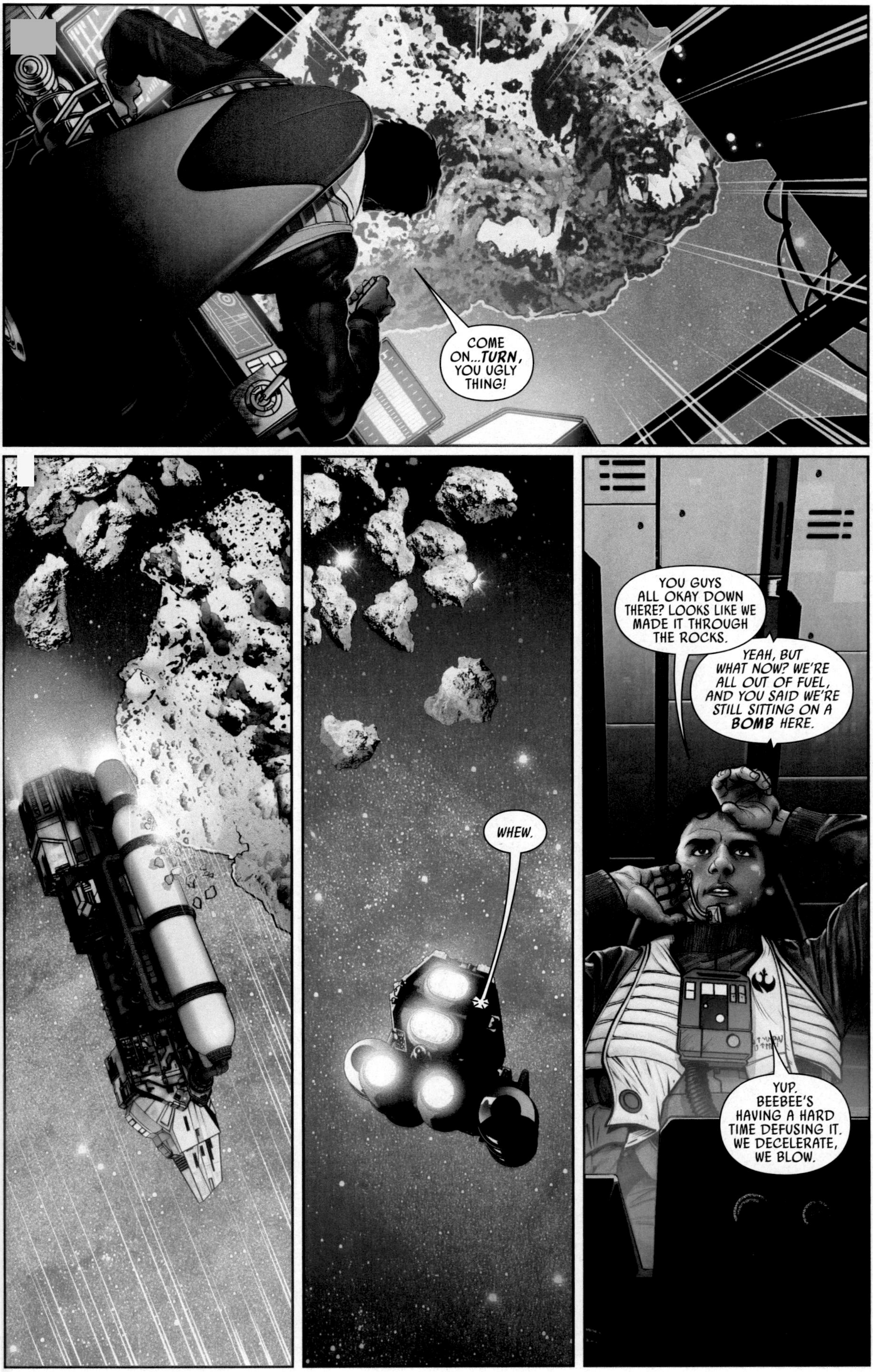
COME ON...TURN, YOU UGLY THING!
WHEW.
YOU GUYS ALL OKAY DOWN THERE? LOOKS LIKE WE MADE IT THROUGH THE ROCKS.
YEAH, BUT WHAT NOW? WE'RE ALL OUT OF FUEL, AND YOU SAID WE'RE STILL SITTING ON A BOMB HERE.
YUP. BEEBEE'S HAVING A HARD TIME DEFUSING IT. WE DECELERATE, WE BLOW.

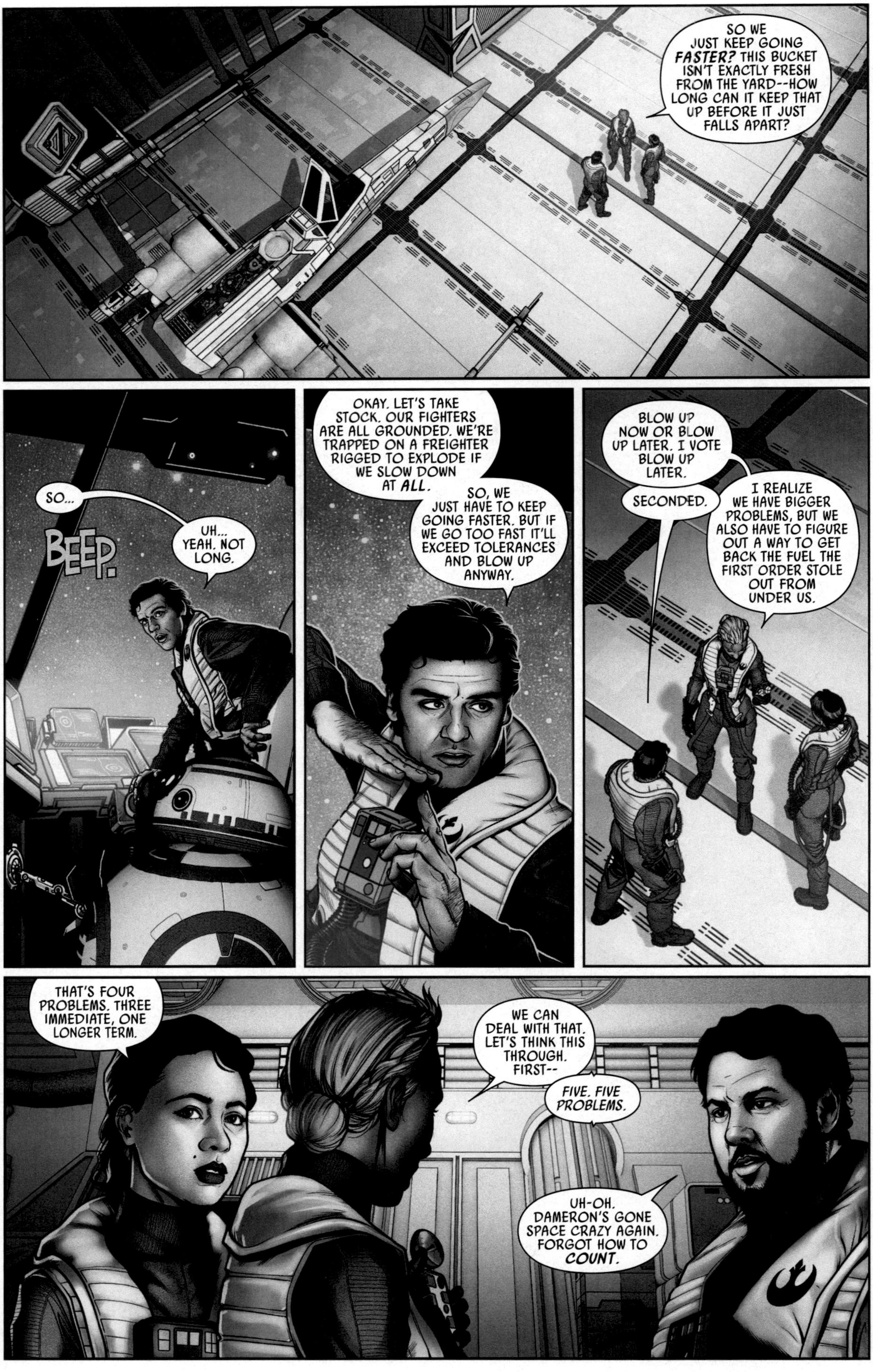
SO WE JUST KEEP GOING FASTER? THIS BUCKET ISN'T EXACTLY FRESH FROM THE YARD--HOW LONG CAN IT KEEP THAT UP BEFORE IT JUST FALLS APART?
SO...
BEEP.
UH... YEAH. NOT LONG.
OKAY. LET'S TAKE STOCK. OUR FIGHTERS ARE ALL GROUNDED. WE'RE TRAPPED ON A FREIGHTER RIGGED TO EXPLODE IF WE SLOW DOWN AT ALL.
SO, WE JUST HAVE TO KEEP GOING FASTER. BUT IF WE GO TOO FAST IT'LL EXCEED TOLERANCES AND BLOW UP ANYWAY.
BLOW UP NOW OR BLOW UP LATER. I VOTE BLOW UP LATER.
SECONDED.
I REALIZE WE HAVE BIGGER PROBLEMS, BUT WE ALSO HAVE TO FIGURE OUT A WAY TO GET BACK THE FUEL THE FIRST ORDER STOLE OUT FROM UNDER US.
THAT'S FOUR PROBLEMS. THREE IMMEDIATE, ONE LONGER TERM.
WE CAN DEAL WITH THAT. LET'S THINK THIS THROUGH. FIRST--
FIVE. FIVE PROBLEMS.
UH-OH. DAMERON'S GONE SPACE CRAZY AGAIN. FORGOT HOW TO COUNT.

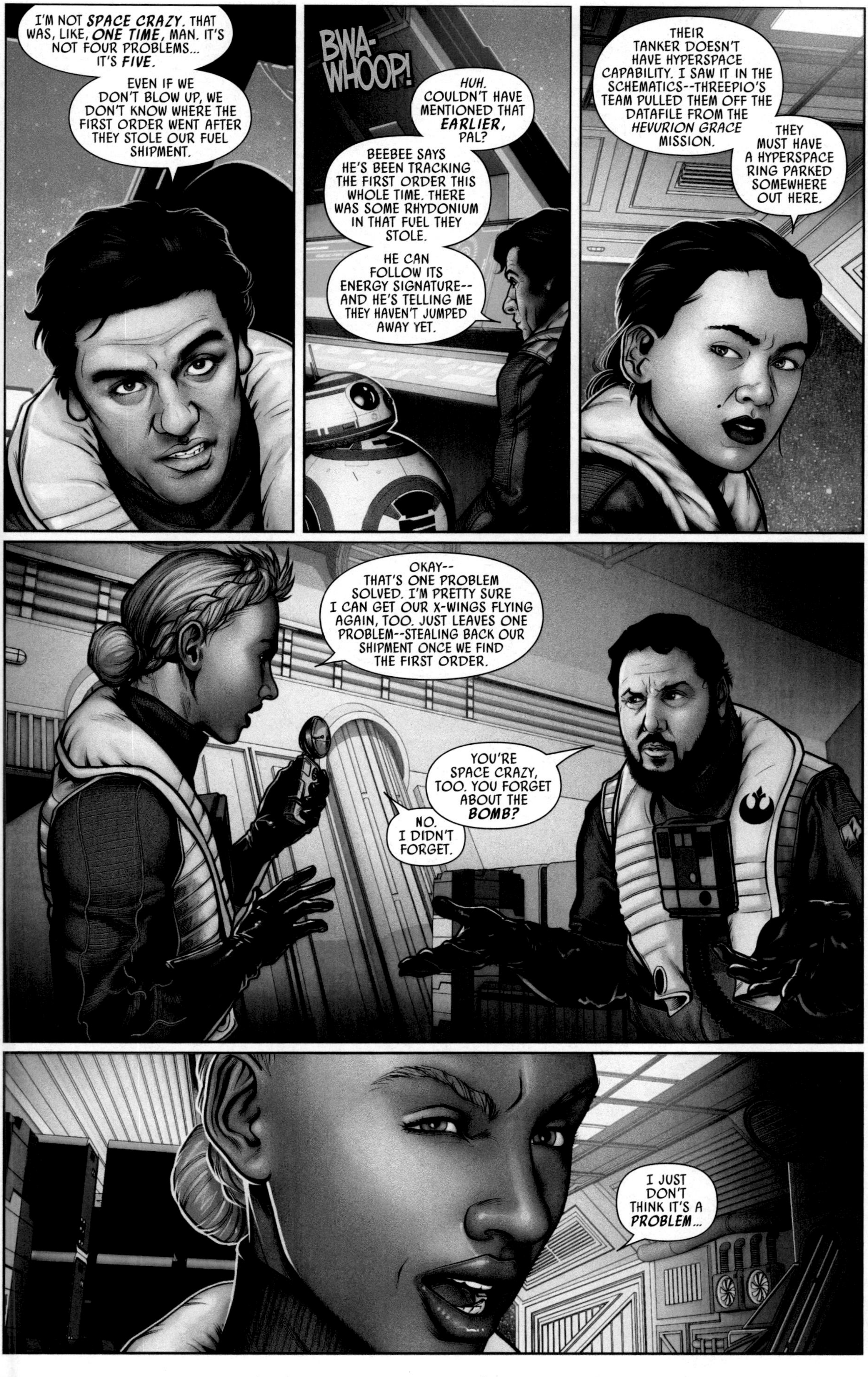
I'M NOT *SPACE CRAZY*. THAT WAS, LIKE, *ONE TIME*, MAN. IT'S NOT FOUR PROBLEMS... IT'S *FIVE*.
EVEN IF WE DON'T BLOW UP, WE DON'T KNOW WHERE THE FIRST ORDER WENT AFTER THEY STOLE OUR FUEL SHIPMENT.
BWA-WHOOP!
HUH. COULDN'T HAVE MENTIONED THAT *EARLIER*, PAL?
BEEBEE SAYS HE'S BEEN TRACKING THE FIRST ORDER THIS WHOLE TIME. THERE WAS SOME RHYDONIUM IN THAT FUEL THEY STOLE.
HE CAN FOLLOW ITS ENERGY SIGNATURE--AND HE'S TELLING ME THEY HAVEN'T JUMPED AWAY YET.
THEIR TANKER DOESN'T HAVE HYPERSPACE CAPABILITY. I SAW IT IN THE SCHEMATICS--THREEPIO'S TEAM PULLED THEM OFF THE DATAFILE FROM THE *HEVURION GRACE* MISSION.
THEY MUST HAVE A HYPERSPACE RING PARKED SOMEWHERE OUT HERE.
OKAY--THAT'S ONE PROBLEM SOLVED. I'M PRETTY SURE I CAN GET OUR X-WINGS FLYING AGAIN, TOO. JUST LEAVES ONE PROBLEM--STEALING BACK OUR SHIPMENT ONCE WE FIND THE FIRST ORDER.
YOU'RE SPACE CRAZY, TOO. YOU FORGET ABOUT THE *BOMB?*
NO. I DIDN'T FORGET.
I JUST DON'T THINK IT'S A *PROBLEM*...

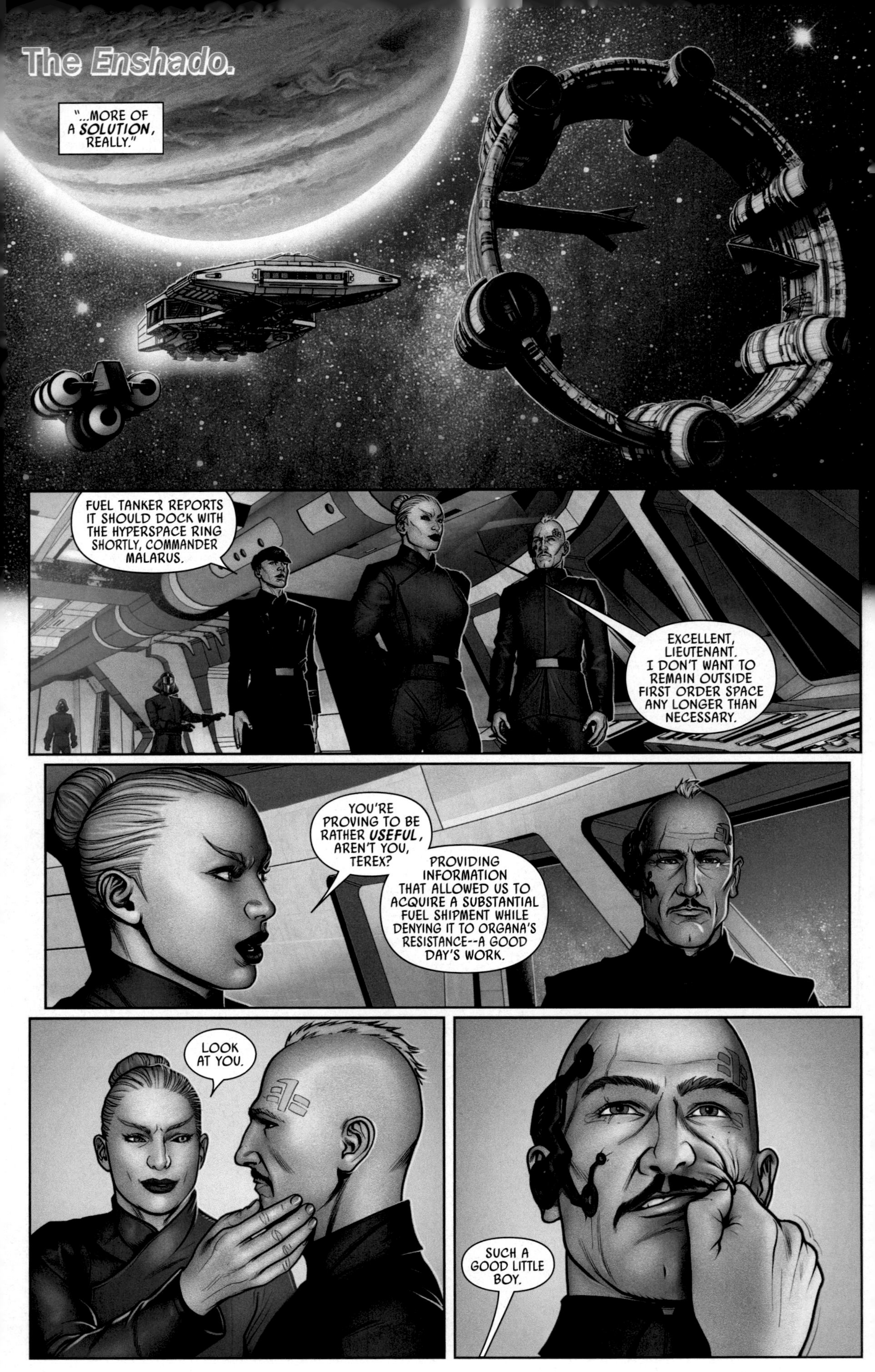
The Enshado.
"...MORE OF A SOLUTION, REALLY."
FUEL TANKER REPORTS IT SHOULD DOCK WITH THE HYPERSPACE RING SHORTLY, COMMANDER MALARUS.
EXCELLENT, LIEUTENANT. I DON'T WANT TO REMAIN OUTSIDE FIRST ORDER SPACE ANY LONGER THAN NECESSARY.
YOU'RE PROVING TO BE RATHER USEFUL, AREN'T YOU, TEREX?
PROVIDING INFORMATION THAT ALLOWED US TO ACQUIRE A SUBSTANTIAL FUEL SHIPMENT WHILE DENYING IT TO ORGANA'S RESISTANCE--A GOOD DAY'S WORK.
LOOK AT YOU.
SUCH A GOOD LITTLE BOY.

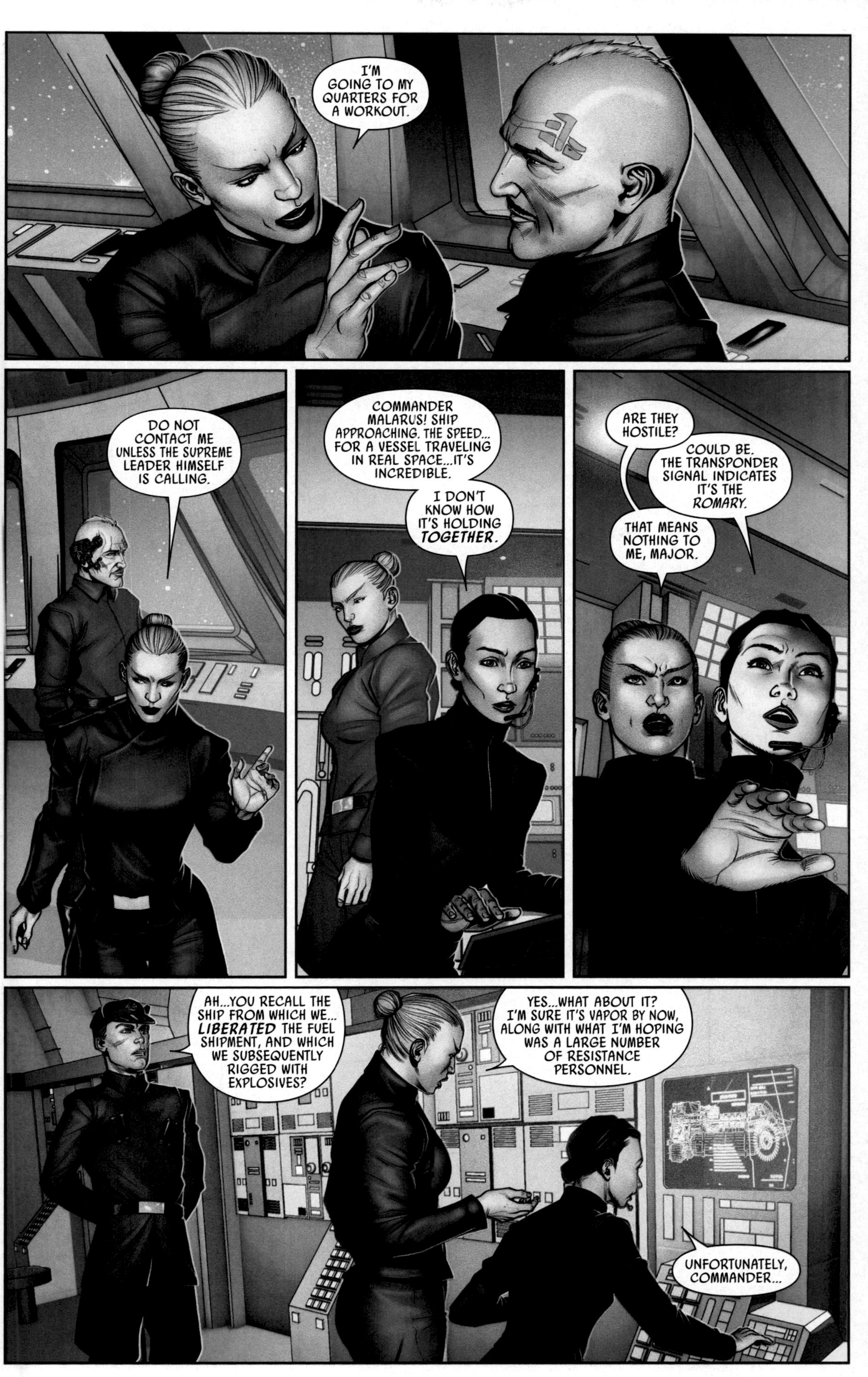
I'M GOING TO MY QUARTERS FOR A WORKOUT.
DO NOT CONTACT ME UNLESS THE SUPREME LEADER HIMSELF IS CALLING.
COMMANDER MALARUS! SHIP APPROACHING. THE SPEED... FOR A VESSEL TRAVELING IN REAL SPACE...IT'S INCREDIBLE.
I DON'T KNOW HOW IT'S HOLDING *TOGETHER*.
ARE THEY HOSTILE?
COULD BE. THE TRANSPONDER SIGNAL INDICATES IT'S THE *ROMARY*.
THAT MEANS NOTHING TO ME, MAJOR.
AH...YOU RECALL THE SHIP FROM WHICH WE... *LIBERATED* THE FUEL SHIPMENT, AND WHICH WE SUBSEQUENTLY RIGGED WITH EXPLOSIVES?
YES...WHAT ABOUT IT? I'M SURE IT'S VAPOR BY NOW, ALONG WITH WHAT I'M HOPING WAS A LARGE NUMBER OF RESISTANCE PERSONNEL.
UNFORTUNATELY, COMMANDER...

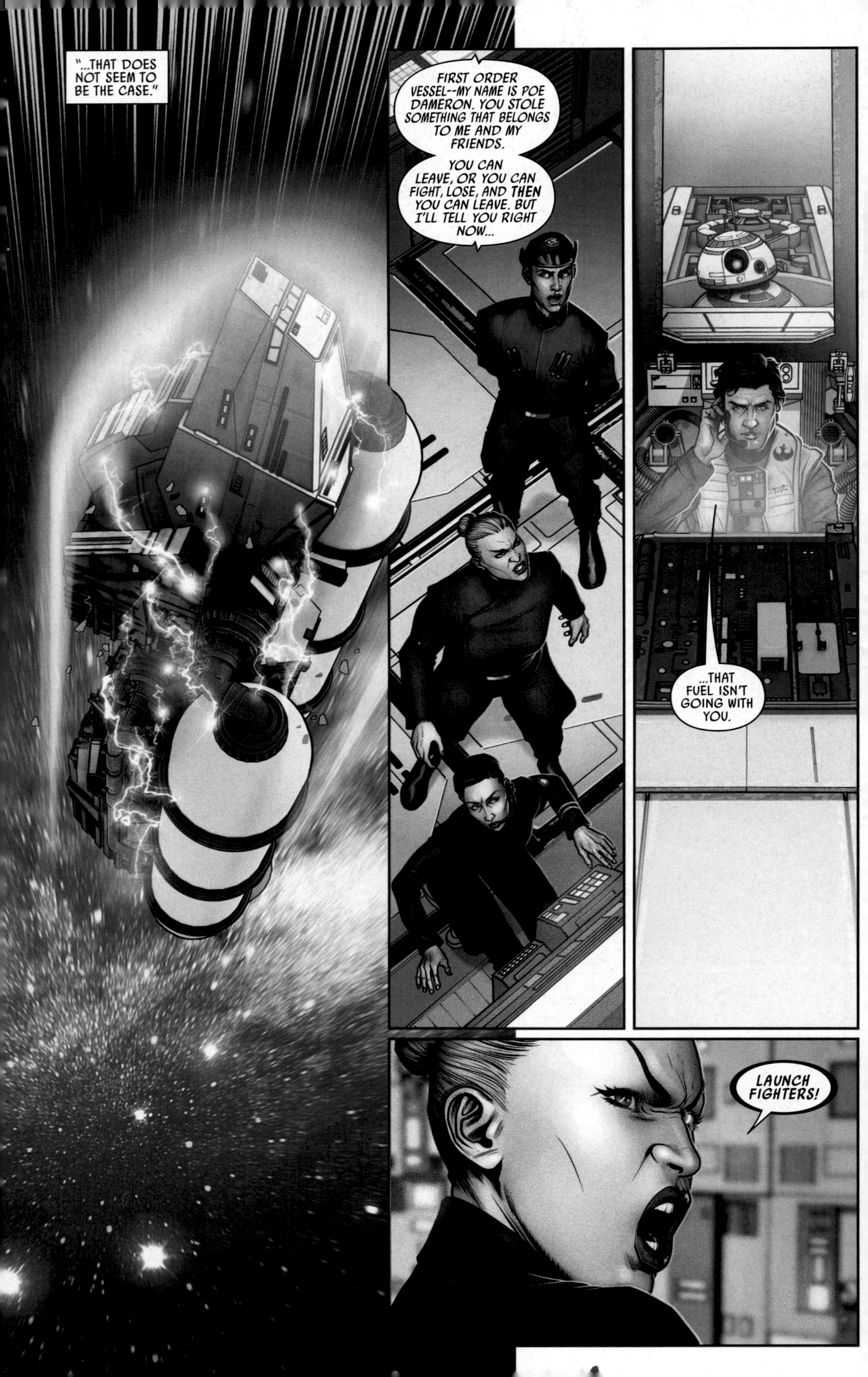
"...THAT DOES NOT SEEM TO BE THE CASE."
FIRST ORDER VESSEL--MY NAME IS POE DAMERON. YOU STOLE SOMETHING THAT BELONGS TO ME AND MY FRIENDS.
YOU CAN LEAVE, OR YOU CAN FIGHT, LOSE, AND THEN YOU CAN LEAVE. BUT I'LL TELL YOU RIGHT NOW...
...THAT FUEL ISN'T GOING WITH YOU.
LAUNCH FIGHTERS!

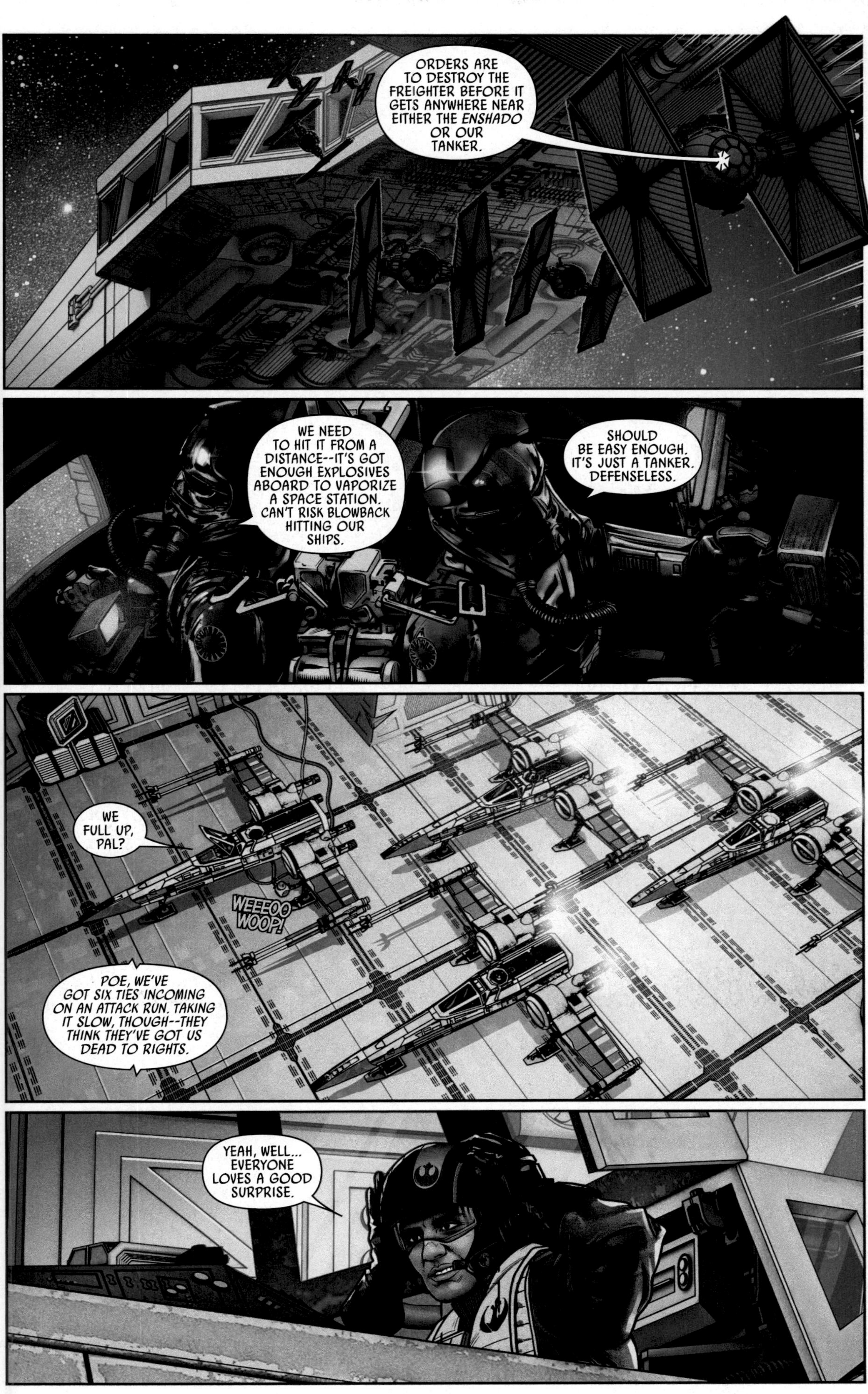
ORDERS ARE TO DESTROY THE FREIGHTER BEFORE IT GETS ANYWHERE NEAR EITHER THE *ENSHADO* OR OUR TANKER.
WE NEED TO HIT IT FROM A DISTANCE--IT'S GOT ENOUGH EXPLOSIVES ABOARD TO VAPORIZE A SPACE STATION. CAN'T RISK BLOWBACK HITTING OUR SHIPS.
SHOULD BE EASY ENOUGH. IT'S JUST A TANKER. DEFENSELESS.
WE FULL UP, PAL?
WEEEOO WOOP!
POE, WE'VE GOT SIX TIES INCOMING ON AN ATTACK RUN. TAKING IT SLOW, THOUGH--THEY THINK THEY'VE GOT US DEAD TO RIGHTS.
YEAH, WELL... EVERYONE LOVES A GOOD SURPRISE.

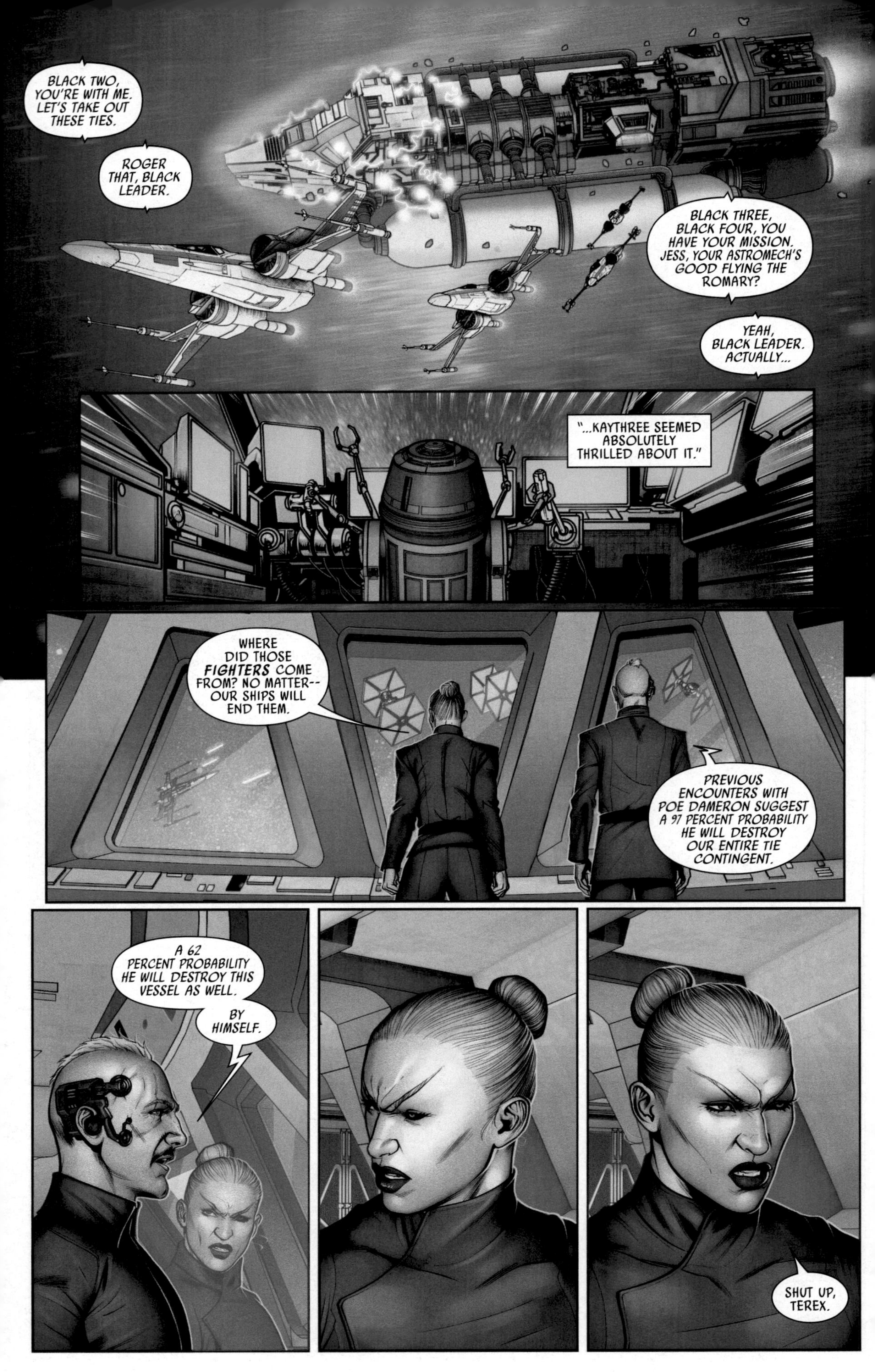
BLACK TWO, YOU'RE WITH ME. LET'S TAKE OUT THESE TIES.
ROGER THAT, BLACK LEADER.
BLACK THREE, BLACK FOUR, YOU HAVE YOUR MISSION. JESS, YOUR ASTROMECH'S GOOD FLYING THE ROMARY?
YEAH, BLACK LEADER. ACTUALLY...
"...KAYTHREE SEEMED ABSOLUTELY THRILLED ABOUT IT."
WHERE DID THOSE **FIGHTERS** COME FROM? NO MATTER--OUR SHIPS WILL END THEM.
PREVIOUS ENCOUNTERS WITH POE DAMERON SUGGEST A 97 PERCENT PROBABILITY HE WILL DESTROY OUR ENTIRE TIE CONTINGENT.
A 62 PERCENT PROBABILITY HE WILL DESTROY THIS VESSEL AS WELL.
BY HIMSELF.
SHUT UP, TEREX.

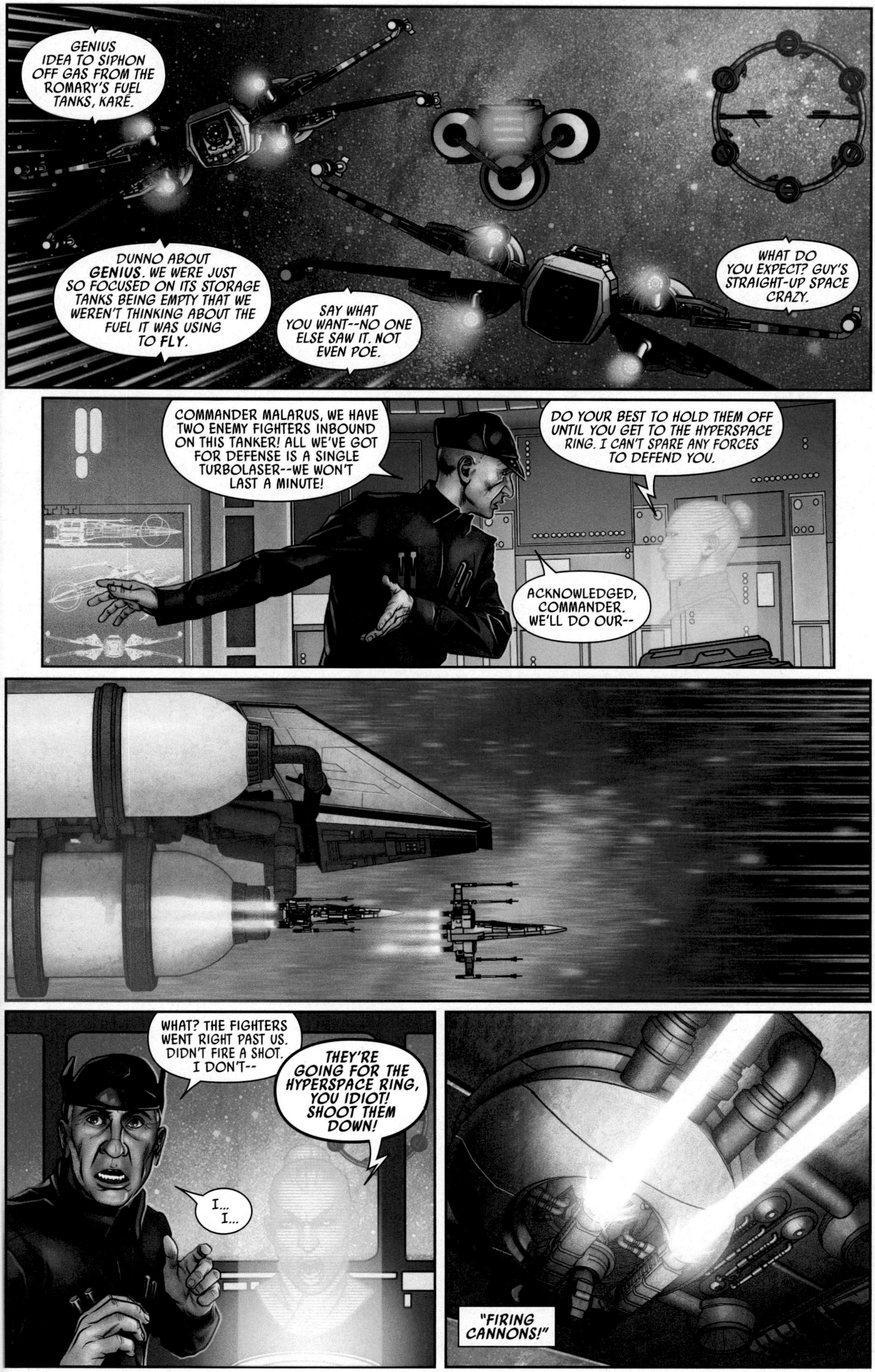
GENIUS IDEA TO SIPHON OFF GAS FROM THE ROMARY'S FUEL TANKS, KARÉ.
DUNNO ABOUT GENIUS. WE WERE JUST SO FOCUSED ON ITS STORAGE TANKS BEING EMPTY THAT WE WEREN'T THINKING ABOUT THE FUEL IT WAS USING TO FLY.
SAY WHAT YOU WANT--NO ONE ELSE SAW IT. NOT EVEN POE.
WHAT DO YOU EXPECT? GUY'S STRAIGHT-UP SPACE CRAZY.
COMMANDER MALARUS, WE HAVE TWO ENEMY FIGHTERS INBOUND ON THIS TANKER! ALL WE'VE GOT FOR DEFENSE IS A SINGLE TURBOLASER--WE WON'T LAST A MINUTE!
DO YOUR BEST TO HOLD THEM OFF UNTIL YOU GET TO THE HYPERSPACE RING. I CAN'T SPARE ANY FORCES TO DEFEND YOU.
ACKNOWLEDGED, COMMANDER. WE'LL DO OUR--
WHAT? THE FIGHTERS WENT RIGHT PAST US. DIDN'T FIRE A SHOT. I DON'T--
THEY'RE GOING FOR THE HYPERSPACE RING, YOU IDIOT! SHOOT THEM DOWN!
I... I...
"FIRING CANNONS!"

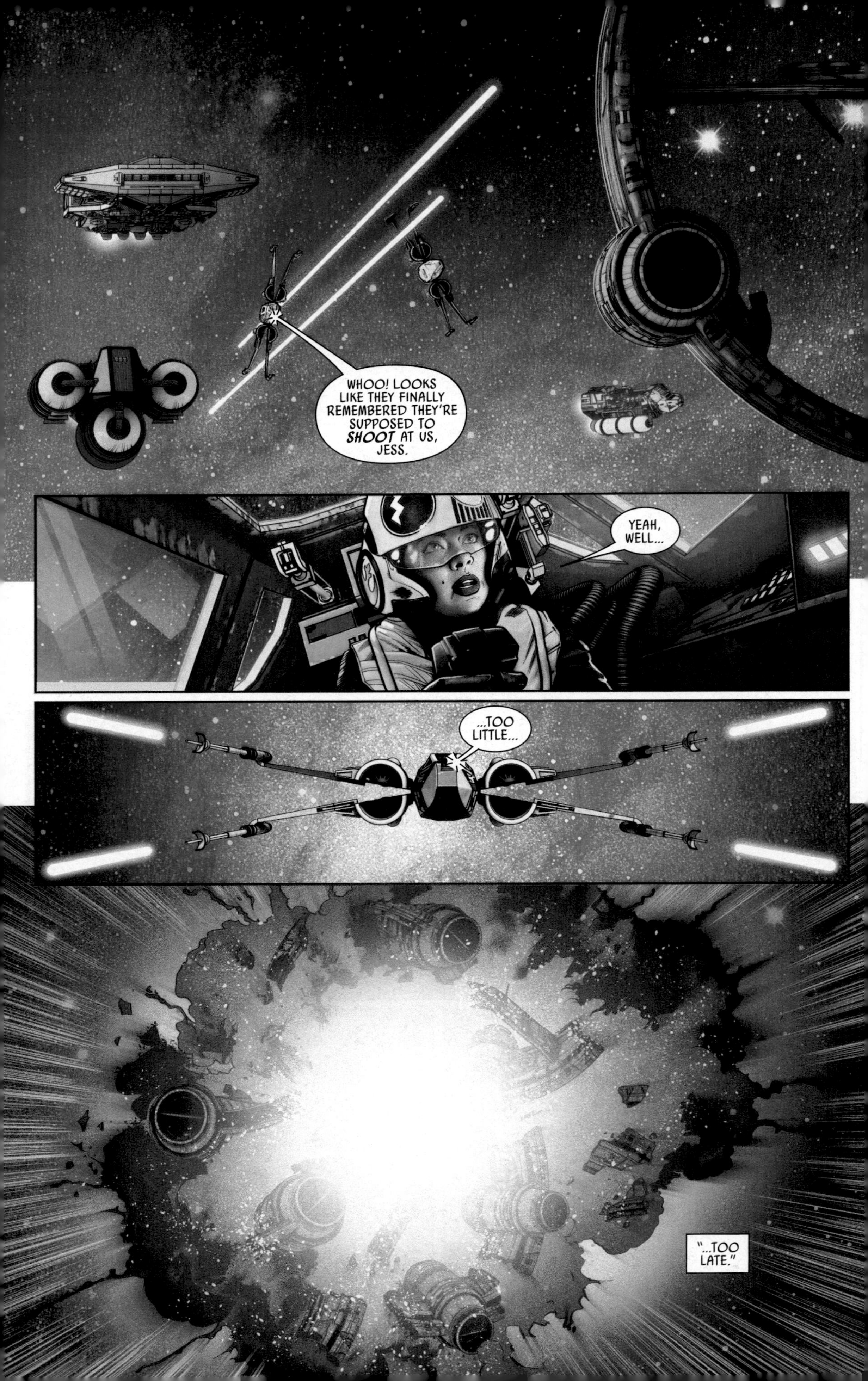
WHOO! LOOKS LIKE THEY FINALLY REMEMBERED THEY'RE SUPPOSED TO *SHOOT* AT US, JESS.
YEAH, WELL...
...TOO LITTLE...
"...TOO LATE."

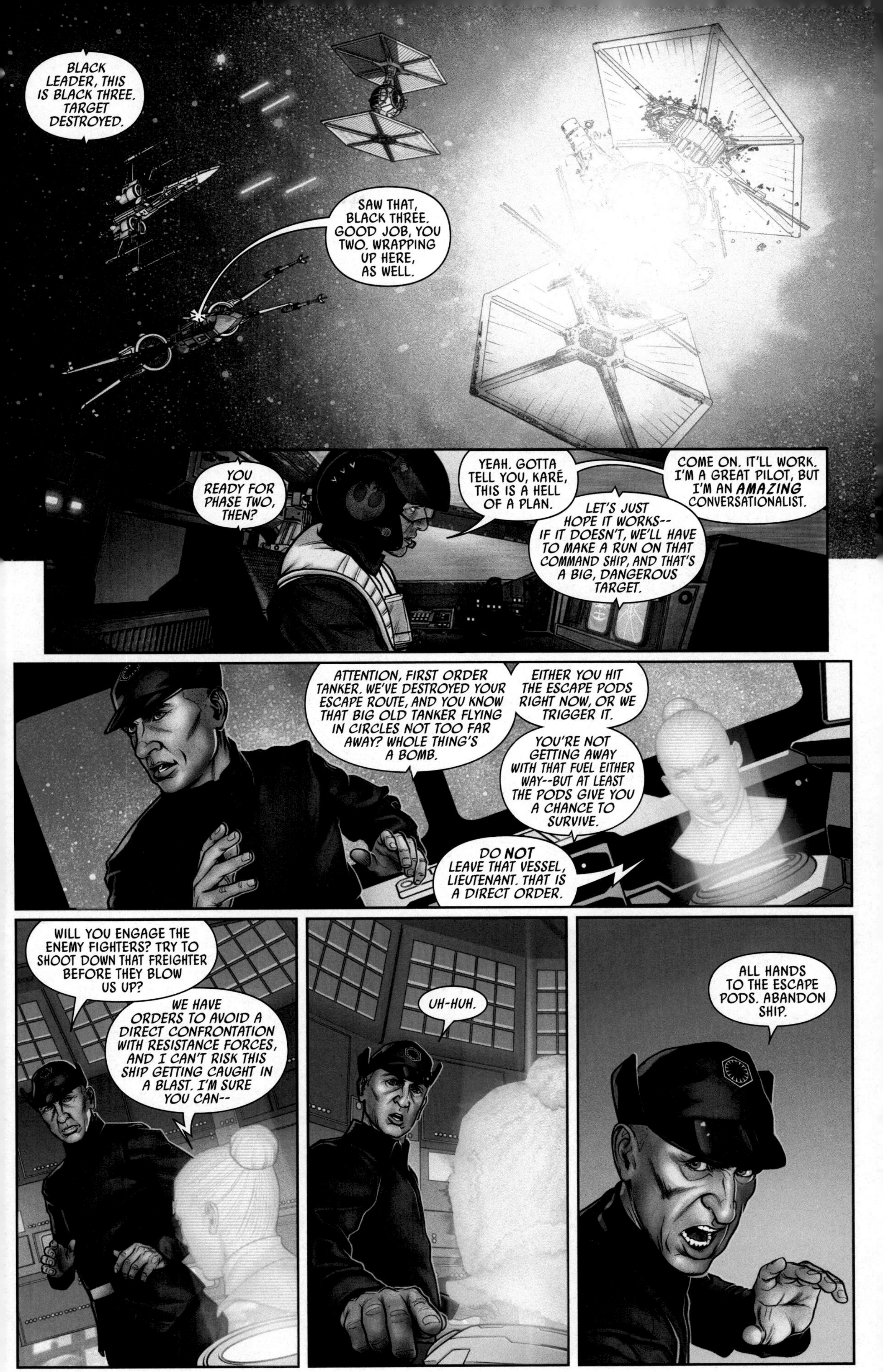
BLACK LEADER, THIS IS BLACK THREE. TARGET DESTROYED.
SAW THAT, BLACK THREE. GOOD JOB, YOU TWO. WRAPPING UP HERE, AS WELL.
YOU READY FOR PHASE TWO, THEN?
YEAH. GOTTA TELL YOU, KARÉ, THIS IS A HELL OF A PLAN.
LET'S JUST HOPE IT WORKS--IF IT DOESN'T, WE'LL HAVE TO MAKE A RUN ON THAT COMMAND SHIP, AND THAT'S A BIG, DANGEROUS TARGET.
COME ON. IT'LL WORK. I'M A GREAT PILOT, BUT I'M AN *AMAZING* CONVERSATIONALIST.
ATTENTION, FIRST ORDER TANKER. WE'VE DESTROYED YOUR ESCAPE ROUTE, AND YOU KNOW THAT BIG OLD TANKER FLYING IN CIRCLES NOT TOO FAR AWAY? WHOLE THING'S A BOMB.
EITHER YOU HIT THE ESCAPE PODS RIGHT NOW, OR WE TRIGGER IT.
YOU'RE NOT GETTING AWAY WITH THAT FUEL EITHER WAY--BUT AT LEAST THE PODS GIVE YOU A CHANCE TO SURVIVE.
DO **NOT** LEAVE THAT VESSEL, LIEUTENANT. THAT IS A DIRECT ORDER.
WILL YOU ENGAGE THE ENEMY FIGHTERS? TRY TO SHOOT DOWN THAT FREIGHTER BEFORE THEY BLOW US UP?
WE HAVE ORDERS TO AVOID A DIRECT CONFRONTATION WITH RESISTANCE FORCES, AND I CAN'T RISK THIS SHIP GETTING CAUGHT IN A BLAST. I'M SURE YOU CAN--
UH-HUH.
ALL HANDS TO THE ESCAPE PODS. ABANDON SHIP.

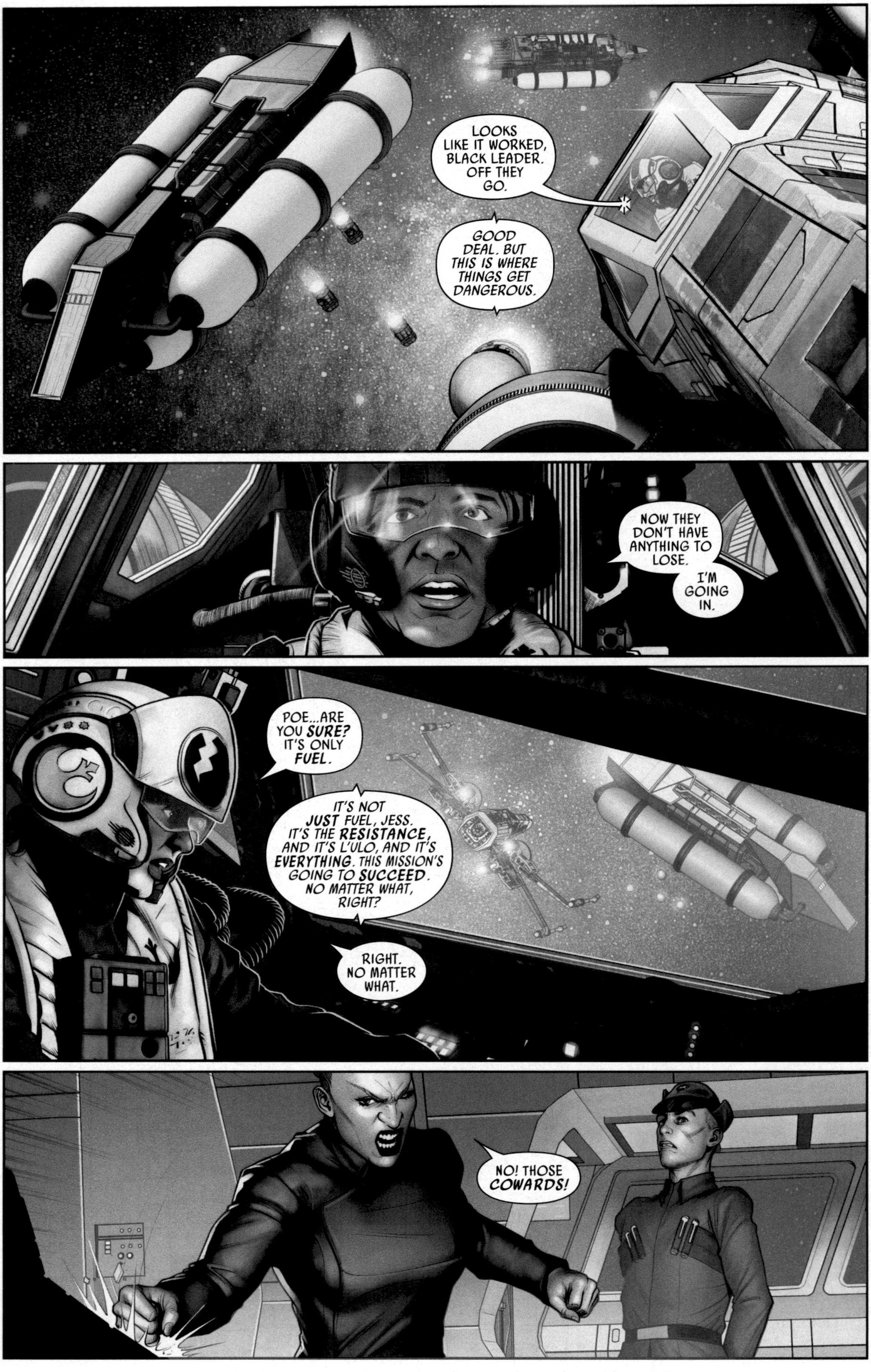
LOOKS LIKE IT WORKED, BLACK LEADER. OFF THEY GO.
GOOD DEAL. BUT THIS IS WHERE THINGS GET DANGEROUS.
NOW THEY DON'T HAVE ANYTHING TO LOSE.
I'M GOING IN.
POE...ARE YOU SURE? IT'S ONLY FUEL.
IT'S NOT JUST FUEL, JESS. IT'S THE RESISTANCE, AND IT'S L'ULO, AND IT'S EVERYTHING. THIS MISSION'S GOING TO SUCCEED. NO MATTER WHAT, RIGHT?
RIGHT. NO MATTER WHAT.
NO! THOSE COWARDS!

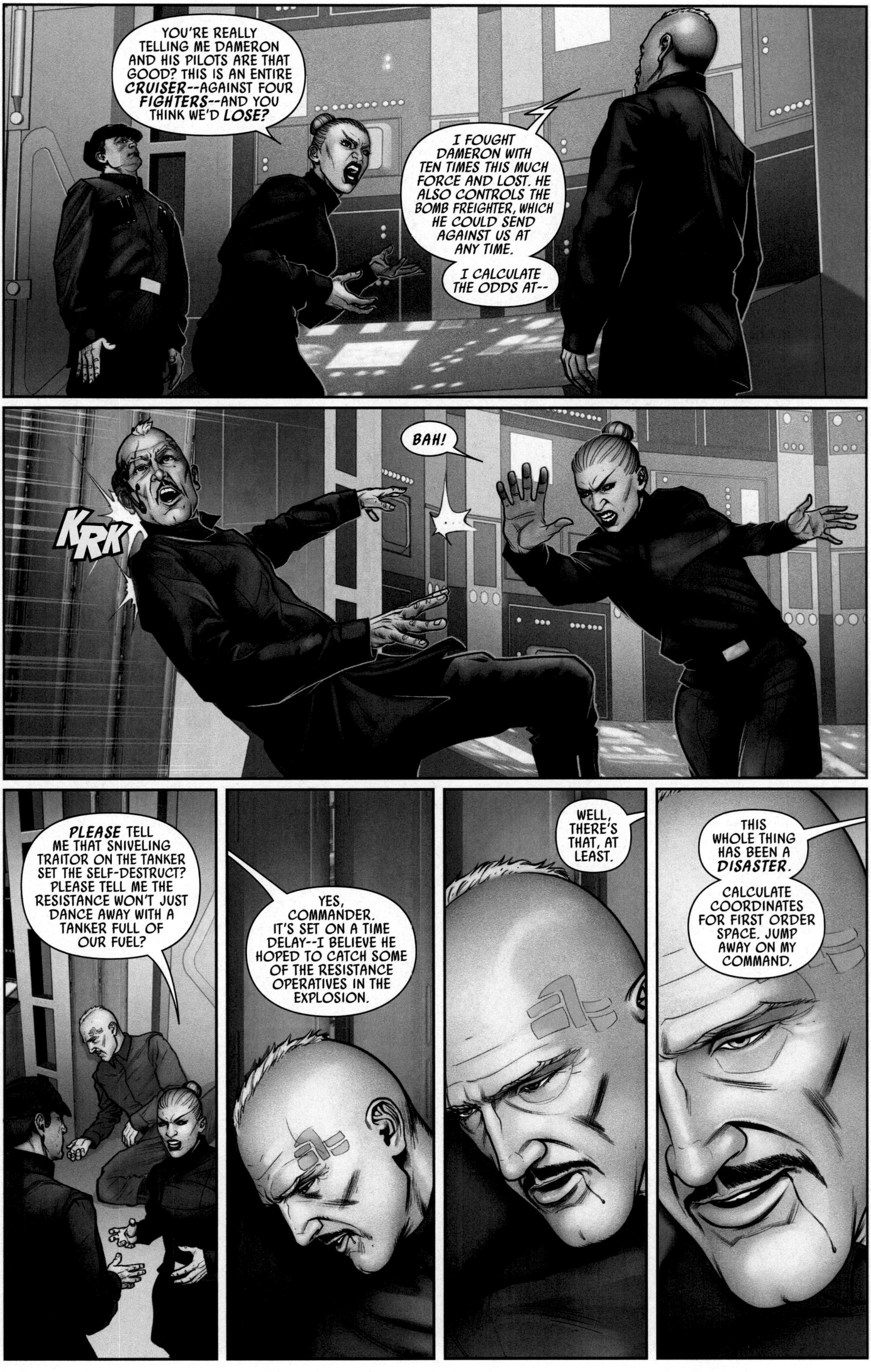
YOU'RE REALLY TELLING ME DAMERON AND HIS PILOTS ARE THAT GOOD? THIS IS AN ENTIRE CRUISER--AGAINST FOUR FIGHTERS--AND YOU THINK WE'D LOSE?
I FOUGHT DAMERON WITH TEN TIMES THIS MUCH FORCE AND LOST. HE ALSO CONTROLS THE BOMB FREIGHTER, WHICH HE COULD SEND AGAINST US AT ANY TIME.
I CALCULATE THE ODDS AT--
BAH!
KRK
PLEASE TELL ME THAT SNIVELING TRAITOR ON THE TANKER SET THE SELF-DESTRUCT? PLEASE TELL ME THE RESISTANCE WON'T JUST DANCE AWAY WITH A TANKER FULL OF OUR FUEL?
YES, COMMANDER. IT'S SET ON A TIME DELAY--I BELIEVE HE HOPED TO CATCH SOME OF THE RESISTANCE OPERATIVES IN THE EXPLOSION.
WELL, THERE'S THAT, AT LEAST.
THIS WHOLE THING HAS BEEN A DISASTER.
CALCULATE COORDINATES FOR FIRST ORDER SPACE. JUMP AWAY ON MY COMMAND.

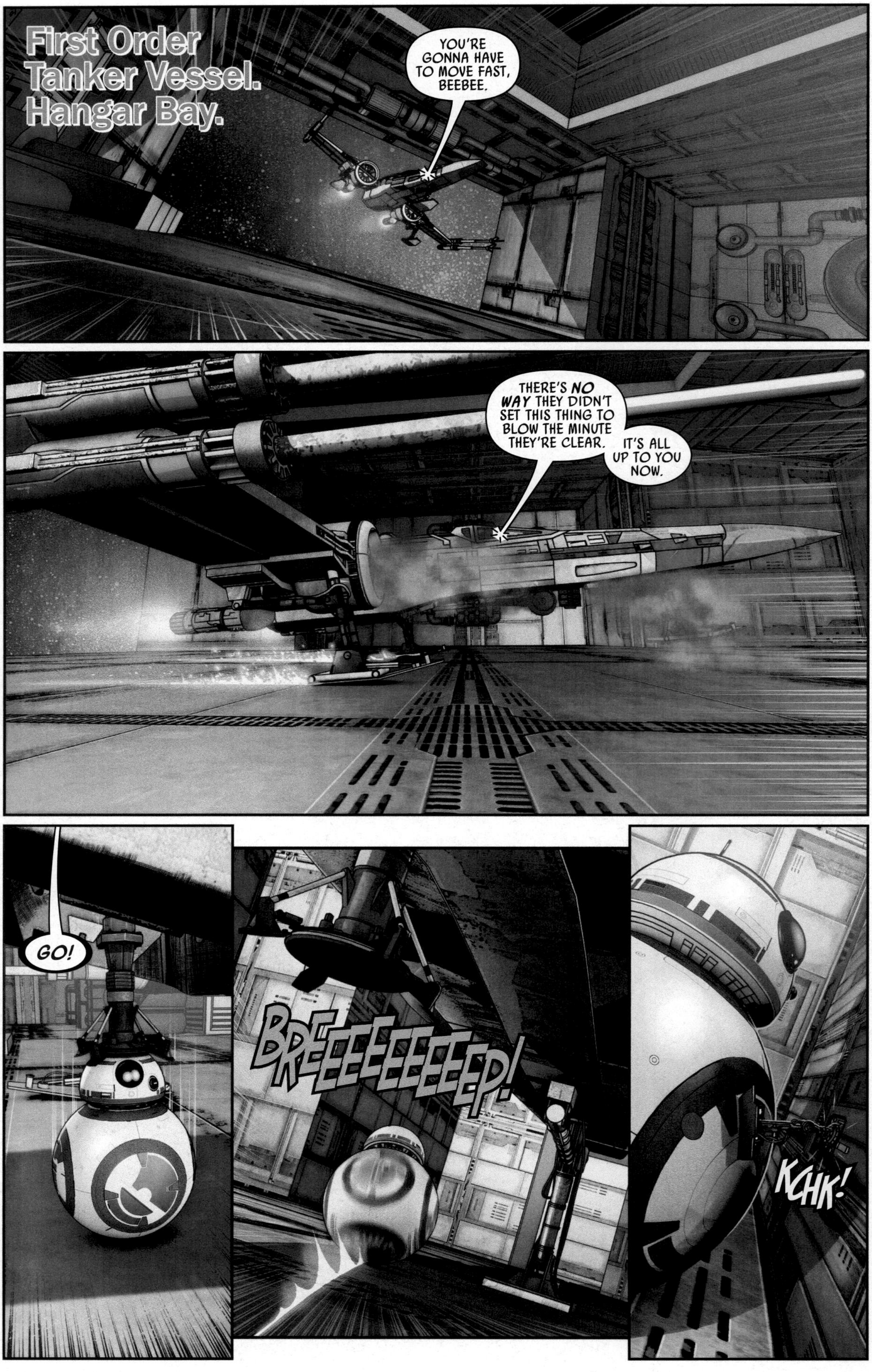
First Order Tanker Vessel. Hangar Bay.
YOU'RE GONNA HAVE TO MOVE FAST, BEEBEE.
THERE'S NO WAY THEY DIDN'T SET THIS THING TO BLOW THE MINUTE THEY'RE CLEAR.
IT'S ALL UP TO YOU NOW.
GO!
BREEEEEEEEEP!
KCHK!

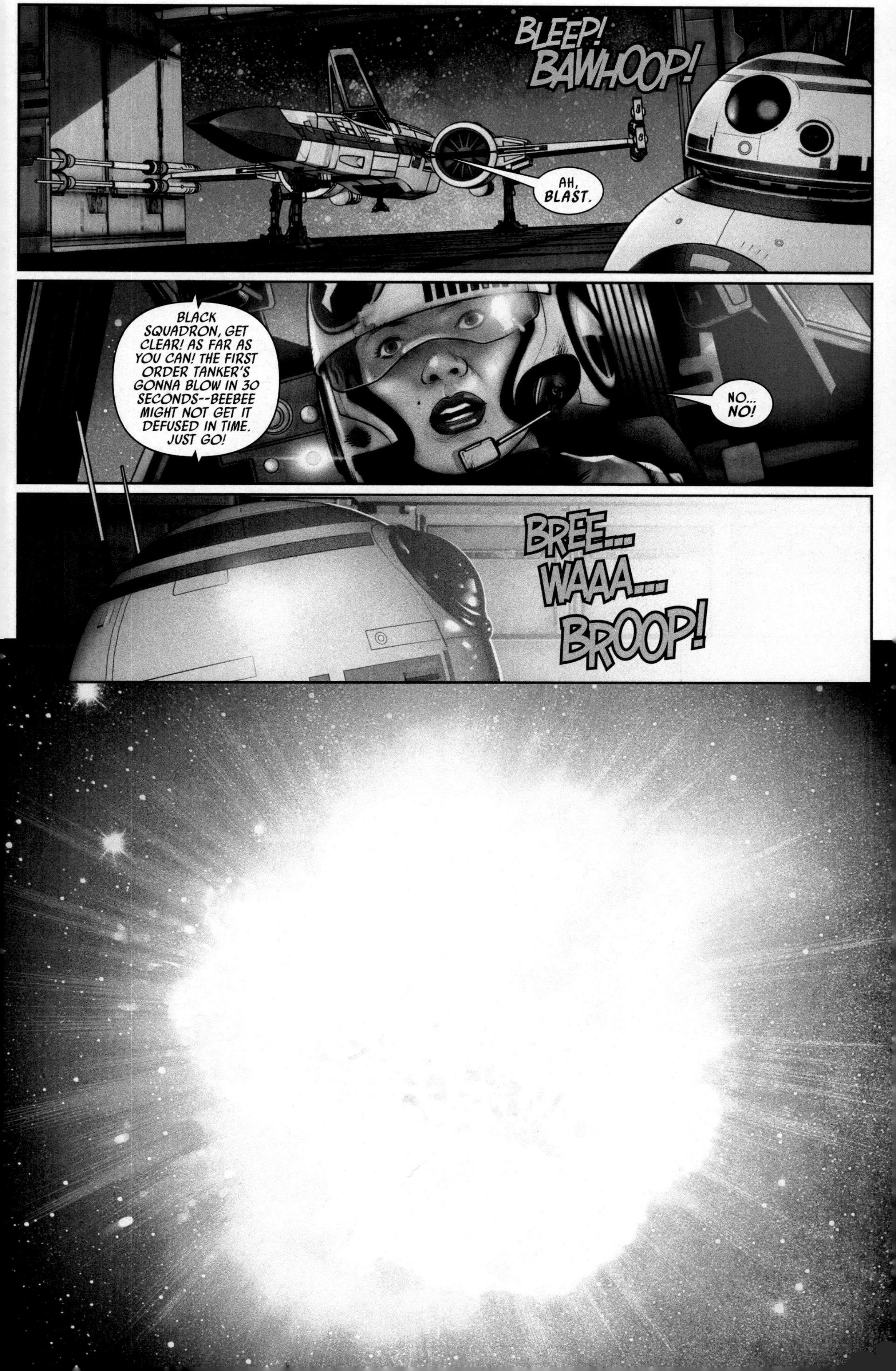
BLEEP! BAWHOOP!
AH, BLAST.
BLACK SQUADRON, GET CLEAR! AS FAR AS YOU CAN! THE FIRST ORDER TANKER'S GONNA BLOW IN 30 SECONDS--BEEBEE MIGHT NOT GET IT DEFUSED IN TIME. JUST GO!
NO... NO!
BREE... WAAA... BROOP!

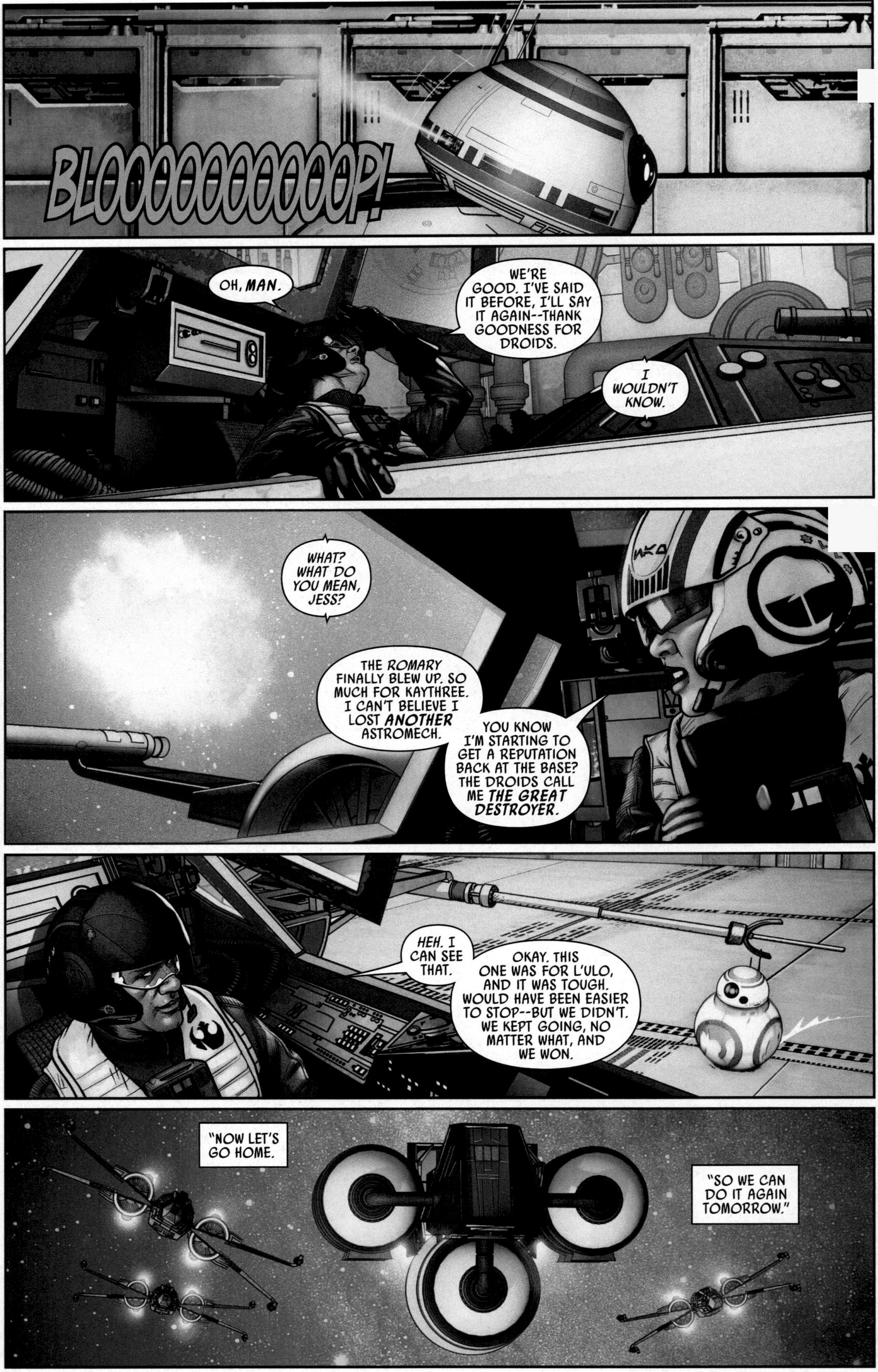
BLOOOOOOOOOOP!
OH, MAN.
WE'RE GOOD. I'VE SAID IT BEFORE, I'LL SAY IT AGAIN--THANK GOODNESS FOR DROIDS.
I WOULDN'T KNOW.
WHAT? WHAT DO YOU MEAN, JESS?
THE ROMARY FINALLY BLEW UP. SO MUCH FOR KAYTHREE. I CAN'T BELIEVE I LOST ANOTHER ASTROMECH.
YOU KNOW I'M STARTING TO GET A REPUTATION BACK AT THE BASE? THE DROIDS CALL ME THE GREAT DESTROYER.
HEH. I CAN SEE THAT.
OKAY. THIS ONE WAS FOR L'ULO, AND IT WAS TOUGH. WOULD HAVE BEEN EASIER TO STOP--BUT WE DIDN'T. WE KEPT GOING, NO MATTER WHAT, AND WE WON.
"NOW LET'S GO HOME.
"SO WE CAN DO IT AGAIN TOMORROW."

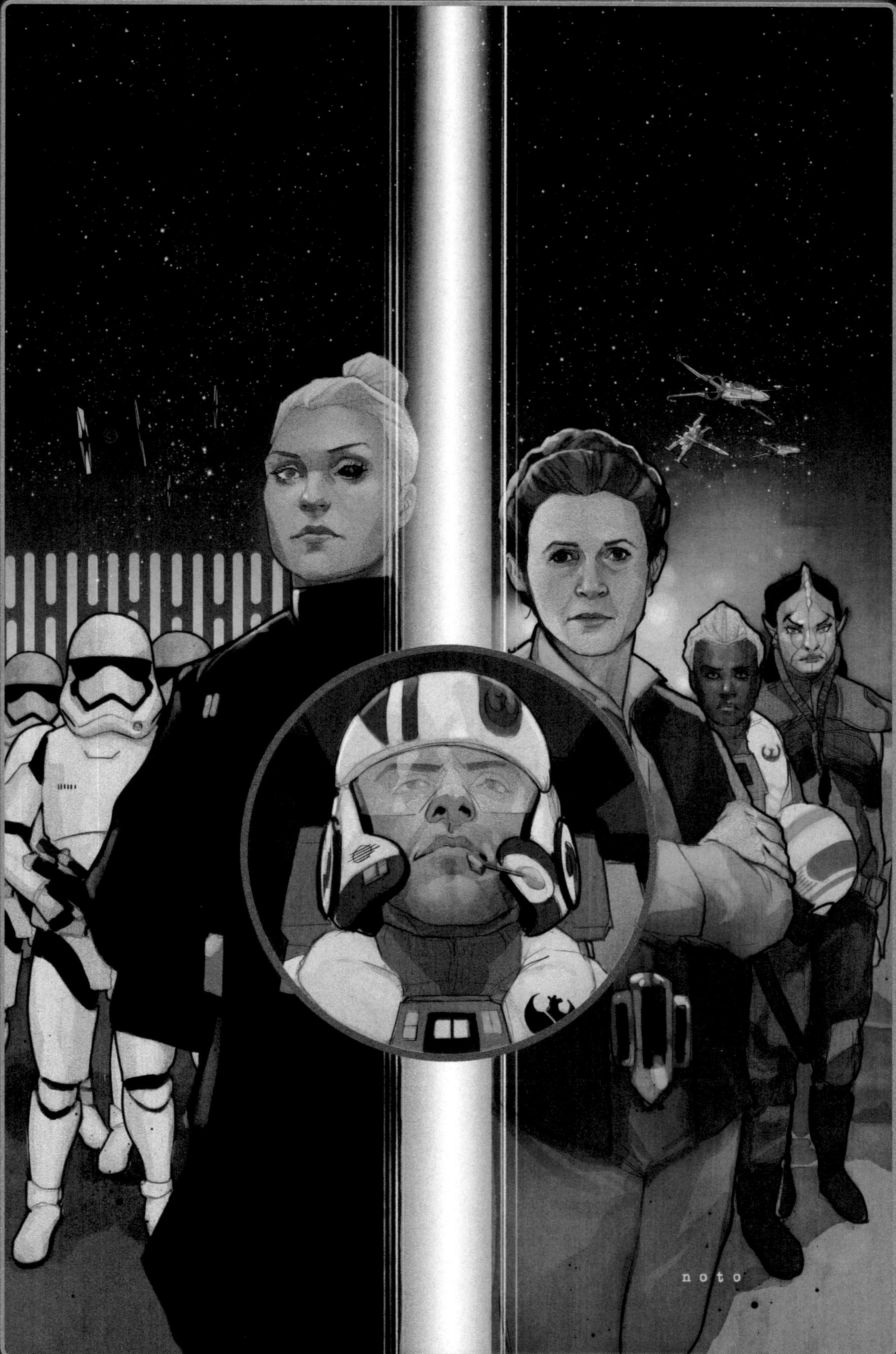
noto

17

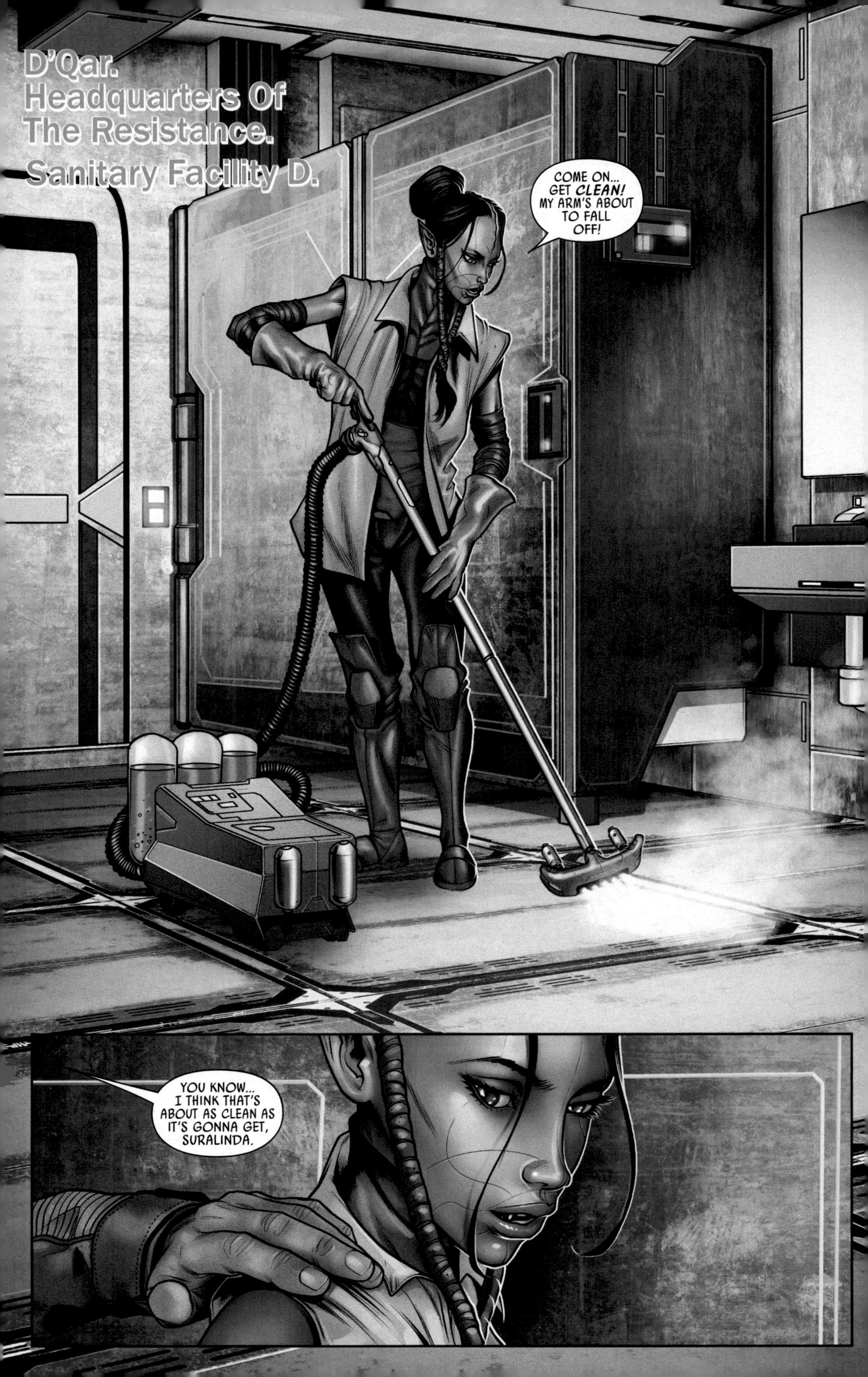
D'Qar.
Headquarters Of
The Resistance.
Sanitary Facility D.
COME ON... GET CLEAN! MY ARM'S ABOUT TO FALL OFF!
YOU KNOW... I THINK THAT'S ABOUT AS CLEAN AS IT'S GONNA GET, SURALINDA.

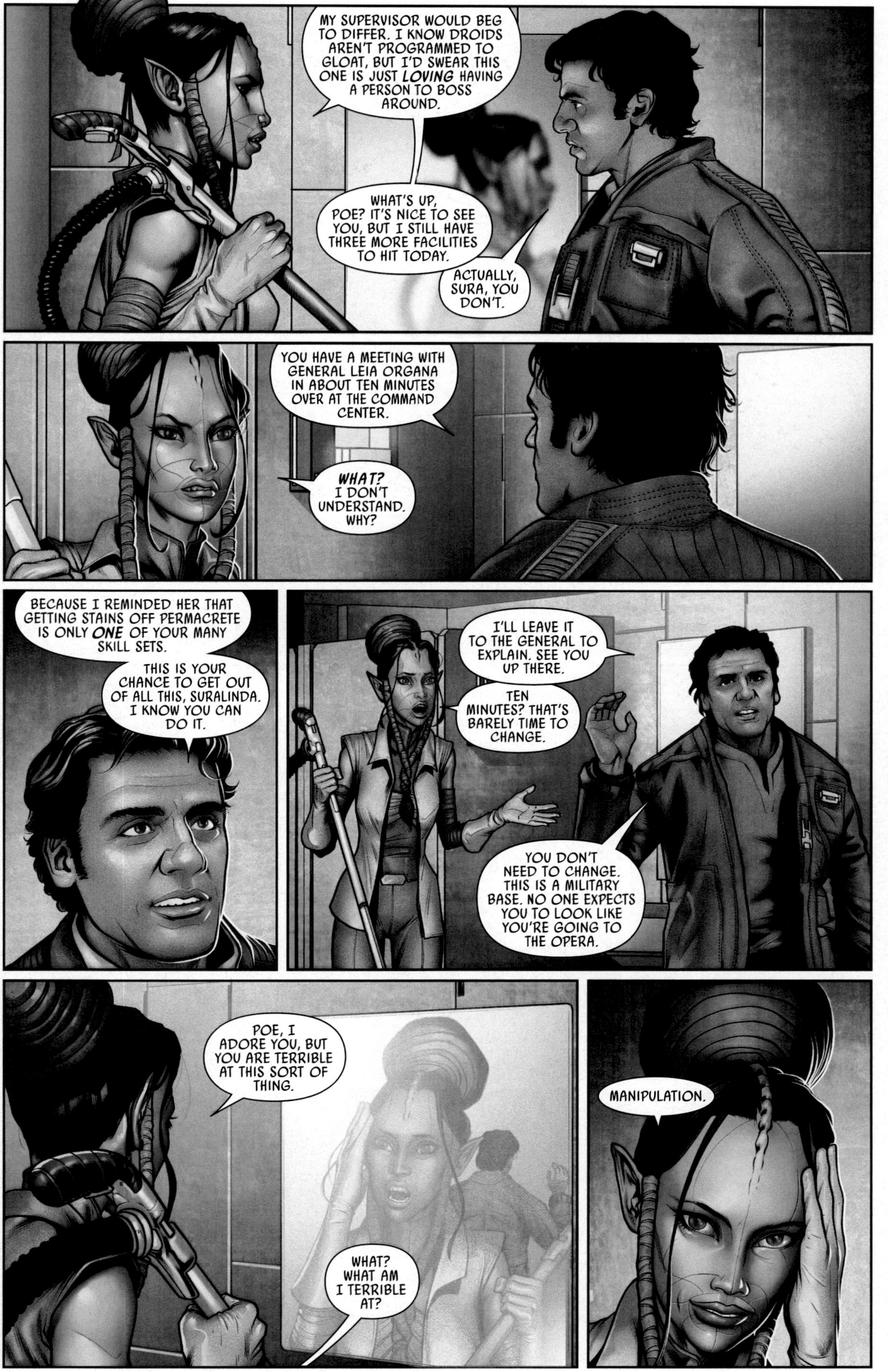
MY SUPERVISOR WOULD BEG TO DIFFER. I KNOW DROIDS AREN'T PROGRAMMED TO GLOAT, BUT I'D SWEAR THIS ONE IS JUST *LOVING* HAVING A PERSON TO BOSS AROUND.
WHAT'S UP, POE? IT'S NICE TO SEE YOU, BUT I STILL HAVE THREE MORE FACILITIES TO HIT TODAY.
ACTUALLY, SURA, YOU DON'T.
YOU HAVE A MEETING WITH GENERAL LEIA ORGANA IN ABOUT TEN MINUTES OVER AT THE COMMAND CENTER.
WHAT? I DON'T UNDERSTAND. WHY?
BECAUSE I REMINDED HER THAT GETTING STAINS OFF PERMACRETE IS ONLY *ONE* OF YOUR MANY SKILL SETS.
THIS IS YOUR CHANCE TO GET OUT OF ALL THIS, SURALINDA. I KNOW YOU CAN DO IT.
I'LL LEAVE IT TO THE GENERAL TO EXPLAIN. SEE YOU UP THERE.
TEN MINUTES? THAT'S BARELY TIME TO CHANGE.
YOU DON'T NEED TO CHANGE. THIS IS A MILITARY BASE. NO ONE EXPECTS YOU TO LOOK LIKE YOU'RE GOING TO THE OPERA.
POE, I ADORE YOU, BUT YOU ARE TERRIBLE AT THIS SORT OF THING.
WHAT? WHAT AM I TERRIBLE AT?
MANIPULATION.

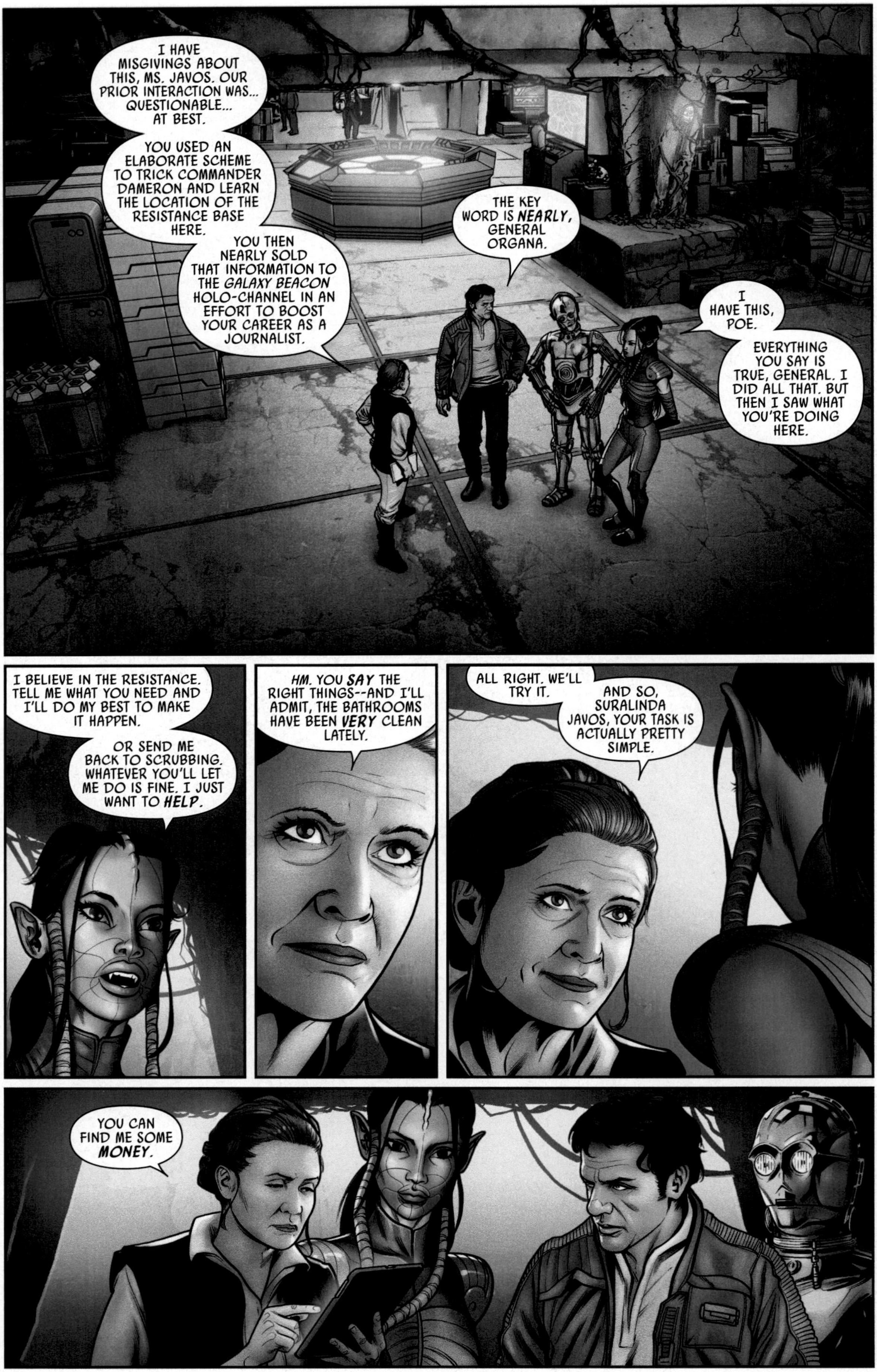
I HAVE MISGIVINGS ABOUT THIS, MS. JAVOS. OUR PRIOR INTERACTION WAS... QUESTIONABLE... AT BEST.
YOU USED AN ELABORATE SCHEME TO TRICK COMMANDER DAMERON AND LEARN THE LOCATION OF THE RESISTANCE BASE HERE.
YOU THEN NEARLY SOLD THAT INFORMATION TO THE *GALAXY BEACON* HOLO-CHANNEL IN AN EFFORT TO BOOST YOUR CAREER AS A JOURNALIST.
THE KEY WORD IS ***NEARLY***, GENERAL ORGANA.
I HAVE THIS, POE.
EVERYTHING YOU SAY IS TRUE, GENERAL. I DID ALL THAT. BUT THEN I SAW WHAT YOU'RE DOING HERE.
I BELIEVE IN THE RESISTANCE. TELL ME WHAT YOU NEED AND I'LL DO MY BEST TO MAKE IT HAPPEN.
OR SEND ME BACK TO SCRUBBING. WHATEVER YOU'LL LET ME DO IS FINE. I JUST WANT TO ***HELP***.
HM. YOU ***SAY*** THE RIGHT THINGS--AND I'LL ADMIT, THE BATHROOMS HAVE BEEN ***VERY*** CLEAN LATELY.
ALL RIGHT. WE'LL TRY IT.
AND SO, SURALINDA JAVOS, YOUR TASK IS ACTUALLY PRETTY SIMPLE.
YOU CAN FIND ME SOME ***MONEY***.

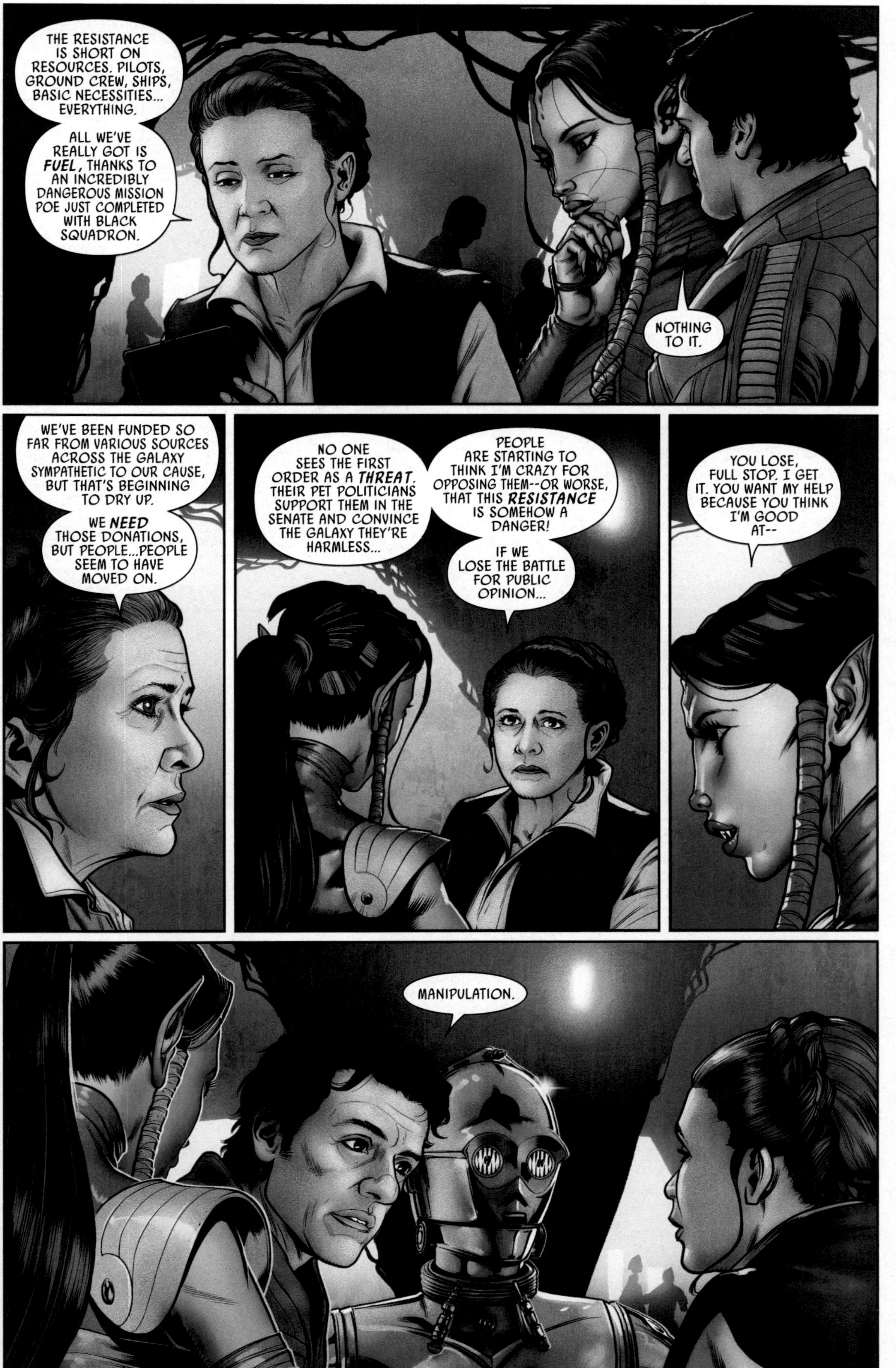
THE RESISTANCE IS SHORT ON RESOURCES. PILOTS, GROUND CREW, SHIPS, BASIC NECESSITIES... EVERYTHING.
ALL WE'VE REALLY GOT IS FUEL, THANKS TO AN INCREDIBLY DANGEROUS MISSION POE JUST COMPLETED WITH BLACK SQUADRON.
NOTHING TO IT.
WE'VE BEEN FUNDED SO FAR FROM VARIOUS SOURCES ACROSS THE GALAXY SYMPATHETIC TO OUR CAUSE, BUT THAT'S BEGINNING TO DRY UP.
WE NEED THOSE DONATIONS, BUT PEOPLE...PEOPLE SEEM TO HAVE MOVED ON.
NO ONE SEES THE FIRST ORDER AS A THREAT. THEIR PET POLITICIANS SUPPORT THEM IN THE SENATE AND CONVINCE THE GALAXY THEY'RE HARMLESS...
PEOPLE ARE STARTING TO THINK I'M CRAZY FOR OPPOSING THEM--OR WORSE, THAT THIS RESISTANCE IS SOMEHOW A DANGER!
IF WE LOSE THE BATTLE FOR PUBLIC OPINION...
YOU LOSE, FULL STOP. I GET IT. YOU WANT MY HELP BECAUSE YOU THINK I'M GOOD AT--
MANIPULATION.

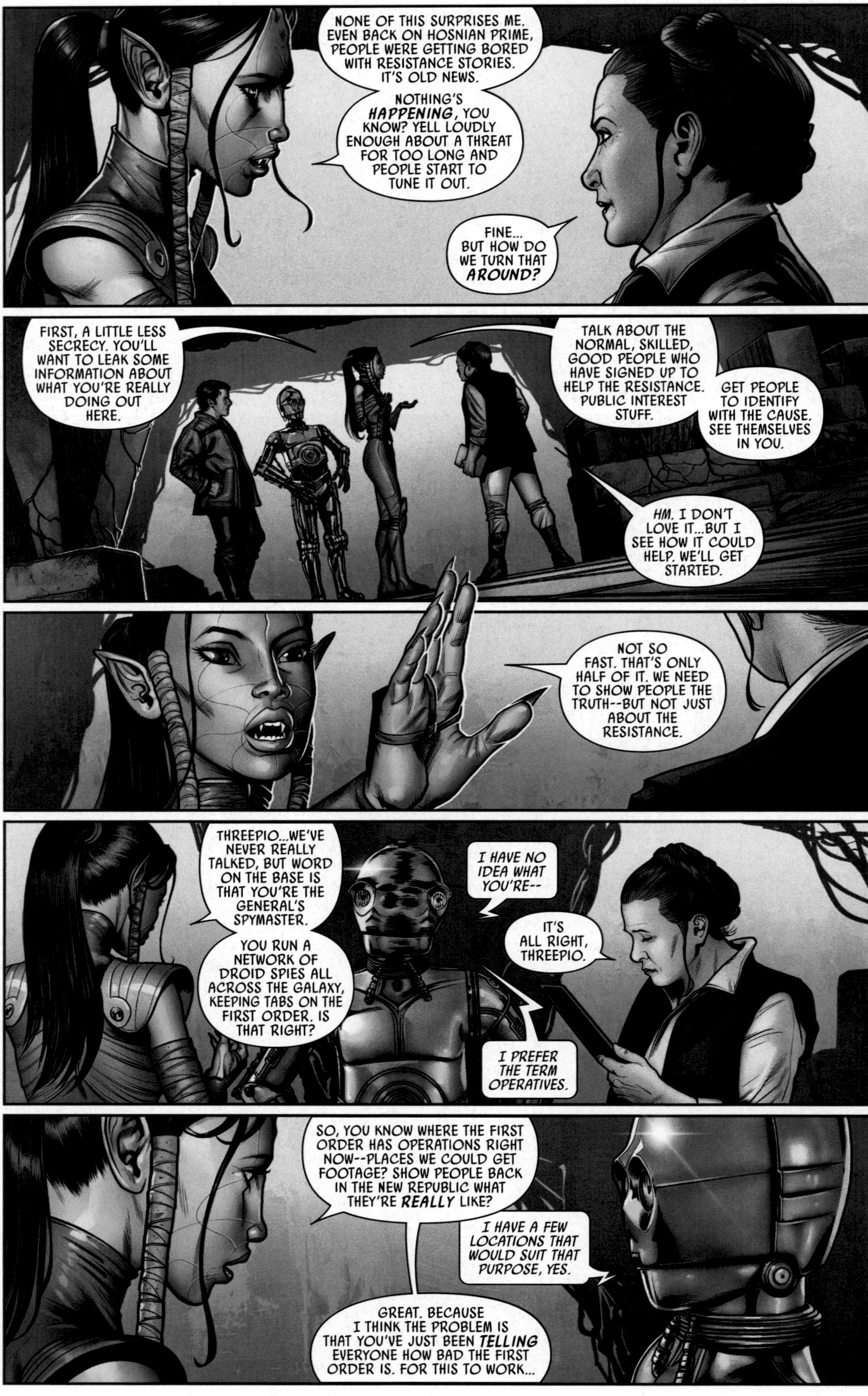
NONE OF THIS SURPRISES ME. EVEN BACK ON HOSNIAN PRIME, PEOPLE WERE GETTING BORED WITH RESISTANCE STORIES. IT'S OLD NEWS.
NOTHING'S *HAPPENING*, YOU KNOW? YELL LOUDLY ENOUGH ABOUT A THREAT FOR TOO LONG AND PEOPLE START TO TUNE IT OUT.
FINE... BUT HOW DO WE TURN THAT *AROUND?*
FIRST, A LITTLE LESS SECRECY. YOU'LL WANT TO LEAK SOME INFORMATION ABOUT WHAT YOU'RE REALLY DOING OUT HERE.
TALK ABOUT THE NORMAL, SKILLED, GOOD PEOPLE WHO HAVE SIGNED UP TO HELP THE RESISTANCE. PUBLIC INTEREST STUFF.
GET PEOPLE TO IDENTIFY WITH THE CAUSE. SEE THEMSELVES IN YOU.
HM. I DON'T LOVE IT...BUT I SEE HOW IT COULD HELP. WE'LL GET STARTED.
NOT SO FAST. THAT'S ONLY HALF OF IT. WE NEED TO SHOW PEOPLE THE TRUTH--BUT NOT JUST ABOUT THE RESISTANCE.
THREEPIO...WE'VE NEVER REALLY TALKED, BUT WORD ON THE BASE IS THAT YOU'RE THE GENERAL'S SPYMASTER.
YOU RUN A NETWORK OF DROID SPIES ALL ACROSS THE GALAXY, KEEPING TABS ON THE FIRST ORDER. IS THAT RIGHT?
I HAVE NO IDEA WHAT YOU'RE--
IT'S ALL RIGHT, THREEPIO.
I PREFER THE TERM OPERATIVES.
SO, YOU KNOW WHERE THE FIRST ORDER HAS OPERATIONS RIGHT NOW--PLACES WE COULD GET FOOTAGE? SHOW PEOPLE BACK IN THE NEW REPUBLIC WHAT THEY'RE *REALLY* LIKE?
I HAVE A FEW LOCATIONS THAT WOULD SUIT THAT PURPOSE, YES.
GREAT. BECAUSE I THINK THE PROBLEM IS THAT YOU'VE JUST BEEN *TELLING* EVERYONE HOW BAD THE FIRST ORDER IS. FOR THIS TO WORK...

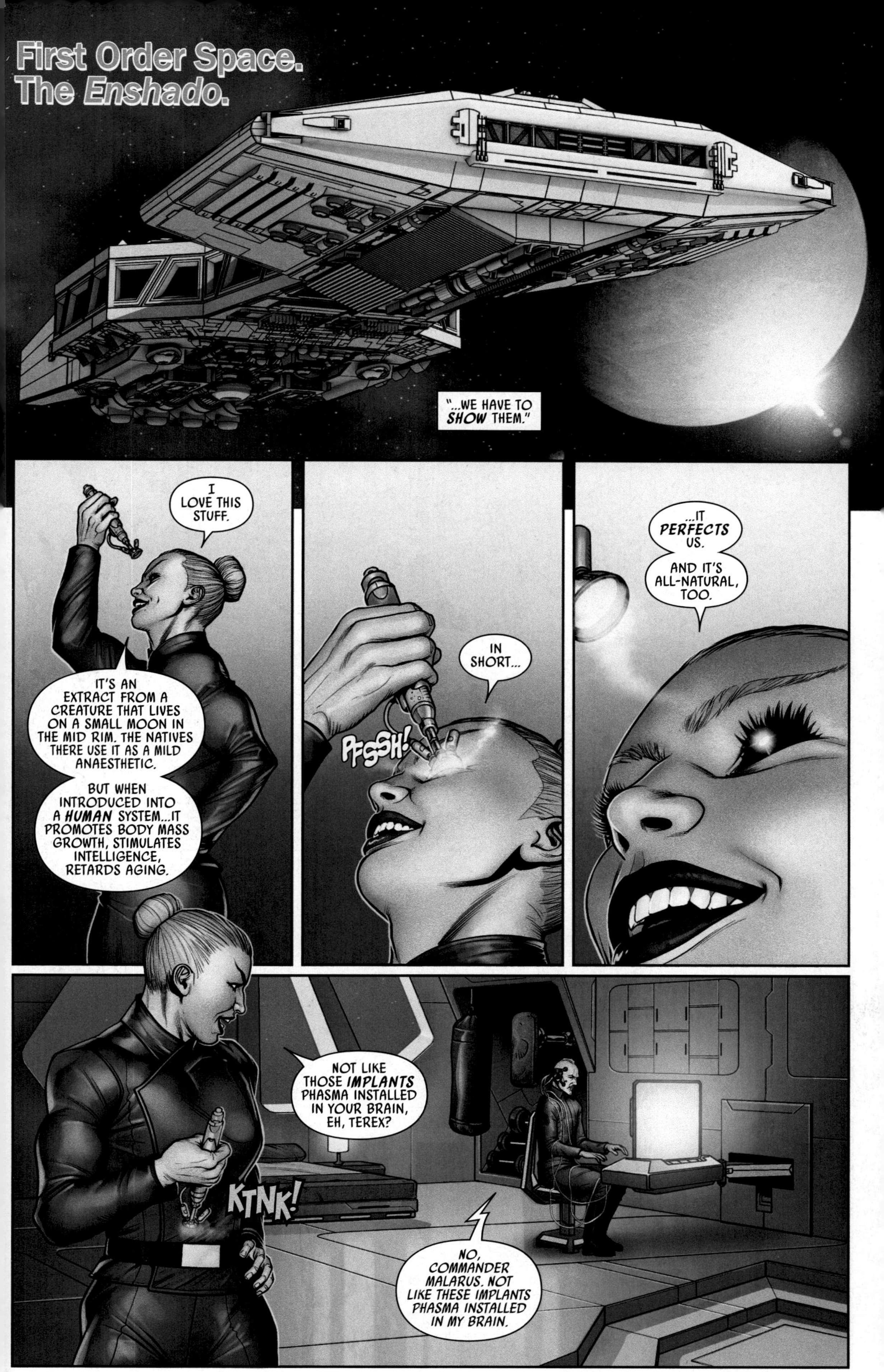
First Order Space.
The *Enshado*.
"...WE HAVE TO SHOW THEM."
I LOVE THIS STUFF.
IT'S AN EXTRACT FROM A CREATURE THAT LIVES ON A SMALL MOON IN THE MID RIM. THE NATIVES THERE USE IT AS A MILD ANAESTHETIC.
BUT WHEN INTRODUCED INTO A HUMAN SYSTEM...IT PROMOTES BODY MASS GROWTH, STIMULATES INTELLIGENCE, RETARDS AGING.
IN SHORT...
PFSSH!
...IT PERFECTS US.
AND IT'S ALL-NATURAL, TOO.
NOT LIKE THOSE IMPLANTS PHASMA INSTALLED IN YOUR BRAIN, EH, TEREX?
KTNK!
NO, COMMANDER MALARUS. NOT LIKE THESE IMPLANTS PHASMA INSTALLED IN MY BRAIN.

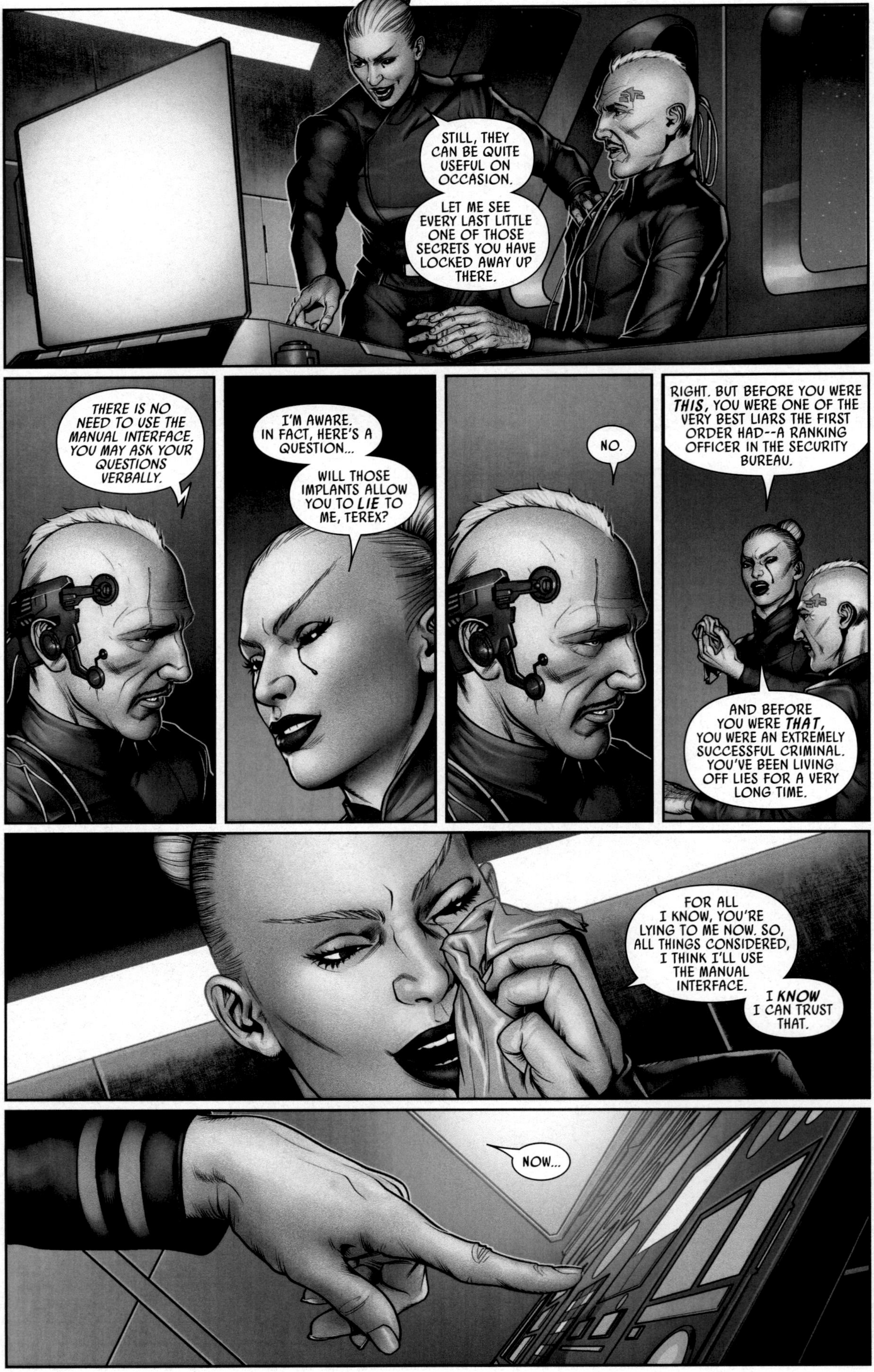
STILL, THEY CAN BE QUITE USEFUL ON OCCASION.
LET ME SEE EVERY LAST LITTLE ONE OF THOSE SECRETS YOU HAVE LOCKED AWAY UP THERE.
THERE IS NO NEED TO USE THE MANUAL INTERFACE. YOU MAY ASK YOUR QUESTIONS VERBALLY.
I'M AWARE. IN FACT, HERE'S A QUESTION...
WILL THOSE IMPLANTS ALLOW YOU TO LIE TO ME, TEREX?
NO.
RIGHT. BUT BEFORE YOU WERE THIS, YOU WERE ONE OF THE VERY BEST LIARS THE FIRST ORDER HAD--A RANKING OFFICER IN THE SECURITY BUREAU.
AND BEFORE YOU WERE THAT, YOU WERE AN EXTREMELY SUCCESSFUL CRIMINAL. YOU'VE BEEN LIVING OFF LIES FOR A VERY LONG TIME.
FOR ALL I KNOW, YOU'RE LYING TO ME NOW. SO, ALL THINGS CONSIDERED, I THINK I'LL USE THE MANUAL INTERFACE.
I KNOW I CAN TRUST THAT.
NOW...

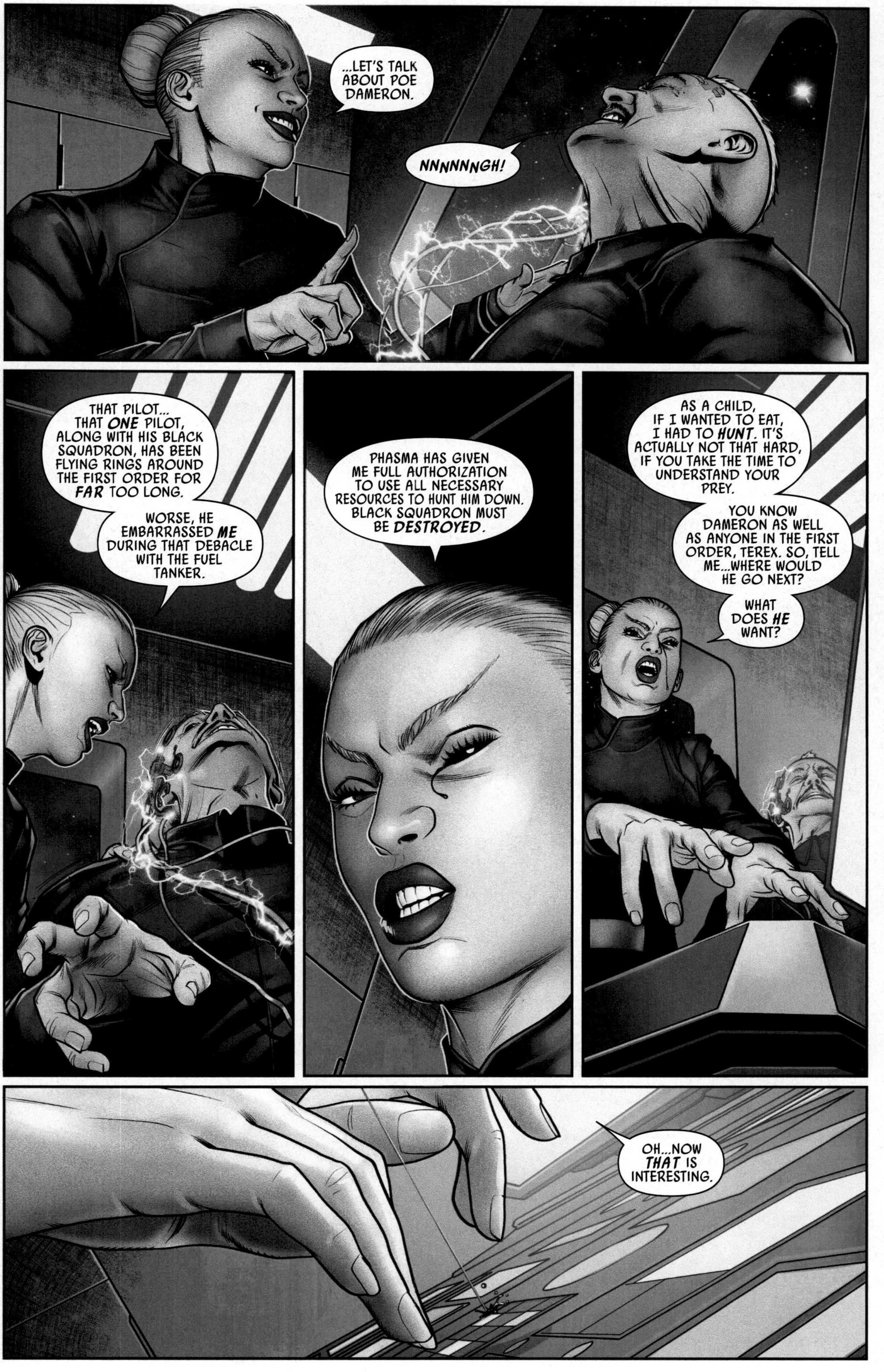
...LET'S TALK ABOUT POE DAMERON.
NNNNNNGH!
THAT PILOT... THAT ONE PILOT, ALONG WITH HIS BLACK SQUADRON, HAS BEEN FLYING RINGS AROUND THE FIRST ORDER FOR FAR TOO LONG.
WORSE, HE EMBARRASSED ME DURING THAT DEBACLE WITH THE FUEL TANKER.
PHASMA HAS GIVEN ME FULL AUTHORIZATION TO USE ALL NECESSARY RESOURCES TO HUNT HIM DOWN. BLACK SQUADRON MUST BE DESTROYED.
AS A CHILD, IF I WANTED TO EAT, I HAD TO HUNT. IT'S ACTUALLY NOT THAT HARD, IF YOU TAKE THE TIME TO UNDERSTAND YOUR PREY.
YOU KNOW DAMERON AS WELL AS ANYONE IN THE FIRST ORDER, TEREX. SO, TELL ME...WHERE WOULD HE GO NEXT?
WHAT DOES HE WANT?
OH...NOW THAT IS INTERESTING.

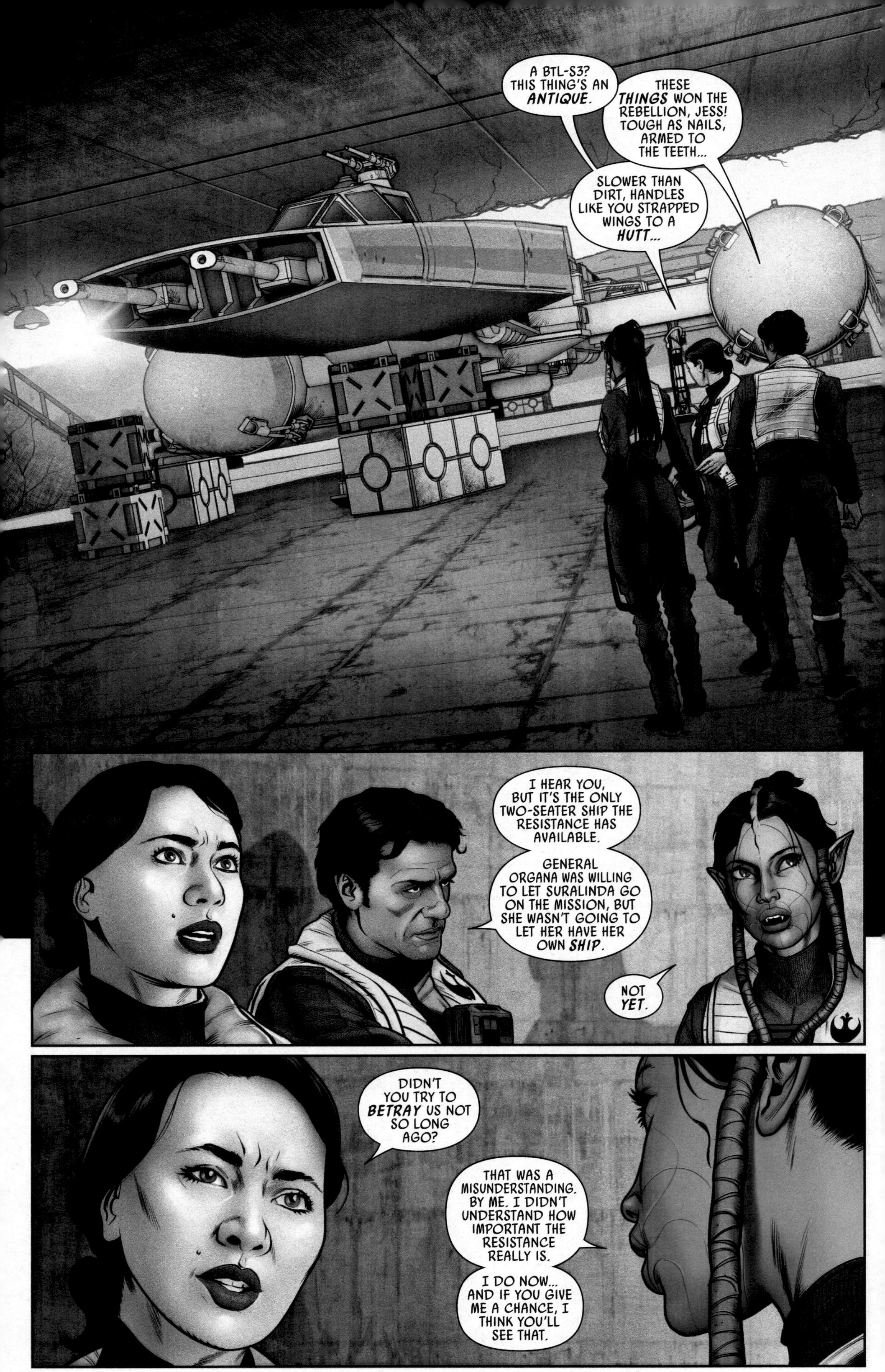

A BTL-S3? THIS THING'S AN ANTIQUE.
THESE THINGS WON THE REBELLION, JESS! TOUGH AS NAILS, ARMED TO THE TEETH...
SLOWER THAN DIRT, HANDLES LIKE YOU STRAPPED WINGS TO A HUTT...
I HEAR YOU, BUT IT'S THE ONLY TWO-SEATER SHIP THE RESISTANCE HAS AVAILABLE.
GENERAL ORGANA WAS WILLING TO LET SURALINDA GO ON THE MISSION, BUT SHE WASN'T GOING TO LET HER HAVE HER OWN SHIP.
NOT YET.
DIDN'T YOU TRY TO BETRAY US NOT SO LONG AGO?
THAT WAS A MISUNDERSTANDING. BY ME. I DIDN'T UNDERSTAND HOW IMPORTANT THE RESISTANCE REALLY IS.
I DO NOW... AND IF YOU GIVE ME A CHANCE, I THINK YOU'LL SEE THAT.

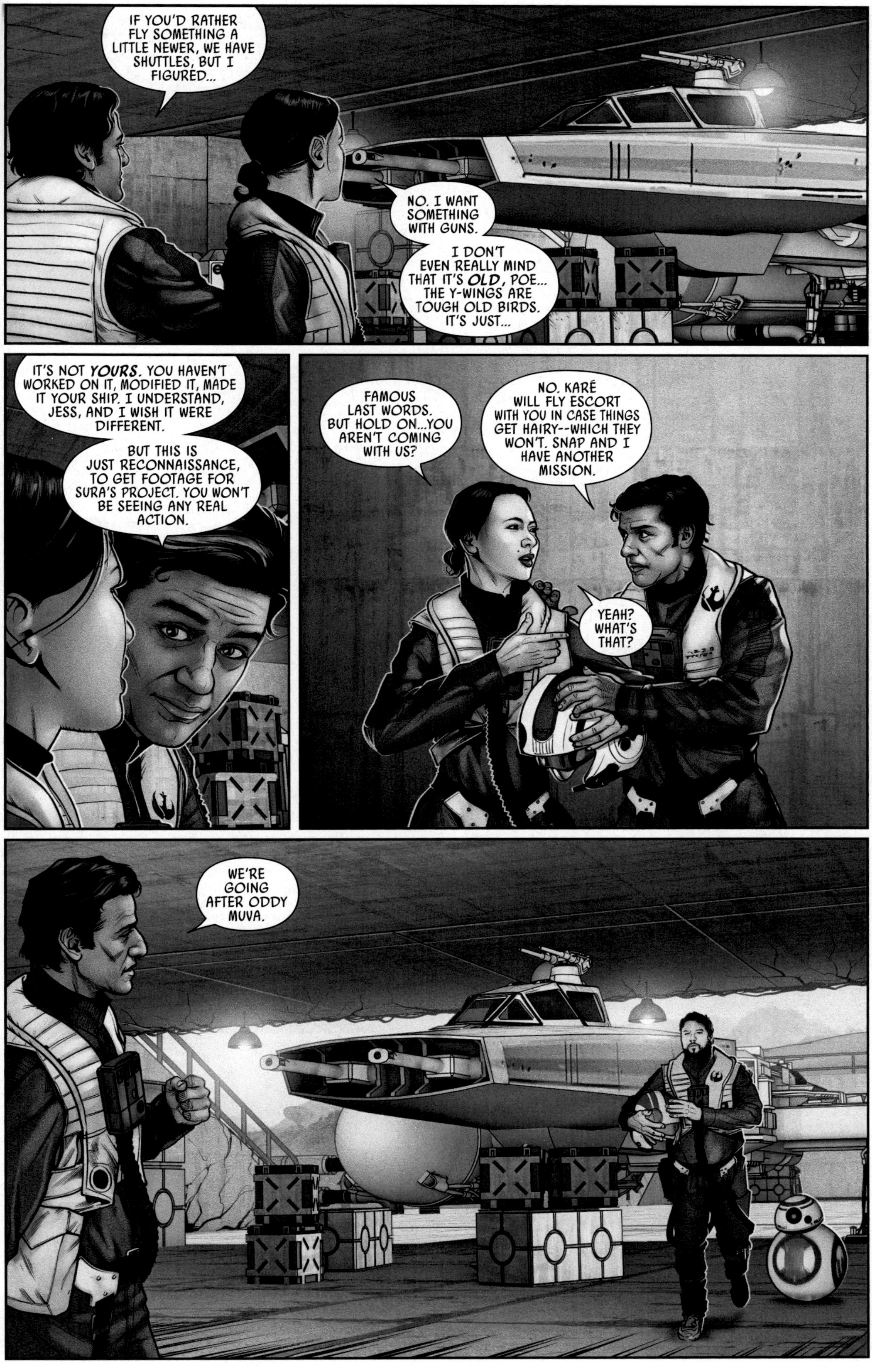
IF YOU'D RATHER FLY SOMETHING A LITTLE NEWER, WE HAVE SHUTTLES, BUT I FIGURED...
NO. I WANT SOMETHING WITH GUNS.
I DON'T EVEN REALLY MIND THAT IT'S *OLD*, POE... THE Y-WINGS ARE TOUGH OLD BIRDS. IT'S JUST...
IT'S NOT *YOURS*. YOU HAVEN'T WORKED ON IT, MODIFIED IT, MADE IT YOUR SHIP. I UNDERSTAND, JESS, AND I WISH IT WERE DIFFERENT.
BUT THIS IS JUST RECONNAISSANCE, TO GET FOOTAGE FOR SURA'S PROJECT. YOU WON'T BE SEEING ANY REAL ACTION.
FAMOUS LAST WORDS. BUT HOLD ON...YOU AREN'T COMING WITH US?
NO. KARÉ WILL FLY ESCORT WITH YOU IN CASE THINGS GET HAIRY--WHICH THEY WON'T. SNAP AND I HAVE ANOTHER MISSION.
YEAH? WHAT'S THAT?
WE'RE GOING AFTER ODDY MUVA.

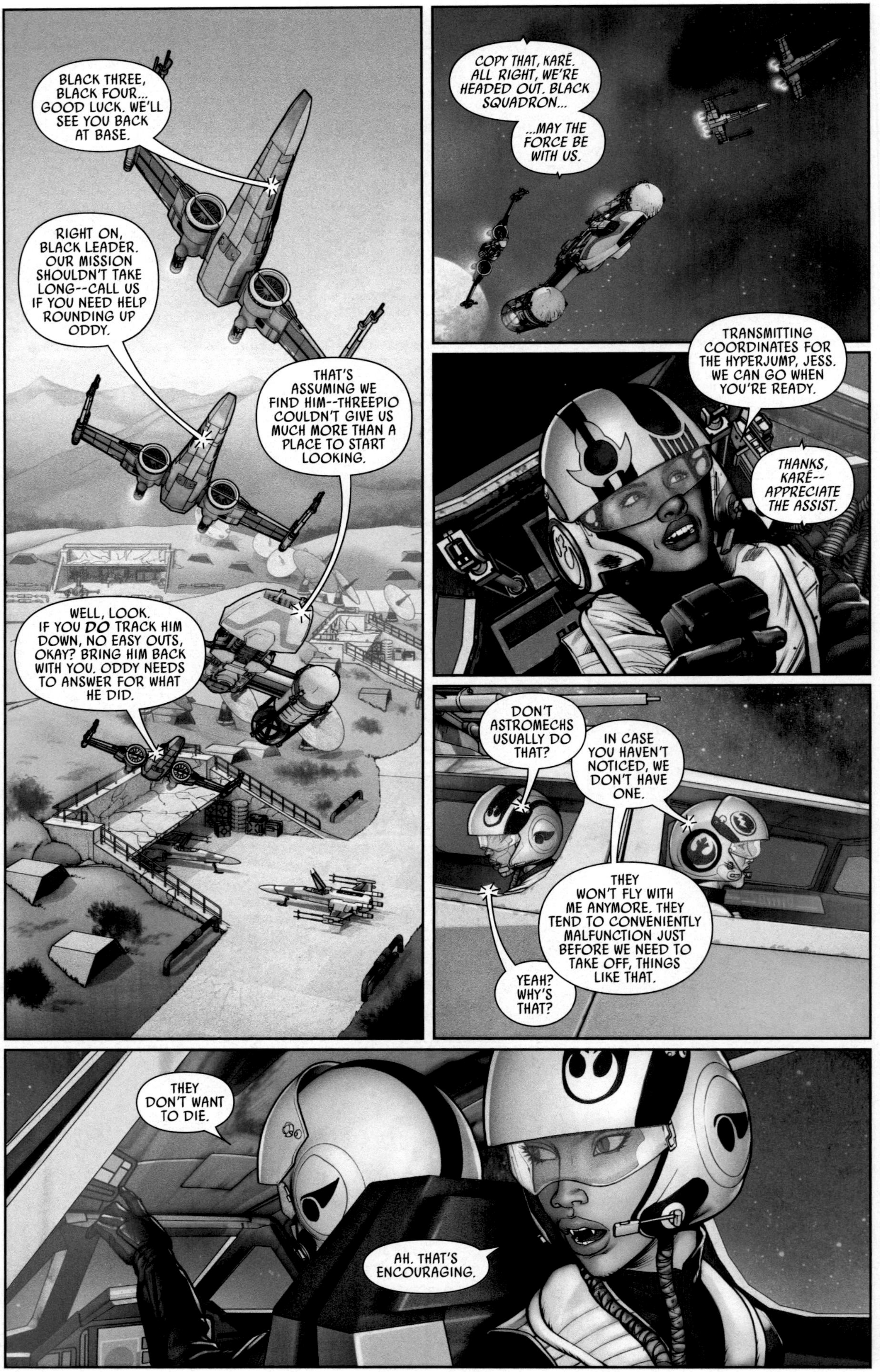
BLACK THREE, BLACK FOUR... GOOD LUCK. WE'LL SEE YOU BACK AT BASE.
RIGHT ON, BLACK LEADER. OUR MISSION SHOULDN'T TAKE LONG--CALL US IF YOU NEED HELP ROUNDING UP ODDY.
THAT'S ASSUMING WE FIND HIM--THREEPIO COULDN'T GIVE US MUCH MORE THAN A PLACE TO START LOOKING.
WELL, LOOK. IF YOU DO TRACK HIM DOWN, NO EASY OUTS, OKAY? BRING HIM BACK WITH YOU. ODDY NEEDS TO ANSWER FOR WHAT HE DID.
COPY THAT, KARÉ. ALL RIGHT, WE'RE HEADED OUT. BLACK SQUADRON...
...MAY THE FORCE BE WITH US.
TRANSMITTING COORDINATES FOR THE HYPERJUMP, JESS. WE CAN GO WHEN YOU'RE READY.
THANKS, KARÉ-- APPRECIATE THE ASSIST.
DON'T ASTROMECHS USUALLY DO THAT?
IN CASE YOU HAVEN'T NOTICED, WE DON'T HAVE ONE.
YEAH? WHY'S THAT?
THEY WON'T FLY WITH ME ANYMORE. THEY TEND TO CONVENIENTLY MALFUNCTION JUST BEFORE WE NEED TO TAKE OFF, THINGS LIKE THAT.
THEY DON'T WANT TO DIE.
AH. THAT'S ENCOURAGING.

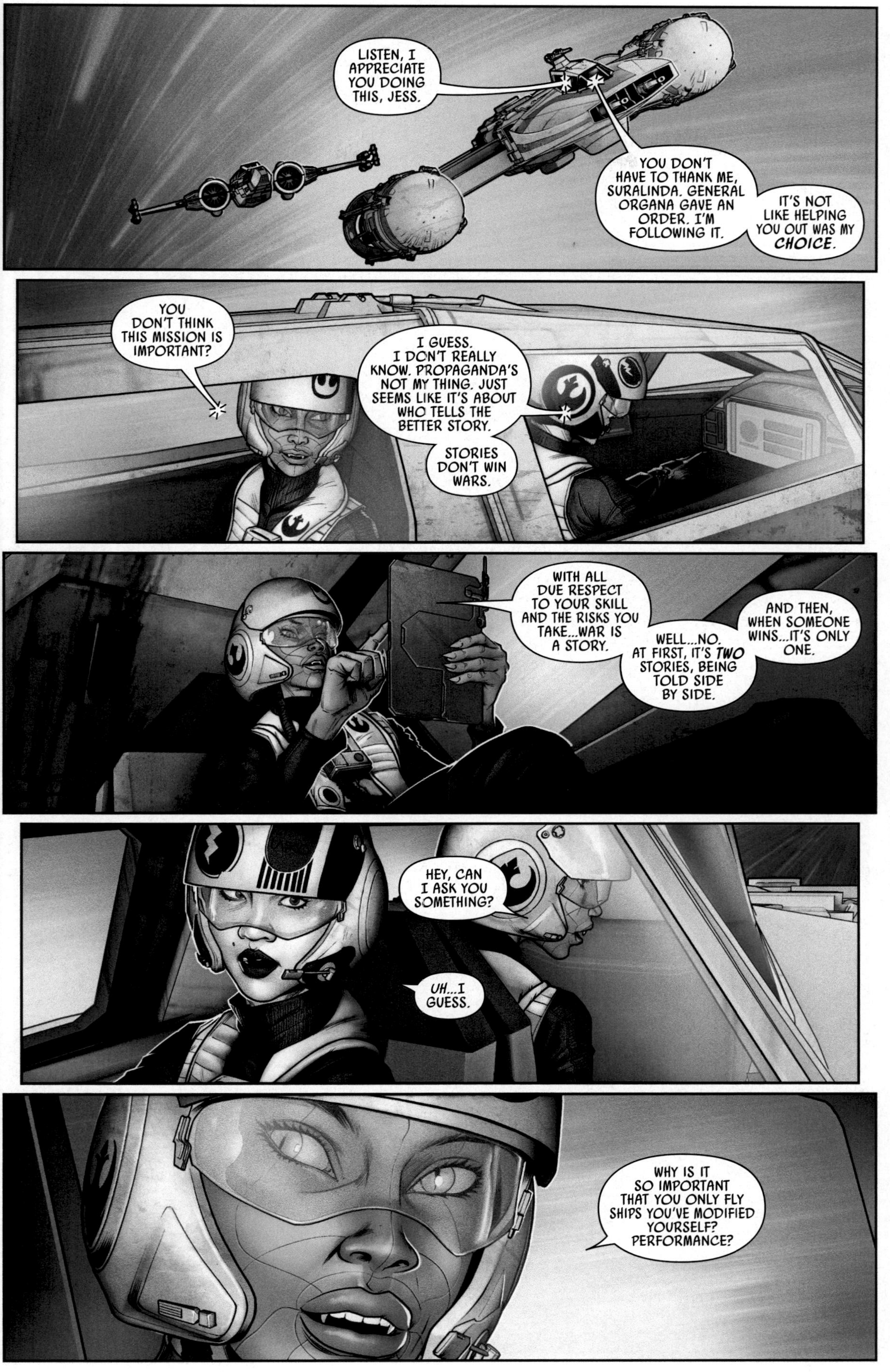
LISTEN, I APPRECIATE YOU DOING THIS, JESS.
YOU DON'T HAVE TO THANK ME, SURALINDA. GENERAL ORGANA GAVE AN ORDER. I'M FOLLOWING IT.
IT'S NOT LIKE HELPING YOU OUT WAS MY *CHOICE*.
YOU DON'T THINK THIS MISSION IS IMPORTANT?
I GUESS. I DON'T REALLY KNOW. PROPAGANDA'S NOT MY THING. JUST SEEMS LIKE IT'S ABOUT WHO TELLS THE BETTER STORY.
STORIES DON'T WIN WARS.
WITH ALL DUE RESPECT TO YOUR SKILL AND THE RISKS YOU TAKE...WAR IS A STORY.
WELL...NO. AT FIRST, IT'S *TWO* STORIES, BEING TOLD SIDE BY SIDE.
AND THEN, WHEN SOMEONE WINS...IT'S ONLY ONE.
HEY, CAN I ASK YOU SOMETHING?
UH...I GUESS.
WHY IS IT SO IMPORTANT THAT YOU ONLY FLY SHIPS YOU'VE MODIFIED YOURSELF? PERFORMANCE?

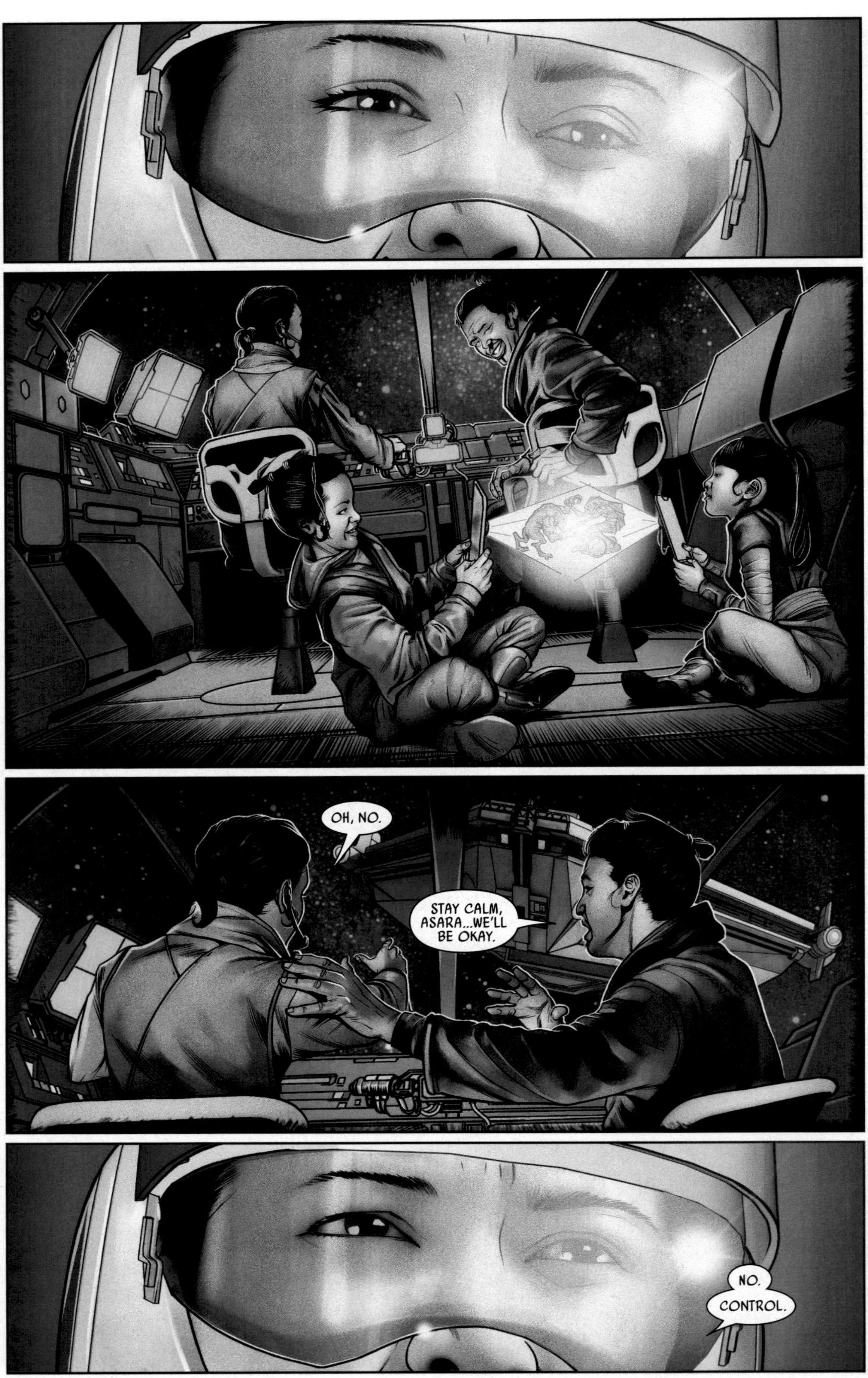
OH, NO.
STAY CALM, ASARA...WE'LL BE OKAY.
NO. CONTROL.

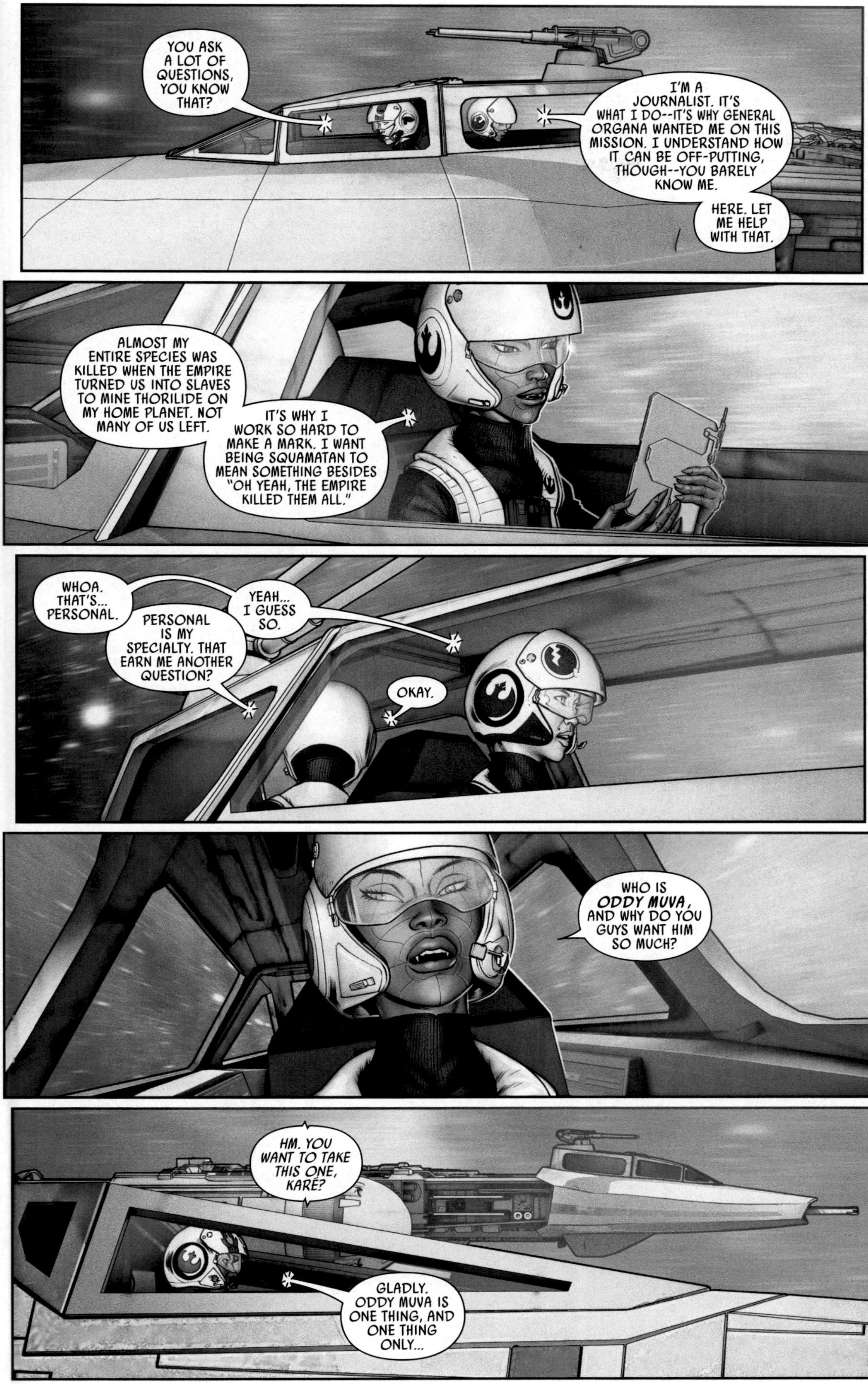
YOU ASK A LOT OF QUESTIONS, YOU KNOW THAT?
I'M A JOURNALIST. IT'S WHAT I DO--IT'S WHY GENERAL ORGANA WANTED ME ON THIS MISSION. I UNDERSTAND HOW IT CAN BE OFF-PUTTING, THOUGH--YOU BARELY KNOW ME.
HERE. LET ME HELP WITH THAT.
ALMOST MY ENTIRE SPECIES WAS KILLED WHEN THE EMPIRE TURNED US INTO SLAVES TO MINE THORILIDE ON MY HOME PLANET. NOT MANY OF US LEFT.
IT'S WHY I WORK SO HARD TO MAKE A MARK. I WANT BEING SQUAMATAN TO MEAN SOMETHING BESIDES "OH YEAH, THE EMPIRE KILLED THEM ALL."
WHOA. THAT'S... PERSONAL.
YEAH... I GUESS SO.
PERSONAL IS MY SPECIALTY. THAT EARN ME ANOTHER QUESTION?
OKAY.
WHO IS *ODDY MUVA*, AND WHY DO YOU GUYS WANT HIM SO MUCH?
HM. YOU WANT TO TAKE THIS ONE, KARÉ?
GLADLY. ODDY MUVA IS ONE THING, AND ONE THING ONLY...

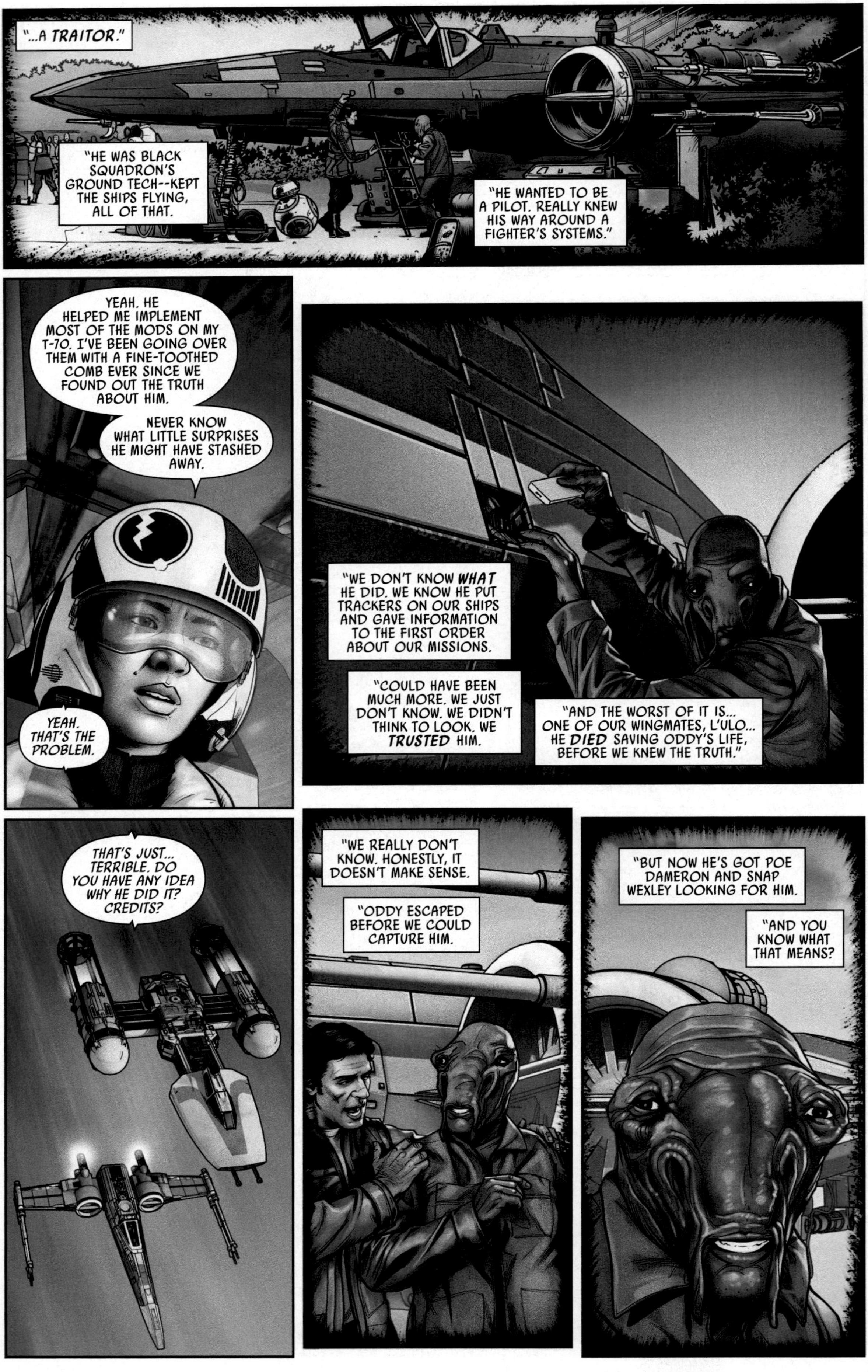
"...A TRAITOR."
"HE WAS BLACK SQUADRON'S GROUND TECH--KEPT THE SHIPS FLYING, ALL OF THAT.
"HE WANTED TO BE A PILOT. REALLY KNEW HIS WAY AROUND A FIGHTER'S SYSTEMS."
YEAH. HE HELPED ME IMPLEMENT MOST OF THE MODS ON MY T-70. I'VE BEEN GOING OVER THEM WITH A FINE-TOOTHED COMB EVER SINCE WE FOUND OUT THE TRUTH ABOUT HIM.
NEVER KNOW WHAT LITTLE SURPRISES HE MIGHT HAVE STASHED AWAY.
YEAH. THAT'S THE PROBLEM.
"WE DON'T KNOW WHAT HE DID. WE KNOW HE PUT TRACKERS ON OUR SHIPS AND GAVE INFORMATION TO THE FIRST ORDER ABOUT OUR MISSIONS.
"COULD HAVE BEEN MUCH MORE. WE JUST DON'T KNOW. WE DIDN'T THINK TO LOOK. WE TRUSTED HIM.
"AND THE WORST OF IT IS... ONE OF OUR WINGMATES, L'ULO... HE DIED SAVING ODDY'S LIFE, BEFORE WE KNEW THE TRUTH."
THAT'S JUST... TERRIBLE. DO YOU HAVE ANY IDEA WHY HE DID IT? CREDITS?
"WE REALLY DON'T KNOW. HONESTLY, IT DOESN'T MAKE SENSE.
"ODDY ESCAPED BEFORE WE COULD CAPTURE HIM.
"BUT NOW HE'S GOT POE DAMERON AND SNAP WEXLEY LOOKING FOR HIM.
"AND YOU KNOW WHAT THAT MEANS?

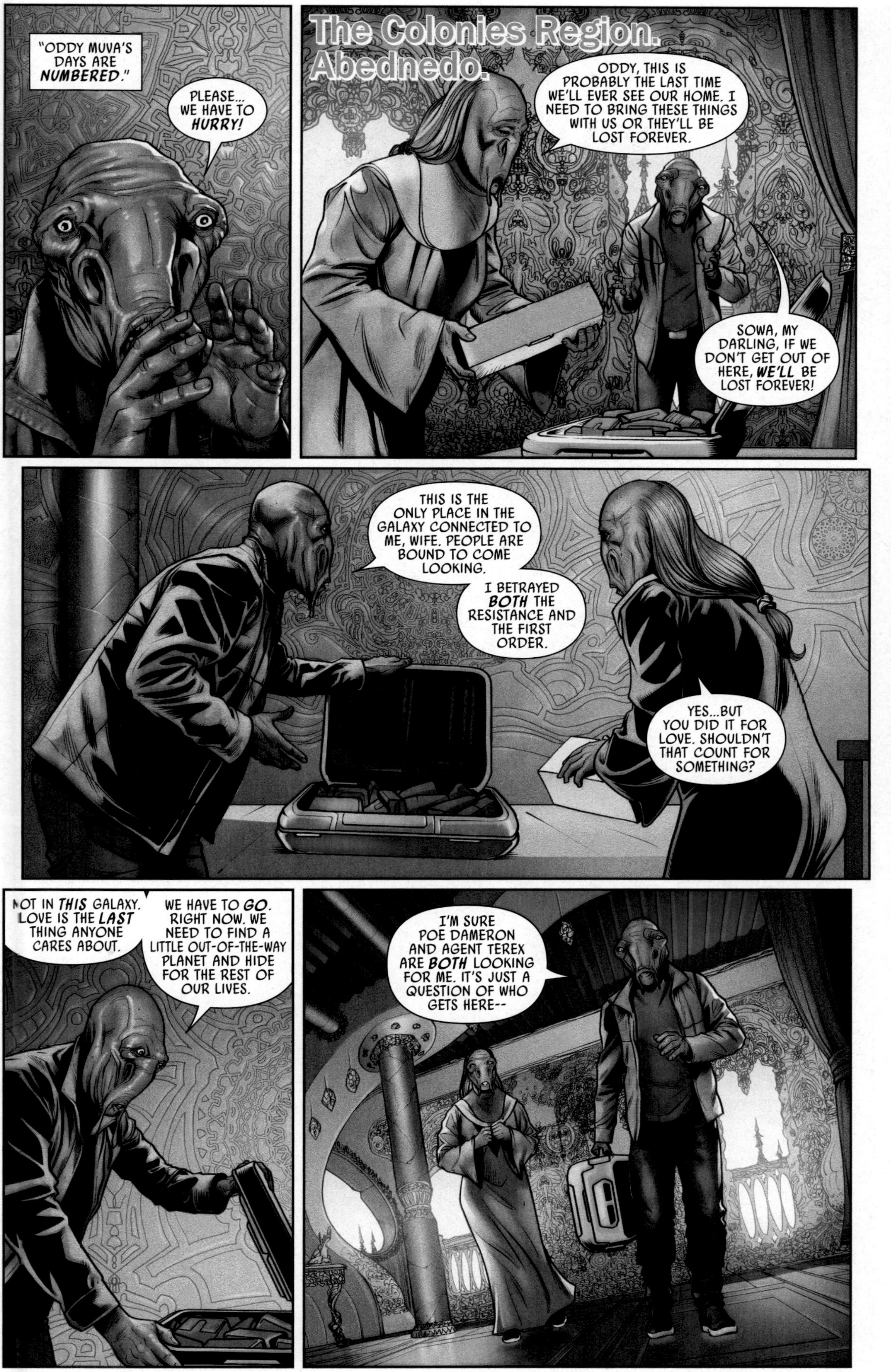
"ODDY MUVA'S DAYS ARE NUMBERED."
PLEASE... WE HAVE TO HURRY!
The Colonies Region. Abednedo.
ODDY, THIS IS PROBABLY THE LAST TIME WE'LL EVER SEE OUR HOME. I NEED TO BRING THESE THINGS WITH US OR THEY'LL BE LOST FOREVER.
SOWA, MY DARLING, IF WE DON'T GET OUT OF HERE, WE'LL BE LOST FOREVER!
THIS IS THE ONLY PLACE IN THE GALAXY CONNECTED TO ME, WIFE. PEOPLE ARE BOUND TO COME LOOKING.
I BETRAYED BOTH THE RESISTANCE AND THE FIRST ORDER.
YES...BUT YOU DID IT FOR LOVE. SHOULDN'T THAT COUNT FOR SOMETHING?
NOT IN THIS GALAXY. LOVE IS THE LAST THING ANYONE CARES ABOUT.
WE HAVE TO GO. RIGHT NOW. WE NEED TO FIND A LITTLE OUT-OF-THE-WAY PLANET AND HIDE FOR THE REST OF OUR LIVES.
I'M SURE POE DAMERON AND AGENT TEREX ARE BOTH LOOKING FOR ME. IT'S JUST A QUESTION OF WHO GETS HERE--

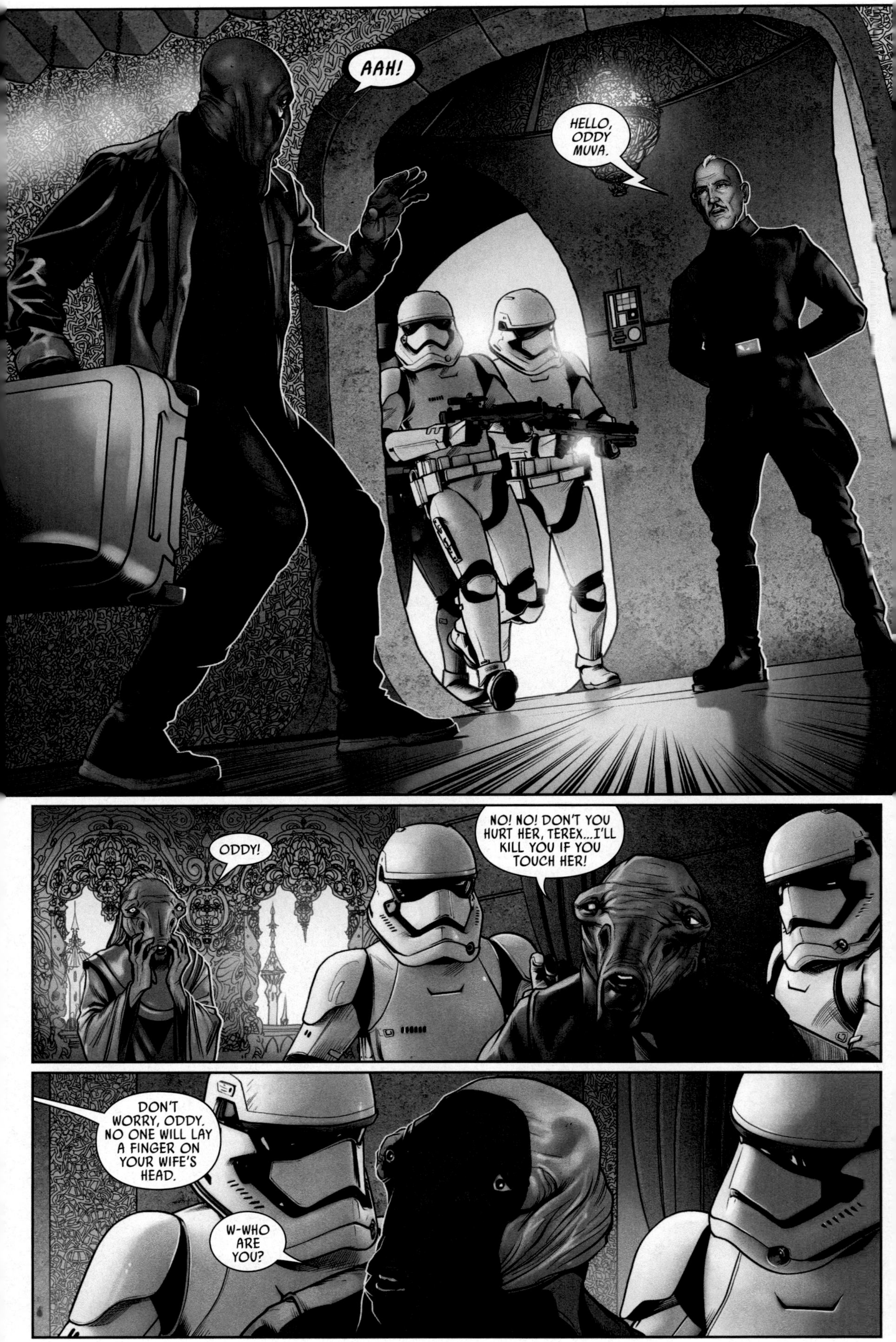
AAH!
HELLO, ODDY MUVA.
ODDY!
NO! NO! DON'T YOU HURT HER, TEREX...I'LL KILL YOU IF YOU TOUCH HER!
DON'T WORRY, ODDY. NO ONE WILL LAY A FINGER ON YOUR WIFE'S HEAD.
W-WHO ARE YOU?

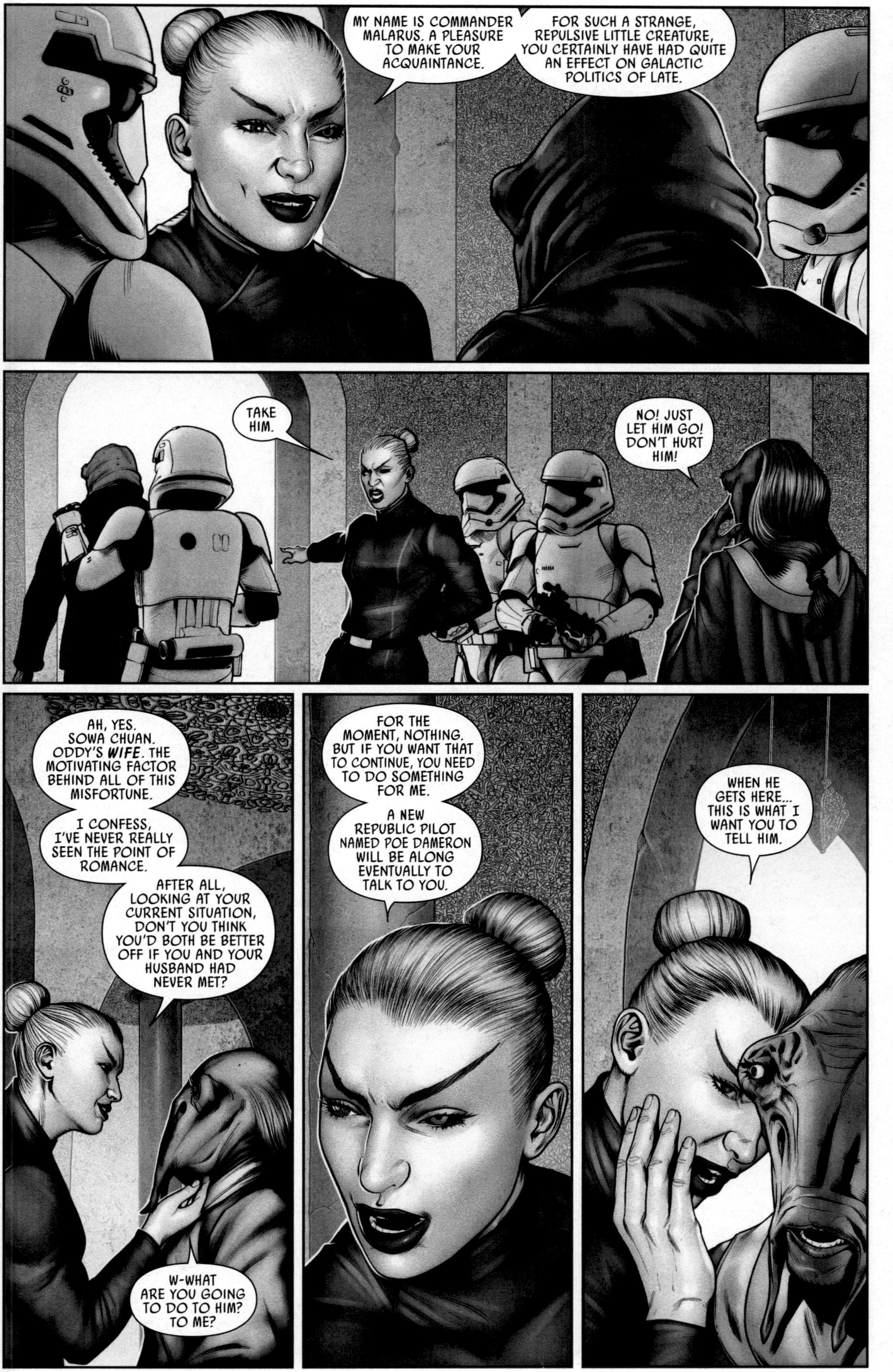
MY NAME IS COMMANDER MALARUS. A PLEASURE TO MAKE YOUR ACQUAINTANCE.
FOR SUCH A STRANGE, REPULSIVE LITTLE CREATURE, YOU CERTAINLY HAVE HAD QUITE AN EFFECT ON GALACTIC POLITICS OF LATE.
TAKE HIM.
NO! JUST LET HIM GO! DON'T HURT HIM!
AH, YES. SOWA CHUAN. ODDY'S WIFE. THE MOTIVATING FACTOR BEHIND ALL OF THIS MISFORTUNE.
I CONFESS, I'VE NEVER REALLY SEEN THE POINT OF ROMANCE.
AFTER ALL, LOOKING AT YOUR CURRENT SITUATION, DON'T YOU THINK YOU'D BOTH BE BETTER OFF IF YOU AND YOUR HUSBAND HAD NEVER MET?
W-WHAT ARE YOU GOING TO DO TO HIM? TO ME?
FOR THE MOMENT, NOTHING. BUT IF YOU WANT THAT TO CONTINUE, YOU NEED TO DO SOMETHING FOR ME.
A NEW REPUBLIC PILOT NAMED POE DAMERON WILL BE ALONG EVENTUALLY TO TALK TO YOU.
WHEN HE GETS HERE... THIS IS WHAT I WANT YOU TO TELL HIM.

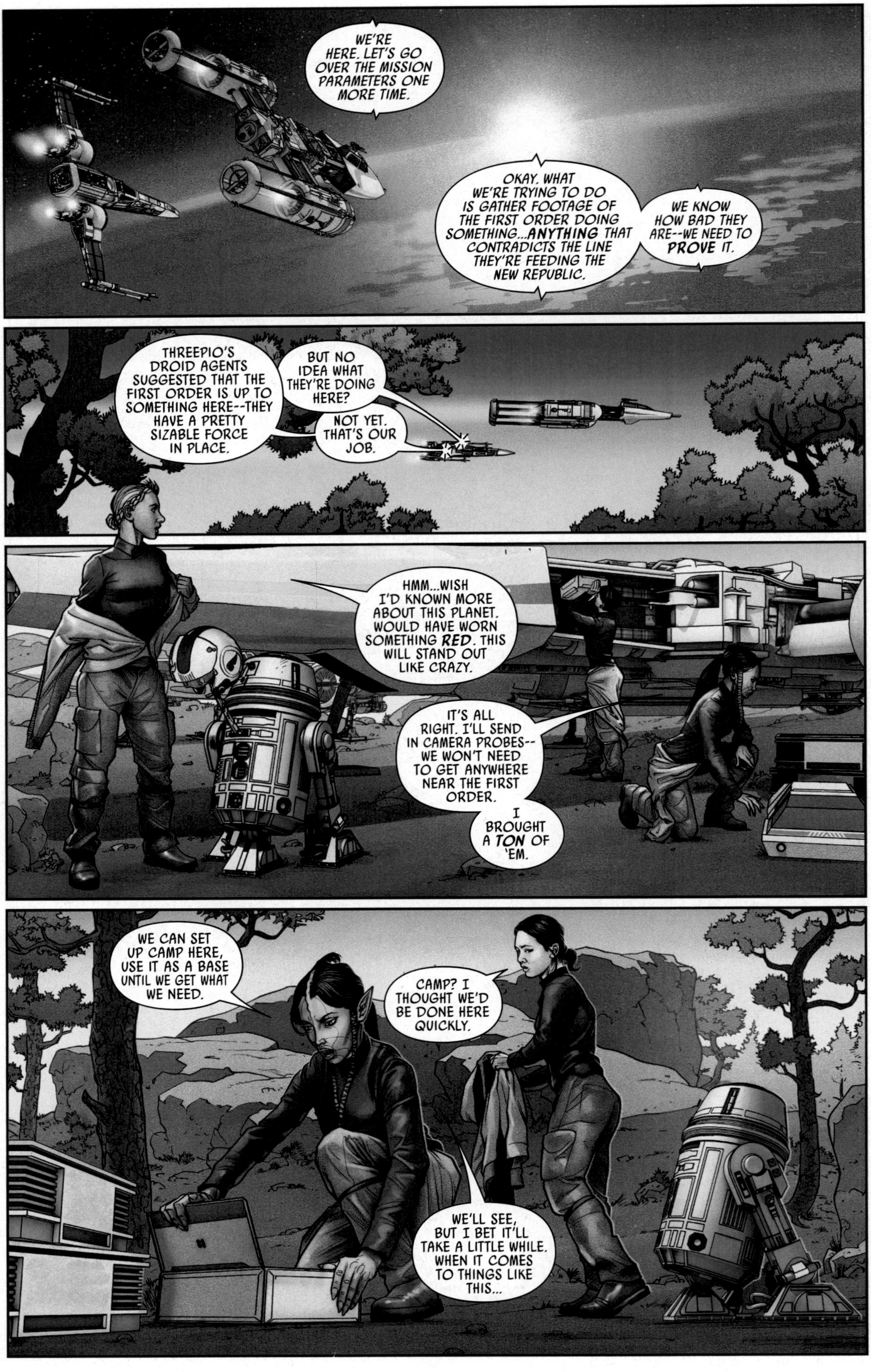
WE'RE HERE. LET'S GO OVER THE MISSION PARAMETERS ONE MORE TIME.
OKAY. WHAT WE'RE TRYING TO DO IS GATHER FOOTAGE OF THE FIRST ORDER DOING SOMETHING...ANYTHING THAT CONTRADICTS THE LINE THEY'RE FEEDING THE NEW REPUBLIC.
WE KNOW HOW BAD THEY ARE--WE NEED TO PROVE IT.
THREEPIO'S DROID AGENTS SUGGESTED THAT THE FIRST ORDER IS UP TO SOMETHING HERE--THEY HAVE A PRETTY SIZABLE FORCE IN PLACE.
BUT NO IDEA WHAT THEY'RE DOING HERE?
NOT YET. THAT'S OUR JOB.
HMM...WISH I'D KNOWN MORE ABOUT THIS PLANET. WOULD HAVE WORN SOMETHING RED. THIS WILL STAND OUT LIKE CRAZY.
IT'S ALL RIGHT. I'LL SEND IN CAMERA PROBES--WE WON'T NEED TO GET ANYWHERE NEAR THE FIRST ORDER.
I BROUGHT A TON OF 'EM.
WE CAN SET UP CAMP HERE, USE IT AS A BASE UNTIL WE GET WHAT WE NEED.
CAMP? I THOUGHT WE'D BE DONE HERE QUICKLY.
WE'LL SEE, BUT I BET IT'LL TAKE A LITTLE WHILE. WHEN IT COMES TO THINGS LIKE THIS...

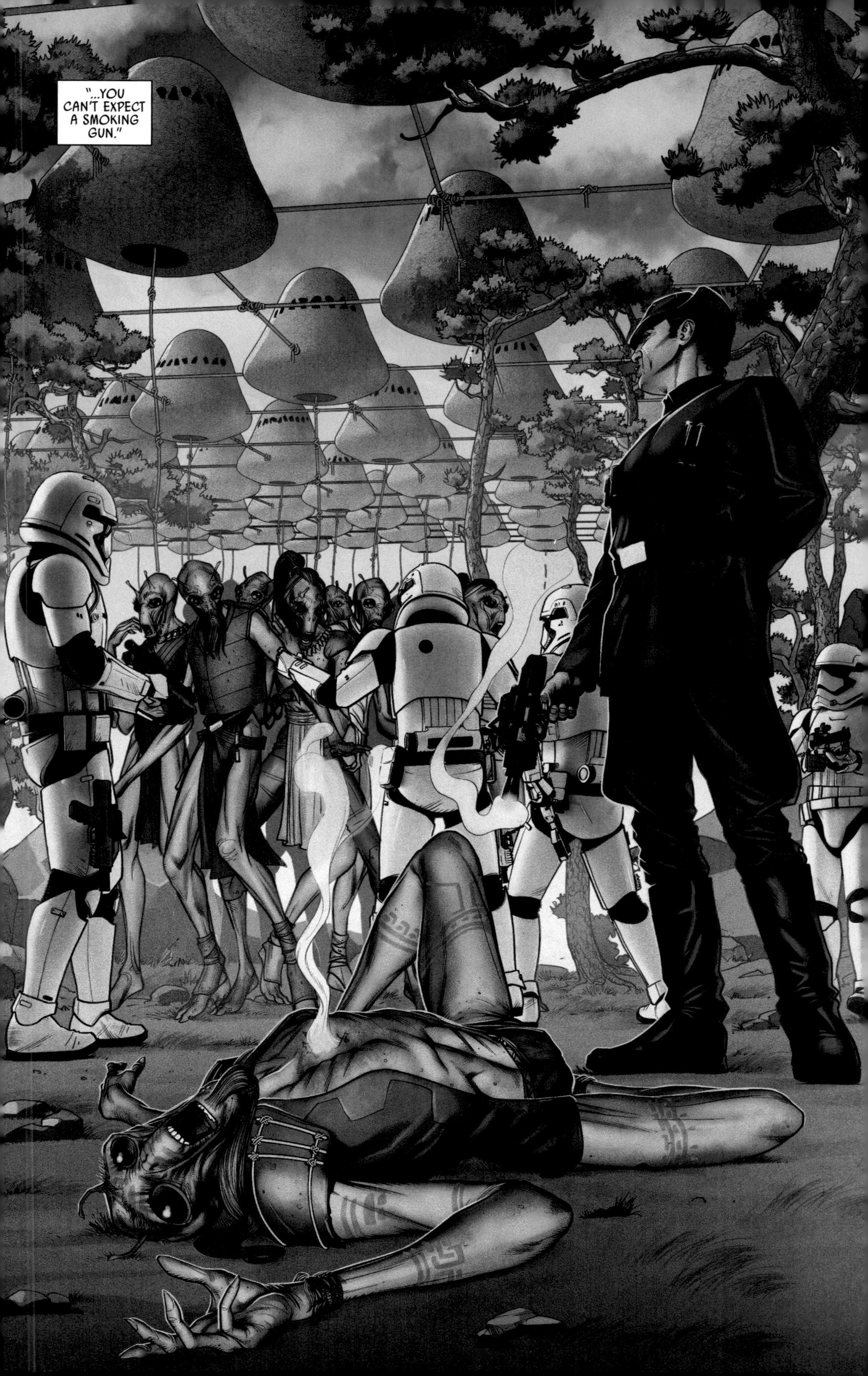
"...YOU CAN'T EXPECT A SMOKING GUN."

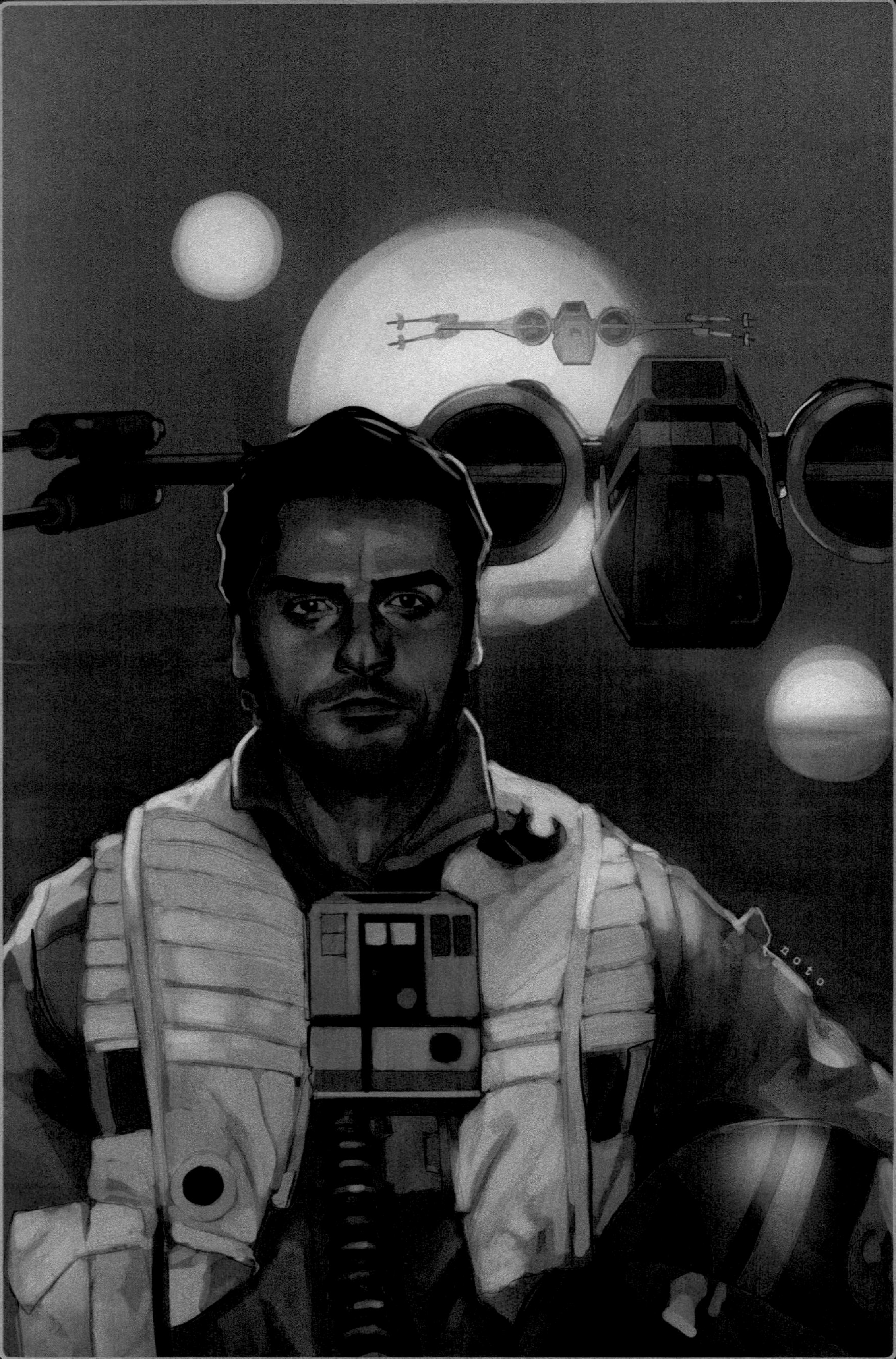
noto

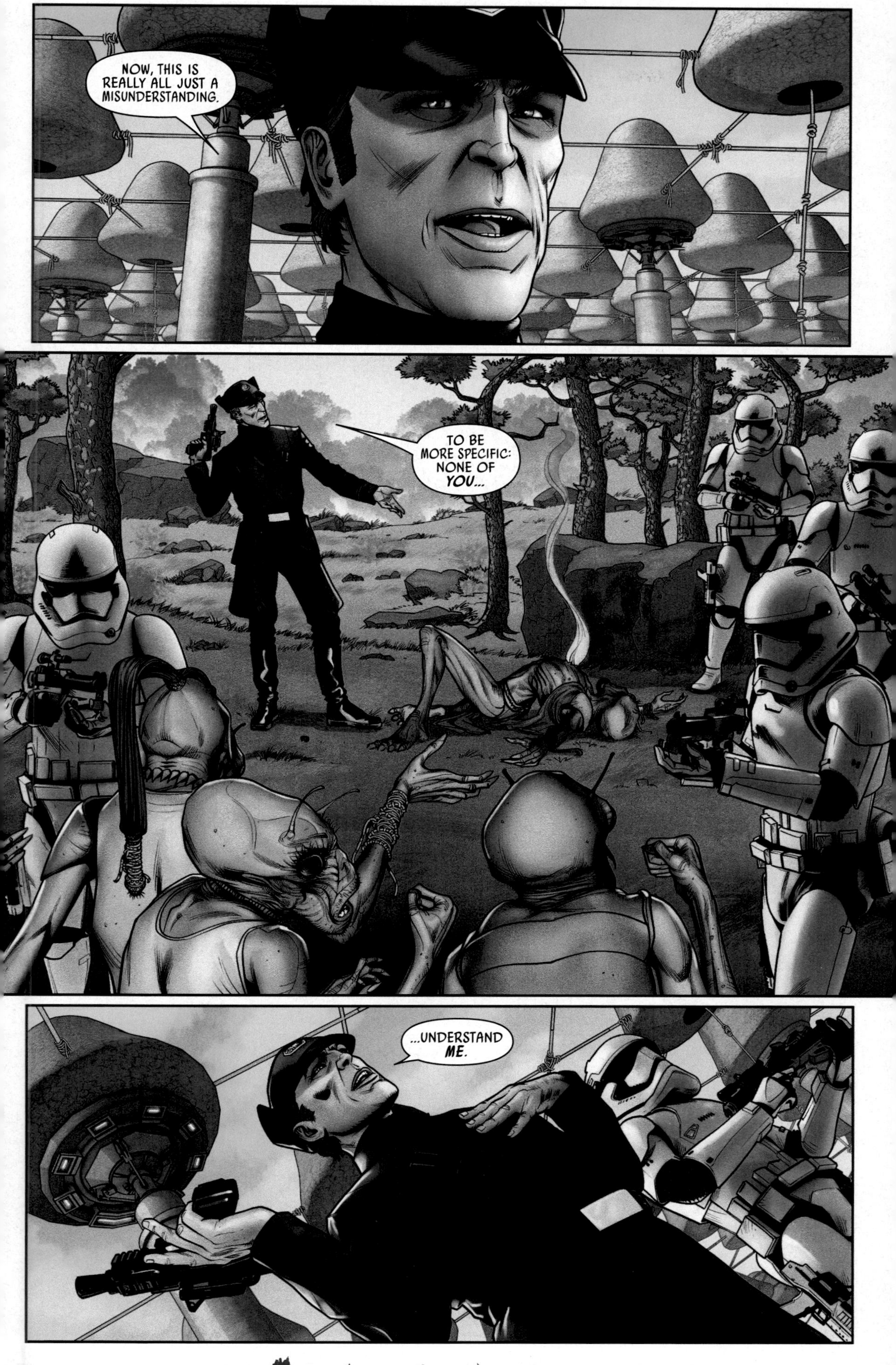
NOW, THIS IS REALLY ALL JUST A MISUNDERSTANDING.
TO BE MORE SPECIFIC: NONE OF YOU...
...UNDERSTAND ME.

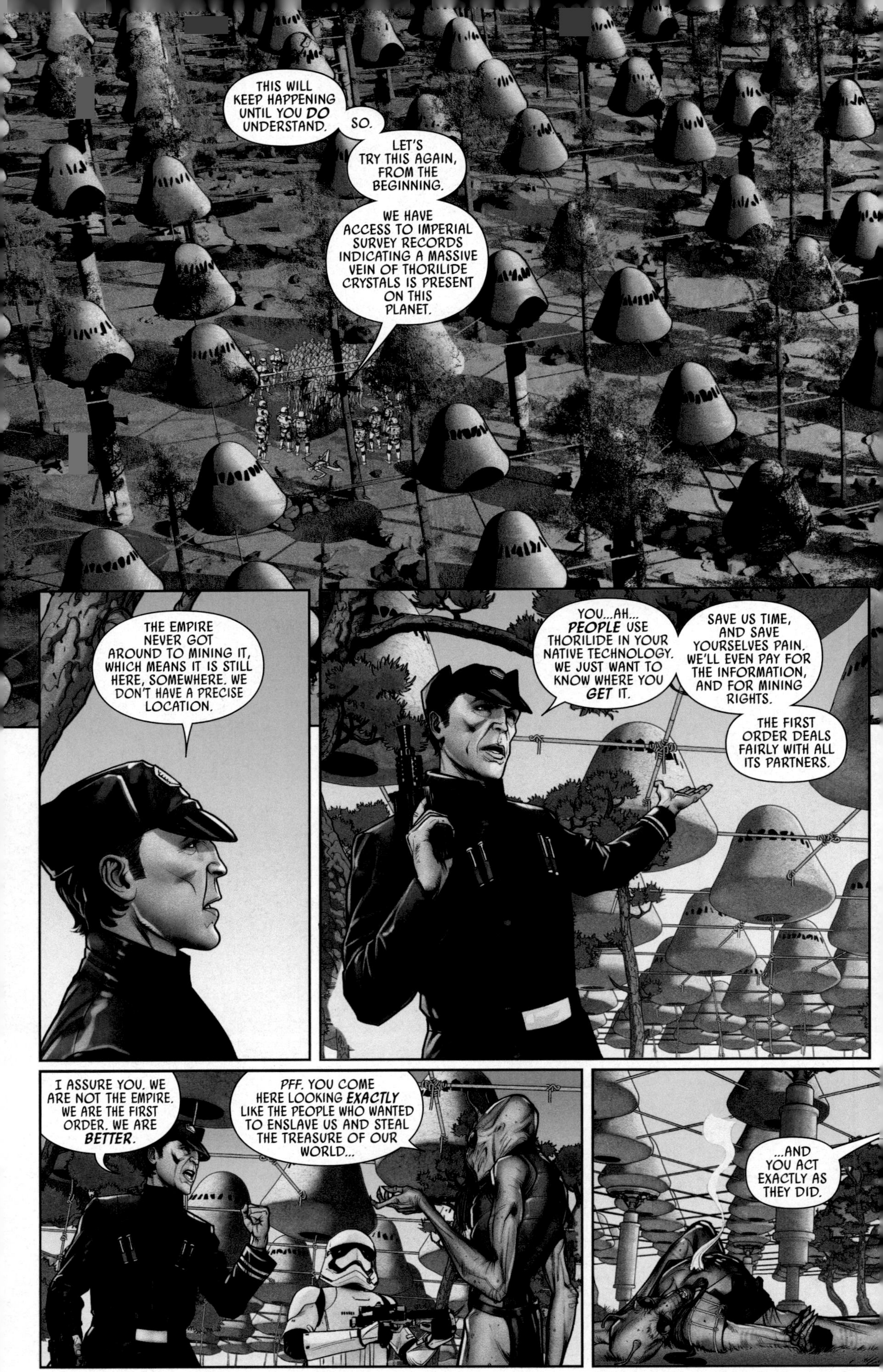
THIS WILL KEEP HAPPENING UNTIL YOU DO UNDERSTAND.
SO.
LET'S TRY THIS AGAIN, FROM THE BEGINNING.
WE HAVE ACCESS TO IMPERIAL SURVEY RECORDS INDICATING A MASSIVE VEIN OF THORILIDE CRYSTALS IS PRESENT ON THIS PLANET.
THE EMPIRE NEVER GOT AROUND TO MINING IT, WHICH MEANS IT IS STILL HERE, SOMEWHERE. WE DON'T HAVE A PRECISE LOCATION.
YOU...AH... PEOPLE USE THORILIDE IN YOUR NATIVE TECHNOLOGY. WE JUST WANT TO KNOW WHERE YOU GET IT.
SAVE US TIME, AND SAVE YOURSELVES PAIN. WE'LL EVEN PAY FOR THE INFORMATION, AND FOR MINING RIGHTS.
THE FIRST ORDER DEALS FAIRLY WITH ALL ITS PARTNERS.
I ASSURE YOU. WE ARE NOT THE EMPIRE. WE ARE THE FIRST ORDER. WE ARE BETTER.
PFF. YOU COME HERE LOOKING EXACTLY LIKE THE PEOPLE WHO WANTED TO ENSLAVE US AND STEAL THE TREASURE OF OUR WORLD...
...AND YOU ACT EXACTLY AS THEY DID.

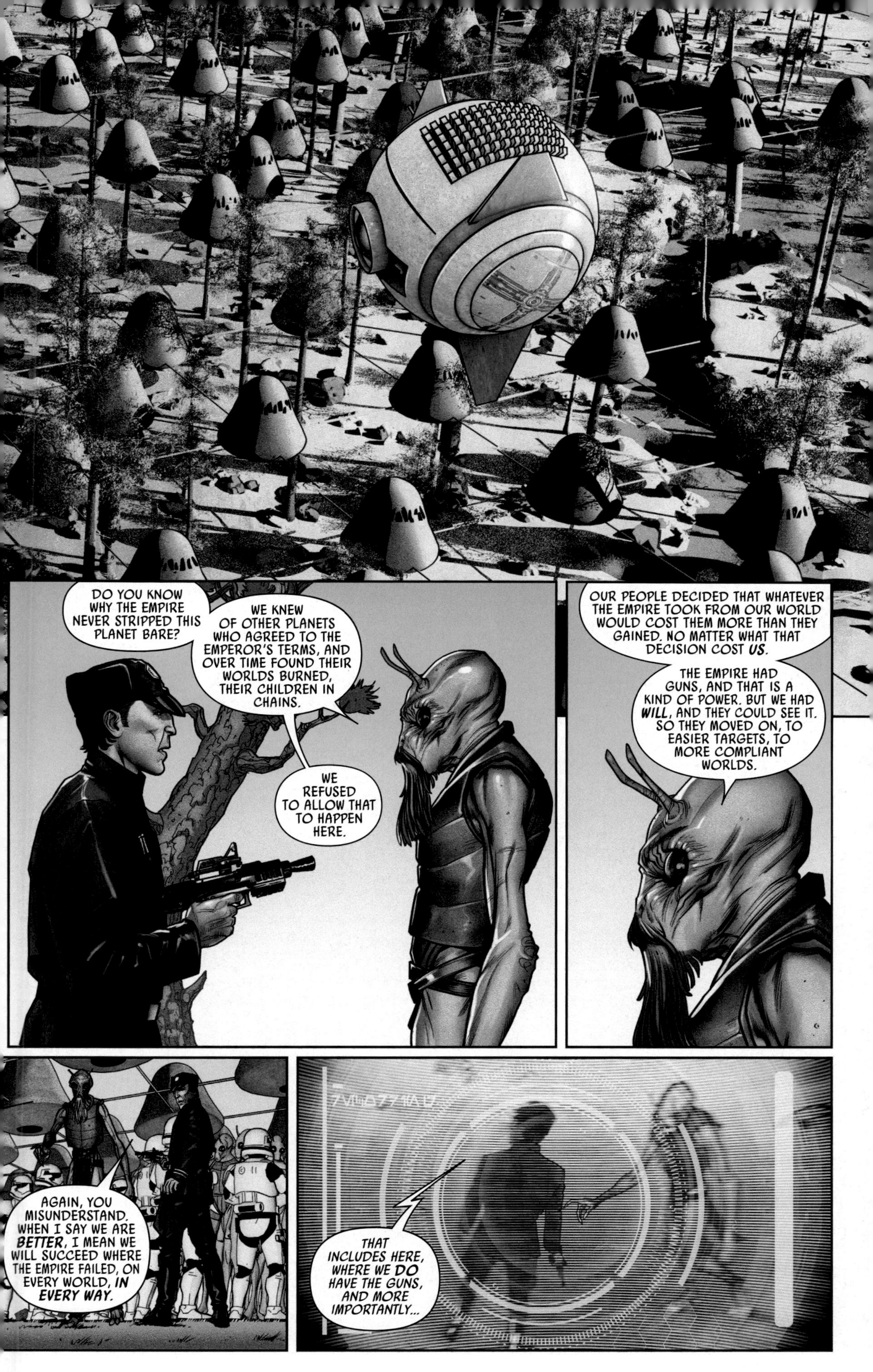
DO YOU KNOW WHY THE EMPIRE NEVER STRIPPED THIS PLANET BARE?
WE KNEW OF OTHER PLANETS WHO AGREED TO THE EMPEROR'S TERMS, AND OVER TIME FOUND THEIR WORLDS BURNED, THEIR CHILDREN IN CHAINS.
WE REFUSED TO ALLOW THAT TO HAPPEN HERE.
OUR PEOPLE DECIDED THAT WHATEVER THE EMPIRE TOOK FROM OUR WORLD WOULD COST THEM MORE THAN THEY GAINED. NO MATTER WHAT THAT DECISION COST *US*.
THE EMPIRE HAD GUNS, AND THAT IS A KIND OF POWER. BUT WE HAD *WILL*, AND THEY COULD SEE IT. SO THEY MOVED ON, TO EASIER TARGETS, TO MORE COMPLIANT WORLDS.
AGAIN, YOU MISUNDERSTAND. WHEN I SAY WE ARE *BETTER*, I MEAN WE WILL SUCCEED WHERE THE EMPIRE FAILED, ON EVERY WORLD, *IN EVERY WAY*.
THAT INCLUDES HERE, WHERE WE DO HAVE THE GUNS, AND MORE IMPORTANTLY...

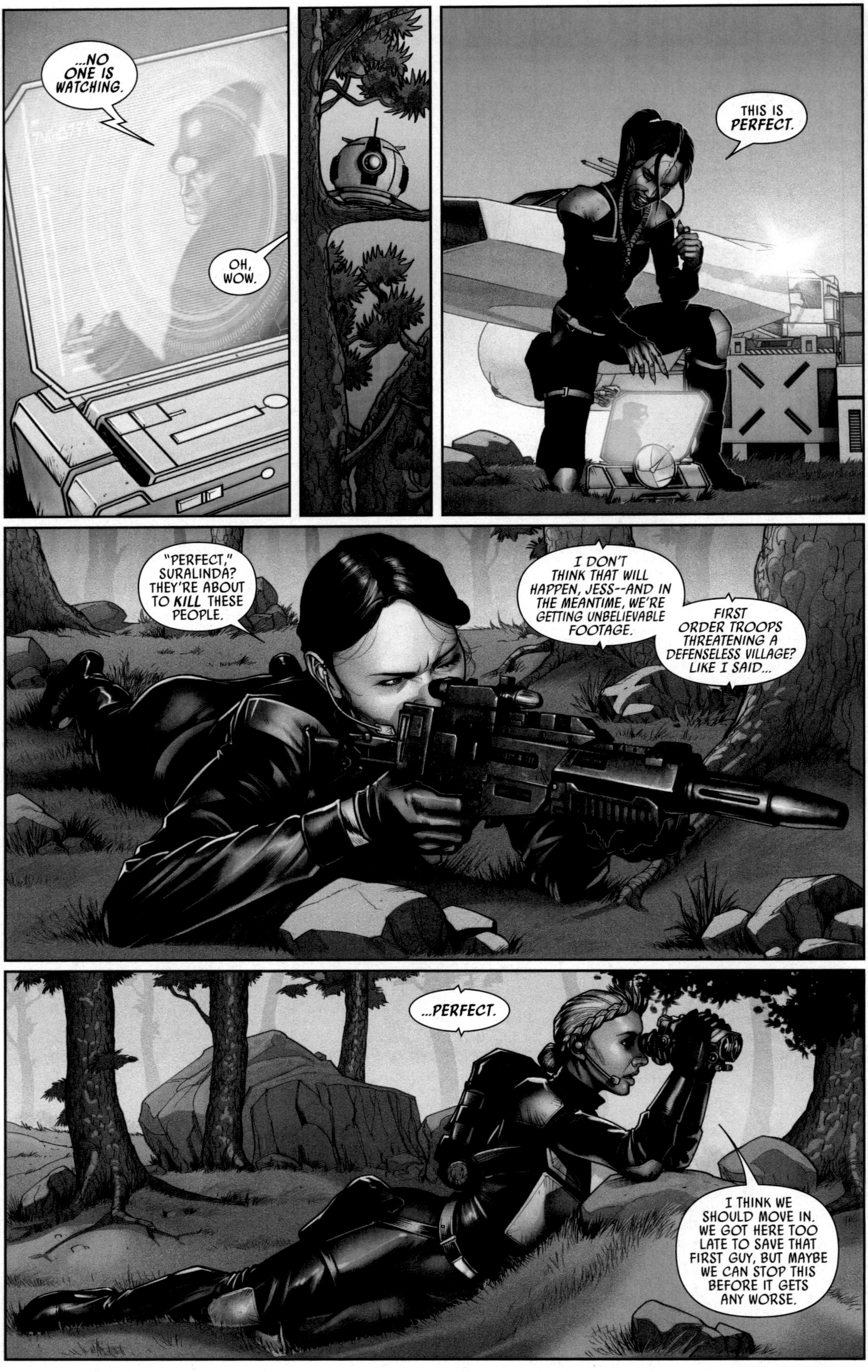
...NO ONE IS WATCHING.
OH, WOW.
THIS IS PERFECT.
"PERFECT," SURALINDA? THEY'RE ABOUT TO KILL THESE PEOPLE.
I DON'T THINK THAT WILL HAPPEN, JESS--AND IN THE MEANTIME, WE'RE GETTING UNBELIEVABLE FOOTAGE.
FIRST ORDER TROOPS THREATENING A DEFENSELESS VILLAGE? LIKE I SAID...
...PERFECT.
I THINK WE SHOULD MOVE IN. WE GOT HERE TOO LATE TO SAVE THAT FIRST GUY, BUT MAYBE WE CAN STOP THIS BEFORE IT GETS ANY WORSE.

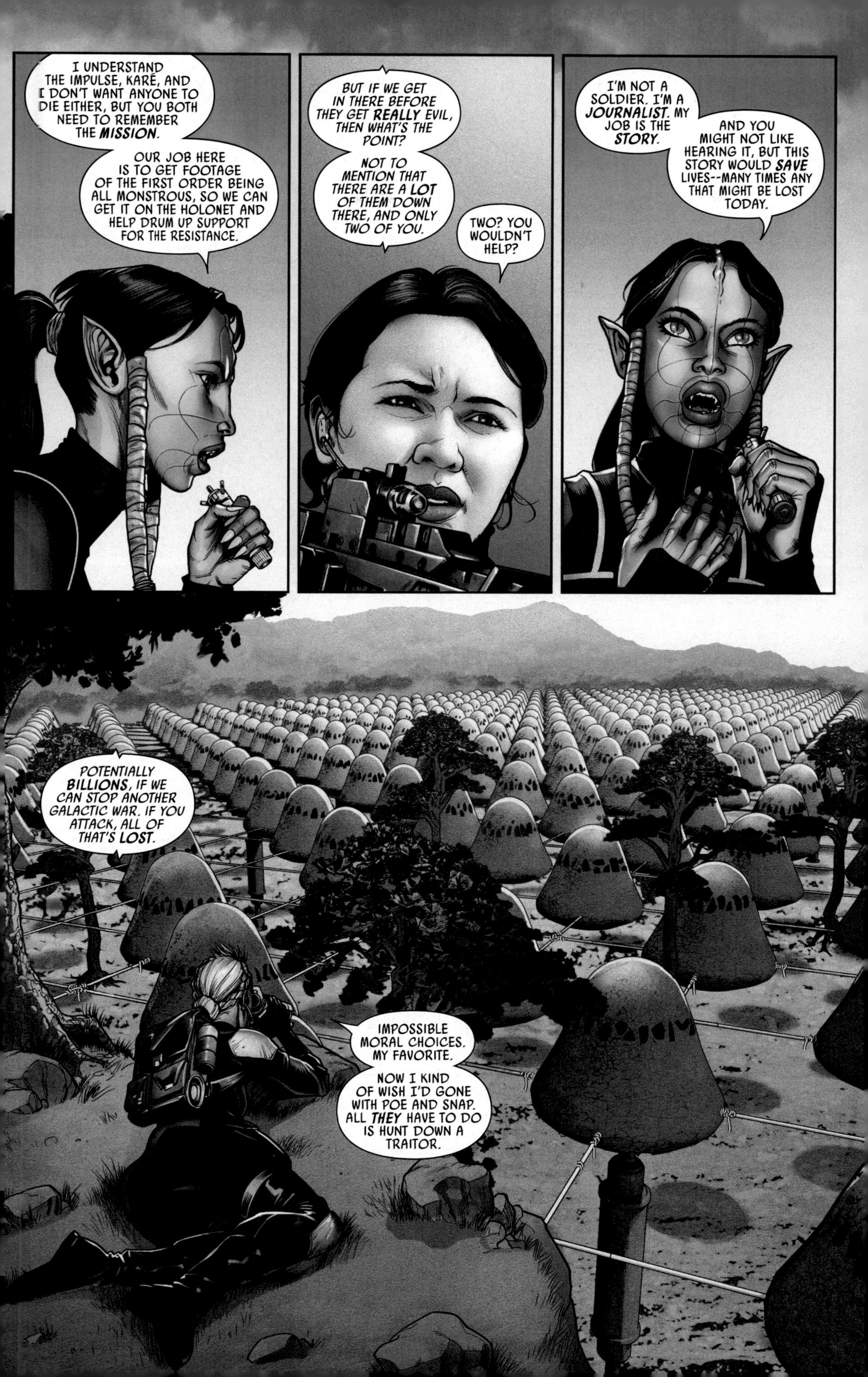
I UNDERSTAND THE IMPULSE, KARÉ, AND I DON'T WANT ANYONE TO DIE EITHER, BUT YOU BOTH NEED TO REMEMBER THE MISSION.
OUR JOB HERE IS TO GET FOOTAGE OF THE FIRST ORDER BEING ALL MONSTROUS, SO WE CAN GET IT ON THE HOLONET AND HELP DRUM UP SUPPORT FOR THE RESISTANCE.
BUT IF WE GET IN THERE BEFORE THEY GET REALLY EVIL, THEN WHAT'S THE POINT?
NOT TO MENTION THAT THERE ARE A LOT OF THEM DOWN THERE, AND ONLY TWO OF YOU.
TWO? YOU WOULDN'T HELP?
I'M NOT A SOLDIER. I'M A JOURNALIST. MY JOB IS THE STORY.
AND YOU MIGHT NOT LIKE HEARING IT, BUT THIS STORY WOULD SAVE LIVES--MANY TIMES ANY THAT MIGHT BE LOST TODAY.
POTENTIALLY BILLIONS, IF WE CAN STOP ANOTHER GALACTIC WAR. IF YOU ATTACK, ALL OF THAT'S LOST.
IMPOSSIBLE MORAL CHOICES. MY FAVORITE.
NOW I KIND OF WISH I'D GONE WITH POE AND SNAP. ALL THEY HAVE TO DO IS HUNT DOWN A TRAITOR.

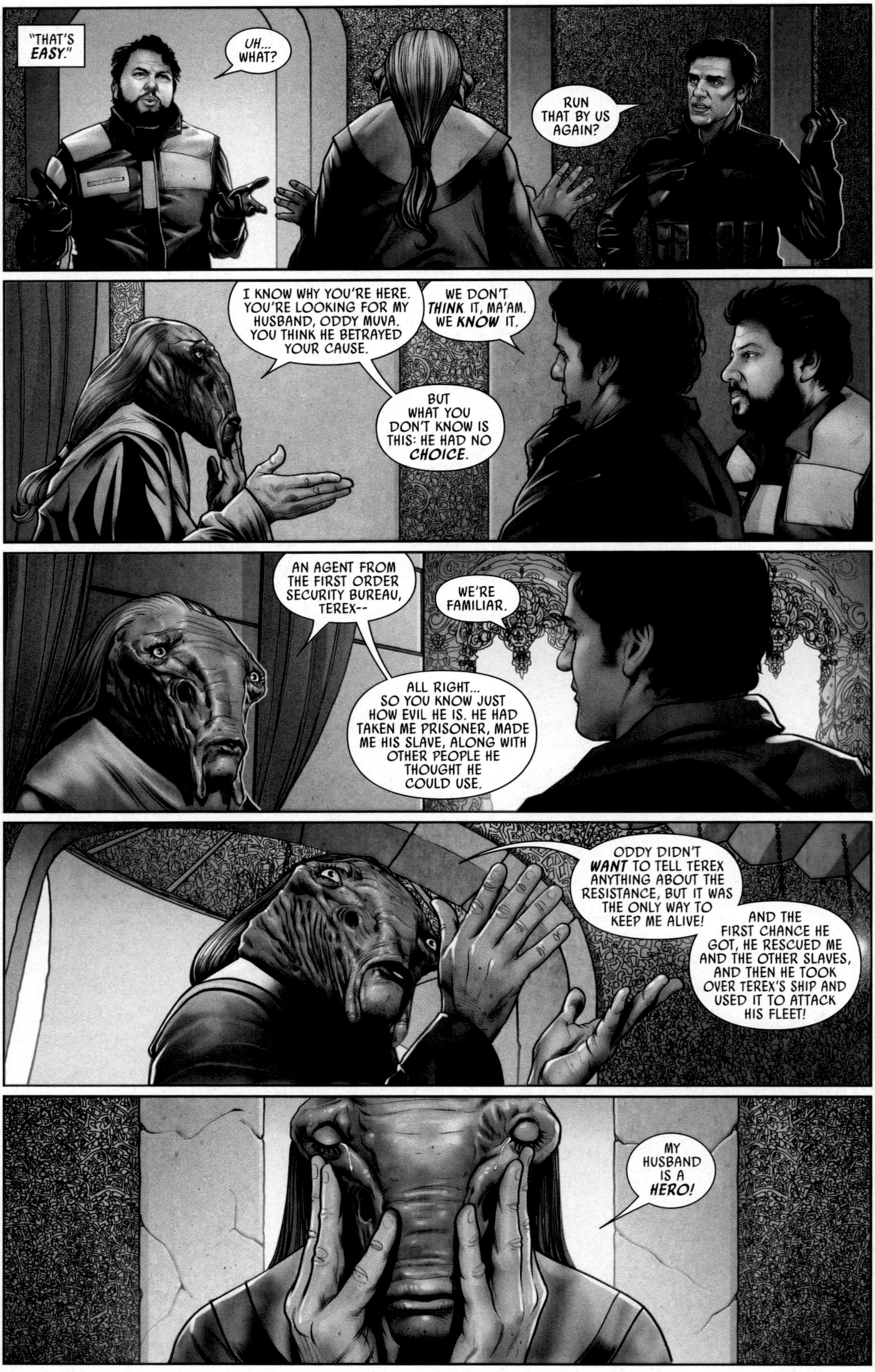
"THAT'S *EASY*."
UH... WHAT?
RUN THAT BY US AGAIN?
I KNOW WHY YOU'RE HERE. YOU'RE LOOKING FOR MY HUSBAND, ODDY MUVA. YOU THINK HE BETRAYED YOUR CAUSE.
WE DON'T *THINK* IT, MA'AM. WE *KNOW* IT.
BUT WHAT YOU DON'T KNOW IS THIS: HE HAD NO *CHOICE*.
AN AGENT FROM THE FIRST ORDER SECURITY BUREAU, TEREX--
WE'RE FAMILIAR.
ALL RIGHT... SO YOU KNOW JUST HOW EVIL HE IS. HE HAD TAKEN ME PRISONER, MADE ME HIS SLAVE, ALONG WITH OTHER PEOPLE HE THOUGHT HE COULD USE.
ODDY DIDN'T *WANT* TO TELL TEREX ANYTHING ABOUT THE RESISTANCE, BUT IT WAS THE ONLY WAY TO KEEP ME ALIVE!
AND THE FIRST CHANCE HE GOT, HE RESCUED ME AND THE OTHER SLAVES, AND THEN HE TOOK OVER TEREX'S SHIP AND USED IT TO ATTACK HIS FLEET!
MY HUSBAND IS A *HERO*!

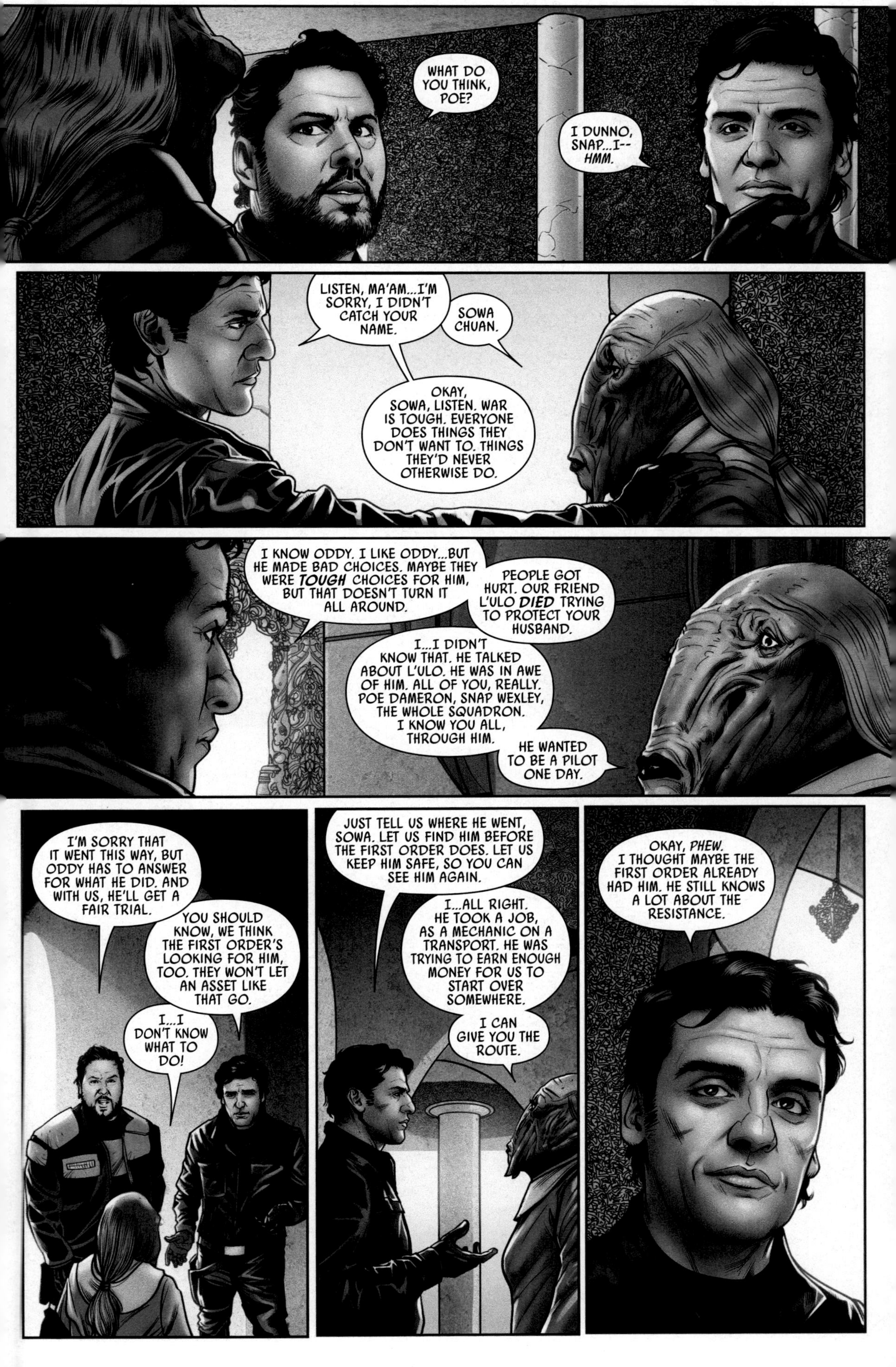
WHAT DO YOU THINK, POE?
I DUNNO, SNAP...I-- HMM.
LISTEN, MA'AM...I'M SORRY, I DIDN'T CATCH YOUR NAME.
SOWA CHUAN.
OKAY, SOWA, LISTEN. WAR IS TOUGH. EVERYONE DOES THINGS THEY DON'T WANT TO. THINGS THEY'D NEVER OTHERWISE DO.
I KNOW ODDY. I LIKE ODDY...BUT HE MADE BAD CHOICES. MAYBE THEY WERE TOUGH CHOICES FOR HIM, BUT THAT DOESN'T TURN IT ALL AROUND.
PEOPLE GOT HURT. OUR FRIEND L'ULO DIED TRYING TO PROTECT YOUR HUSBAND.
I...I DIDN'T KNOW THAT. HE TALKED ABOUT L'ULO. HE WAS IN AWE OF HIM. ALL OF YOU, REALLY. POE DAMERON, SNAP WEXLEY, THE WHOLE SQUADRON. I KNOW YOU ALL, THROUGH HIM.
HE WANTED TO BE A PILOT ONE DAY.
I'M SORRY THAT IT WENT THIS WAY, BUT ODDY HAS TO ANSWER FOR WHAT HE DID. AND WITH US, HE'LL GET A FAIR TRIAL.
YOU SHOULD KNOW, WE THINK THE FIRST ORDER'S LOOKING FOR HIM, TOO. THEY WON'T LET AN ASSET LIKE THAT GO.
I...I DON'T KNOW WHAT TO DO!
JUST TELL US WHERE HE WENT, SOWA. LET US FIND HIM BEFORE THE FIRST ORDER DOES. LET US KEEP HIM SAFE, SO YOU CAN SEE HIM AGAIN.
I...ALL RIGHT. HE TOOK A JOB, AS A MECHANIC ON A TRANSPORT. HE WAS TRYING TO EARN ENOUGH MONEY FOR US TO START OVER SOMEWHERE.
I CAN GIVE YOU THE ROUTE.
OKAY, PHEW. I THOUGHT MAYBE THE FIRST ORDER ALREADY HAD HIM. HE STILL KNOWS A LOT ABOUT THE RESISTANCE.

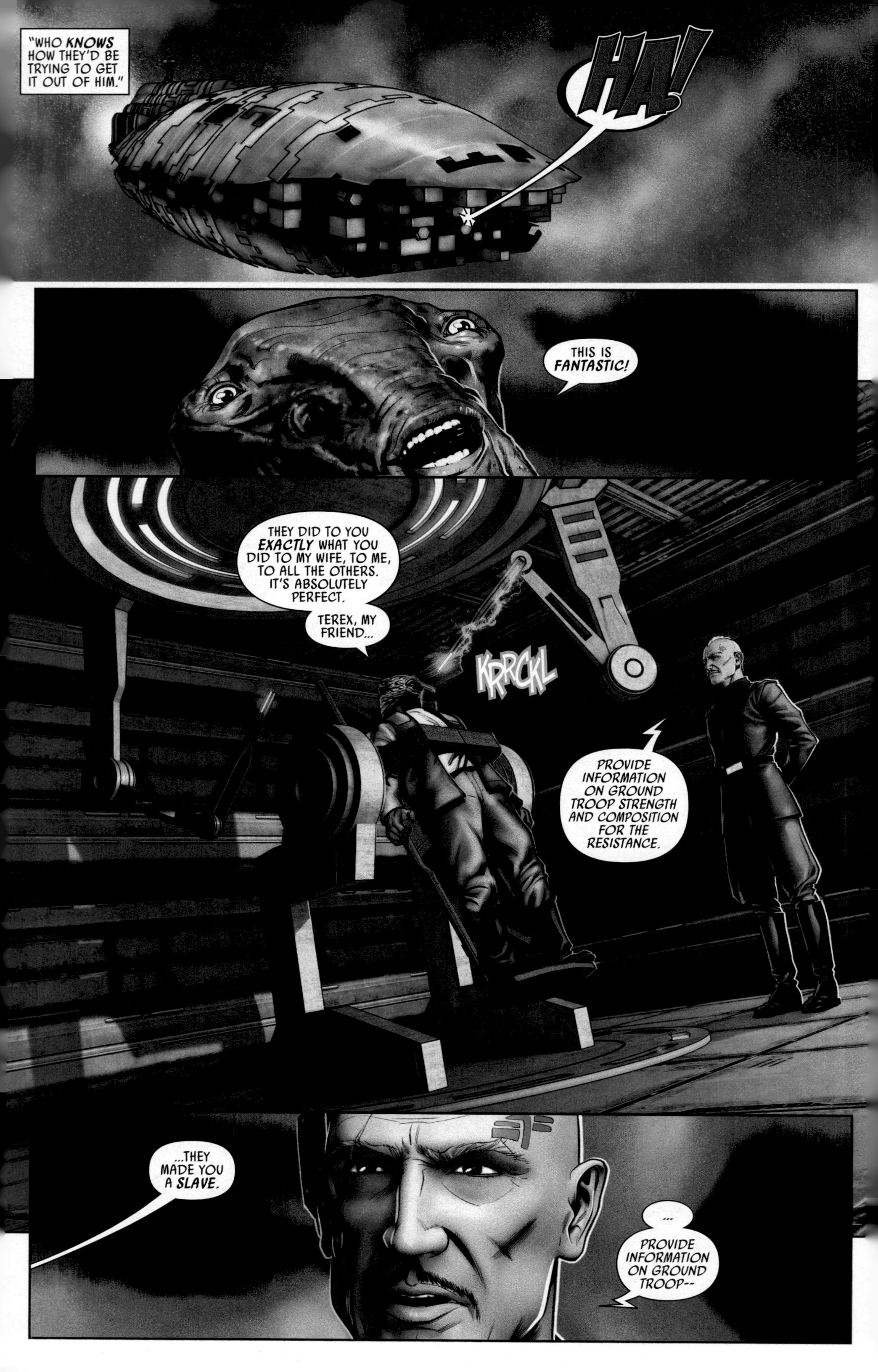
"WHO KNOWS HOW THEY'D BE TRYING TO GET IT OUT OF HIM."
HA!
THIS IS FANTASTIC!
THEY DID TO YOU EXACTLY WHAT YOU DID TO MY WIFE, TO ME, TO ALL THE OTHERS. IT'S ABSOLUTELY PERFECT.
TEREX, MY FRIEND...
KRRCKL
PROVIDE INFORMATION ON GROUND TROOP STRENGTH AND COMPOSITION FOR THE RESISTANCE.
...THEY MADE YOU A SLAVE.
...
PROVIDE INFORMATION ON GROUND TROOP--

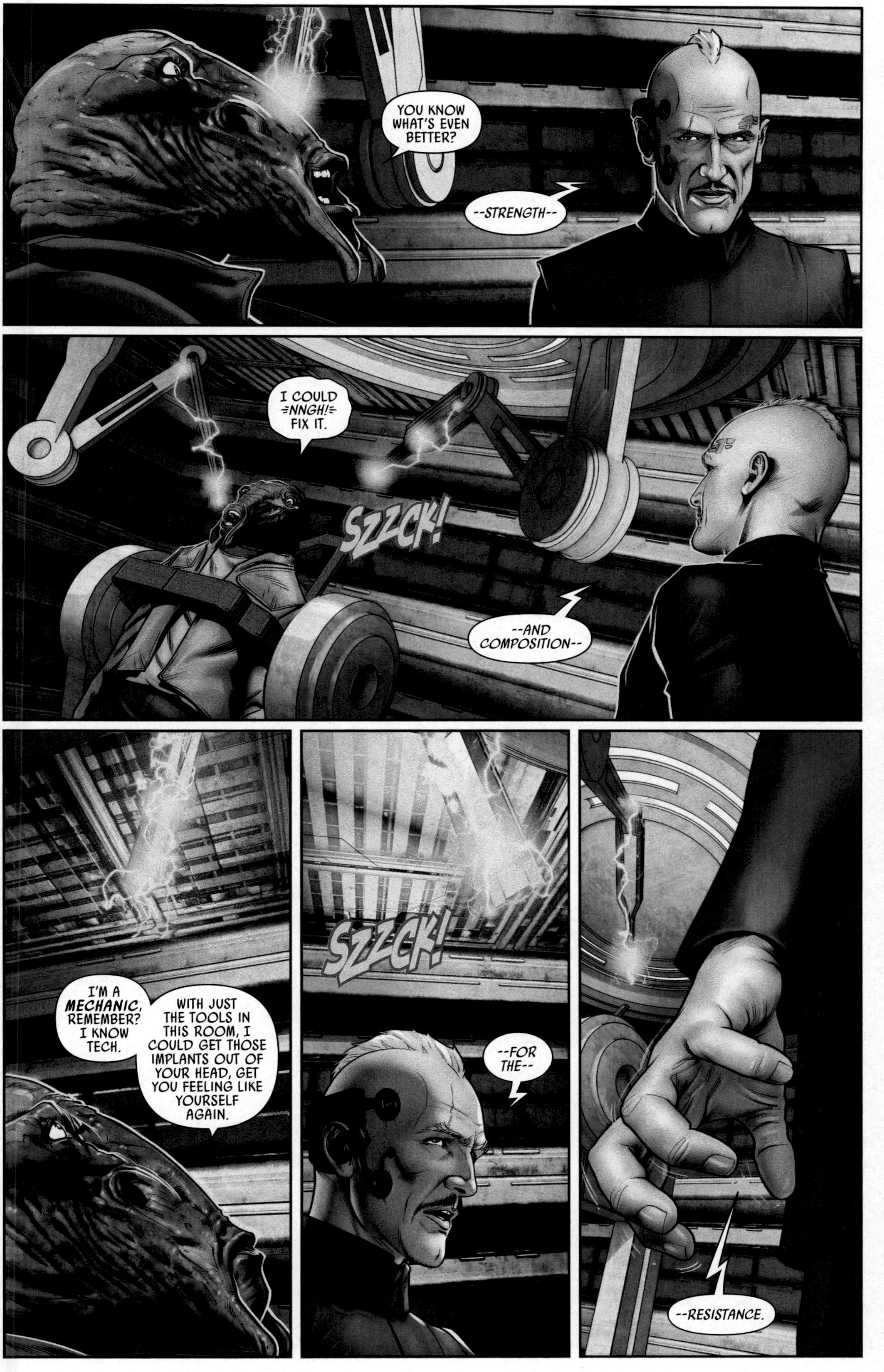
YOU KNOW WHAT'S EVEN BETTER?
--STRENGTH--
I COULD =NNGH!= FIX IT.
SZZCK!
--AND COMPOSITION--
I'M A *MECHANIC*, REMEMBER? I KNOW TECH.
WITH JUST THE TOOLS IN THIS ROOM, I COULD GET THOSE IMPLANTS OUT OF YOUR HEAD, GET YOU FEELING LIKE YOURSELF AGAIN.
SZZCK!
--FOR THE--
--RESISTANCE.

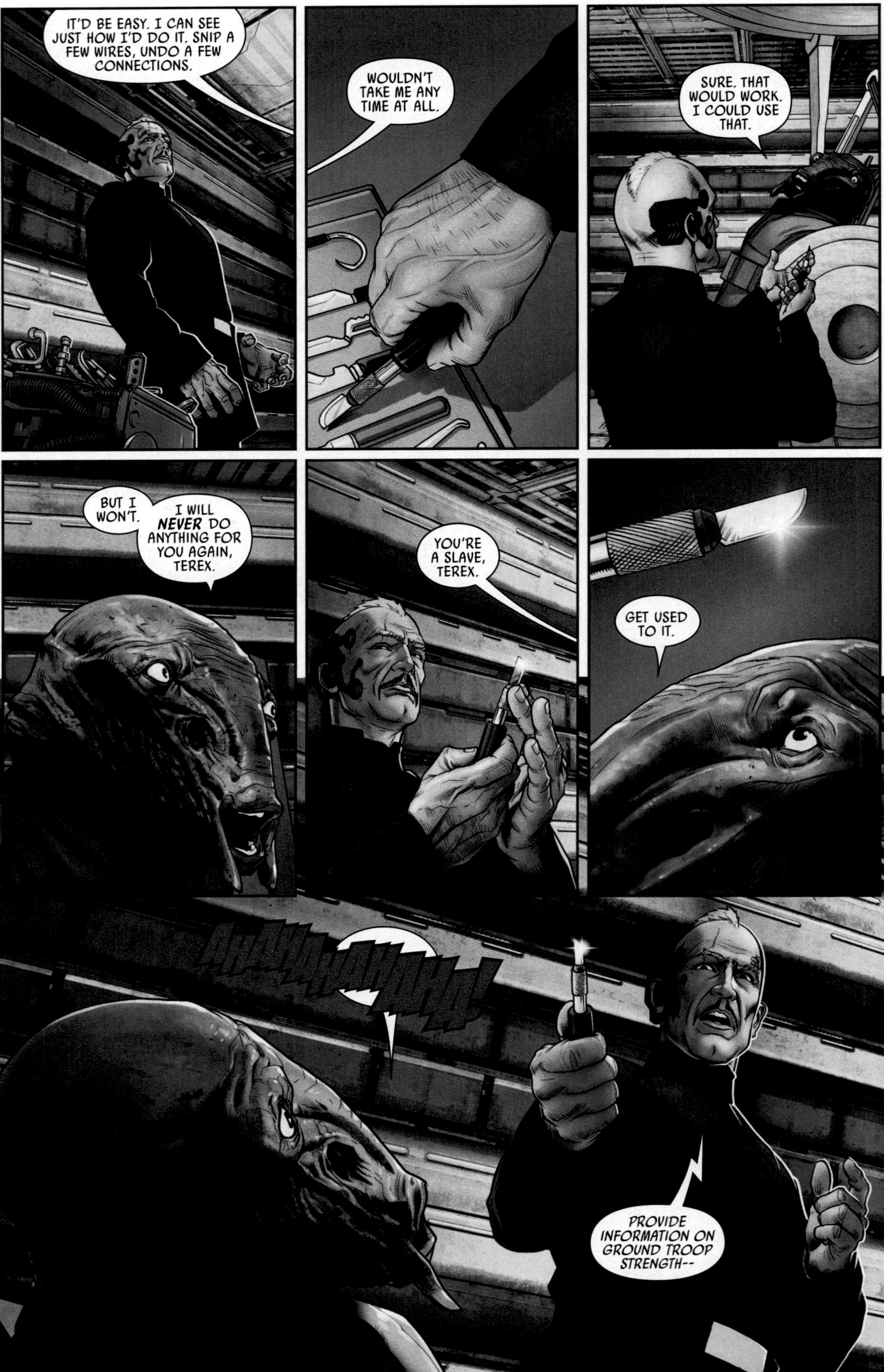
IT'D BE EASY. I CAN SEE JUST HOW I'D DO IT. SNIP A FEW WIRES, UNDO A FEW CONNECTIONS.
WOULDN'T TAKE ME ANY TIME AT ALL.
SURE. THAT WOULD WORK. I COULD USE THAT.
BUT I WON'T.
I WILL **NEVER** DO ANYTHING FOR YOU AGAIN, TEREX.
YOU'RE A SLAVE, TEREX.
GET USED TO IT.
PROVIDE INFORMATION ON GROUND TROOP STRENGTH--

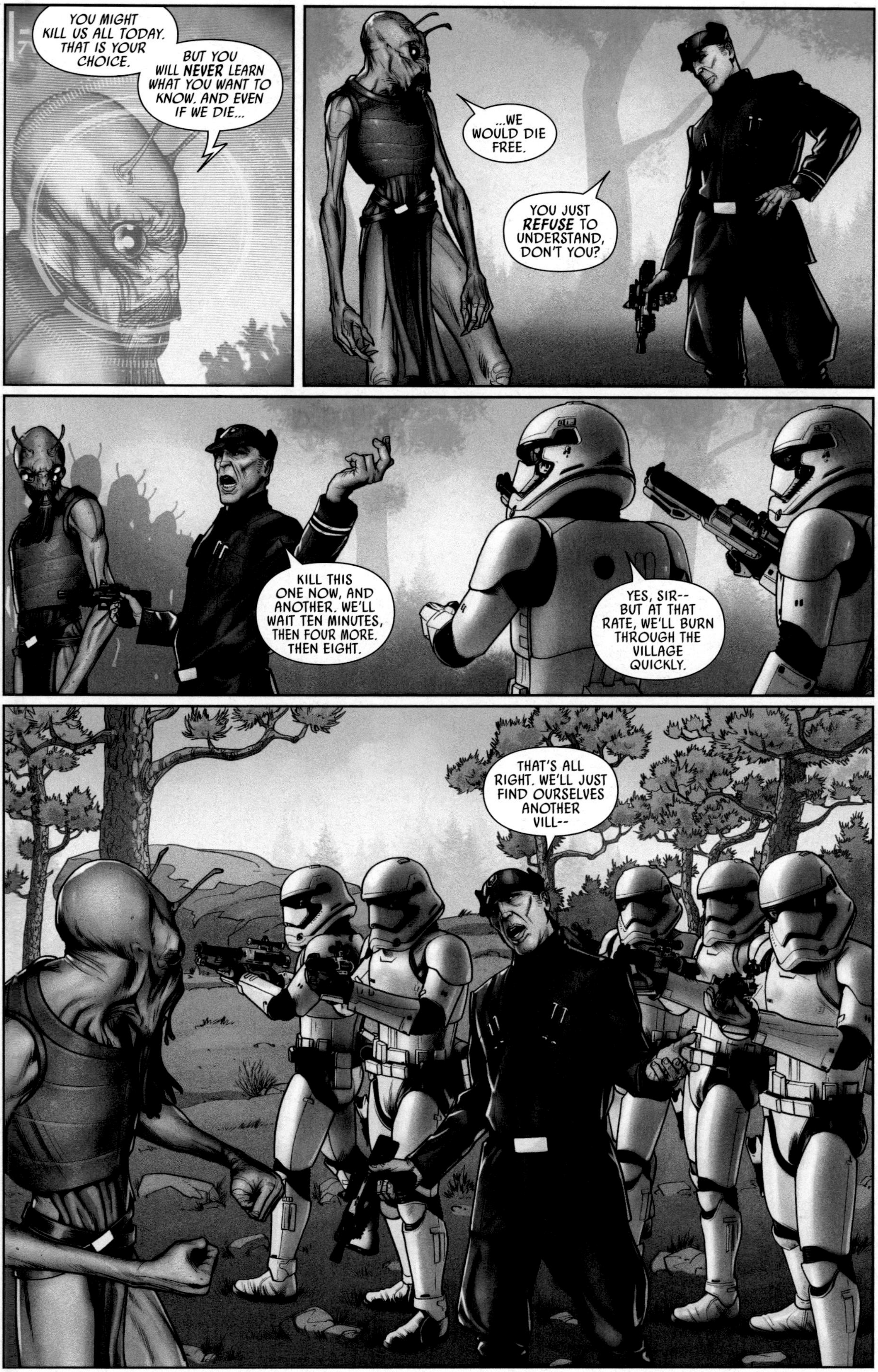
YOU MIGHT KILL US ALL TODAY. THAT IS YOUR CHOICE.
BUT YOU WILL NEVER LEARN WHAT YOU WANT TO KNOW. AND EVEN IF WE DIE...
...WE WOULD DIE FREE.
YOU JUST REFUSE TO UNDERSTAND, DON'T YOU?
KILL THIS ONE NOW, AND ANOTHER. WE'LL WAIT TEN MINUTES, THEN FOUR MORE. THEN EIGHT.
YES, SIR-- BUT AT THAT RATE, WE'LL BURN THROUGH THE VILLAGE QUICKLY.
THAT'S ALL RIGHT. WE'LL JUST FIND OURSELVES ANOTHER VILL--

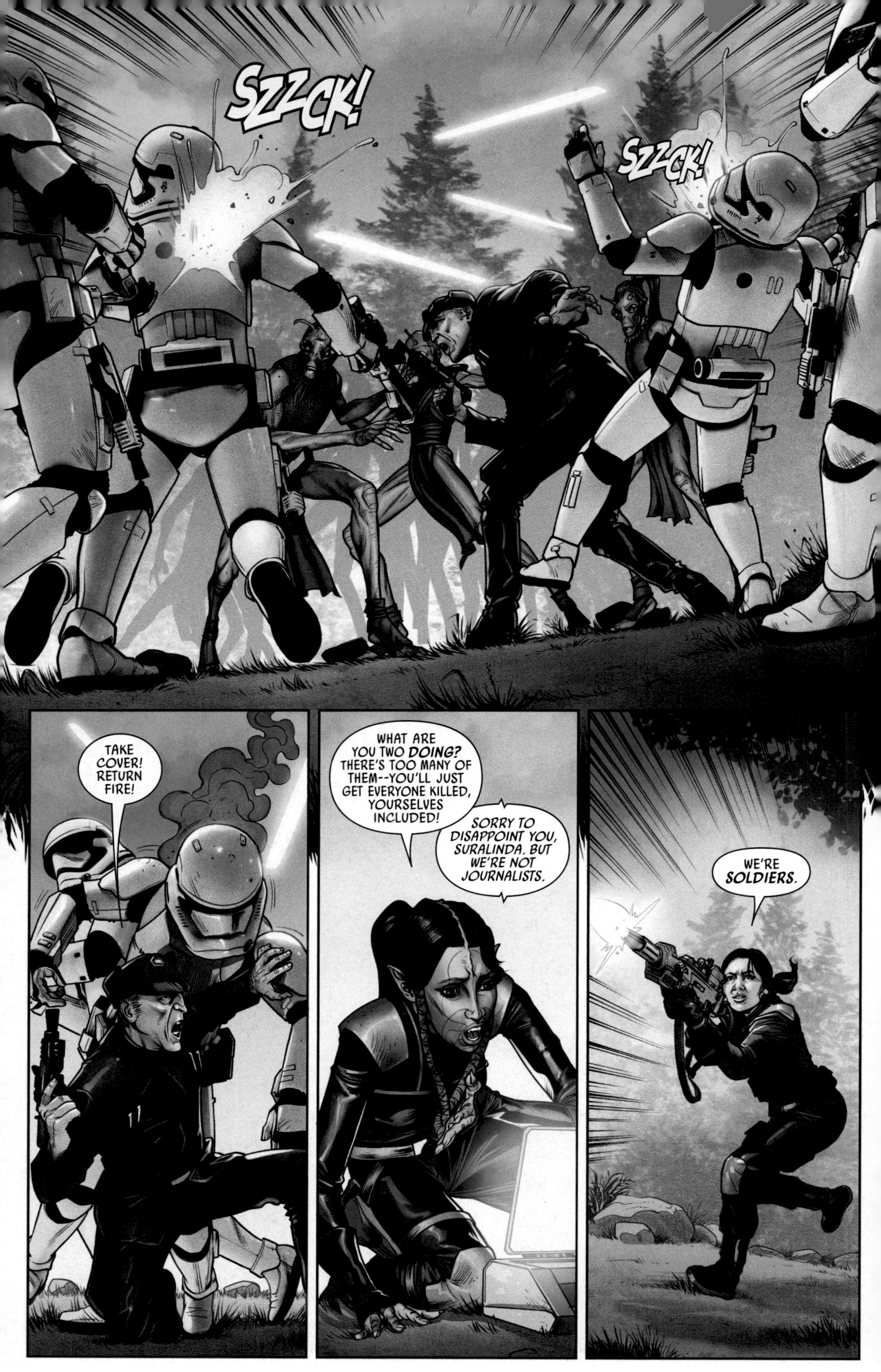
SZZCK!
SZZCK!
TAKE COVER! RETURN FIRE!
WHAT ARE YOU TWO DOING? THERE'S TOO MANY OF THEM--YOU'LL JUST GET EVERYONE KILLED, YOURSELVES INCLUDED!
SORRY TO DISAPPOINT YOU, SURALINDA. BUT WE'RE NOT JOURNALISTS.
WE'RE SOLDIERS.

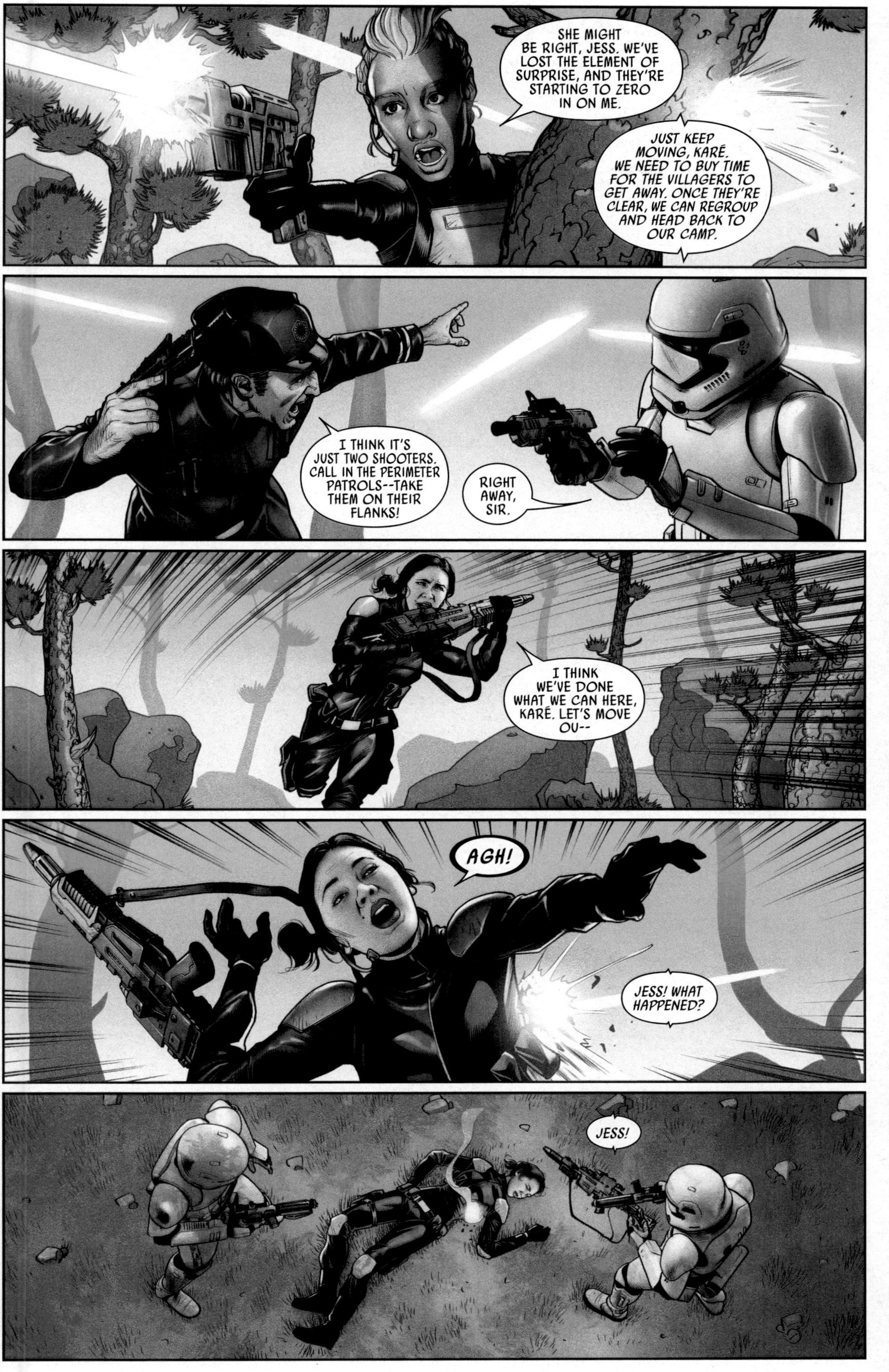
SHE MIGHT BE RIGHT, JESS. WE'VE LOST THE ELEMENT OF SURPRISE, AND THEY'RE STARTING TO ZERO IN ON ME.
JUST KEEP MOVING, KARÉ. WE NEED TO BUY TIME FOR THE VILLAGERS TO GET AWAY. ONCE THEY'RE CLEAR, WE CAN REGROUP AND HEAD BACK TO OUR CAMP.
I THINK IT'S JUST TWO SHOOTERS. CALL IN THE PERIMETER PATROLS--TAKE THEM ON THEIR FLANKS!
RIGHT AWAY, SIR.
I THINK WE'VE DONE WHAT WE CAN HERE, KARÉ. LET'S MOVE OU--
AGH!
JESS! WHAT HAPPENED?
JESS!

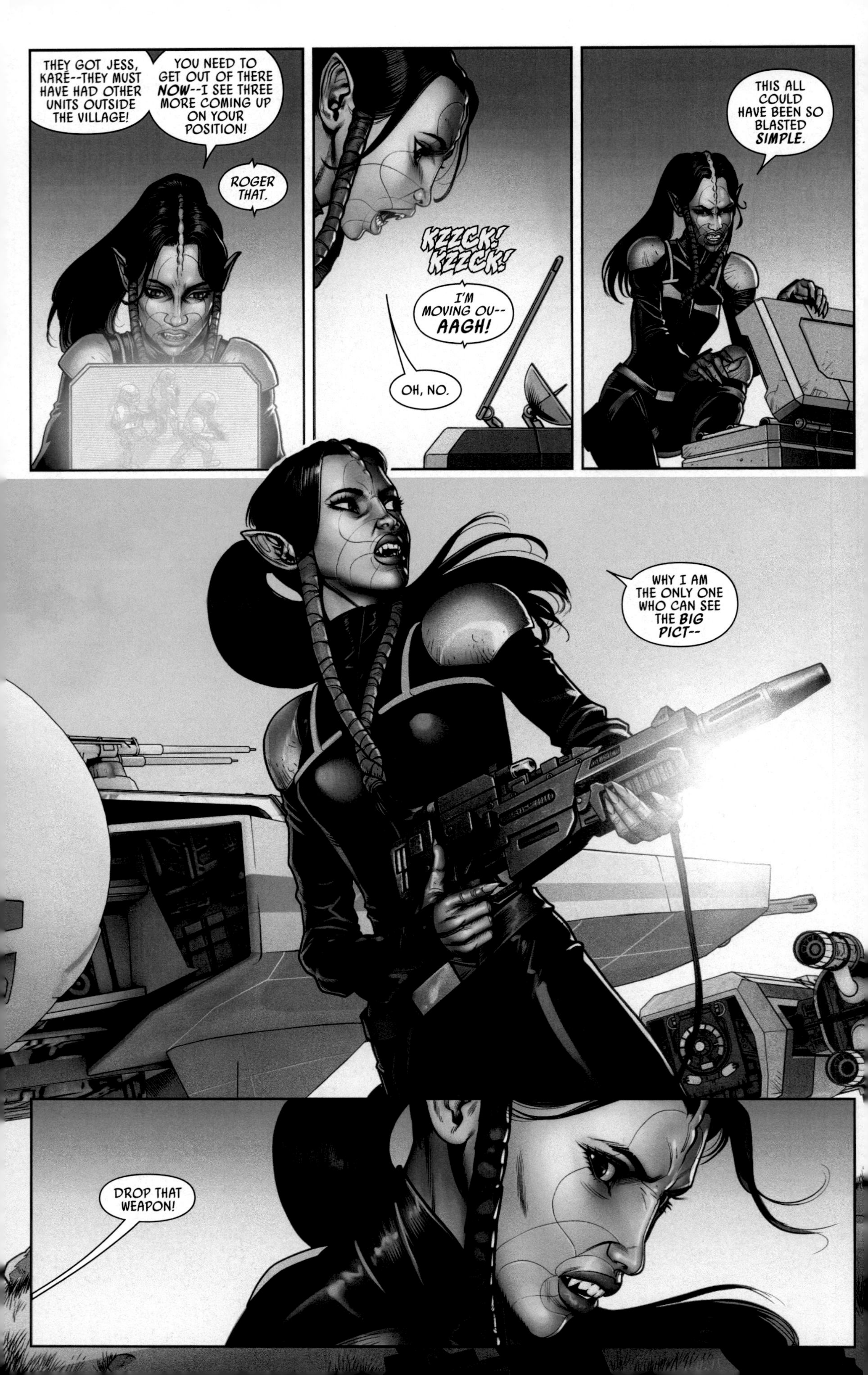
THEY GOT JESS, KARÉ--THEY MUST HAVE HAD OTHER UNITS OUTSIDE THE VILLAGE!
YOU NEED TO GET OUT OF THERE NOW--I SEE THREE MORE COMING UP ON YOUR POSITION!
ROGER THAT.
KZZCK! KZZCK!
I'M MOVING OU-- AAGH!
OH, NO.
THIS ALL COULD HAVE BEEN SO BLASTED SIMPLE.
WHY I AM THE ONLY ONE WHO CAN SEE THE BIG PICT--
DROP THAT WEAPON!

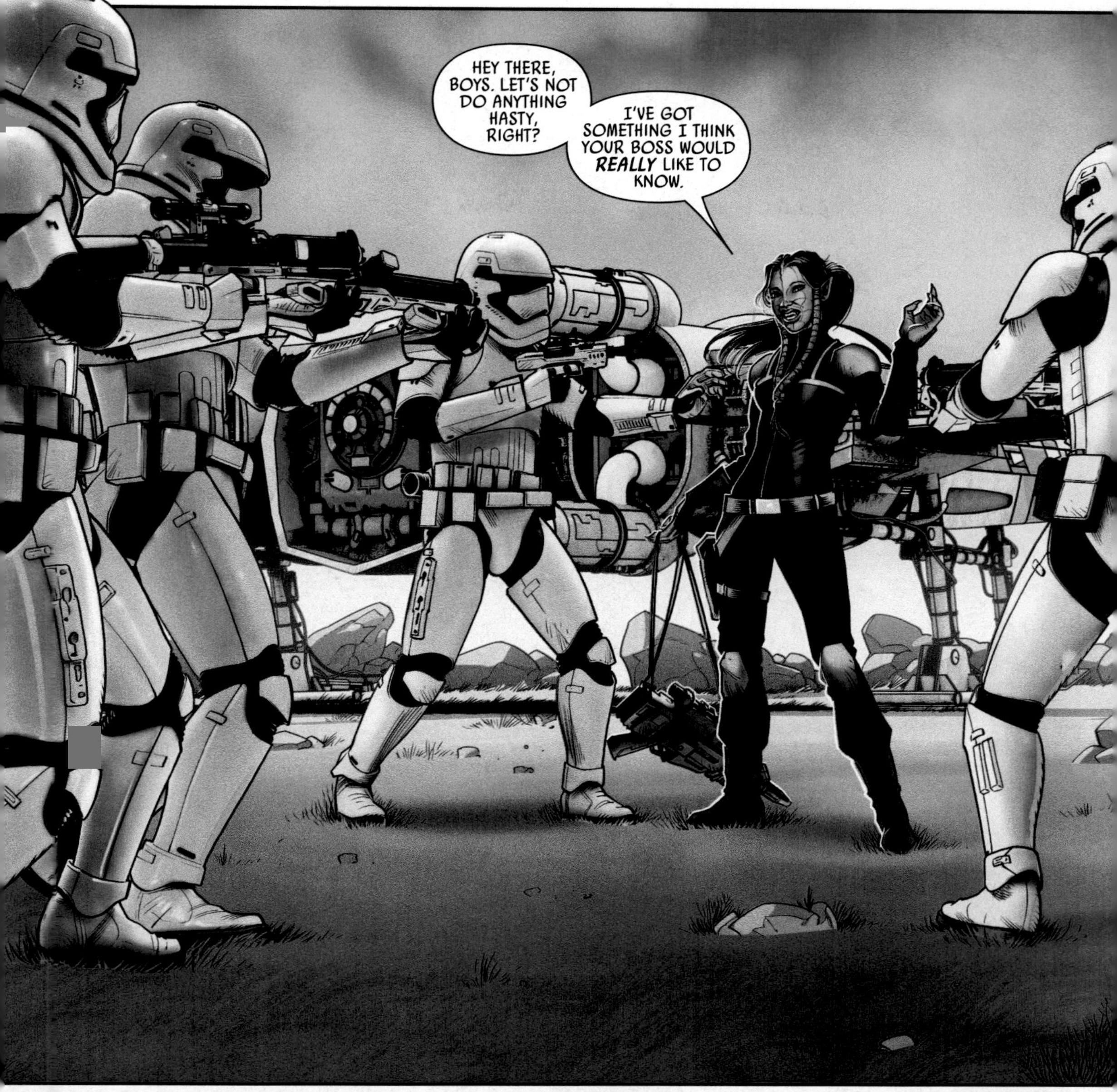
HEY THERE, BOYS. LET'S NOT DO ANYTHING HASTY, RIGHT?
I'VE GOT SOMETHING I THINK YOUR BOSS WOULD *REALLY* LIKE TO KNOW.

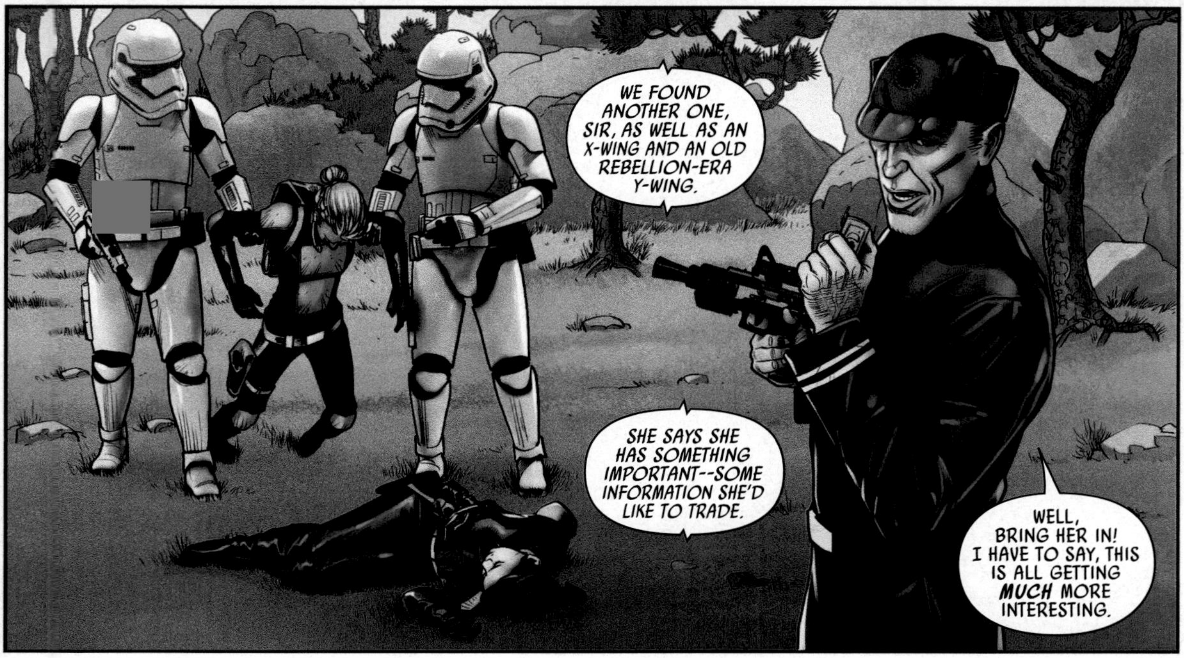
WE FOUND ANOTHER ONE, SIR, AS WELL AS AN X-WING AND AN OLD REBELLION-ERA Y-WING.
SHE SAYS SHE HAS SOMETHING IMPORTANT--SOME INFORMATION SHE'D LIKE TO TRADE.
WELL, BRING HER IN! I HAVE TO SAY, THIS IS ALL GETTING *MUCH* MORE INTERESTING.

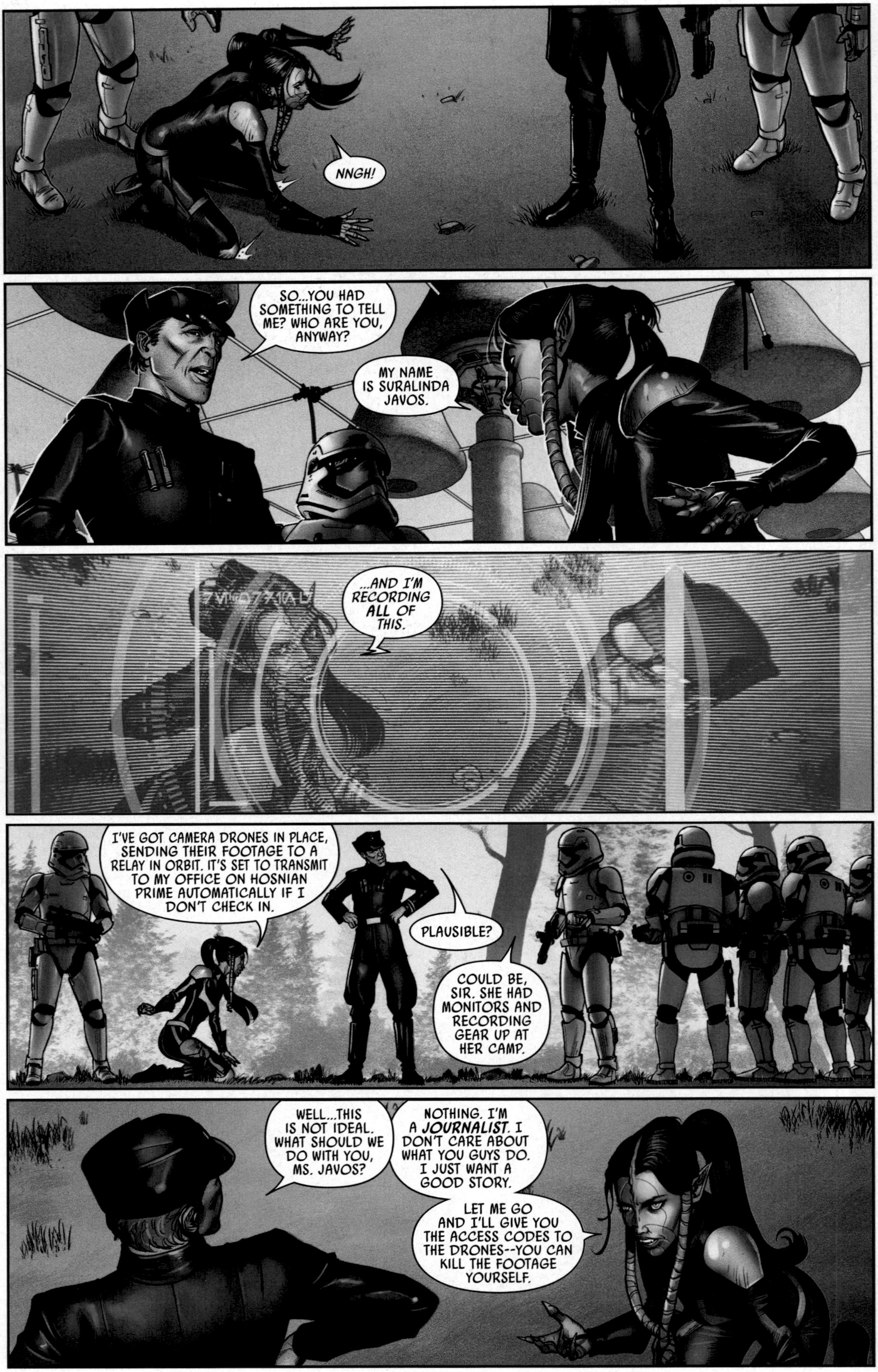
NNGH!
SO...YOU HAD SOMETHING TO TELL ME? WHO ARE YOU, ANYWAY?
MY NAME IS SURALINDA JAVOS.
...AND I'M RECORDING ALL OF THIS.
I'VE GOT CAMERA DRONES IN PLACE, SENDING THEIR FOOTAGE TO A RELAY IN ORBIT. IT'S SET TO TRANSMIT TO MY OFFICE ON HOSNIAN PRIME AUTOMATICALLY IF I DON'T CHECK IN.
PLAUSIBLE?
COULD BE, SIR. SHE HAD MONITORS AND RECORDING GEAR UP AT HER CAMP.
WELL...THIS IS NOT IDEAL. WHAT SHOULD WE DO WITH YOU, MS. JAVOS?
NOTHING. I'M A JOURNALIST. I DON'T CARE ABOUT WHAT YOU GUYS DO. I JUST WANT A GOOD STORY.
LET ME GO AND I'LL GIVE YOU THE ACCESS CODES TO THE DRONES--YOU CAN KILL THE FOOTAGE YOURSELF.

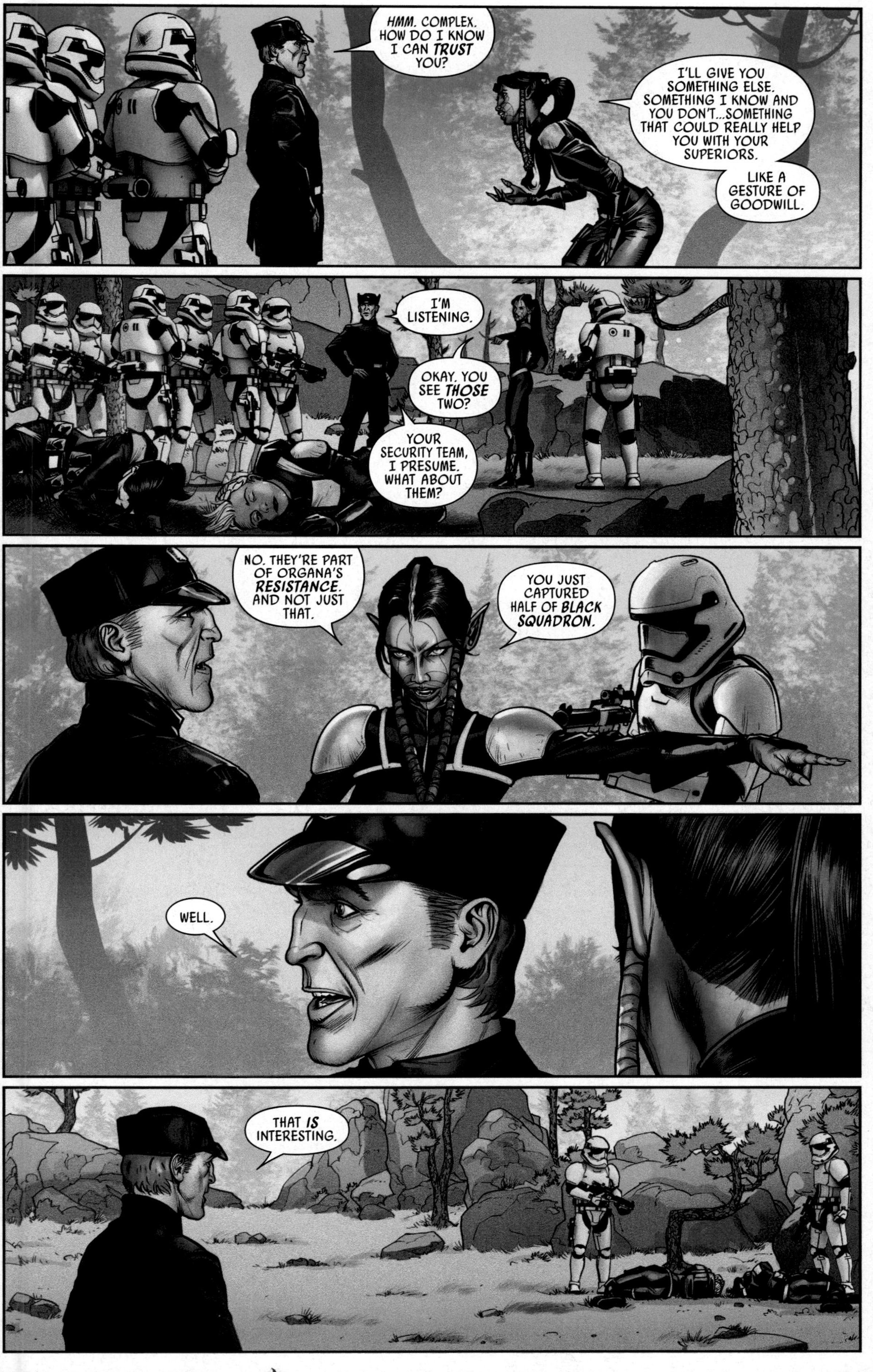
HMM. COMPLEX. HOW DO I KNOW I CAN TRUST YOU?
I'LL GIVE YOU SOMETHING ELSE. SOMETHING I KNOW AND YOU DON'T...SOMETHING THAT COULD REALLY HELP YOU WITH YOUR SUPERIORS.
LIKE A GESTURE OF GOODWILL.
I'M LISTENING.
OKAY. YOU SEE THOSE TWO?
YOUR SECURITY TEAM, I PRESUME. WHAT ABOUT THEM?
NO. THEY'RE PART OF ORGANA'S RESISTANCE. AND NOT JUST THAT.
YOU JUST CAPTURED HALF OF BLACK SQUADRON.
WELL.
THAT IS INTERESTING.

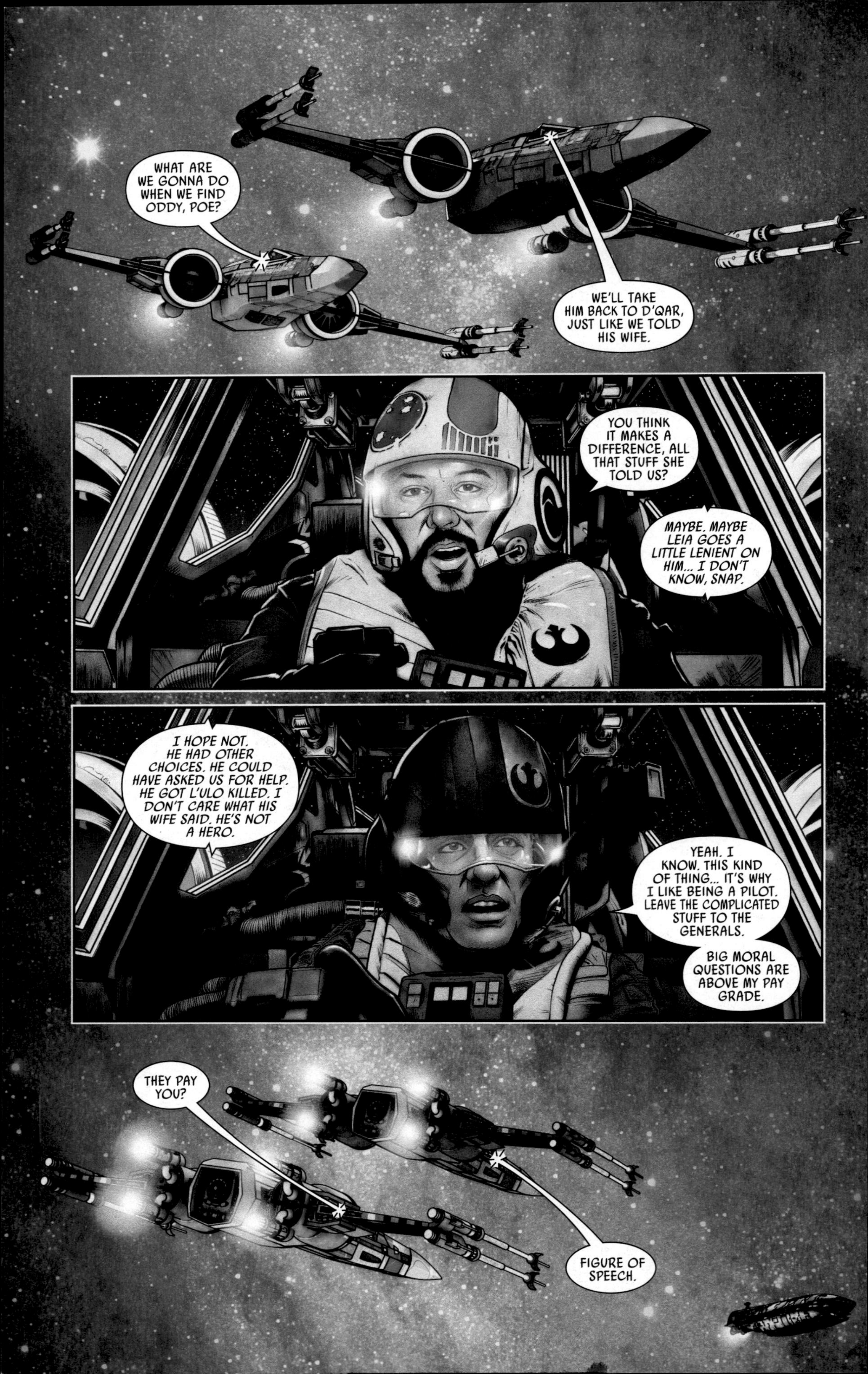
WHAT ARE WE GONNA DO WHEN WE FIND ODDY, POE?
WE'LL TAKE HIM BACK TO D'QAR, JUST LIKE WE TOLD HIS WIFE.
YOU THINK IT MAKES A DIFFERENCE, ALL THAT STUFF SHE TOLD US?
MAYBE. MAYBE LEIA GOES A LITTLE LENIENT ON HIM... I DON'T KNOW, SNAP.
I HOPE NOT. HE HAD OTHER CHOICES. HE COULD HAVE ASKED US FOR HELP. HE GOT L'ULO KILLED. I DON'T CARE WHAT HIS WIFE SAID. HE'S NOT A HERO.
YEAH. I KNOW. THIS KIND OF THING... IT'S WHY I LIKE BEING A PILOT. LEAVE THE COMPLICATED STUFF TO THE GENERALS.
BIG MORAL QUESTIONS ARE ABOVE MY PAY GRADE.
THEY PAY YOU?
FIGURE OF SPEECH.

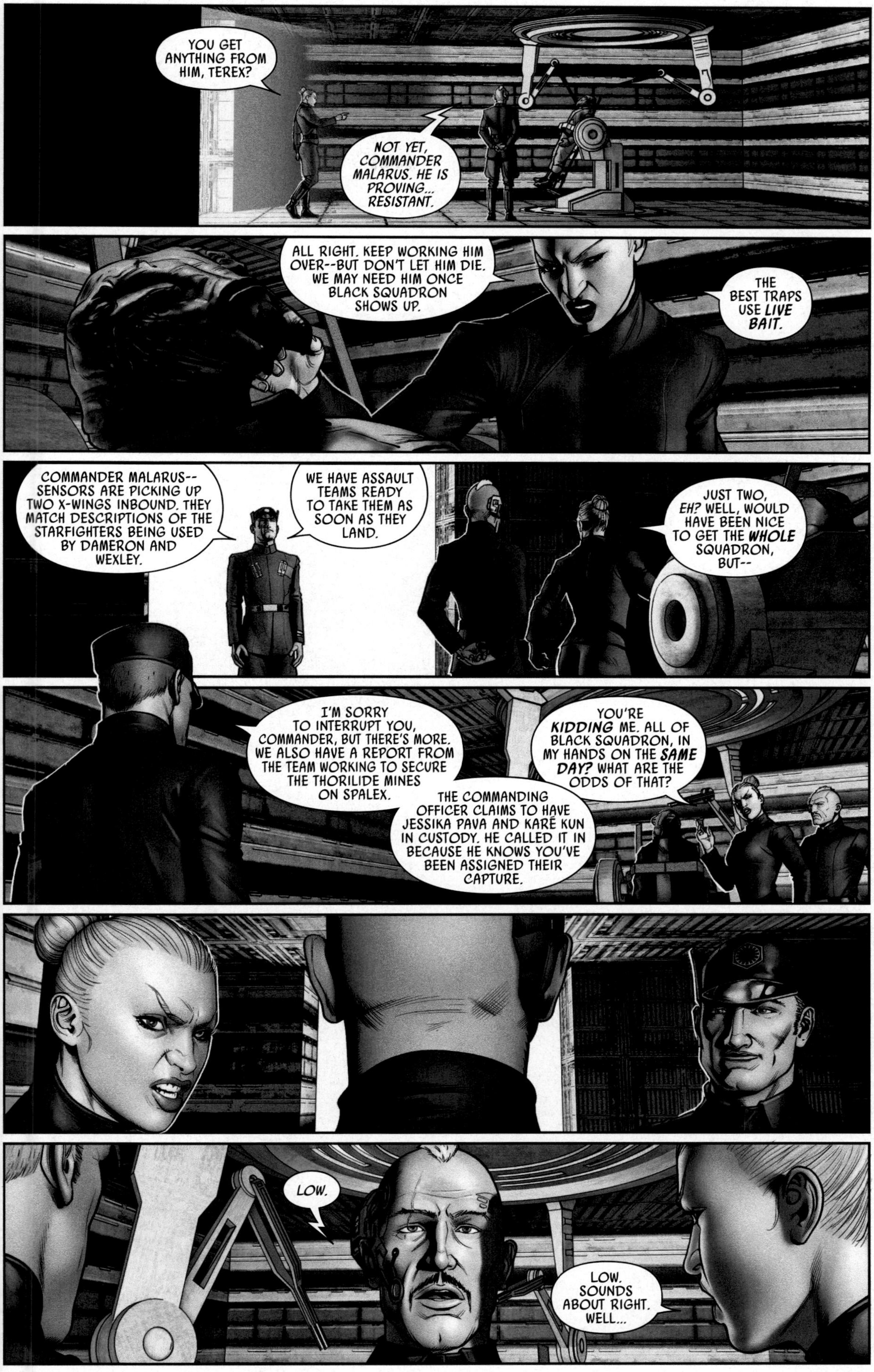
YOU GET ANYTHING FROM HIM, TEREX?
NOT YET, COMMANDER MALARUS. HE IS PROVING... RESISTANT.
ALL RIGHT. KEEP WORKING HIM OVER--BUT DON'T LET HIM DIE. WE MAY NEED HIM ONCE BLACK SQUADRON SHOWS UP.
THE BEST TRAPS USE LIVE BAIT.
COMMANDER MALARUS--SENSORS ARE PICKING UP TWO X-WINGS INBOUND. THEY MATCH DESCRIPTIONS OF THE STARFIGHTERS BEING USED BY DAMERON AND WEXLEY.
WE HAVE ASSAULT TEAMS READY TO TAKE THEM AS SOON AS THEY LAND.
JUST TWO, EH? WELL, WOULD HAVE BEEN NICE TO GET THE WHOLE SQUADRON, BUT--
I'M SORRY TO INTERRUPT YOU, COMMANDER, BUT THERE'S MORE. WE ALSO HAVE A REPORT FROM THE TEAM WORKING TO SECURE THE THORILIDE MINES ON SPALEX.
THE COMMANDING OFFICER CLAIMS TO HAVE JESSIKA PAVA AND KARÉ KUN IN CUSTODY. HE CALLED IT IN BECAUSE HE KNOWS YOU'VE BEEN ASSIGNED THEIR CAPTURE.
YOU'RE KIDDING ME. ALL OF BLACK SQUADRON, IN MY HANDS ON THE SAME DAY? WHAT ARE THE ODDS OF THAT?
LOW.
LOW. SOUNDS ABOUT RIGHT. WELL...

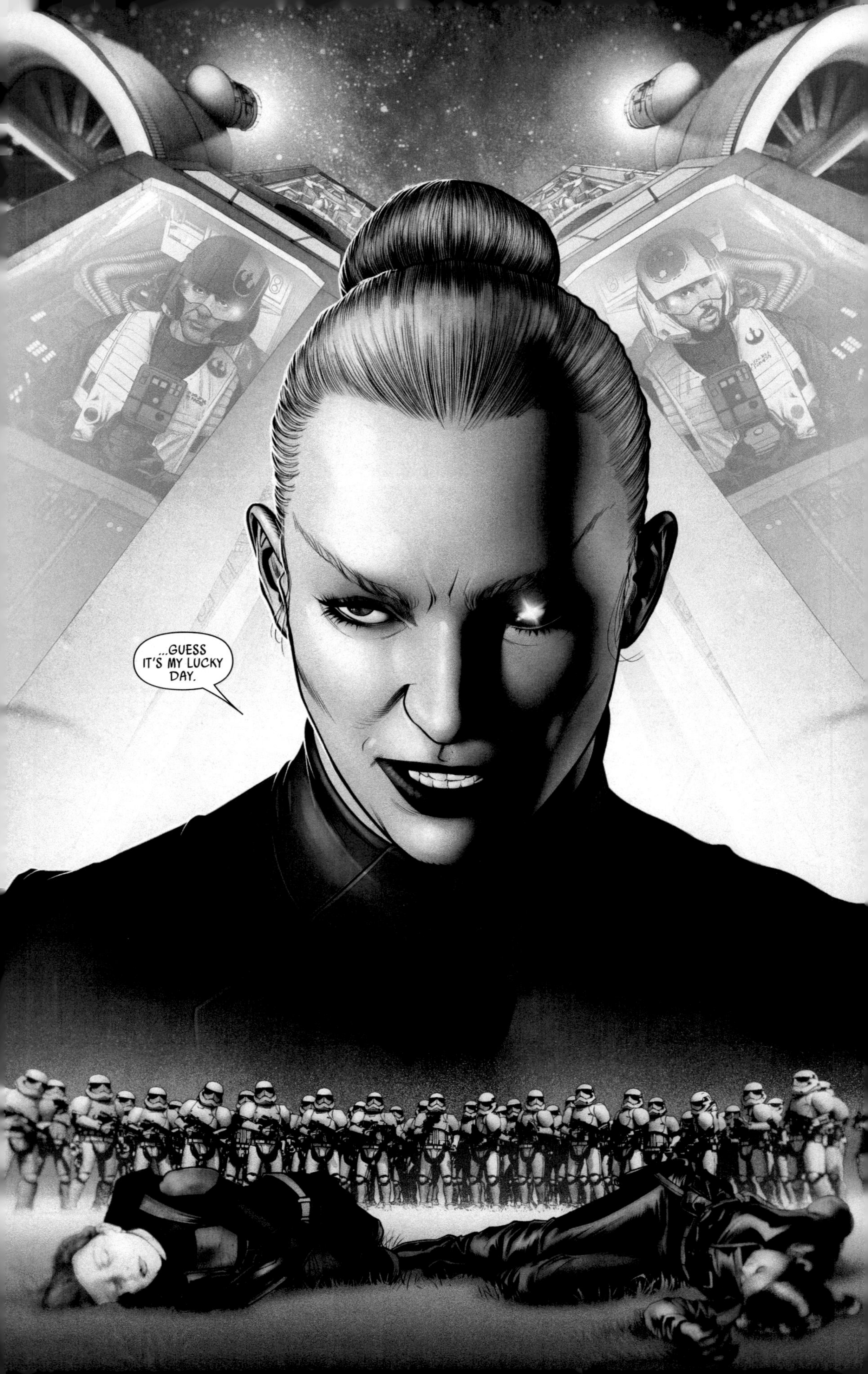
...GUESS IT'S MY LUCKY DAY.

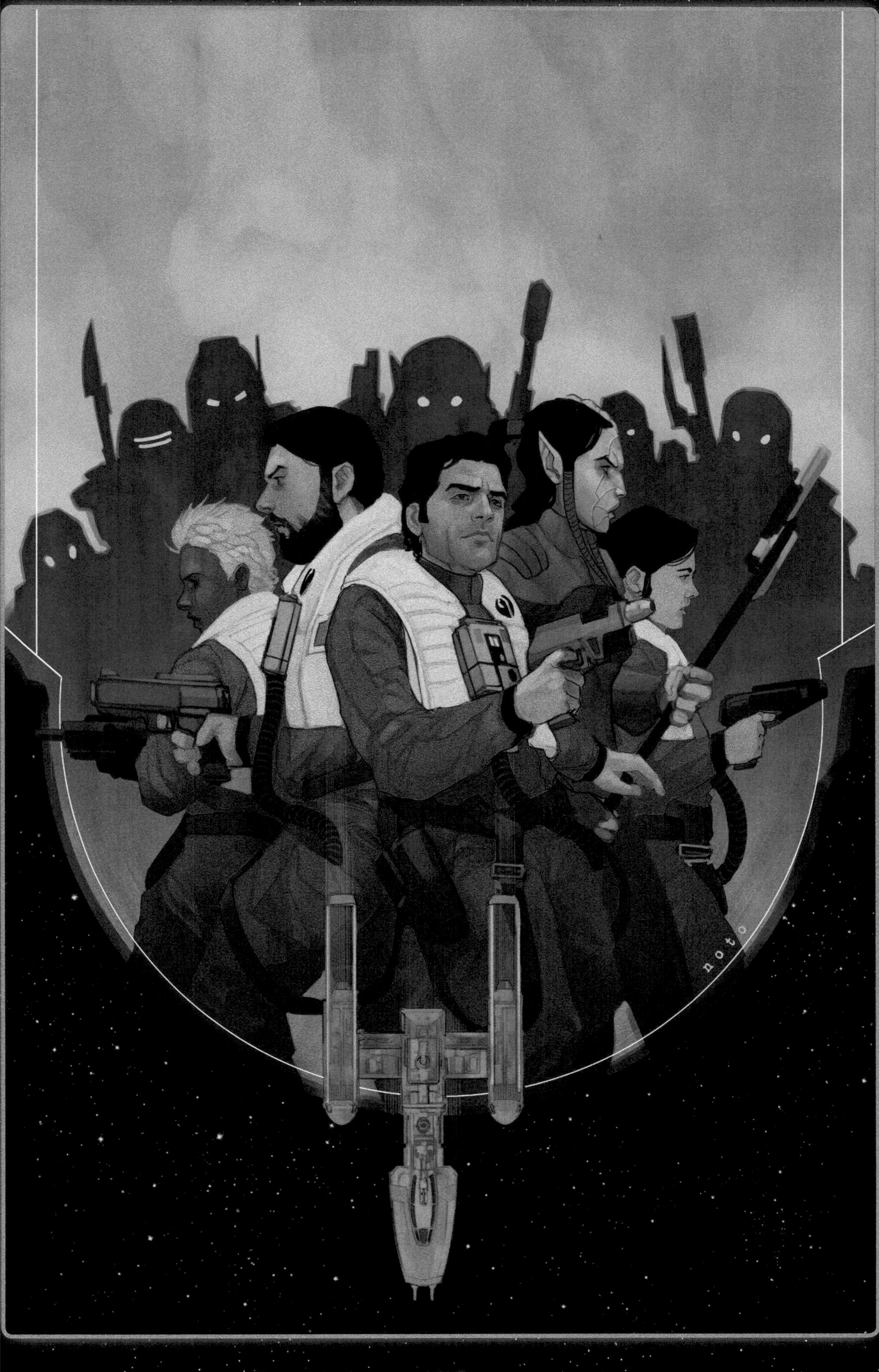
noto

19

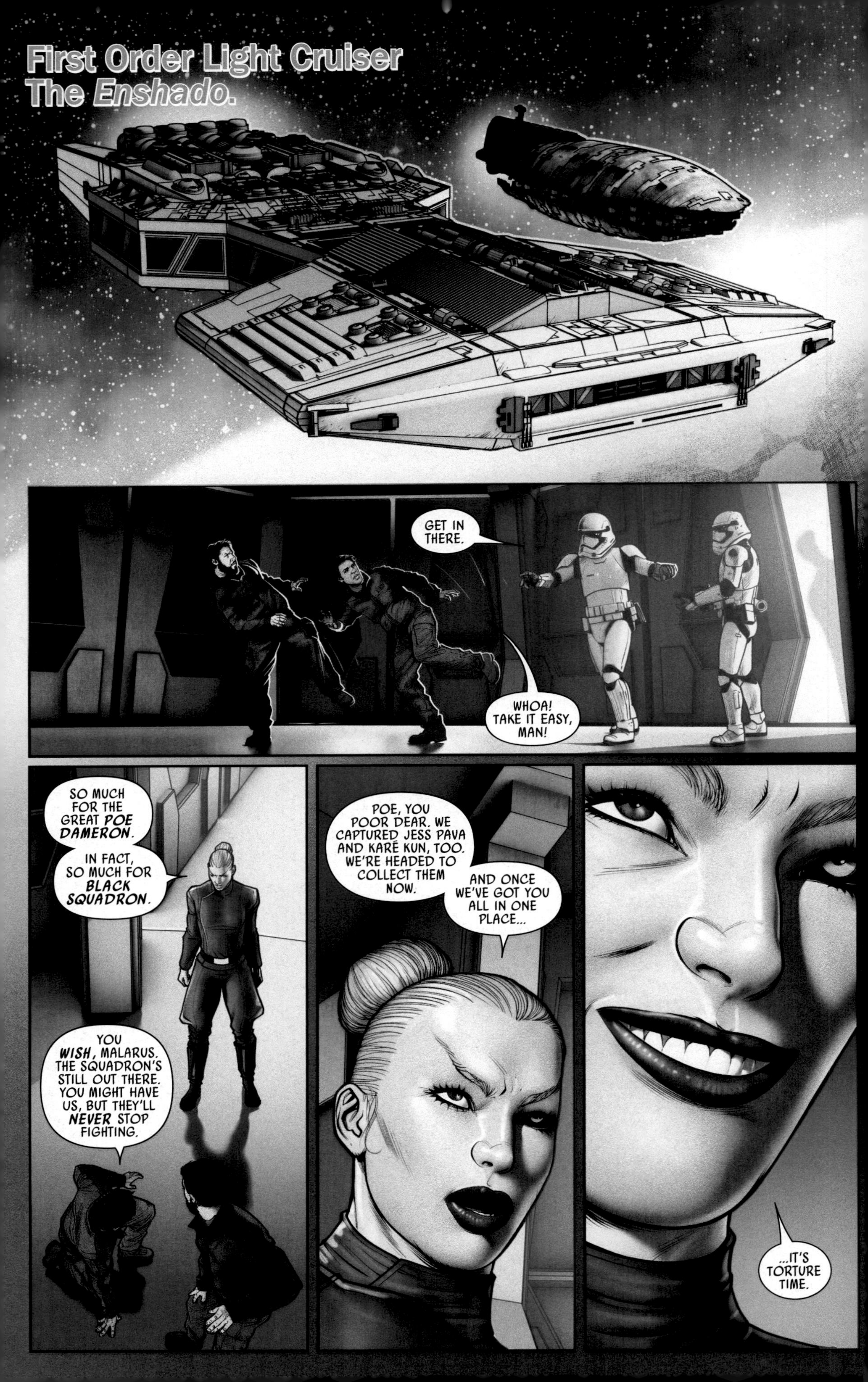
First Order Light Cruiser The Enshado.
GET IN THERE.
WHOA! TAKE IT EASY, MAN!
SO MUCH FOR THE GREAT POE DAMERON.
IN FACT, SO MUCH FOR BLACK SQUADRON.
YOU WISH, MALARUS. THE SQUADRON'S STILL OUT THERE. YOU MIGHT HAVE US, BUT THEY'LL NEVER STOP FIGHTING.
POE, YOU POOR DEAR. WE CAPTURED JESS PAVA AND KARÉ KUN, TOO. WE'RE HEADED TO COLLECT THEM NOW.
AND ONCE WE'VE GOT YOU ALL IN ONE PLACE...
...IT'S TORTURE TIME.

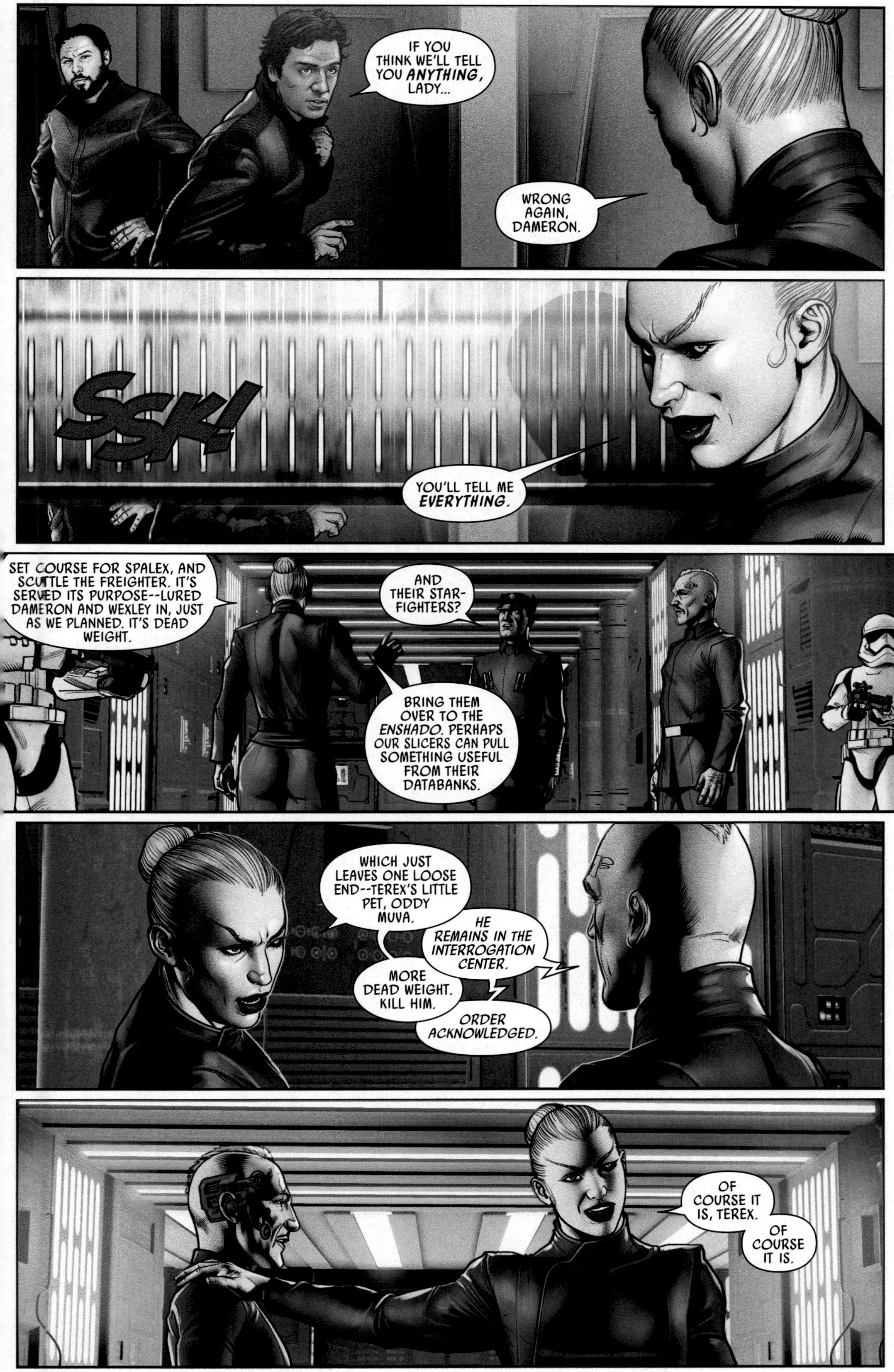
IF YOU THINK WE'LL TELL YOU ANYTHING, LADY...
WRONG AGAIN, DAMERON.
SSK!
YOU'LL TELL ME EVERYTHING.
SET COURSE FOR SPALEX, AND SCUTTLE THE FREIGHTER. IT'S SERVED ITS PURPOSE--LURED DAMERON AND WEXLEY IN, JUST AS WE PLANNED. IT'S DEAD WEIGHT.
AND THEIR STAR-FIGHTERS?
BRING THEM OVER TO THE ENSHADO. PERHAPS OUR SLICERS CAN PULL SOMETHING USEFUL FROM THEIR DATABANKS.
WHICH JUST LEAVES ONE LOOSE END--TEREX'S LITTLE PET, ODDY MUVA.
HE REMAINS IN THE INTERROGATION CENTER.
MORE DEAD WEIGHT. KILL HIM.
ORDER ACKNOWLEDGED.
OF COURSE IT IS, TEREX.
OF COURSE IT IS.

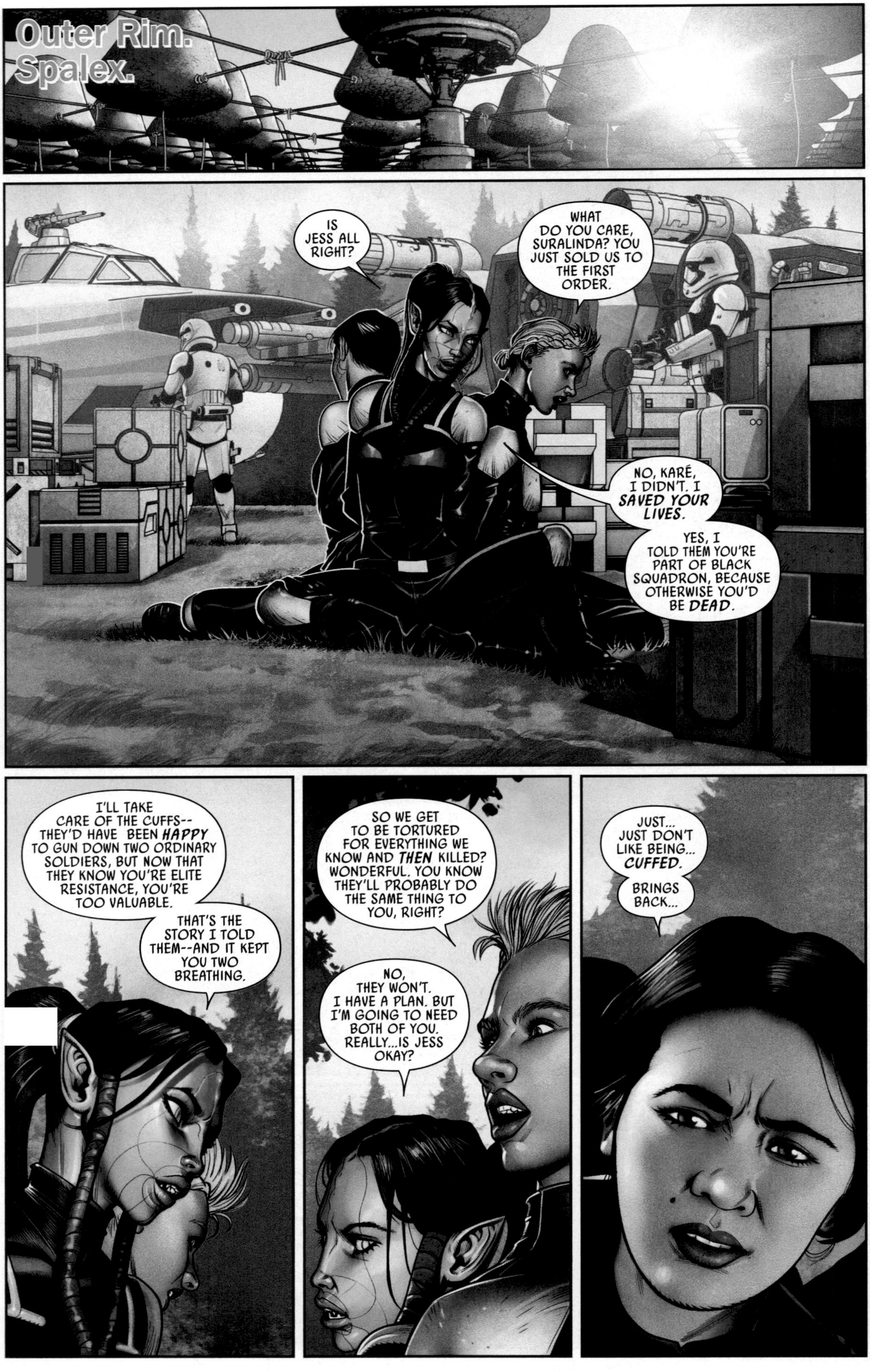
Outer Rim.
Spalex.
IS JESS ALL RIGHT?
WHAT DO YOU CARE, SURALINDA? YOU JUST SOLD US TO THE FIRST ORDER.
NO, KARÉ, I DIDN'T. I *SAVED YOUR LIVES*.
YES, I TOLD THEM YOU'RE PART OF BLACK SQUADRON, BECAUSE OTHERWISE YOU'D BE *DEAD*.
I'LL TAKE CARE OF THE CUFFS--THEY'D HAVE BEEN *HAPPY* TO GUN DOWN TWO ORDINARY SOLDIERS, BUT NOW THAT THEY KNOW YOU'RE ELITE RESISTANCE, YOU'RE TOO VALUABLE.
THAT'S THE STORY I TOLD THEM--AND IT KEPT YOU TWO BREATHING.
SO WE GET TO BE TORTURED FOR EVERYTHING WE KNOW AND *THEN* KILLED? WONDERFUL. YOU KNOW THEY'LL PROBABLY DO THE SAME THING TO YOU, RIGHT?
NO, THEY WON'T. I HAVE A PLAN. BUT I'M GOING TO NEED BOTH OF YOU. REALLY...IS JESS OKAY?
JUST... JUST DON'T LIKE BEING... *CUFFED.*
BRINGS BACK...

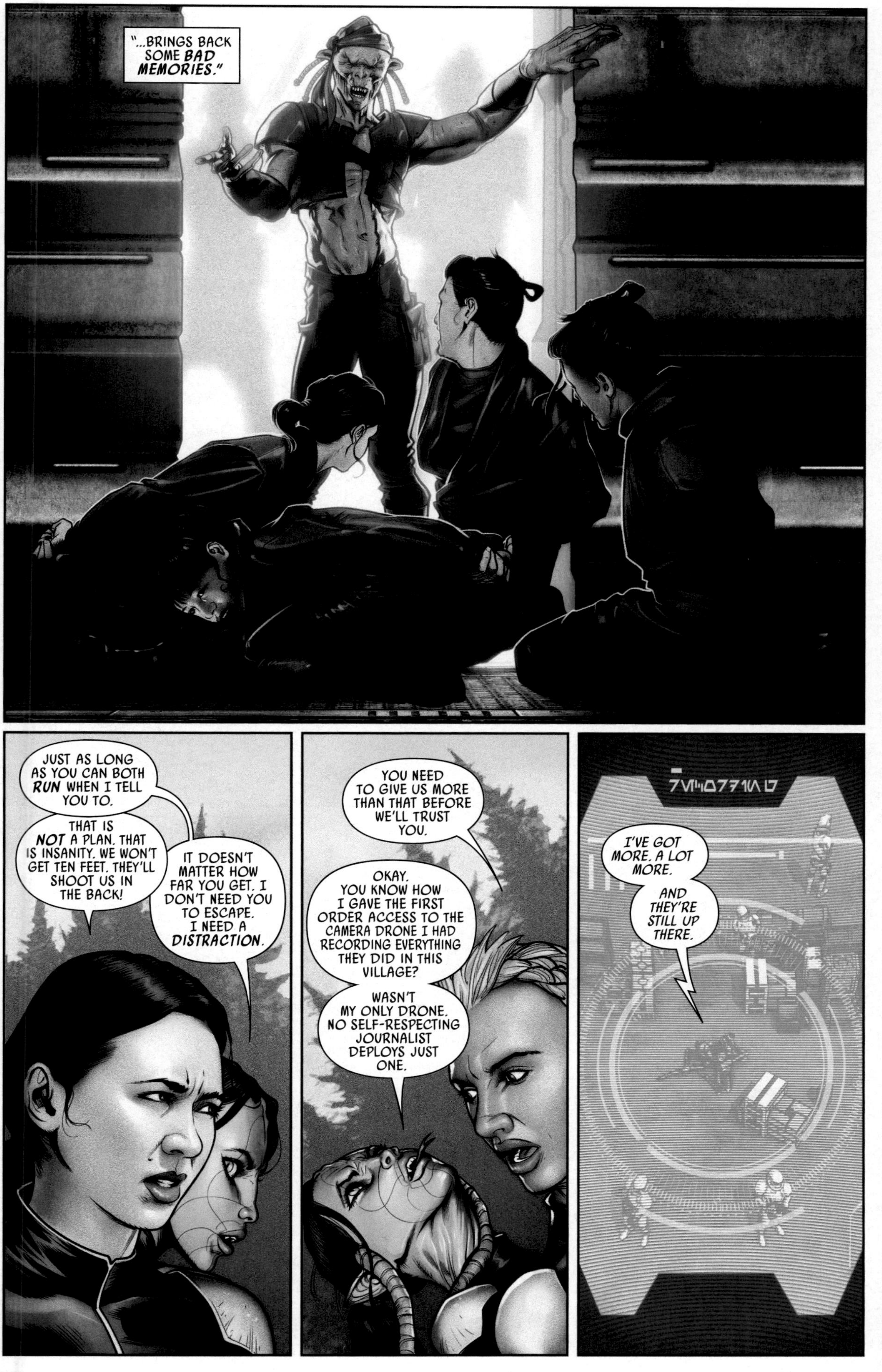
"...BRINGS BACK SOME BAD MEMORIES."
JUST AS LONG AS YOU CAN BOTH RUN WHEN I TELL YOU TO.
THAT IS NOT A PLAN. THAT IS INSANITY. WE WON'T GET TEN FEET. THEY'LL SHOOT US IN THE BACK!
IT DOESN'T MATTER HOW FAR YOU GET. I DON'T NEED YOU TO ESCAPE. I NEED A DISTRACTION.
YOU NEED TO GIVE US MORE THAN THAT BEFORE WE'LL TRUST YOU.
OKAY. YOU KNOW HOW I GAVE THE FIRST ORDER ACCESS TO THE CAMERA DRONE I HAD RECORDING EVERYTHING THEY DID IN THIS VILLAGE?
WASN'T MY ONLY DRONE. NO SELF-RESPECTING JOURNALIST DEPLOYS JUST ONE.
I'VE GOT MORE. A LOT MORE.
AND THEY'RE STILL UP THERE.

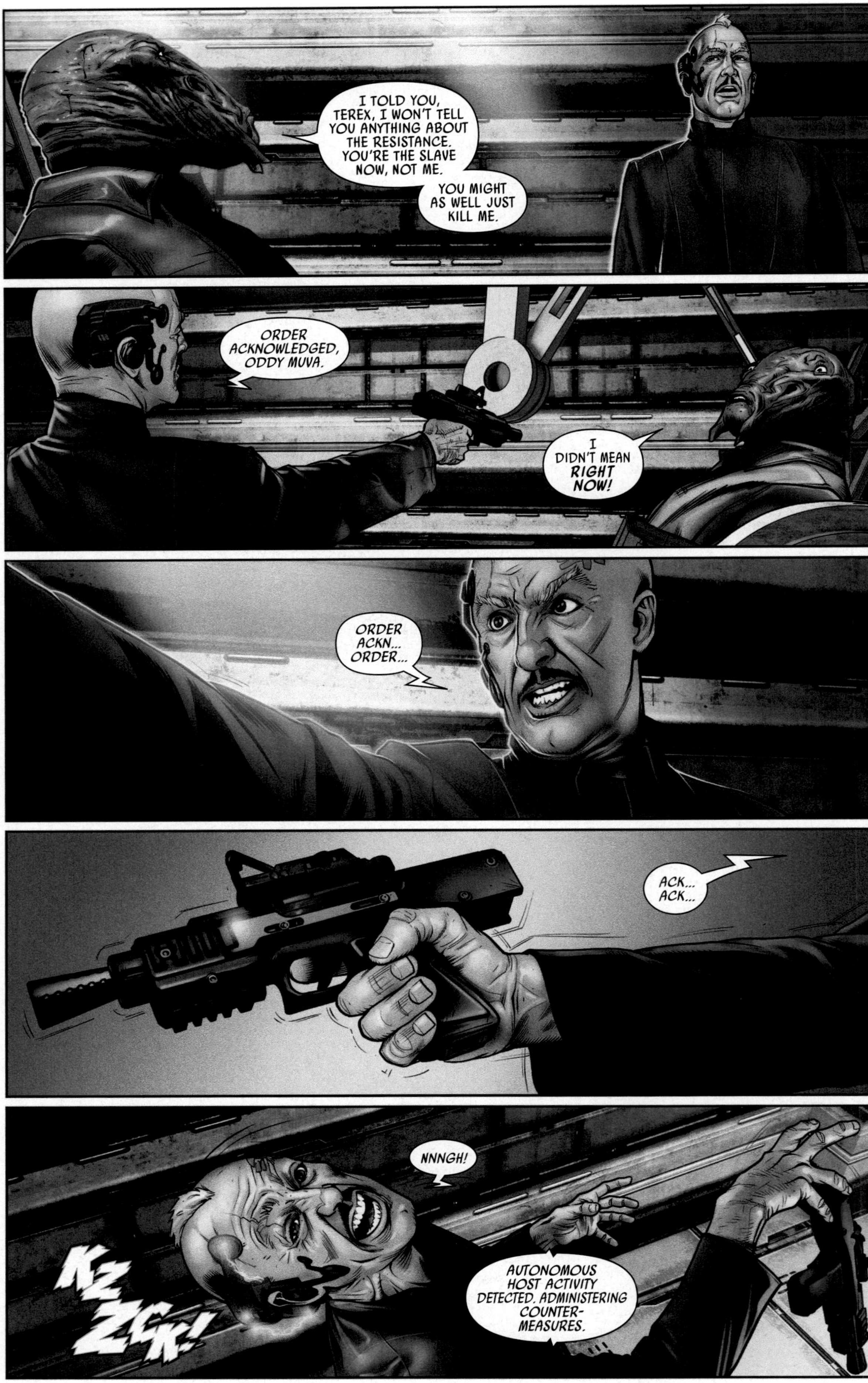
I TOLD YOU, TEREX, I WON'T TELL YOU ANYTHING ABOUT THE RESISTANCE. YOU'RE THE SLAVE NOW, NOT ME.
YOU MIGHT AS WELL JUST KILL ME.
ORDER ACKNOWLEDGED, ODDY MUVA.
I DIDN'T MEAN RIGHT NOW!
ORDER ACKN... ORDER...
ACK... ACK...
NNNGH!
KZZCK!
AUTONOMOUS HOST ACTIVITY DETECTED. ADMINISTERING COUNTER-MEASURES.

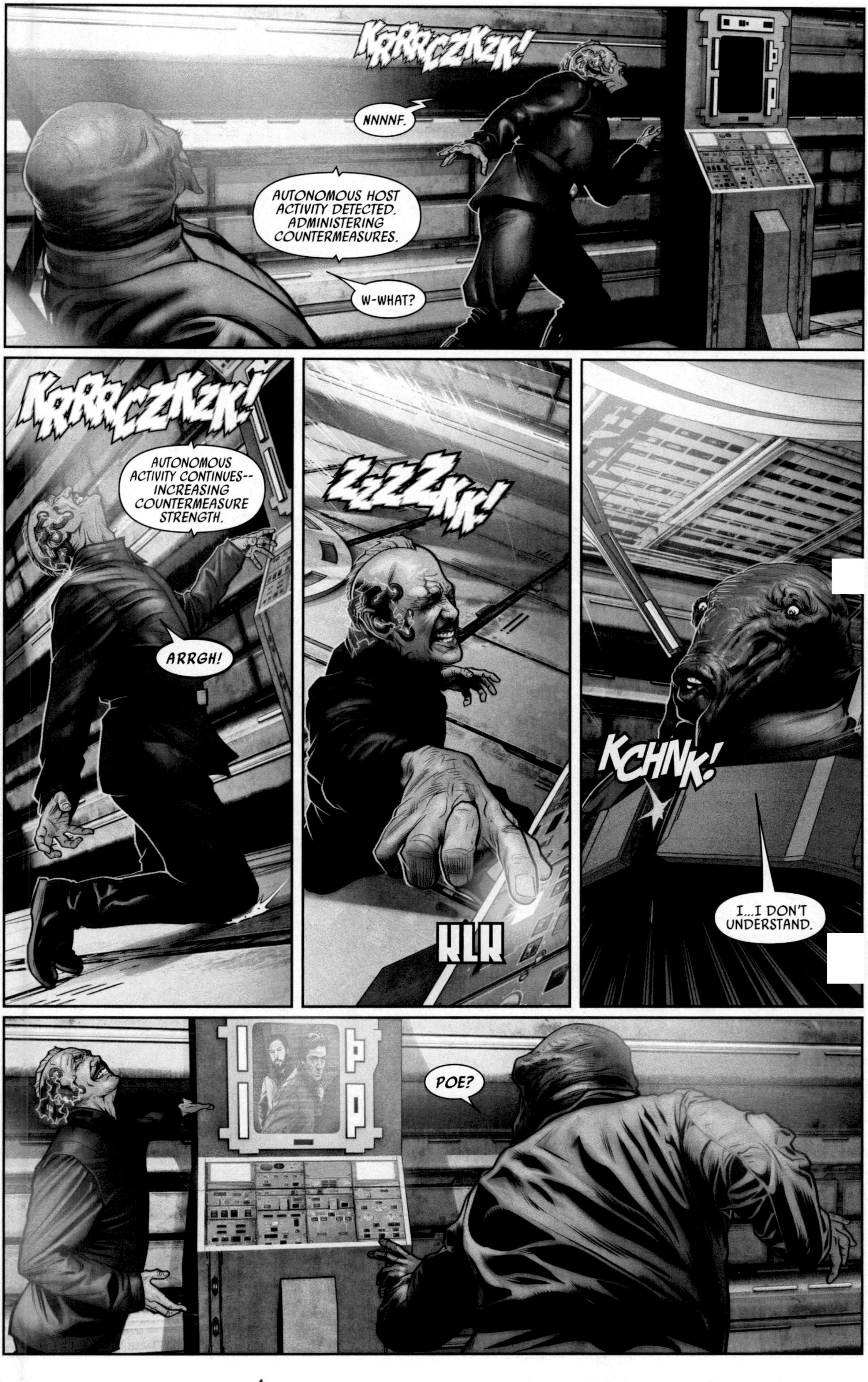
KRRRRCZKZK!
NNNNF.
AUTONOMOUS HOST ACTIVITY DETECTED. ADMINISTERING COUNTERMEASURES.
W-WHAT?
KRRRRCZKZK!
AUTONOMOUS ACTIVITY CONTINUES-- INCREASING COUNTERMEASURE STRENGTH.
ARRGH!
ZZZZKK!
KLK
KCHINK!
I...I DON'T UNDERSTAND.
POE?

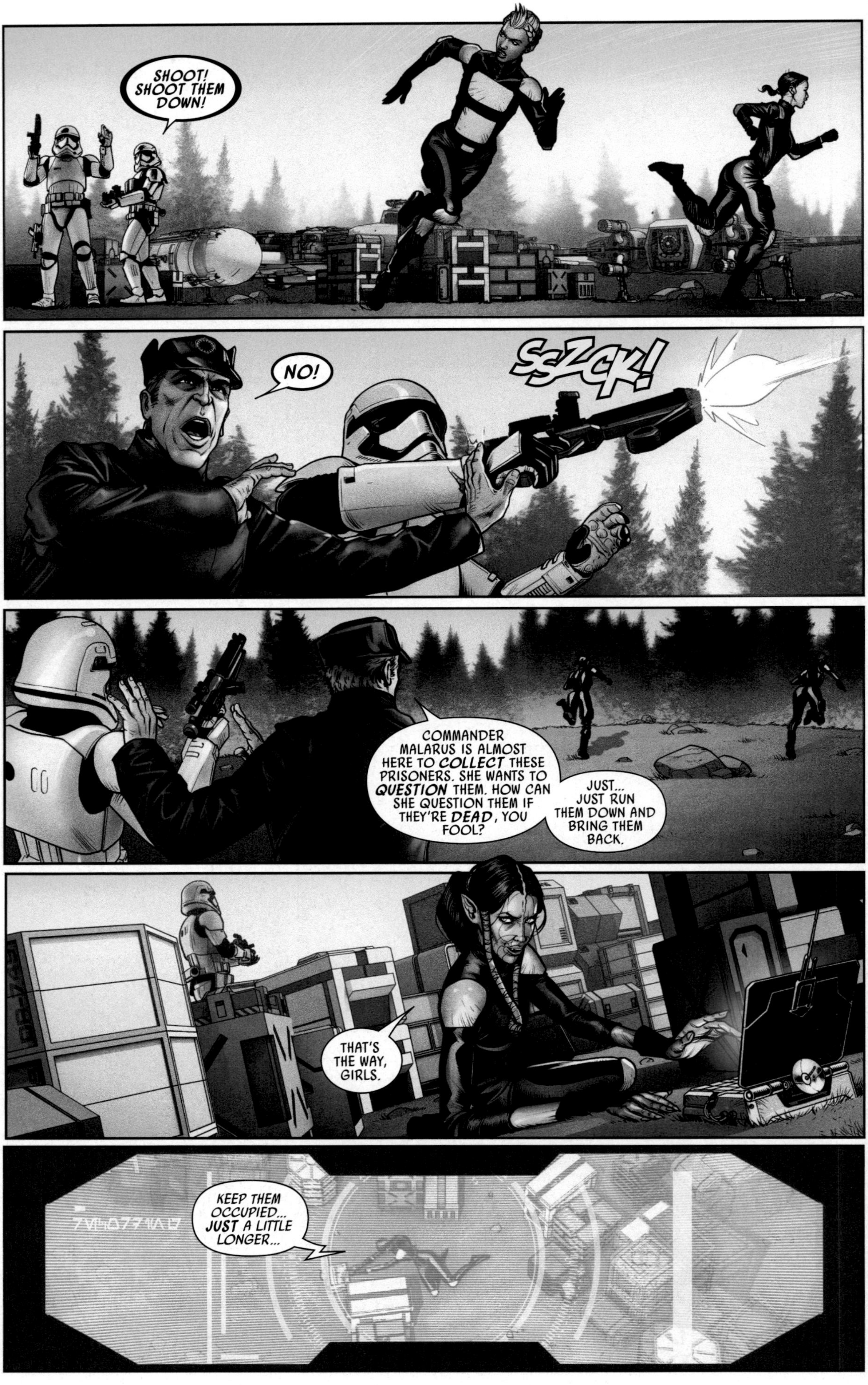

SHOOT! SHOOT THEM DOWN!
NO!
SSZCK!
COMMANDER MALARUS IS ALMOST HERE TO COLLECT THESE PRISONERS. SHE WANTS TO QUESTION THEM. HOW CAN SHE QUESTION THEM IF THEY'RE DEAD, YOU FOOL?
JUST... JUST RUN THEM DOWN AND BRING THEM BACK.
THAT'S THE WAY, GIRLS.
KEEP THEM OCCUPIED... JUST A LITTLE LONGER...

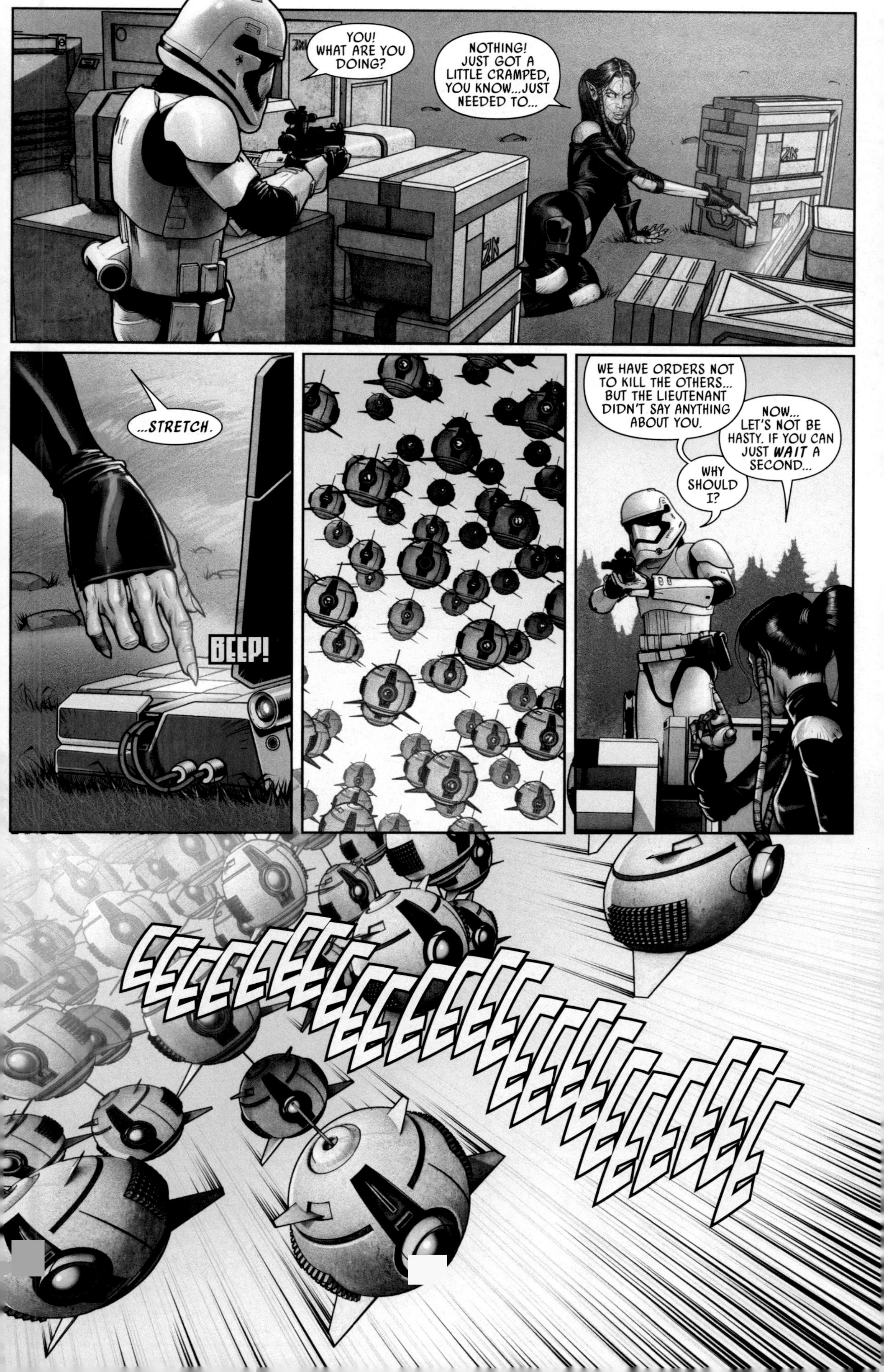
YOU! WHAT ARE YOU DOING?
NOTHING! JUST GOT A LITTLE CRAMPED, YOU KNOW...JUST NEEDED TO...
...STRETCH.
BEEP!
WE HAVE ORDERS NOT TO KILL THE OTHERS... BUT THE LIEUTENANT DIDN'T SAY ANYTHING ABOUT YOU.
NOW... LET'S NOT BE HASTY. IF YOU CAN JUST WAIT A SECOND...
WHY SHOULD I?

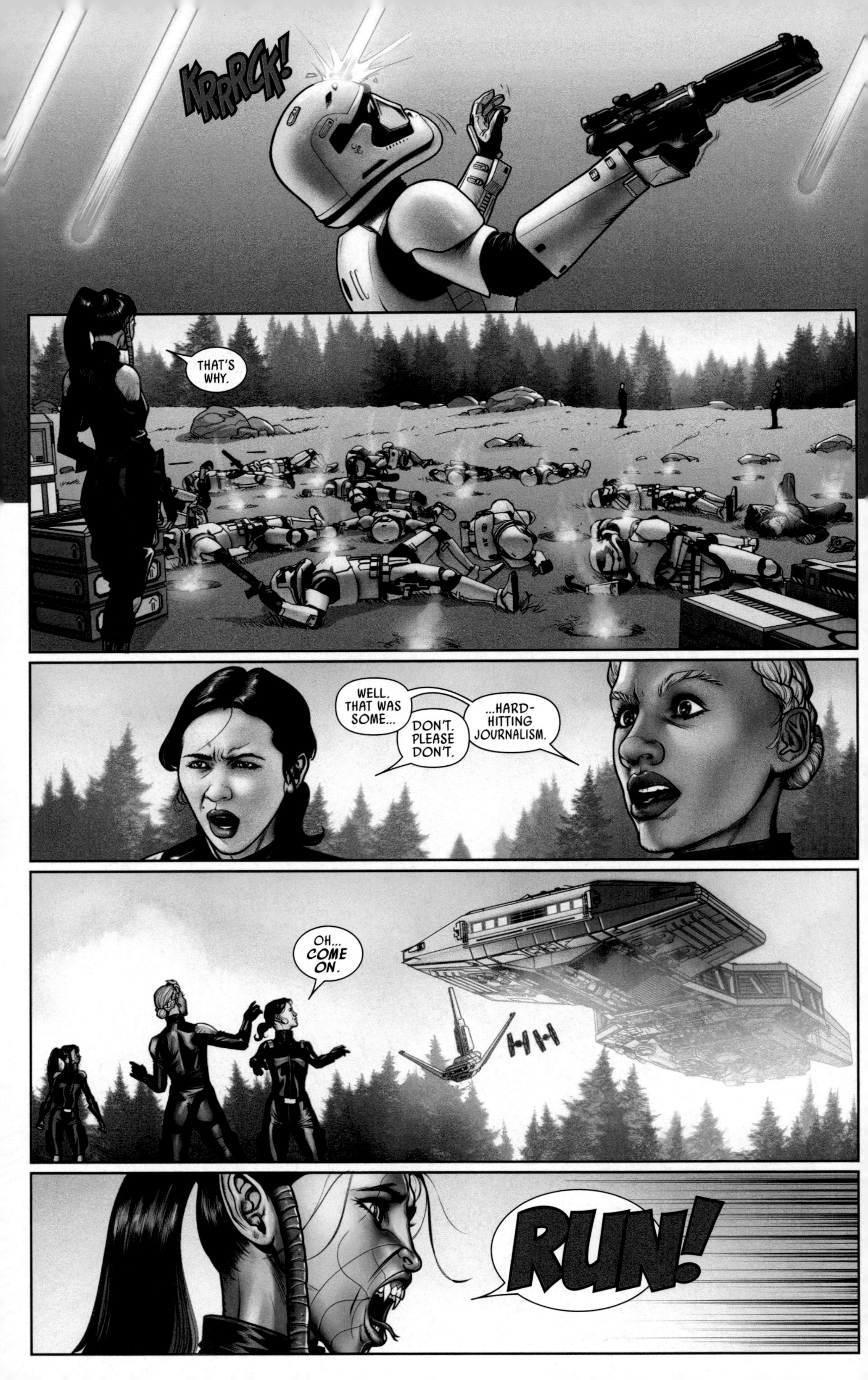
KRRRCK!
THAT'S WHY.
WELL. THAT WAS SOME...
DON'T. PLEASE DON'T.
...HARD-HITTING JOURNALISM.
OH... COME ON.
RUN!

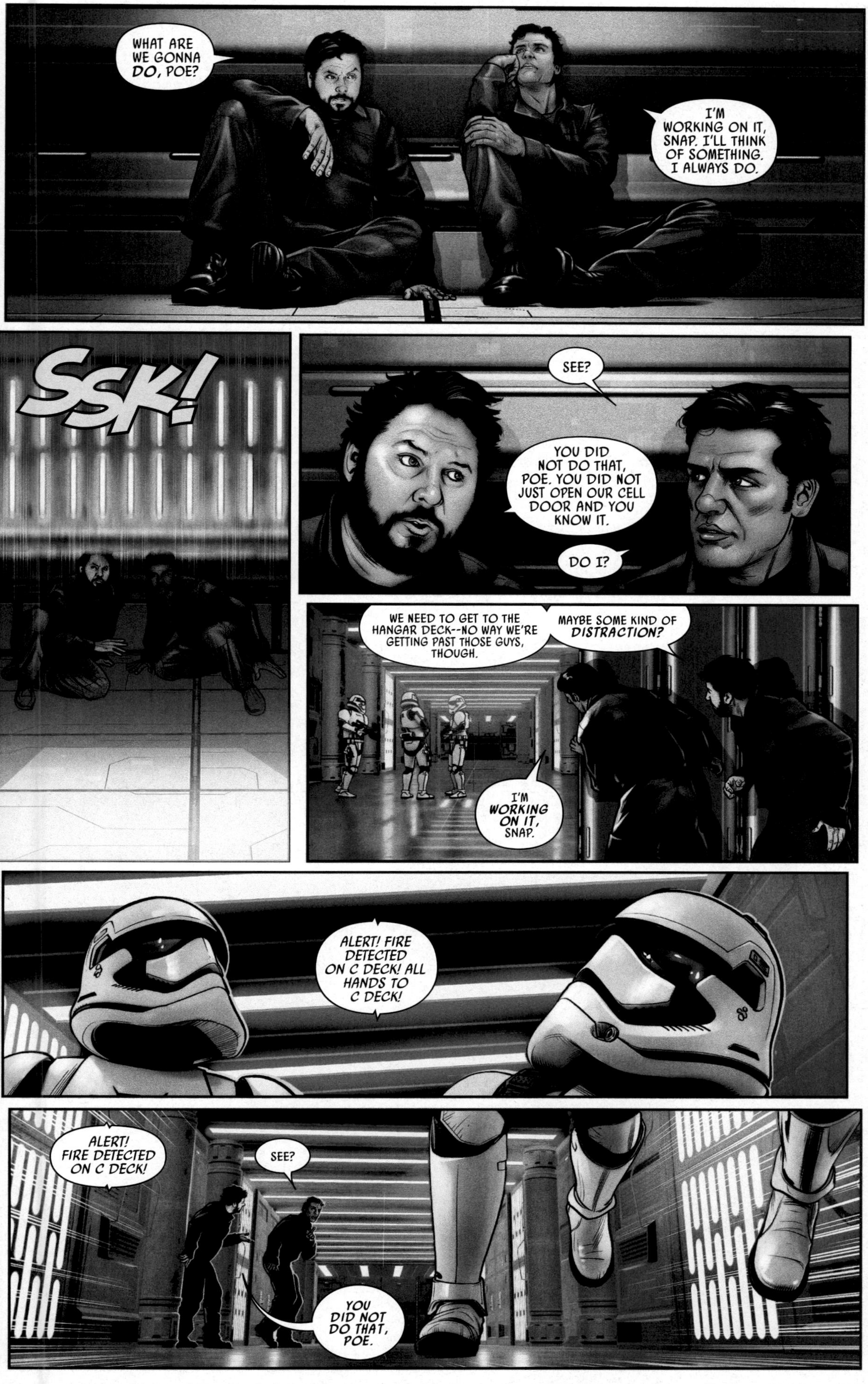
WHAT ARE WE GONNA DO, POE?
I'M WORKING ON IT, SNAP. I'LL THINK OF SOMETHING. I ALWAYS DO.
SSK!
SEE?
YOU DID NOT DO THAT, POE. YOU DID NOT JUST OPEN OUR CELL DOOR AND YOU KNOW IT.
DO I?
WE NEED TO GET TO THE HANGAR DECK--NO WAY WE'RE GETTING PAST THOSE GUYS, THOUGH.
MAYBE SOME KIND OF DISTRACTION?
I'M WORKING ON IT, SNAP.
ALERT! FIRE DETECTED ON C DECK! ALL HANDS TO C DECK!
ALERT! FIRE DETECTED ON C DECK!
SEE?
YOU DID NOT DO THAT, POE.

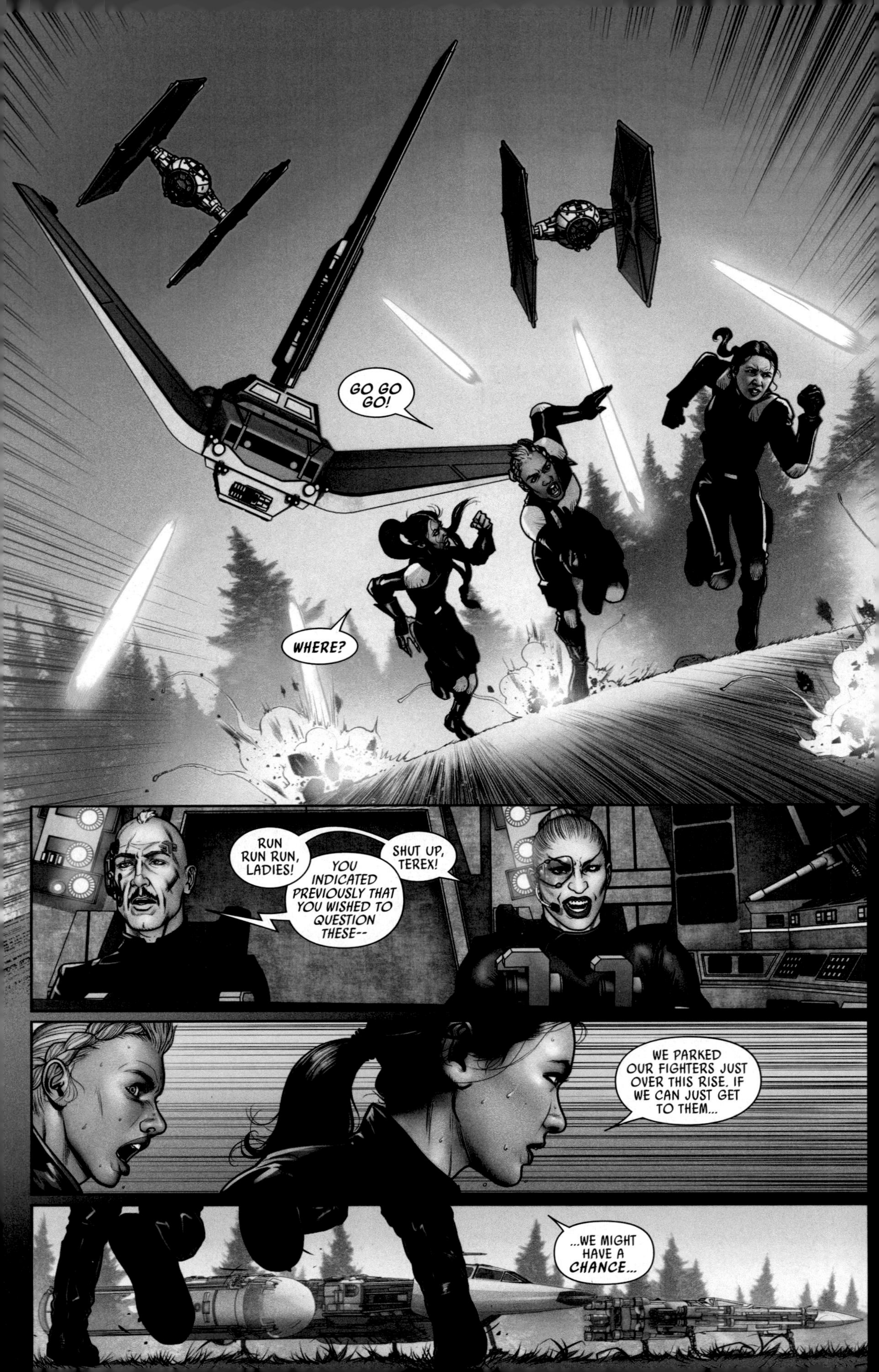
GO GO GO!
WHERE?
RUN RUN RUN, LADIES!
SHUT UP, TEREX!
YOU INDICATED PREVIOUSLY THAT YOU WISHED TO QUESTION THESE--
WE PARKED OUR FIGHTERS JUST OVER THIS RISE. IF WE CAN JUST GET TO THEM...
...WE MIGHT HAVE A CHANCE...

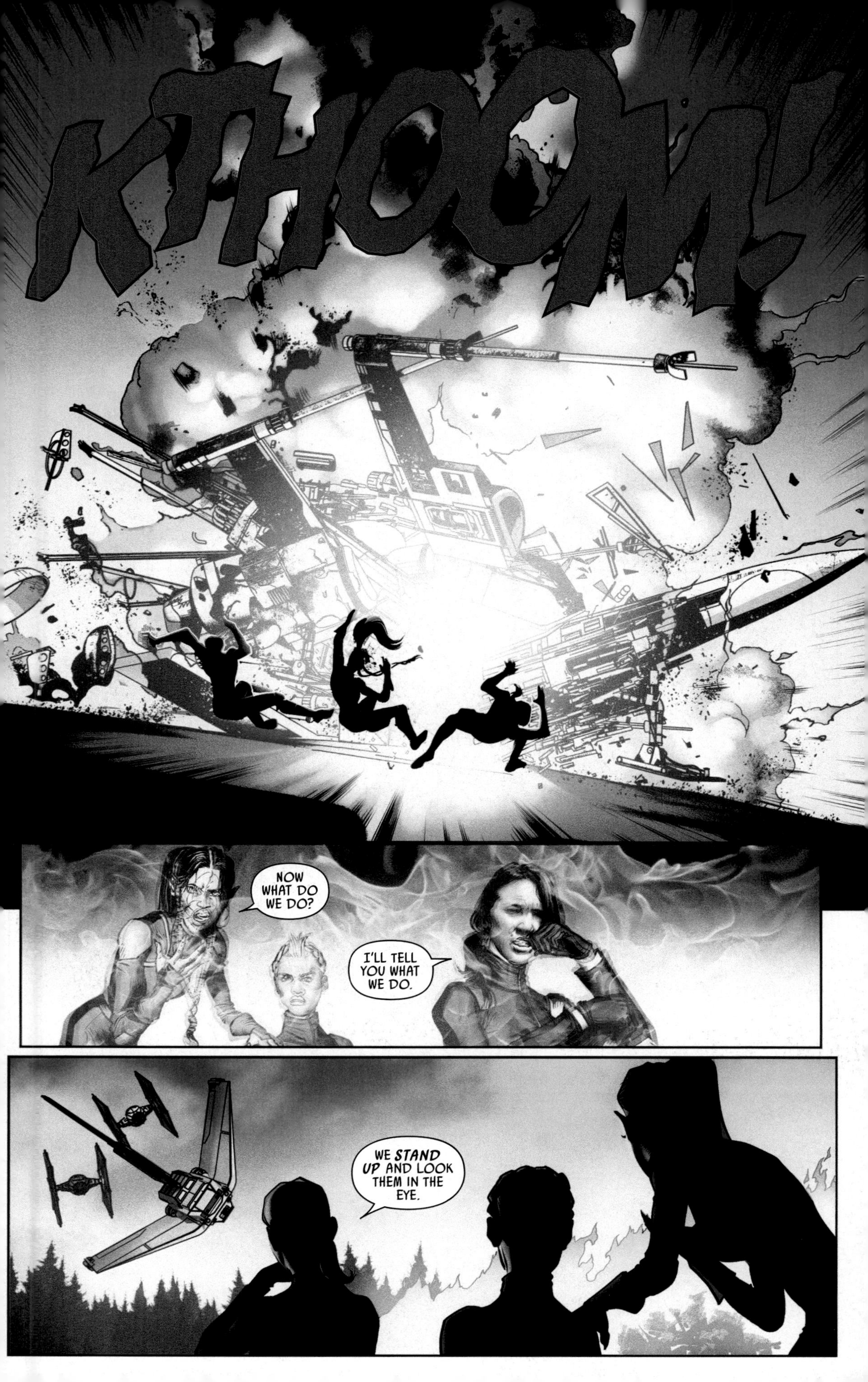
KTHOOM!
NOW WHAT DO WE DO?
I'LL TELL YOU WHAT WE DO.
WE STAND UP AND LOOK THEM IN THE EYE.

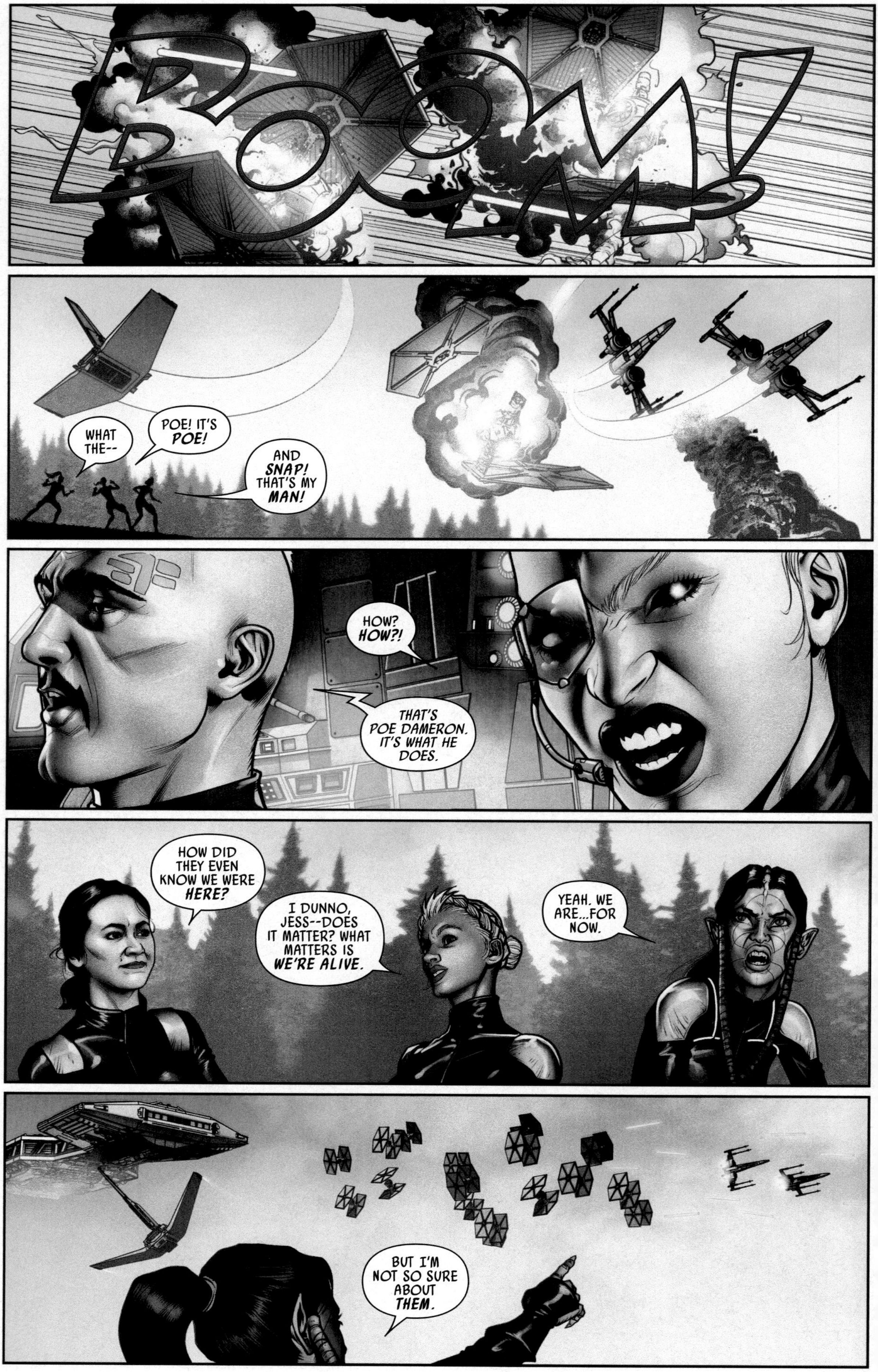
BOOM! BOOM!
WHAT THE--
POE! IT'S POE!
AND SNAP! THAT'S MY MAN!
HOW? HOW?!
THAT'S POE DAMERON. IT'S WHAT HE DOES.
HOW DID THEY EVEN KNOW WE WERE HERE?
I DUNNO, JESS--DOES IT MATTER? WHAT MATTERS IS WE'RE ALIVE.
YEAH. WE ARE...FOR NOW.
BUT I'M NOT SO SURE ABOUT THEM.

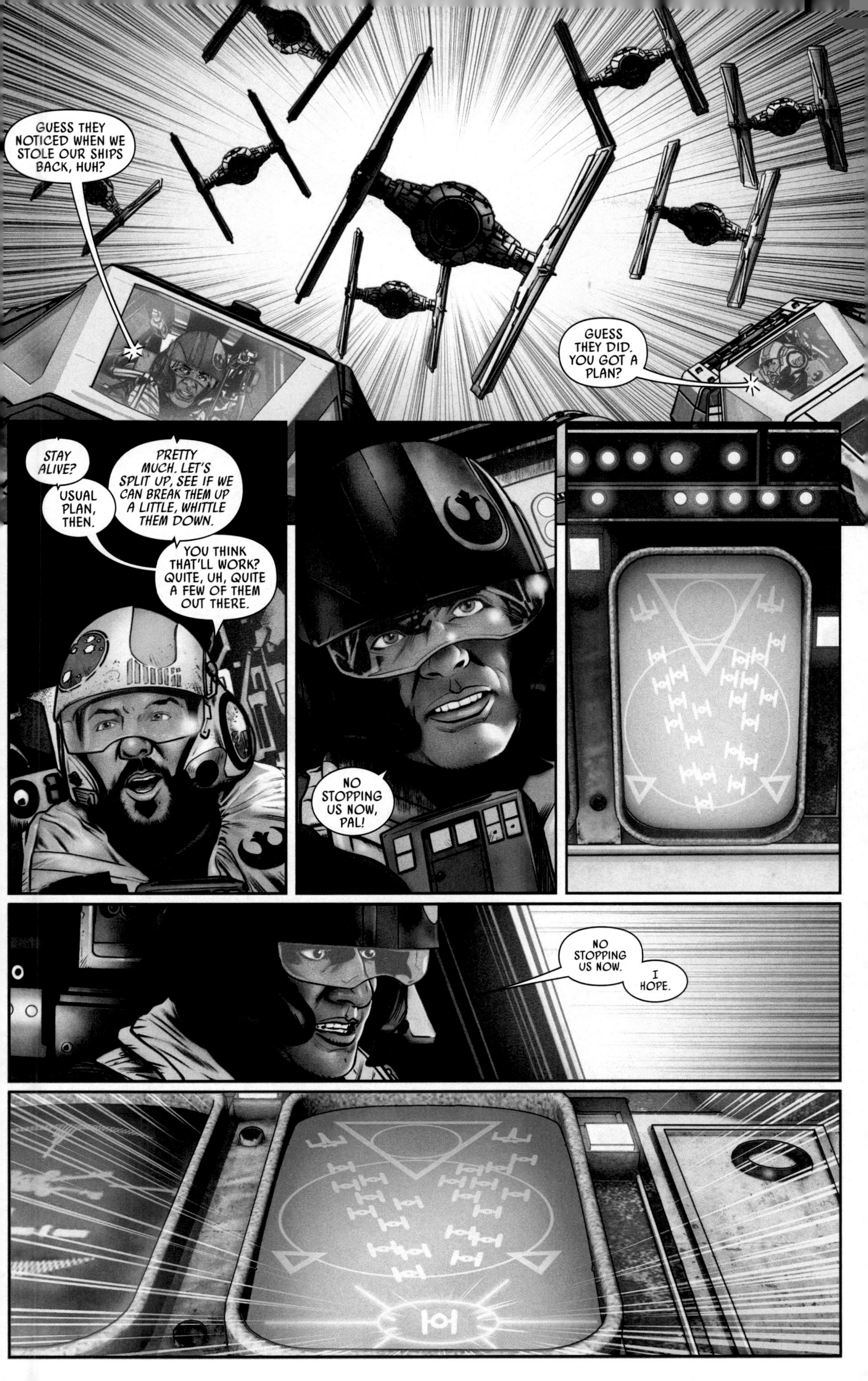
GUESS THEY NOTICED WHEN WE STOLE OUR SHIPS BACK, HUH?
GUESS THEY DID. YOU GOT A PLAN?
STAY ALIVE?
PRETTY MUCH. LET'S SPLIT UP, SEE IF WE CAN BREAK THEM UP A LITTLE, WHITTLE THEM DOWN.
USUAL PLAN, THEN.
YOU THINK THAT'LL WORK? QUITE, UH, QUITE A FEW OF THEM OUT THERE.
NO STOPPING US NOW, PAL!
NO STOPPING US NOW.
I HOPE.

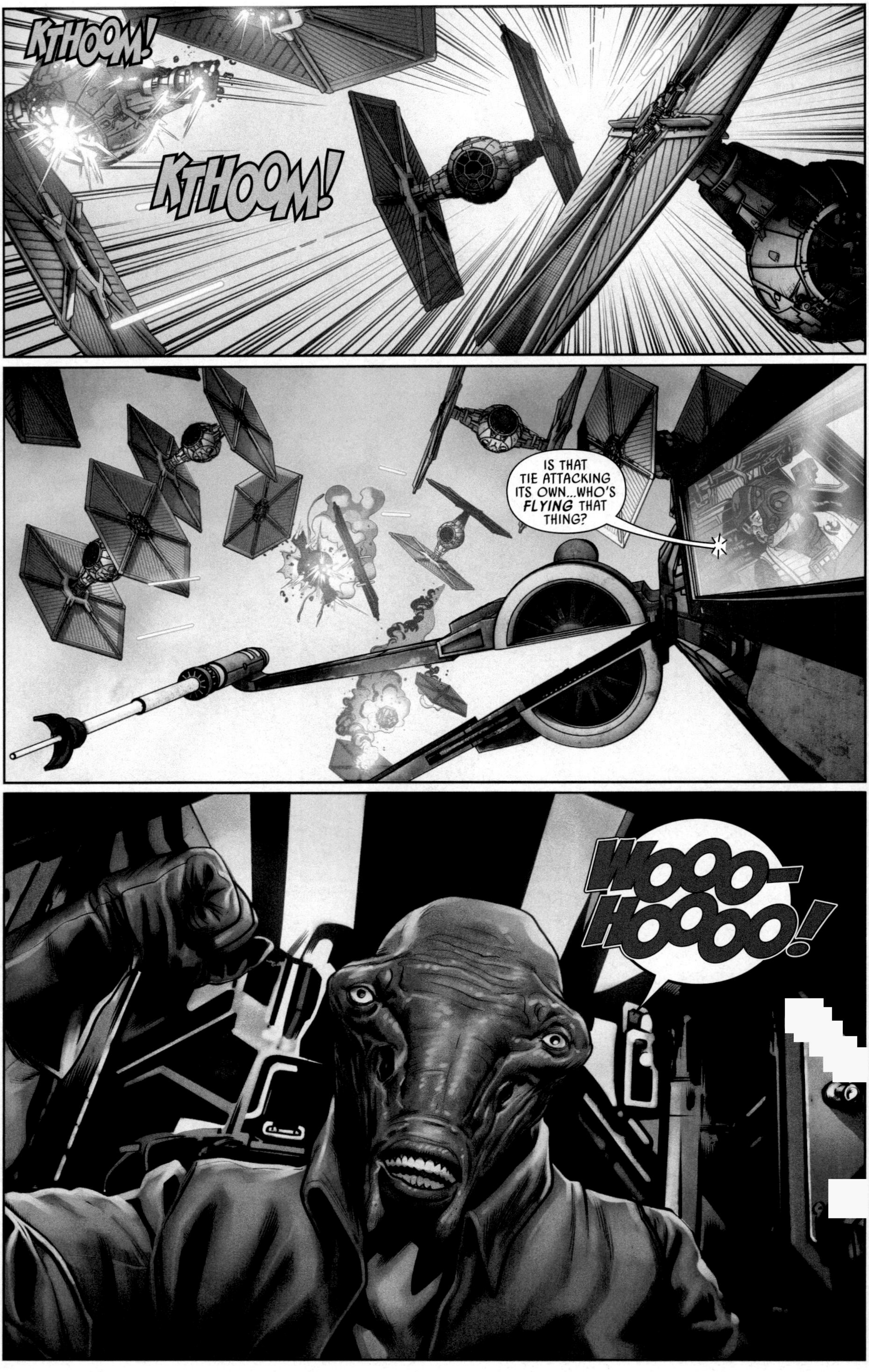
KTHOOM!
KTHOOM!
IS THAT TIE ATTACKING ITS OWN...WHO'S *FLYING* THAT THING?
WOOO-HOOOOO!

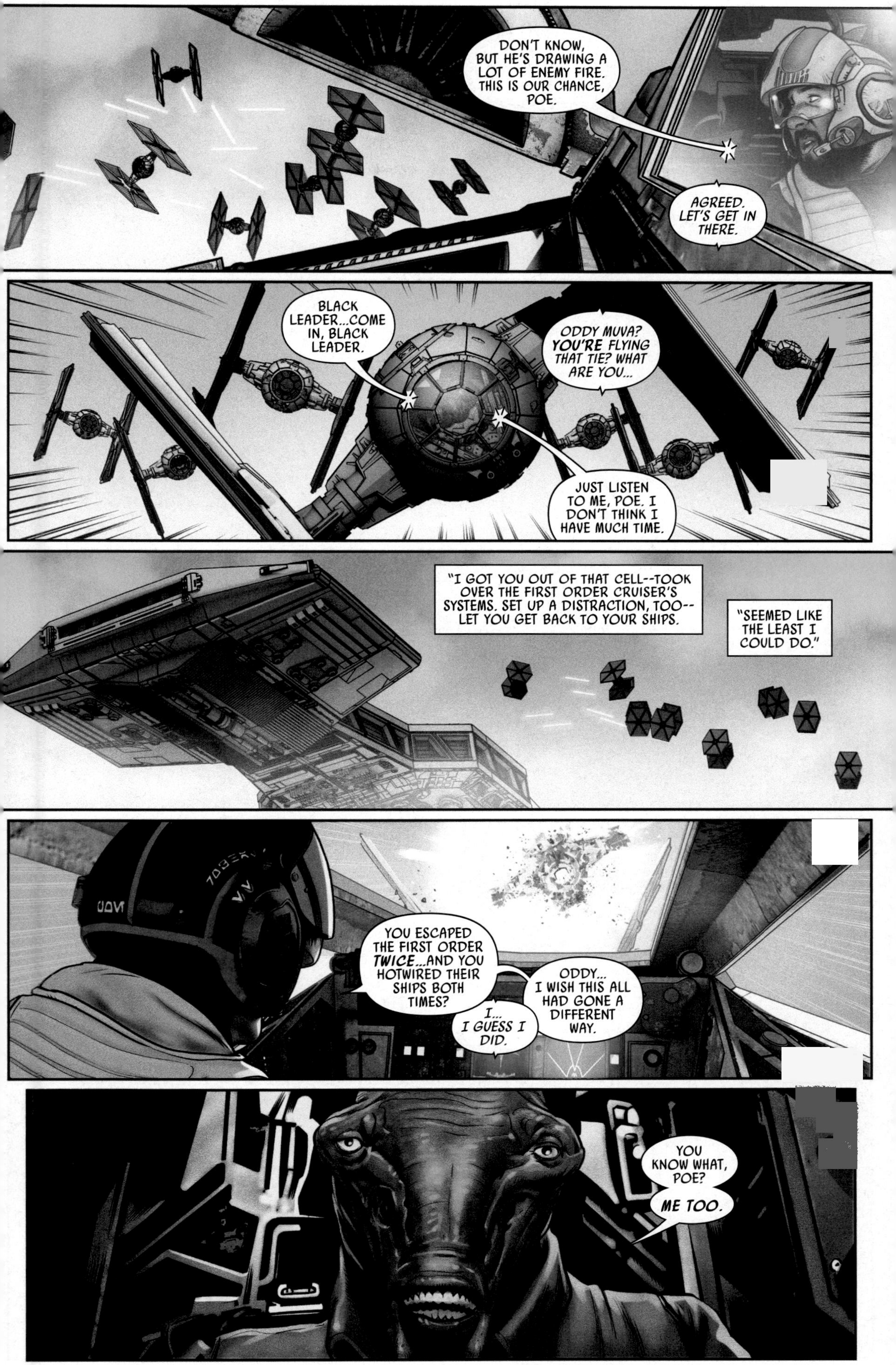
DON'T KNOW, BUT HE'S DRAWING A LOT OF ENEMY FIRE. THIS IS OUR CHANCE, POE.
AGREED. LET'S GET IN THERE.
BLACK LEADER...COME IN, BLACK LEADER.
ODDY MUVA? YOU'RE FLYING THAT TIE? WHAT ARE YOU...
JUST LISTEN TO ME, POE. I DON'T THINK I HAVE MUCH TIME.
"I GOT YOU OUT OF THAT CELL--TOOK OVER THE FIRST ORDER CRUISER'S SYSTEMS. SET UP A DISTRACTION, TOO--LET YOU GET BACK TO YOUR SHIPS.
"SEEMED LIKE THE LEAST I COULD DO."
YOU ESCAPED THE FIRST ORDER TWICE...AND YOU HOTWIRED THEIR SHIPS BOTH TIMES?
I... I GUESS I DID.
ODDY... I WISH THIS ALL HAD GONE A DIFFERENT WAY.
YOU KNOW WHAT, POE?
ME TOO.

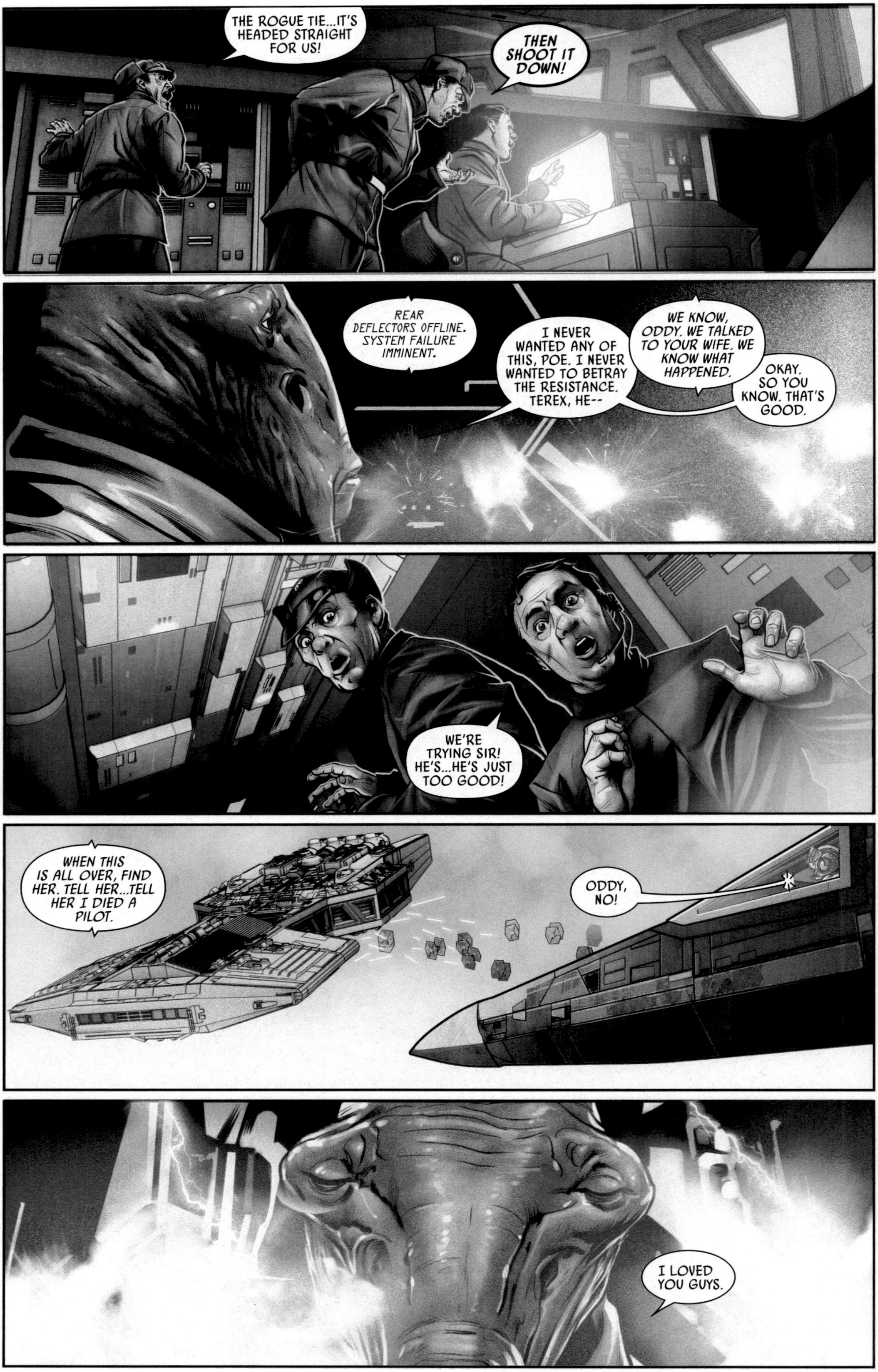
THE ROGUE TIE...IT'S HEADED STRAIGHT FOR US!
THEN SHOOT IT DOWN!
REAR DEFLECTORS OFFLINE. SYSTEM FAILURE IMMINENT.
I NEVER WANTED ANY OF THIS, POE. I NEVER WANTED TO BETRAY THE RESISTANCE. TEREX, HE--
WE KNOW, ODDY. WE TALKED TO YOUR WIFE. WE KNOW WHAT HAPPENED.
OKAY. SO YOU KNOW. THAT'S GOOD.
WE'RE TRYING SIR! HE'S...HE'S JUST TOO GOOD!
WHEN THIS IS ALL OVER, FIND HER. TELL HER...TELL HER I DIED A PILOT.
ODDY, NO!
I LOVED YOU GUYS.

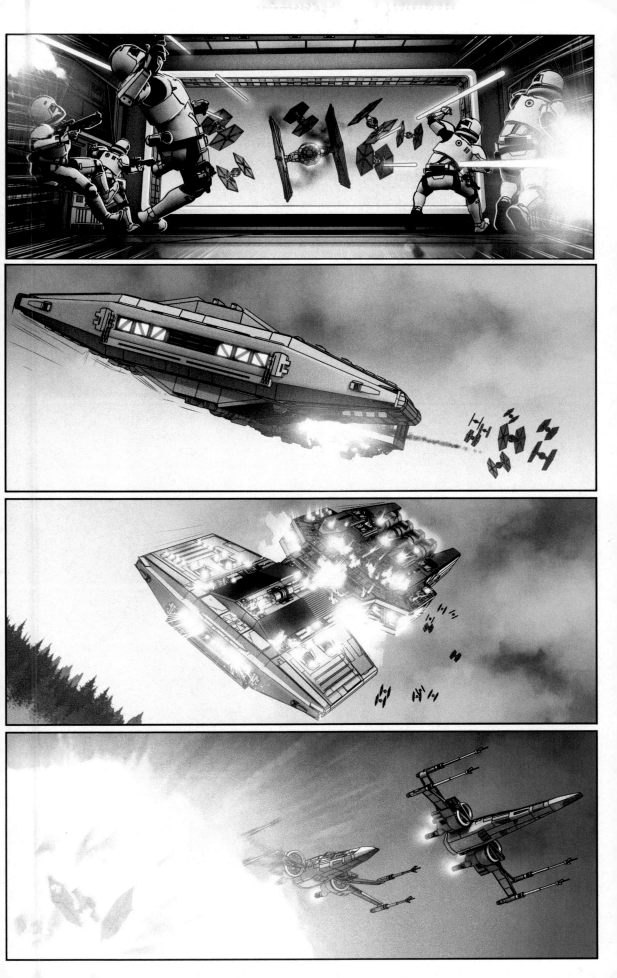

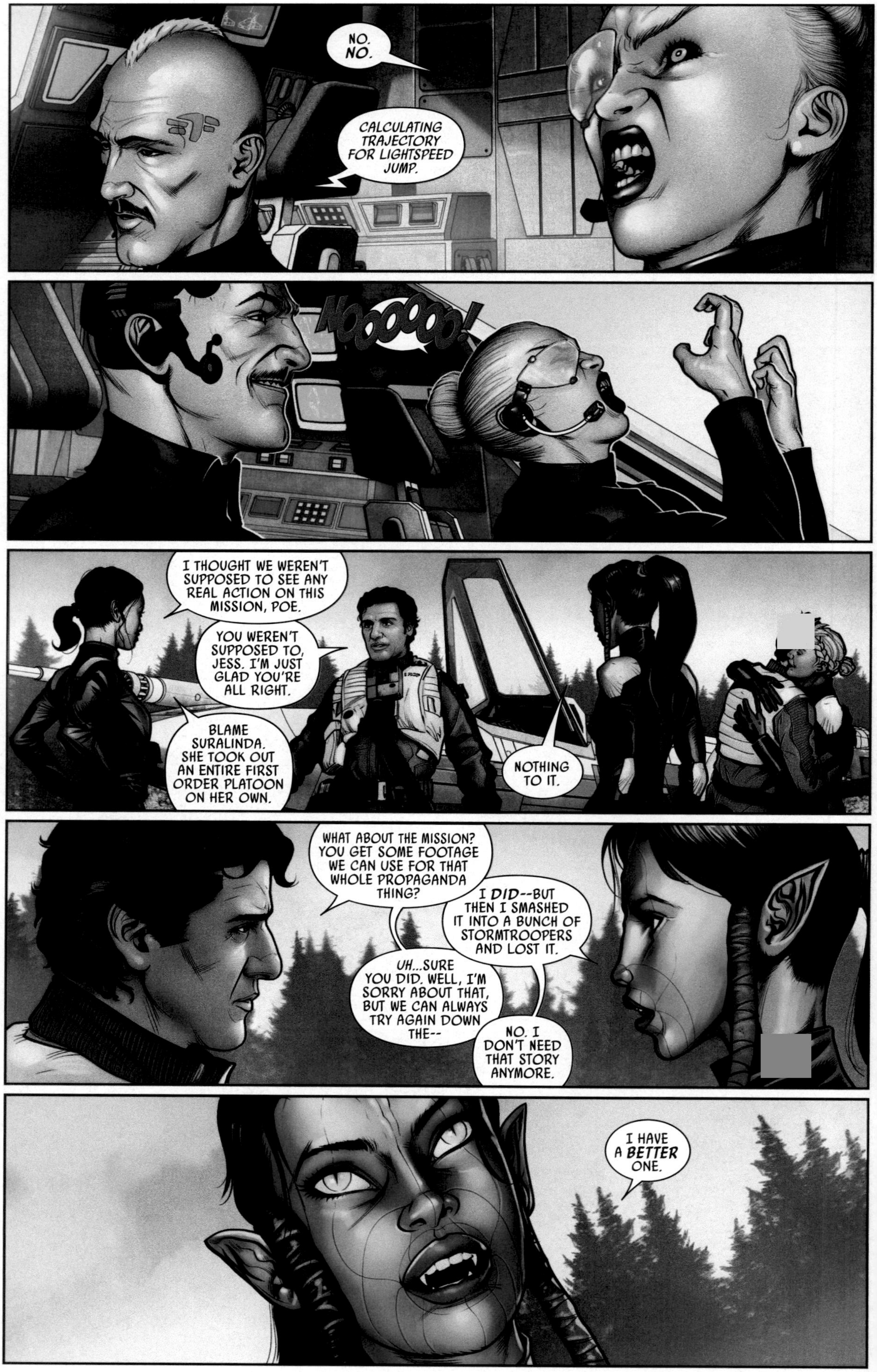
NO. NO.
CALCULATING TRAJECTORY FOR LIGHTSPEED JUMP.
NOOOOOO!
I THOUGHT WE WEREN'T SUPPOSED TO SEE ANY REAL ACTION ON THIS MISSION, POE.
YOU WEREN'T SUPPOSED TO, JESS. I'M JUST GLAD YOU'RE ALL RIGHT.
BLAME SURALINDA. SHE TOOK OUT AN ENTIRE FIRST ORDER PLATOON ON HER OWN.
NOTHING TO IT.
WHAT ABOUT THE MISSION? YOU GET SOME FOOTAGE WE CAN USE FOR THAT WHOLE PROPAGANDA THING?
I DID--BUT THEN I SMASHED IT INTO A BUNCH OF STORMTROOPERS AND LOST IT.
UH...SURE YOU DID. WELL, I'M SORRY ABOUT THAT, BUT WE CAN ALWAYS TRY AGAIN DOWN THE--
NO. I DON'T NEED THAT STORY ANYMORE.
I HAVE A BETTER ONE.

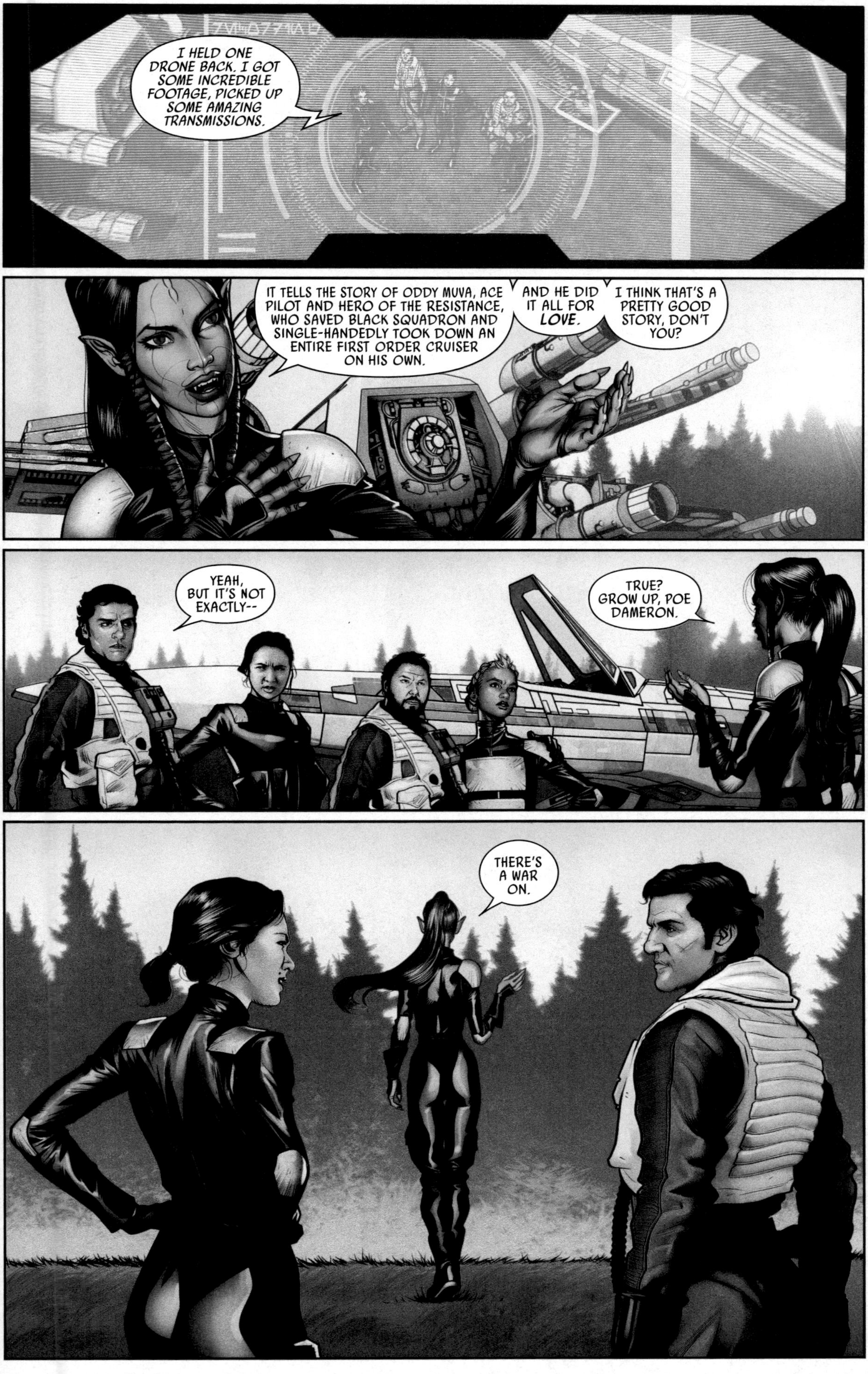
I HELD ONE DRONE BACK. I GOT SOME INCREDIBLE FOOTAGE, PICKED UP SOME AMAZING TRANSMISSIONS.
IT TELLS THE STORY OF ODDY MUVA, ACE PILOT AND HERO OF THE RESISTANCE, WHO SAVED BLACK SQUADRON AND SINGLE-HANDEDLY TOOK DOWN AN ENTIRE FIRST ORDER CRUISER ON HIS OWN.
AND HE DID IT ALL FOR *LOVE*.
I THINK THAT'S A PRETTY GOOD STORY, DON'T YOU?
YEAH, BUT IT'S NOT EXACTLY--
TRUE? GROW UP, POE DAMERON.
THERE'S A WAR ON.

RETURN TO A GALAXY FAR, FAR AWAY!

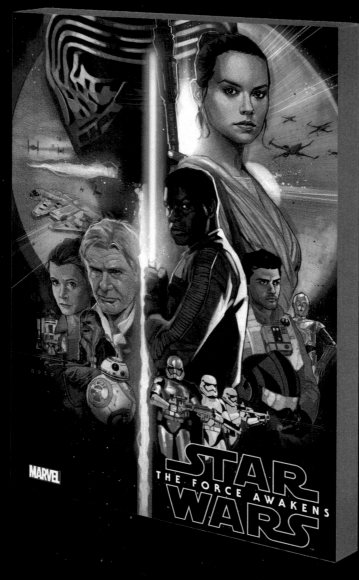

STAR WARS: THE FORCE AWAKENS ADAPTATION TPB
978-1302902032

ON SALE NOVEMBER 2017
WHEREVER BOOKS ARE SOLD

TO FIND A COMIC SHOP NEAR YOU, VISIT COMICSHOPLOCATOR.COM

WHAT HORRORS AWAIT IN THE SCREAMING CITADEL?

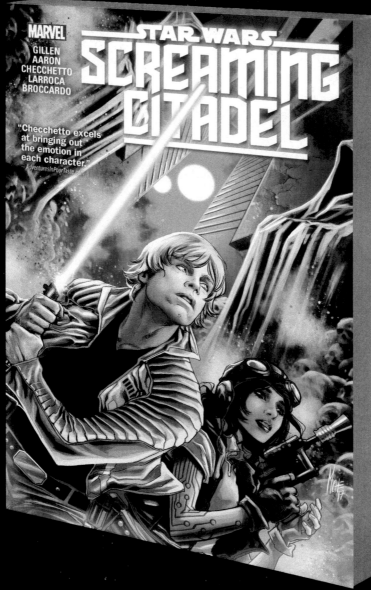

STAR WARS: THE SCREAMING CITADEL TPB
978-1302906788

ON SALE NOW
WHEREVER BOOKS ARE SOLD

TO FIND A COMIC SHOP NEAR YOU, VISIT COMICSHOPLOCATOR.COM

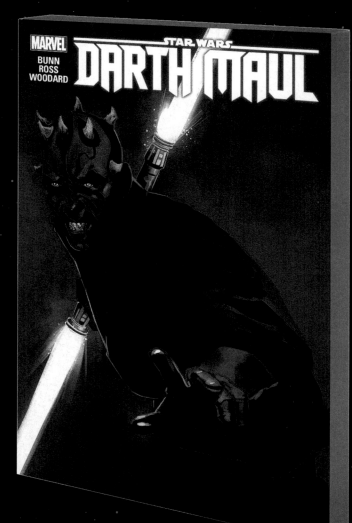